Feminist Theories and Feminist Economics

Feminist Theories and Feminist Economics

A Multi-Paradigmatic Approach

Kavous Ardalan

LEXINGTON BOOKS

Lanham • Boulder • New York • London

Published by Lexington Books
An imprint of The Rowman & Littlefield Publishing Group, Inc.
4501 Forbes Boulevard, Suite 200, Lanham, Maryland 20706
www.rowman.com

6 Tinworth Street, London SE11 5AL, United Kingdom

British Library Cataloguing in Publication Information Available

Library of Congress Cataloging-in-Publication Data

Names: Ardalan, Kavous, author.
Title: Feminist theories and feminist economics : a multi-paradigmatic approach / Kavous Ardalan.
Description: Lanham : Lexington Books, [2021] | Includes bibliographical references and index. | Summary: "This book is about understanding feminist theories and feminist economics through a multi-paradigmatic approach. It discusses four paradigms, offers four paradigmatic viewpoints of several social concerns of feminism, and emphasizes that the four views provide a broader and balanced understanding of feminism" —Provided by publisher.
Identifiers: LCCN 2021037950 (print) | LCCN 2021037951 (ebook) | ISBN 9781793648853 (cloth) | ISBN 9781793648860 (ebook) Subjects:
LCSH: Feminism. | Feminist economics.
Classification: LCC HQ1155 .A73 2021 (print) | LCC HQ1155 (ebook) | DDC 305.42—dc23
LC record available at https://lccn.loc.gov/2021037950
LC ebook record available at https://lccn.loc.gov/2021037951

This work is dedicated to my family.

Contents

Introduction

This book is the eighth book that reflects the change in the way that I think about the world, and in writing it I hope that it will do the same for others. The writing of my first book[1] began a few years after I received my PhD in Finance from York University in Toronto, Ontario, Canada. But, the origin of it goes back to the time I was a doctoral candidate and took a course in "Philosophy and Method" with Professor Gareth Morgan. At that time, I was exposed to ideas which were totally new to me. They occupied my mind and every day I found them more helpful than the day before in explaining what I experienced in my daily, practical, and intellectual life.

When in high school, I grew up overseas and I was raised to appreciate mathematics and science at the expense of other fields of study. Then in college, I was exposed only to economics to receive my bachelor of arts. Afterward, in order to obtain my master's and doctoral degrees in economics, I attended University of California, Santa Barbara and I received my specialized training in economics. My further specialized studies in finance at York University ended in a second doctoral degree. As is clear, throughout the years of my education, I was trained to see the world in a special narrow way.

Among all courses, which I took during all these years of training, one course stood out as being different and, in the final analysis, as being most influential. It was the "Philosophy and Method" course which I took with Professor Gareth Morgan at York University. It was most influential because none of the other courses gave me the vision that this one did. Whereas all the other courses trained me to see the world in one special narrow way, this course provided me with the idea that the world can be seen from different vantage points, where each one would be insightful in its own way. Over the years, constant applications of this idea in my daily, practical, and intellectual life were quite an eye-opener for me, such that, I naturally converted to this new way of thinking about the world. This happened in spite of the fact that my entire education, almost exclusively, trained me to see the world in a narrow and limited way. Since then, I have been writing based on this new approach, and the current book represents what has been accumulated since the publication of my first seven books.[2]

This book crosses two existing lines of literature; philosophy of social science and feminism. More specifically, its frame of reference is Burrell and Morgan (1979) and Morgan (1983), and applies their ideas and insights to various dimensions of feminism. Clearly, a thorough treatment of all the relevant issues referred to in this work is well beyond just one book. Within such limits, this book aims at only providing an overview, a review, a taxonomy, or a map of the topics and leaving further discussions of all the relevant issues to the references cited herein. In other words, the aim of this work is not so much to create a new piece of puzzle as it is to fit the existing pieces of puzzle together in order to make sense of it. To implement this aim, and given the specialized and abstract nature of the philosophy of social science, this book first discusses the framework of Burrell and Morgan (1979), and in this context, thereafter, the following chapters bring some of the important dimensions of feminism into focus. The chapters in this book put the pieces of puzzle together into the bigger picture. The choice of what to be included in the book and what to be excluded has been a hard one. In numerous occasions, it is decided to refer to some massive topics very briefly. In any case, this book is only an overview, but it provides a comprehensive set of references to avoid some of its shortcomings.

The main theme of the book is as follows. Social theory can usefully be conceived in terms of four key paradigms: functionalist, interpretive, radical humanist, and radical structuralist. The four paradigms are founded upon different assumptions about the nature of social science and the nature of society. Each generates theories, concepts, and analytical tools that are different from those of the other paradigms.

These four paradigms are not airtight compartments into which all theories must be squeezed. They are heuristic devices which are created to make sense of the messy reality of any real-life phenomenon. They are merely useful constructs to aid understanding. They are not claimed to be the only constructs to aid understanding. They are not claimed to be the best constructs to aid understanding. They are only one such construct, among many possible constructs, to aid understanding. They provide an analytically clear and compelling map of the terrain. They help in differentiating the various perspectives that exist with respect to a given phenomenon. Their purpose is to help to understand differences, but not to make invidious comparisons. There is no one paradigm that can capture the essence of reality. Paradigm diversity provides enhanced understanding. In intellectual as well as natural environments, diversity is a sine qua non of robust good health. There is no singular approach that, in its universality, can apprehend the totality of reality. Since academic models are inevitably the product of a partial viewpoint, they will always be biased, and hence a multiplicity of perspectives is required to represent the complexity and diversity of phenomena and activities. The four paradigms provide a full-circle worldview.

The mainstream in most academic fields of study is based upon the functionalist paradigm; and, for the most part, mainstream scholars are not always entirely aware of the tradition to which they belong. Their understanding of different paradigms leads to a better understanding of the multifaceted nature of their academic field of study. Although a researcher may decide to conduct research from the point of view of a certain paradigm, an understanding of the nature of other paradigms leads to a better understanding of what one is doing.

Knowledge of any phenomenon is ultimately a product of the researcher's paradigmatic approach to that multifaceted phenomenon. Viewed from this angle, the pursuit of knowledge is seen as much an ethical, moral, ideological, and political activity, as a technical one. Each paradigm can gain much from the contributions of the other paradigms.

The ancient parable of six blind scholars and their experience with the elephant illustrates the benefits of paradigm diversity. There were six blind scholars who did not know what the elephant looked like and had never even heard its name. They decided to obtain a mental picture —that is, knowledge— by touching the animal. The first blind scholar felt the elephant's trunk and argued that the elephant was like a lively snake. The second blind scholar rubbed along one of the elephant's enormous legs and likened the animal to a rough column of massive proportions. The third blind scholar took hold of the elephant's tail and insisted that the elephant resembled a large, flexible brush. The fourth blind scholar felt the elephant's sharp tusk and declared it to be like a great spear. The fifth blind scholar examined the elephant's waving ear and was convinced that the animal was some sort of a fan. The sixth blind scholar, who occupied the space between the elephant's front and hind legs, could not touch any parts of the elephant and consequently asserted that there were no such beasts as elephant at all and accused his colleagues of making up fantastic stories about nonexisting things. Each of the six blind scholars held firmly to their understanding of an elephant, and they argued and fought about which story contained the correct understanding of the elephant. As a result, their entire community was torn apart, and suspicion and distrust became the order of the day.

This parable contains many valuable lessons. First, probably reality is too complex to be fully grasped by imperfect human beings. Second, although each person might correctly identify one aspect of reality, each may incorrectly attempt to reduce the entire phenomenon to their own partial and narrow experience. Third, the maintenance of communal peace and harmony might be worth much more than stubbornly clinging to one's understanding of the world. Fourth, it might be wise for each person to return to reality and exchange positions with others to better appreciate the whole of the reality.[3]

This book, as in my previous seven books, advocates a multi-paradigmatic approach that employs the method of juxtaposing heterogeneous viewpoints in order to illuminate more comprehensively the phenomenon under consideration. The multi-paradigmatic approach uses a systematic and structured method to explain the phenomenon from the viewpoint of each paradigm, and juxtaposes them in order to transcend the limitations of each of the worldviews.

The current book, entitled "Feminist Theories and Feminist Economics: A Multi-Paradigmatic Approach," is about understanding feminist theories and feminist economics through a multi-paradigmatic approach. For this purpose, chapter 1 discusses the four paradigms, that is, the book starts with a discussion of four most diverse worldviews or paradigms: functionalist, interpretive, radical humanist, radical structuralist. Then, chapters 2 through 7, in turn, apply the four paradigmatic framework to the extant literature about six relevant dimensions of social life: human nature, feminist theories, family, patriarchy, discrimination, and feminist economics. Afterward, chapters 8 through 11, in turn, apply the four paradigmatic framework to four relevant scholarly pieces of research: feminist research, feminist education, economics versus sociology, and men versus women. Chapter 12 concludes the book by recommending paradigm diversity.

In short, chapter 1 discusses the four paradigms. Chapters 2 through 7 apply the four paradigmatic framework to six different lines of scholarly literature. Chapters 8 through 11 apply the four paradigmatic framework to four singular pieces of scholarly research. Chapter 12 recommends paradigm diversity. In this way, this book shows, among other things, that the four paradigmatic framework can be used not only as a classificatory device, but also as an analytical tool.

This book follows one general approach, that is, to approach any "topic" through the four paradigmatic framework. In this way, if the "topic" under consideration consists of the entirety of a literature, then, it will be more extensive, and the four paradigmatic discussion, most likely, will involve all four paradigms—as in chapters 1 through 7. However, if the "topic" under consideration consists of only one piece of scholarship, then, the discussion will be shorter and, most likely, will involve a limited number of paradigms—as in chapters 8 through 11. So, the book manuscript follows one general approach, but the outcome looks different when the same approach is applied to different contexts, that is, an entire literature versus one piece in a literature.

On a more conceptual level, this book crosses two existing lines of literature; social philosophy on the one hand and feminist theories and feminist economics on the other hand. The main theme of the book is as follows. Social theory can usefully be conceived in terms of four key paradigms: functionalist, interpretive, radical humanist, and radical structuralist. The four paradigms are founded upon different assumptions about the nature of social science and the nature of society. Each paradigm generates theories, concepts, and analytical tools which are different from those of other paradigms. The book emphasizes that the four views expressed are equally scientific and informative; they look at the phenomenon under consideration from a certain paradigmatic viewpoint. An understanding of different paradigms leads to a more comprehensive and a more balanced understanding of the multifaceted nature of the subject matter. A multi-paradigmatic approach promotes self-reflexivity and reduces the risk of excessive dogmatism. Consequently, in the final chapter, the book concludes by recommending paradigm diversity. This book shows, among other things, the versatility and utility of the multi-paradigmatic approach.

Each categorization of a literature provides a different view of the literature to the reader. This book categorizes the literature, written on various dimensions of feminism, through the four paradigmatic framework. This book, however, does not claim that the four paradigmatic framework leads to the best categorization; it claims that it is only another categorization that provides another way of looking at the literature, and therefore, provides new insight to the reader about the literature.

In this book, chapters 2 through 7 discuss six aspects, or dimensions, of social life. Each chapter focuses on one aspect, or dimension, of social life and discusses that aspect, or dimension, from the four most diverse paradigmatic viewpoints: functionalist, interpretive, radical humanist, and radical structuralist. Each chapter allocates the same space, in terms of the number of book pages, to each of the four viewpoints, which is the same principle as followed in my previous books as well. In each chapter, for each of the four paradigmatic viewpoints, a list of publications that share similar paradigmatic characteristics is offered, and then, one of them which is regarded as the "ideal-typical" publication is discussed in the section. That is, each of the four paradigmatic viewpoints is represented by a typical, "ideal-typical," viewpoint. These four different perspectives should be regarded as typical polar viewpoints. The work of certain authors helps to define the logically coherent form of a certain polar viewpoint. But, the work of many authors who share more than one perspective is located between the poles of the spectrum defined by the polar viewpoints. For instance, some critical realists believe that they offer a meta-theoretical perspective that actually subsumes all four paradigms treated in this book by explicitly theorizing the subjective-objective and the reproduction-transformation dialectics. The purpose of this book is not to put people into boxes. It is, rather, to recommend that a satisfactory perspective may draw upon several of the typical polar viewpoints.

The main purpose of this book is to see the philosophical differences between the four paradigmatic views expressed with respect to the phenomenon under consideration. Therefore, the book avoids distractions caused by literal reference to the literature, whether in terms of authors of scholarly manuscripts, dates of scholarly manuscripts, or the sources of sets of data used in scholarly manuscripts.

This book is unique due to its especial characteristics as follows:

1. It is systematic and methodic: It discusses each of the six aspects/dimensions of feminism and feminist economics from the same four paradigmatic viewpoints. This method of analysis can be applied to any phenomenon, that is, each phenomenon can be viewed from these four perspectives. This method is, indeed, versatile and resilient.
2. It is fundamental and applied: It applies four fundamental viewpoints to each of the six aspects/dimensions of human social life in feminism and feminist economics.
3. It is fair and unbiased: In each chapter, it allocates the same number of pages of the book to each paradigmatic viewpoint.
4. It is enlightening: It provides four different views with respect to the same phenomenon, and therefore, it provides a broader and a balanced understanding of the phenomenon under consideration.
5. It is multidimensional and multiperspectival: It regards and treats any phenomenon as being multidimensional, and in addition, it looks at each dimension of the phenomenon from four various multi-paradigmatic perspectives. There are other books, but they are either on feminism or feminist economics; however, this book regards feminism and feminist economics to be inseparable, and therefore, discusses both of them side-by-side and with the same multi-paradigmatic approach. Furthermore, other books focus on particular aspects/dimensions of feminism or feminist economics and their explanations are made from a specific viewpoint. But, this book emphasizes as many aspects/dimensions of feminism and feminist economics as a book's space allows, and, in this way, proposes a comprehensive approach to the understanding of feminism and feminist economics. Moreover, the approach used in this book, when learned, can be applied to any other phenomenon.

6. It is multidisciplinary and interdisciplinary: It is based on philosophy, incorporates sociology and humanities, and goes on to include discussions about economics, culture, and politics.

In terms of the audience for this book, one can say that this book will be useful to everyone in society. As a textbook, it can be used in upper-level undergraduate and master-level courses in a variety of disciplines because the book discusses various fundamental aspects/dimensions of human social life. Especially, this book will be useful to students in gender studies, women's studies, economics, political science, sociology, social studies, liberal studies, sociology, humanities, and philosophy. This book can be used as either the main text or a supplementary reading. This book is about fundamental aspects/dimensions of human social life, and therefore, it can be used in any country.

The writing of the chapters of this book involved extensive work over several years. It required peace of mind and extended uninterrupted research time. My deepest expressions of gratitude go to my wife Haleh, my son Arash, and my daughter Camellia for their prolonged patience, unlimited understanding, sustained support, constant cooperation, and individual independence during all these long years. I hold much respect for my late parents (Javad and Afagholmolouk) who instilled in their children (Ghobad, Golnar, Alireza, and Kavous) the grand Ardalan family's values of respect, openness, and love of learning, among others. I sincerely appreciate the heartfelt support of my in-laws (Farideh, Parviz, and Houman) who have always been in close contact with us since the formation of my immediate family.

The ideas expressed in this work are based on the teachings, writings, and insights of Professor Gareth Morgan, to whom the nucleus of this work is owed. Needless to say, I stand responsible for all the errors and omissions. I would like to thank Professor Gareth Morgan who taught me how to diversely view the world, and accordingly inspired my work.

I am thankful of the Marist College library staff for their timely provision of the requested literature, which they obtained from various sources. I would also like to thank the publishers, referenced in the endnotes, who allowed me to use their materials. Certainly, I would like to thank the respectable people who work at Rowman and Littlefield for their recognition of the significance of my work, and for their publication of the book with utmost professionalism.

Kavous Ardalan, PhD
Professor of Finance
School of Management
Marist College
Poughkeepsie, New York 12601
United States of America

NOTES

1. Ardalan (2008).
2. Ardalan (2008, 2014, 2016, 2018, 2019a, 2019b, 2020).
3. This parable is taken from Steger (2002).

REFERENCES

Ardalan, Kavous, 2008, *On the Role of Paradigms in Finance*, Aldershot, Hampshire: Ashgate Publishing Limited, and Burlington, VT: Ashgate Publishing Company.

Ardalan, Kavous, 2014, *Understanding Globalization: A Multi-Dimensional Approach*, Piscataway, NJ: Transaction Publishers.

Ardalan, Kavous, 2016, *Paradigms in Political Economy*, New York, NY: Routledge.

Ardalan, Kavous, 2018, *Case Method and Pluralist Economics: Philosophy, Methodology, and Practice*, New York, NY; and Cham, Switzerland: Springer International Publishing AG.

Ardalan, Kavous, 2019a, *Global Political Economy: A Multi-Paradigmatic Approach*, New York, NY; and Cham, Switzerland: Springer International Publishing AG.

Ardalan, Kavous, 2019b, *Equity Home Bias in International Finance: A Place-Attachment Perspective*, Abingdon, Oxon; and New York, NY: Routledge.

Ardalan, Kavous, 2020, *Understanding Revolution: A Multi-Paradigmatic Approach*, New York, NY; and Cham, Switzerland: Springer International Publishing AG.

Burrell, Gibson and Morgan, Gareth, 1979, *Sociological Paradigms and Organizational Analysis*, Hants, Britain: Gower Publishing Company Limited.

Morgan, Gareth, 1983, *Beyond Method: Strategies for Social Research*, Beverley Hills, CA: Sage Publications.

Steger, Manfred B., 2002, *Globalism: The New Market Ideology*, New York, NY: Rowan & Littlefield Publishers, Inc.

Chapter 1

Four Paradigms

Social theory can usefully be conceived in terms of four key paradigms: functionalist, interpretive, radical humanist, and radical structuralist. The four paradigms are founded upon different assumptions about the nature of social science and the nature of society. Each generates theories, concepts, and analytical tools which are different from those of other paradigms.[1]

All theories are based on a philosophy of science and a theory of society. Many theorists appear to be unaware of, or ignore, the assumptions underlying these philosophies. They emphasize only some aspects of the phenomenon and ignore others. Unless they bring out the basic philosophical assumptions of the theories, their analysis can be misleading; since by emphasizing differences between theories, they imply diversity in approach. Although there appear to be different kinds of theory, they are founded on a certain philosophy, worldview, or paradigm. This becomes evident when these theories are related to the wider background of social theory.

The functionalist paradigm has provided the framework for current mainstream academic fields, and accounts for the largest proportion of theory and research in their respective academic fields.

In order to understand a new paradigm, theorists should be fully aware of assumptions upon which their own paradigm is based. Moreover, to understand a new paradigm one has to explore it from within, since the concepts in one paradigm cannot easily be interpreted in terms of those of another. No attempt should be made to criticize or evaluate a paradigm from the outside. This is self-defeating since it is based on a separate paradigm. All four paradigms can be easily criticized and ruined in this way.

These four paradigms are of paramount importance to any scientist, because the process of learning about a favored paradigm is also the process of learning what that paradigm is not. The knowledge of paradigms makes scientists aware of the boundaries within which they approach their subject. Each of the four paradigms implies a different way of social theorizing.

Before discussing each paradigm, it is useful to look at the notion of "paradigm." Burrell and Morgan (1979)[2] regard the:

> ... four paradigms as being defined by very basic meta-theoretical assumptions which underwrite the frame of reference, mode of theorizing and modus operandi of the social theorists who operate within them. It is a term which is intended to emphasize the commonality of perspective which binds the work of a group of theorists together in such a way that they can be usefully regarded as approaching social theory within the bounds of the same problematic.

> The paradigm does ... have an underlying unity in terms of its basic and often "taken for granted" assumptions, which separate a group of theorists in a very fundamental way from theorists located in other paradigms. The "unity" of the paradigm thus derives from reference to alternative views of reality which lie outside its boundaries and which may not necessarily even be recognized as existing. (pages 23–24)

Each theory can be related to one of the four broad worldviews. These adhere to different sets of fundamental assumptions about; the nature of science—that is, the subjective-objective dimension—and the nature of society—that is, the dimension of regulation-radical change—as in figure 1.1.[3]

Assumptions related to the nature of science are assumptions with respect to ontology, epistemology, human nature, and methodology.

The assumptions about ontology are assumptions regarding the very essence of the phenomenon under investigation. That is, to what extent the phenomenon is objective and external to the individual or it is subjective and the product of individual's mind.

The assumptions about epistemology are assumptions about the nature of knowledge. That is, they are assumptions about how one might go about understanding the world, and communicate such knowledge to others. That is, what constitutes knowledge and to what extent it is something which can be acquired or it is something which has to be personally experienced.

The assumptions about human nature are concerned with human nature and, in particular, the relationship between individuals and their environment, which is the object and subject of social sciences. That is, to what extent human beings and their experiences are the products of their environment or human beings are creators of their environment.

The assumptions about methodology are related to the way in which one attempts to investigate and obtain knowledge about the social world. That is, to what extent the methodology treats the social world as being real hard

The Sociology of Radical Change

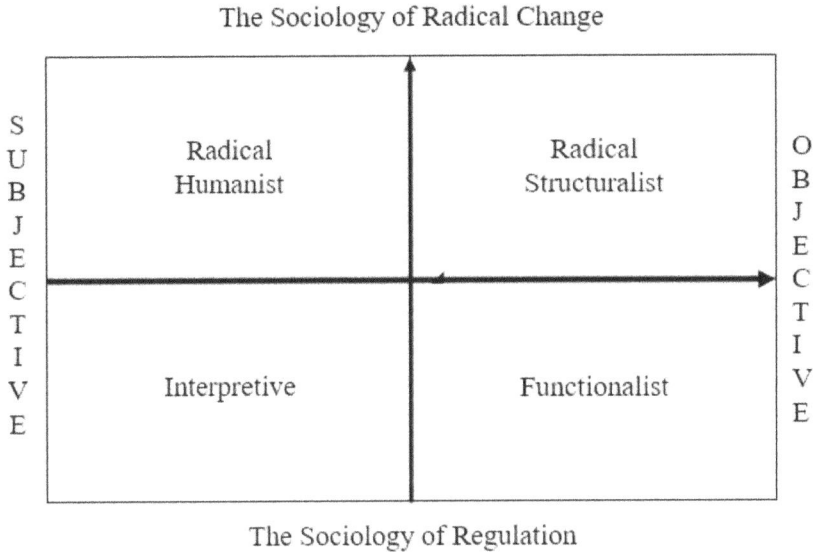

Figure 1.1 **The Four Paradigms: Each paradigm adheres to a set of fundamental assumptions about the nature of science (i.e., the subjective-objective dimension), and the nature of society (i.e., the dimension of regulation-radical change).** *Source*: Burrell and Morgan (1979, page 22).

and external to the individual or it is as being of a much softer, personal and more subjective quality. In the former, the focus is on the universal relationship among elements of the phenomenon, whereas in the latter, the focus is on the understanding of the way in which the individual creates, modifies, and interprets the situation which is experienced.

The assumptions related to the nature of society are concerned with the extent of regulation of the society or radical change in the society.

Sociology of regulation provides explanation of society based on the assumption of its unity and cohesiveness. It focuses on the need to understand and explain why society tends to hold together rather than fall apart.

Sociology of radical change provides explanation of society based on the assumption of its deep-seated structural conflict, modes of domination, and structural contradiction. It focuses on the deprivation of human beings, both material and psychic, and it looks toward alternatives rather than the acceptance of status quo.

The subjective-objective dimension and the regulation-radical change dimension together define four paradigms, each of which share common fundamental assumptions about the nature of social science and the nature of society. Each paradigm has a fundamentally unique perspective for the analysis of social phenomena.

FUNCTIONALIST PARADIGM

The functionalist paradigm assumes that society has a concrete existence and follows certain order. These assumptions lead to the existence of an objective and value-free social science which can produce true explanatory and predictive knowledge of the reality "out there." It assumes scientific theories can be assessed objectively by reference to empirical evidence. Scientists do not see any roles for themselves, within the phenomenon which they analyze, through the rigor and technique of the scientific method. It attributes independence to the observer from the observed. That is, an ability to observe "what is" without affecting it. It assumes there are universal standards of science, which determine what constitutes an adequate explanation of what is observed. It assumes there are external rules and regulations governing the external world. The goal of scientists is to find the orders that prevail within that phenomenon.

The functionalist paradigm seeks to provide rational explanations of social affairs and generate regulative sociology. It assumes a continuing order, pattern, and coherence and tries to explain what is. It emphasizes the importance of understanding order, equilibrium and stability in society and the way in which these can be maintained. It is concerned with the regulation and control of social affairs. It believes in social engineering as a basis for social reform.

The rationality which underlies functionalist science is used to explain the rationality of society. Science provides the basis for structuring and ordering the social world, similar to the structure and order in the natural world. The methods of natural science are used to generate explanations of the social world. The use of mechanical and biological analogies for modeling and understanding the social phenomena are particularly favored.

Functionalists are individualists. That is, the properties of the aggregate are determined by the properties of its units. Their approach to social science is rooted in the tradition of positivism. It assumes that the social world is concrete, meaning it can be identified, studied and measured through approaches derived from the natural sciences.

Functionalists believe that the positivist methods which have triumphed in natural sciences should prevail in social sciences, as well. In addition, the functionalist paradigm has become dominant in academic sociology. The social world is treated as a place of concrete reality, characterized by uniformities and regularities which can be understood and explained in terms of causes and effects. Given these assumptions, the individuals are regarded as taking on a passive role; their behavior is being determined by the social environment.

Functionalists are pragmatic in orientation and are concerned to understand society so that the knowledge thus generated can be used in society. It is problem orientated in approach as it is concerned to provide practical solutions to practical problems.

In figure 1.1, the functionalist paradigm occupies the south-east quadrant. Schools of thought within this paradigm can be located on the objective-subjective continuum. From right to left they are: Objectivism, Social System Theory, Integrative Theory, Interactionism, and Social Action Theory.[4]

INTERPRETIVE PARADIGM

The interpretive paradigm assumes that social reality is the result of the subjective interpretations of individuals. It sees the social world as a process which is created by individuals. Social reality, insofar as it exists outside the consciousness of any individual, is regarded as being a network of assumptions and intersubjectively shared meanings. This assumption leads to the belief there are shared multiple realities which are sustained and changed. Researchers recognize their role within the phenomenon under investigation. Their frame of reference is one of participant, as opposed to observer. The goal of the interpretive researchers is to find the orders that prevail within the phenomenon under consideration; however, they are not objective.

The interpretive paradigm is concerned with understanding the world as it is, at the level of subjective experience. It seeks explanations within the realm of individual consciousness and subjectivity. Its analysis of the social world produces sociology of regulation. Its views are underwritten by the assumptions that the social world is cohesive, ordered, and integrated.

Interpretive sociologists seek to understand the source of social reality. They often delve into the depth of human consciousness and subjectivity in their quest for the meanings in social life. They reject the use of mathematics and biological analogies in learning about the society and their approach places emphasis on understanding the social world from the vantage point of the individuals who are actually engaged in social activities.

The interpretive paradigm views the functionalist position as unsatisfactory for two reasons. First, human values affect the process of scientific enquiry. That is, scientific method is not value-free, since the frame of reference of the scientific observer determines the way in which scientific knowledge is obtained. Second, in cultural sciences the subject matter is spiritual in nature. That is, human beings cannot be studied by the methods of the natural sciences, which aim to establish general laws. In the cultural sphere, human beings are perceived as free. An understanding of their lives and actions can be obtained by the intuition of the total wholes, which is bound to break down by atomistic analysis of functionalist paradigm.

Cultural phenomena are seen as the external manifestations of inner expe-rience. The cultural sciences, therefore, need to apply analytical methods based on "understanding;" through which the scientist can seek to under-stand human beings, their minds, and their feelings, and the way these are expressed in their outward actions. The notion of "understanding" is a defin-ing characteristic of all theories located within this paradigm.

The interpretive paradigm believes that science is based on "taken for granted" assumptions; and, like any other social practice, must be understood within a specific context. Therefore, it cannot generate objective and value-free knowledge. Scientific knowledge is socially constructed and socially sustained; its significance and meaning can only be understood within its immediate social context.

The interpretive paradigm regards mainstream social theorists as belong-ing to a small and self-sustaining community, who believe that corporations and financial markets exist in a concrete world. They theorize about concepts which have little significance to people outside the community, who practice social theory, and the limited community whom social theorists may attempt to serve.

Functionalist social theorists tend to treat their subject of study as a hard, concrete, and tangible empirical phenomenon which exists "out there" in the "real world." Interpretive researchers are opposed to such structural absolu-tion. They emphasize that the social world is no more than the subjective construction of individual human beings who create and sustain a social world of intersubjectively shared meaning, which is in a continuous process of reaffirmation or change. Therefore, there are no universally valid social rules. Interpretive social research enables scientists to examine social behav-ior together with ethical, cultural, political, and social issues.

In figure 1.1, the interpretive paradigm occupies the south-west quadrant. Schools of thought within this paradigm can be located on the objective-subjective continuum. From left to right they are: Solipsism, Phenomenology, Phenomenological Sociology, and Hermeneutics.[5]

RADICAL HUMANIST PARADIGM

The radical humanist paradigm provides critiques of the status quo and is concerned to articulate, from a subjective standpoint, the sociology of radical change, modes of domination, emancipation, deprivation, and potentiality. Based on its subjectivist approach, it places great emphasis on human con-sciousness. It tends to view society as anti-human. It views the process of reality creation as feeding back on itself; such that individuals and society are prevented from reaching their highest possible potential. That is, the consciousness of human beings is dominated by the ideological superstructures of the social system, which results in their alienation or false consciousness. This, in turn, prevents true human fulfillment. The social theorist regards the orders that prevail in the society as instruments of ideological domination.

The major concern for theorists is with the way this occurs and finding ways in which human beings can release themselves from constraints which existing social arrangements place upon realization of their full potential. They seek to change the social world through a change in consciousness.

Radical humanists believe that everything must be grasped as a whole, because the whole dominates the parts in an all-embracing sense. Moreover, truth is historically specific, relative to a given set of circumstances, so that one should not search for generalizations for the laws of motion of societies.

The radical humanists believe the functionalist paradigm accepts purposive rationality, logic of science, positive functions of technology, and neutrality of language, and uses them in the construction of "value-free" social theories. The radical humanist theorists intend to demolish this structure, emphasizing the political and repressive nature of it. They aim to show the role that science, ideology, technology, language, and other aspects of the superstructure play in sustaining and developing the system of power and domination, within the totality of the social formation. Their function is to influence the consciousness of human beings for eventual emancipation and formation of alternative social formations.

The radical humanists note that functionalist sociologists create and sustain a view of social reality which maintains the status quo and which forms one aspect of the network of ideological domination of the society.

The focus of the radical humanists upon the "superstructural" aspects of society reflects their attempt to move away from the economism of orthodox Marxism and emphasize the Hegelian dialectics. It is through the dialectic that the objective and subjective aspects of social life interact. The superstructure of society is believed to be the medium through which the consciousness of human beings is controlled and molded to fit the requirements of the social formation as a whole. The concepts of structural conflict, contradiction, and crisis do not play a major role in this paradigm, because these are more objectivist view of social reality, that is, the ones which fall in the radical structuralist paradigm. In the radical humanist paradigm, the concepts of consciousness, alienation, and critique form their concerns.

In figure 1.1, the radical humanist paradigm occupies the north-west quadrant. Schools of thought within this paradigm can be located on the objective-subjective continuum. From left to right they are: Solipsism, French Existentialism, Anarchistic Individualism, and Critical Theory.[6]

RADICAL STRUCTURALIST PARADIGM

The radical structuralist paradigm assumes that reality is objective and concrete, as it is rooted in the materialist view of natural and social world. The social world, similar to the natural world, has an independent existence, that is, it exists outside the minds of human beings. Sociologists aim at discovering and understanding the patterns and regularities which characterize the social world. Scientists do not see any roles for themselves in the phenomenon under investigation. They use scientific methods to find the order that prevails in the phenomenon. This paradigm views society as a potentially dominating force. Sociologists working within this paradigm have an objectivist standpoint and are committed to radical change, emancipation, and potentiality. In their analysis they emphasize structural conflict, modes of domination, contradiction, and deprivation. They analyze the basic interrelationships within the total social formation and emphasize the fact that radical change is inherent in the structure of society and the radical change takes place though political and economic crises. This radical change necessarily disrupts the status quo and replaces it by a radically different social formation. It is through this radical change that the emancipation of human beings from the social structure is materialized.

For radical structuralists, an understanding of classes in society is essential for understanding the nature of knowledge. They argue that all knowledge is class specific. That is, it is determined by the place one occupies in the productive process. Knowledge is more than a reflection of the material world in thought. It is determined by one's relation to that reality. Since different classes occupy different positions in the process of material transformation, there are different kinds of knowledge. Hence class knowledge is produced by and for classes, and exists in a struggle for domination. Knowledge is thus ideological. That is, it formulates views of reality and solves problems from class points of view.

Radical structuralists reject the idea that it is possible to verify knowledge in an absolute sense through comparison with socially neutral theories or data. But, emphasize that there is the possibility of producing a "correct" knowledge from a class standpoint. They argue that the dominated class is uniquely positioned to obtain an objectively "correct" knowledge of social reality and its contradictions. It is the class with the most direct and widest access to the process of material transformation that ultimately produces and reproduces that reality.

Radical structuralists' analysis indicates that the social scientist, as a producer of class-based knowledge, is a part of the class struggle.

Radical structuralists believe truth is the whole, and emphasize the need to understand the social order as a totality rather than as a collection of small truths about various parts and aspects of society. The economic empiricists are seen as relying almost exclusively upon a number of seemingly disparate, data-packed, problem-centered studies. Such studies, therefore, are irrelevant exercises in mathematical methods.

This paradigm is based on four central notions. First, there is the notion of totality. All theories address the total social formation. This notion emphasizes that the parts reflect the totality, not the totality the parts.

Second, there is the notion of structure. The focus is upon the configurations of social relationships, called structures, which are treated as persistent and enduring concrete facilities.

The third notion is that of contradiction. Structures, or social formations, contain contradictory and antagonistic relationships within them which act as seeds of their own decay.

The fourth notion is that of crisis. Contradictions within a given totality reach a point at which they can no longer be contained. The resulting political, economic crises indicate the point of transformation from one totality to another, in which one set of structures is replaced by another of a fundamentally different kind.

In figure 1.1, the radical structuralist paradigm occupies the north-east quadrant. Schools of thought within this paradigm can be located on the objective-subjective continuum. From right to left they are: Russian Social Theory, Conflict Theory, and Contemporary Mediterranean Marxism.[7]

CONCLUSION

This chapter briefly discussed social theory, its complexity, and diversity. It indicated that theorists are not always entirely aware of the traditions to which they belong. The diversity of theories presented in this section is vast. Although each paradigm advocates a research strategy that is logically coherent, in terms of underlying assumptions, these vary from paradigm to paradigm. The phenomenon to be researched is conceptualized and studied in many different ways, each generating distinctive kinds of insight and understanding. There are many different ways of studying the same social phenomenon, and given that the insights generated by any one approach are at best partial and incomplete, the social researcher can gain much by reflecting on the nature and merits of different approaches before engaging in a particular mode of research practice.

Social knowledge is ultimately a product of the researcher's paradigmatic approach to this multifaceted phenomenon. Viewed from this angle, the pursuit of social knowledge is seen as much an ethical, moral, ideological, and political activity, as a technical one. Economists can gain much by exploiting the new insights coming from other paradigms.

NOTES

1. For the literature on paradigms, see Bottomore (1975), Clark (1985), Denisoff (1974), Eckburg and Hill (1979), Effrat (1973), Evered and Louis (1981), Friedheim (1979), Gioia and Pitre (1990), Goles and Hirschheim (2000), Guba (1985), Guba and Lincoln (1994), Hassard (1988, 1991a, b, 1993, 2013), Holland (1990), Jackson and Carter (1991), Jackson and Carter (2008), Jennings, Perren, and Carter (2005), Jick (1979), Kirkwood and Campbell-Hunt (2007), Knudsen (2003), Kuhn (1962, 1970a, b, 1974, 1977), Lammers (1974), Lehmann and Young (1974), Lewis and Grimes (1999), Lincoln (1985), Martin (1990), Maruyama (1974), Masterman (1970), McKelvey (2008), Mir and Mir (2002), Morgan (1990), Okhuysen and Bonardi (2011), Parsons (1967), Ritzer (1975), Romani, Primecz, and Topcu (2011), Schultz and Hatch (1996), Shapere (1971), Siehl and Martin (1988), Snizek (1976), Steinle (1983), van de Berge (1963), White (1983), and Willmott (1990, 1993).

2. This work borrows heavily from the ideas and insights of Burrell and Morgan (1979) and Morgan (1983) and applies them to revolution. Burrell and Morgan (1979) state "The scope for applying the analytical scheme to other field of study is enormous … readers interested in applying the scheme in this way should find little difficulty in proceeding from the sociological analyses ... to an analysis of the literature in their own sphere of specialised interest." (page 35)

3. This can be used as both a classificatory device, or more importantly, as an analytical tool.

4. For classics in this literature, see Blau (1955, 1964), Buckley (1967), Comte (1953), Durkheim (1938, 1947), James (1890), Mead (1932a, b, 1934, 1938), Merton (1968), Pareto (1935), Simmel (1936, 1955), Skinner (1953, 1957, 1972), and Spencer (1873).

5. For classics in this literature, see Berkeley (1962), Dilthey (1976), Gadamer (1965), Garfinkel (1967), Hegel (1931), Husserl (1929), Schutz (1964, 1966, 1967), Winch (1958), and Wittgenstein (1963).

6. For classics in this literature, see Bookchin (1974), Fichte (1970), Goldmann (1969), Gouldner (1954a, b, 1970, 1973, 1976), Gramsci (1971), Habermas (1970a, b, 1971, 1972, 1974, 1976), Horkheimer (1972), Lukacs (1971), Marcuse (1954, 1964, 1966, 1968), Marx (1975), Meszaros (1970, 1971), Sartre (1966, 1974, 1976), and Stirner (1907).

7. For classics in this literature, see Althusser (1969, 1971), Althusser and Balibar (1970), Bukharin (1965), Colletti (1972, 1974, 1975), Dahrendorf (1959), Marx (1973, 1976), Marx and Engels (1965, 1968), Plekhanov (1974), and Rex (1961, 1974).

REFERENCES

Althusser, L. 1969. *For Marx.* Harmondsworth, England: Penguin.
Althusser, L. 1971. *Lenin and Philosophy and Other Essays.* London, England: New Left Books.

Althusser, L., and E. Balibar. 1970. *Reading Capital.* London, England: New Left Books.

Berkeley, G. 1962. *The Principles of Human Knowledge and Three Dialogues between Hylas and Philonous.* London, England: Collins.

Blau, P.M. 1955. *The Dynamics of Bureaucracy.* Chicago, IL: University of Chicago Press.

Blau, P.M. 1964. *Exchange and Power in Social Life.* New York, NY: John Wiley.

Bookchin, Murray. 1974. *Post-Scarcity Anarchism.* London, England: Wildwood House.

Bottomore, T. 1975. "Competing Paradigms in Macrosociology." In *Annual Review of Sociology*, edited by A. Inkeles, 191–202. New York, NY: Annual Reviews.

Buckley, William. 1967. *Sociology and Modern Systems Theory.* Englewood Cliffs, NJ: Prentice-Hall.

Bukharin, N. 1965. *Historical Materialism: A System of Sociology.* New York, NY: Russell and Russell.

Burrell, Gibson, and Gareth Morgan. 1979. *Sociological Paradigms and Organizational Analysis*, Hants, England: Gower Publishing Company Limited.

Clark, D.L. 1985. "Emerging Paradigms in Organization Theory." In *Organizational Theory and Inquiry*, edited by Y. Lincoln, 43–78. Beverly Hills, CA: Sage.

Colletti, L. 1972. *From Rousseau to Lenin.* London, England: New Left Books.

Colletti, L. 1974. "A Political and Philosophical Interview." *New Left Review* 86: 3–28.

Colletti, L. 1975. "Marxism and the Dialectics." *New Left Review* 93: 3–29.

Comte, Auguste. 1953. *The Positivist Philosophy*, Vol. I. London, England: Chapman.

Dahrendorf, R. 1959. *Class and Class Conflict in Industrial Society.* London, England: Routledge and Kegan Paul.

Denisoff, R. et al. 1974. *Theories and Paradigms in Contemporary Sociology.* New York, NY: Peacock.

Dilthey, Wilhelm. 1976. *Selected Writings*, edited by H.P. Rickman. London, England: Cambridge University Press.

Durkheim, Emile. 1938. *The Rules of Sociological Method.* Glencoe, IL: Free Press.

Durkheim, Emile. 1947. *The Division of Labor in Society.* Glencoe, IL: Free Press.

Eckburg, D., and L. Hill, Jr. 1979. "The Paradigm Concept and Sociology: A Critical Review." *Annual Sociological Review* 44(4): 925–937.

Effrat, A. 1973. "Power to the Paradigms." In *Perspectives in Political Sociology*, edited by A. Effrat, 3–33. New York, NY: Bobbs-Merrill.

Evered, R., and M. Louis. 1981. "Alternative Perspectives in Organizational Sciences." *Academy of Management Review* 6(3): 385–395.

Fichte, J.F. 1970. *Science of Knowledge*, edited by P. Heath, and J. Lachs, New York, NY: Century Philosophy Sourcebooks.

Friedheim, E.A. 1979. "An Empirical Comparison of Ritzer's Paradigms and Similar Metatheories." *Social Forces* 58(1): 59–66.

Gadamer, H.G. 1965. *Wahrheit und Method.* Tubingen, Germany: J.C.B. Mohr.

Garfinkel, Harold. 1967. *Studies in Ethnomethodology.* Englewood Cliffs, NJ: Prentice-Hall.

Gioia, D., and E. Pitre. 1990. "Multi-Paradigmatic Perspectives in Theory Building." *Academy of Management Review* 15: 584–602.

Goldmann, Lucien. 1969. *The Human Sciences and Philosophy*. London, England: Cape.

Goles, T., and R. Hirschheim 2000. "The Paradigm Is Dead, the Paradigm Is Dead … Long Live the Paradigm: The Legacy of Burrell and Morgan." *Omega* 28: 249–268.

Gouldner, Alvin W. 1954a. *Patterns of Industrial Bureaucracy*. Glencoe, IL: Free Press.

Gouldner, Alvin W. 1954b. *Wildcat Strike*. New York, NY: Antioch Press.

Gouldner, Alvin W. 1970. *The Coming Crisis of Western Sociology*. London, England: Heinemann.

Gouldner, Alvin W. 1973. *For Sociology*. Harmondsworth, England: Allen Lane.

Gouldner, Alvin W. 1976. *The Dialectic of Ideology and Technology*. New York, NY: Macmillan.

Gramsci, Antonio. 1971. *Selections from the Prison Notebooks of Antonio Gramsci*, edited by Hoare, Quinton and Nowell-Smith, Geoffrey, London, England: Lawrence and Wishart.

Guba, E.G. 1985. "The Context of Emergent Paradigm Research." In *Organizational Theory and Inquiry*, edited by Y.S, 79–105. Lincoln. Beverly Hills, CA: Sage.

Guba, E.G., and Y.S. Lincoln. 1994. "Competing Paradigms in Qualitative Research." In *Handbook of Qualitative Research*, edited by N.K. Denzin, and Y.S. Lincoln, 105–117. Thousand Oaks, CA: Sage Publications.

Habermas, Jurgen. 1970a. "On Systematically Distorted Communications." *Inquiry* 13: 205–218.

Habermas, Jurgen. 1970b. "Towards a Theory of Communicative Competence." *Inquiry* 13: 360–375.

Habermas, Jurgen. 1971. *Toward a Rational Society*. London, England: Heinemann.

Habermas, Jurgen. 1972. *Knowledge and Human Interests*. London, England: Heinemann.

Habermas, Jurgen. 1974. *Theory and Practice*. London, England: Heinemann.

Habermas, Jurgen. 1976. *Legitimation Crisis*, London, England: Heinemann.

Hassard, John. 1988. "Overcoming Hermeticism in Organization Theory: An Alternative to Paradigm Incommensurability." *Human Relations* 41(3): 247–259.

Hassard, John. 1991a. "Multiple Paradigm Analysis: A Methodology for Management Research." In *The Management Research Handbook*, edited by C. Smith, and P. Dainty, 23–43. London, England: Routledge.

Hassard, John. 1991b. "Multiple Paradigm Research in Organizations: A Case Study." *Organization Studies* 12(2): 275–299.

Hassard, John. 1993. *Sociology and Organizational Theory: Positivism, Paradigms, and Postmodernity*. Cambridge, England: Cambridge University Press.

Hassard, John. 2013. "Can Sociological Paradigms Still Inform Organizational Analysis? A Paradigm Model for Post-Paradigm Times." *Organizational Studies* 34(11): 1701–1728.

Hegel, G. 1931. *The Phenomenology of Mind*. London, England: George Allen and Unwin.

Holland, R. 1990. "The Paradigm Plague: Prevention, Cure, and Innoculation." *Human Relations* 43(1): 23–48.

Horkheimer, M. 1972. *Critical Theory: Selected Essays.* New York, NY: Herder.

Husserl, Edmund. 1936, "Phenomenology," In *Encyclopedia Britannica*, 14th edition 825–831. Chicago, Illinois: Encyclopedia Britannica Inc.

Jackson, N., and P. Carter. 1991. "In Defense of Paradigm Incommensurability." *Organization Studies* 12(1): 109–127.

Jackson, N., and P. Carter. 2008. "Baffling Bill McKelvey, the Commensurability Kid." *Epherma* 8: 403–419.

James, William. 1890. *Principles of Psychology.* London, England: Macmillan.

Jennings, P., L. Perren, and S. Carter. 2005. "Guest Editor's Introduction: Alternative Perspectives on Entrepreneurship Research." *Entrepreneurship Theory and Practice* 29: 145–152.

Jick, T. 1979 "Mixing Quantitative and Qualitative Methods: Triangulation in Action." *Administrative Science Quarterly* 24(4): 602–611.

Kirkwood, J., and C. Campbell-Hunt. 2007. "Using Multiple Paradigm Research Methodologies to Gain New Insights into Entrepreneurial Motivations." *Journal of Enterprise Culture* 15: 219–241.

Knudsen, C. 2003. "Pluralism, Scientific Progress and the Structure of Organization Theory." In *The Oxford Handbook of Organization Theory*, edited by H. Tsoukas, and C. Knudsen, 262–288. Oxford, England: Oxford University Press.

Kuhn, T.S. 1962. *The Structure of Scientific Revolutions.* Chicago, IL: Chicago University Press.

Kuhn, T.S. 1970a. *The Structure of Scientific Revolutions.* Chicago, IL: University of Chicago Press, Second Edition with Postscript.

Kuhn, T.S. 1970b. "Reflections on My Critics." In *Criticism and the Growth of Knowledge*, edited by I. Lakatos, and A. Musgrave, 237–278. Cambridge, England: Cambridge University Press.

Kuhn, T.S. 1974. "Second Thoughts on Paradigms." In *The Structure of Scientific Theories*, edited by F. Suppe, 459–482. Chicago, IL: University of Illinois Press.

Kuhn, T.S. 1977. *The Essential Tension.* Chicago, IL: University of Chicago Press.

Lammers, C. 1974. "Mono- and Poly-Paradigmatic Developments in the Natural and Social Sciences," In *Social Processes of Scientific Development*, edited by R. Whitely. London, England: Routledge and Kegan Paul.

Lehmann, T., and R. Young. 1974. "From Conflict Theory to Conflict Methodology: An Emerging Paradigm for Sociology." *Sociological Inquiry* 44(1): 15–28.

Lewis, M., and A. Grimes. 1999. "Metatriangulation: Building Theory from Multiple Paradigms." *Academy of Management Review* 24: 672–690.

Lincoln, Y.S., ed. 1985. *Organizational Theory and Inquiry: The Paradigm Revolution.* Beverly Hills, CA: Sage Publications.

Lukacs, Georg. 1971. *History and Class Consciousness.* London, England: Merlin.

Marcuse, H. 1954. *Reason and Revolution.* New York, NY: Humanities Press.

Marcuse, H. 1964. *One-Dimensional Man.* London, England: Routledge and Kegan Paul.

Marcuse, H. 1966. *Eros and Civilisation.* Boston, MA: Beason.

Marcuse, H. 1968. *Negations: Essays in Critical Theory.* London, England: Heinemann.

Martin, J. 1990. "Breaking up the Mono-Method Monopolies in Organizational Research." In *The Theory and Philosophy of Organizations*, edited by J. Hassard, and D. Pym, 30-43. London, England: Routledge.

Maruyama, M. 1974. "Paradigms and Communication." *Technological Forecasting and Social Change* 6: 3–32.

Marx, Karl. 1973. *Grundrisse: Foundations of the Critique of Political Economy.* Harmondsworth, England: Penguin.

Marx, Karl. 1975. *Early Writings.* Harmondsworth, England: Penguin.

Marx, Karl. 1976. *Capital: A Critique of Political Economy*, Vols. I–III. Harmondsworth, England: Penguin.

Marx, Karl, and Fredrick Engels. 1965. *The German Ideology.* London, England: Lawrence and Wishart.

Marx, Karl, and Fredrick Engels. 1968. *Selected Works.* London, England: Lawrence and Wishart Ltd.

Masterman, M. 1970. "The Nature of Paradigms." In *Criticism and Growth of Knowledge*, edited by I. Lakatos, and A. Musgrave, 59–90. Cambridge, England: Cambridge University Press.

McKelvey, B. 2008. "Commensurability, Rhetoric, and Ephemera: Searching for Clarity in a Cloud of Critique." *Epherma* 8: 420–432.

Mead, George Herbert. 1932a. *Movements of Thought in the Nineteenth Century*, edited by M.N. Moore. Chicago, IL: University of Chicago Press.

Mead, George Herbert. 1932b. *The Philosophy of the Present*, edited by A.E. Murphy. Chicago, IL: Open Court Publishing.

Mead, George Herbert. 1934. *Mind, Self and Society*, edited by Charles Morris. Chicago, IL: University of Chicago Press.

Mead, George Herbert. 1938. *The Philosophy of the Act*, edited by Charles Morris. Chicago, IL: University of Chicago Press.

Merton, Robert K. 1968. *Social Theory and Social Structure.* New York, NY: Free Press.

Meszaros, I. 1970. *Marx's Theory of Alienation.* London, England: Merlin.

Meszaros, I. 1971 *Aspects of History and Class Consciousness.* London, England: Routledge and Kegan Paul.

Mir, R., and A. Mir. 2002. "The Organizational Imagination from Paradigm Wars to Praxis." *Organizational Research Methods* 5: 105–125.

Morgan, Gareth, ed. 1983. *Beyond Method: Strategies for Social Research.* Beverly Hills, CA: Sage Publications, Inc.

Morgan, Gareth. 1990. "Paradigm Diversity in Organizational Research." In *The Theory and Philosophy of Organizations*, edited by J. Hassard, and D. Pym, 13–29. London, England: Routledge.

Okhuysen, G., and J.P. Bonardi. 2011. "Editors' Comments: The Challenge of Building Theory by Combining Lenses." *Academy of Management Review* 36: 6–11.

Pareto, Vilfredo. 1935. *The Mind and Society*, 4 Volumes. New York, NY: Harcourt, Brace, Jovanovich.

Parsons, T. 1967. "A Paradigm for the Analysis of Social Systems and Change." In *System, Change, and Conflict*, edited by N. Demerath, and R. Peterson, 189–212. New York, NY: Free Press.

Plekhanov, G. 1974. *Selected Philosophical Works*, Vol. I. Moscow, Russia: Progress.

Rex, J. 1961. *Key Problems in Sociological Theory*. London, England: Routledge and Kegan Paul.

Rex, J. 1974. *Approaches to Sociology*. London, England: Routledge and Kegan Paul.

Ritzer, G. 1975. *Sociology: A Multiple-Paradigm Science*. New York, NY: Allyn and Bacon.

Romani, L., H. Primecz, and K. Topcu, K. 2011. "Paradigm Interplay for Theory Development: A Methodological Example with the Kulturstandard Method." *Organizational Research Method* 14: 432–455.

Sartre, Jean-Paul. 1966. *Being and Nothingness*. New York, NY: Washington Square Press.

Sartre, Jean-Paul. 1974. *Between Existentialism and Marxism*. London, England: Pantheon.

Sartre, Jean-Paul. 1976. *Critique of Dialectical Reason*, Vol. I. London, England: New Left Books.

Schultz, M., and M.J. Hatch. 1996. "Living with Multiple Paradigms: The Case of Paradigm Interplay in Organizational Culture Studies." *Academy of Management Review* 21: 529–557.

Schutz, Alfred. 1964. *Collected Papers II: Studies in Social Theory*. The Hague, The Netherlands: Martinus Nijhoff.

Schutz, Alfred. 1966. *Collected Papers III: Studies in Phenomenological Philosophy*. The Hague, The Netherlands: Martinus Nijhoff.

Schutz, Alfred. 1967. *Collected Papers I: The Problem of Social Reality*, 2nd edition. The Hague, The Netherlands: Martinus Nijhoff.

Shapere, D. 1971. "The Paradigm Concept." *Science* 17: 706–709.

Siehl, C., and J. Martin. 1988. "Measuring Organizational Culture: Mixing Qualitative and Quantitative Methods." In *Inside Organizations*, edited by M. Jones, D. Moore, and R. Snyder, 79–103. Beverly Hills, CA: Sage.

Simmel, Georg. 1936. *The Metropolis and Mental Life*. Chicago, IL: University of Chicago Press.

Simmerl, Georg. 1955. *Conflict and the Web of Group Affiliations*. Glencoe, IL: Free Press.

Skinner, B.F. 1953. *Science and Human Behaviour*. New York, NY: Macmillan.

Skinner, B.F. 1957. *Verbal Behavior*. New York, NY: Appleton-Century-Crofts.

Skinner, B.F. 1972. *Beyond Freedom and Dignity*. New York, NY: Alfred Knopf.

Snizek, W. 1976. "An Empirical Assessment of 'Sociology: A Multi-Paradigm Science.'" *American Sociologist* 1(2): 217–219.

Spencer, Herbert. 1873. *The Study of Sociology*. London, England: Kegan Paul and Tench.

Steinle, C. 1983. "Organization Theory and Multiple Plane Analysis." *Management International Review* 23: 31–46.

Stirner, Max. 1907. *The Ego and His Own*. New York, NY: Libertarian Book Club.

van de Berge, P. 1963. "Dialectics and Functionalism: Toward a Theoretical Synthesis." *American Sociological Review* 28(5): 695–705.

White, O. 1983. "Improving the Prospects for Heterodoxy in Organization Theory." *Administration and Society* 15(2): 257–272.

Willmott, H. 1990. "Beyond Paradigmatic Closure in Organizational Inquiry." In *The Theory and Philosophy of Organizations*, edited by J. Hassard, and D. Pym, 44–62. London, England: Routledge.

Willmott, H. 1993. "Breaking the Paradigm Mentality." *Organization Studies* 14: 681–719.

Winch, P. 1958. *The Idea of a Social Science.* London, England: Routledge and Kegan Paul.

Wittgenstein, L. 1963. *Philosophical Investigations.* Oxford, England: Blackwell.

Chapter 2

Human Nature

Four Paradigmatic Views

Any explanation of human nature is based on a worldview. The premise of this book is that any worldview can be associated with one of the four broad paradigms: functionalist, interpretive, radical humanist, and radical structuralist. This chapter takes the case of human nature and discusses it from the four different viewpoints. It emphasizes that the four views expressed are equally scientific and informative; they look at the phenomenon from their certain paradigmatic viewpoint; and together they provide a more balanced understanding of the phenomenon under consideration. In this chapter, the first four sections present the four perspectives, and the fifth section concludes the chapter.

FUNCTIONALIST VIEW

Liberal philosophy developed with the rise of capitalism. It advocated democracy and political liberties that reflected deeply-held moral convictions about the inherent equality of human beings. It led to the demands of the rising merchant, and later the industrial capitalist, class that challenged the restrictions set by the feudal system on travel, finance, and manufacture that hampered the growth of trade and industry. The climax of the confrontation between feudalism and capitalism was experienced at different times in different countries. For instance, in England, it took place in the mid-seventeenth century with the Civil War. Such social transformation affected both women and men. However, the changing circumstance of women's lives, together with the persuasiveness of the new ideas, led women to ask why the new egalitarianism was not applied to them. In the same way that the new bourgeois man revolted against the monarch's claim to absolute authority, which was based on divine right; the new bourgeois woman started to rebel against traditional male's claim to authority over her. Women stated that if the state should not have absolute sovereignty in the country, then, males should not have sovereignty in the family. Women also stated that if all men are born free, then, there is no reason for women to be born slaves, that is, be subjected to the inconstant, uncertain, unknown, arbitrary will of men.[1]

Liberal feminism has been a constant voice throughout the three hundred-year history of liberal political theory, although it has often gone unheard. Liberal feminists have consistently demanded that the liberal ideals that have been applies to men should also be applied to women. In the eighteenth century, liberal feminists demanded that women should have the natural rights that men had; in the nineteenth century, liberal feminists, based on utilitarianism, demanded that women should have equal rights as men under the law; and in the twentieth century, liberal feminists, based on the liberal theory of the welfare state, demanded that the state should actively pursue a variety of social reforms in order to ensure equal opportunities for women as men.

Over its long history, the liberal philosophy has produced in a number of strands, not all of which are consistent with each other. However, liberal theory is unified through its assumptions about human nature, which constitute the philosophical foundation of the theory. Liberal feminism, as well, is built on this foundation. Liberal feminism has always used liberal principles as its frame of reference, but it has always operated on the progressive end of liberal thought, and has pushed those ideals to their logical conclusion.

Liberal theory regards human beings as essentially rational agents. This may not seem particularly different, because the notion of rationality had always been prominent in the western philosophical tradition, from Aristotle to the medieval philosophers. However, liberal theorists have a particular conception of reason that uniquely distinguishes the liberal conception of human nature from others.

First, liberals consider rationality as a "mental" capacity. The classical liberal theorists believed in metaphysical dualism. That is, they believed the human mind and the human body represented two quite different realms, each of which is irreducible to the other, and each of which is only contingently connected with the other. Contemporary liberal theorists are not explicitly committed to metaphysical dualism, but their theories rest on a dualism which may be called "normative dualism." Normative dualists believe that an especially valuable characteristic of human beings is their "mental" capacity, that is, the capacity for rationality. Liberals assume that the physical basis of this capacity is irrelevant to their theory. An example of the expression of this view is the discussion by John Locke, a seventeenth-century liberal philosopher, of the case of the abbot of St. Martin. When abbot was born, his body did not look like the figure of a man, but more like a monster. People were not sure whether he should be baptized or not. However, he was finally baptized, and he was declared a man only provisionally, until he would prove it. In other words, Locke believed that what made the abbot a "man" was not his physical shape, but his capacity to reason, which was not possible to be determined at birth. Similar to Locke, contemporary liberal theorists believe that political rights should be given to people who have the specifically human capacity for rationality; and liberal theorists disregard people's "merely physical" capacities and incapacities.

Second, liberals consider rationality as a property of individuals rather than of groups. Similar to "normative dualism," this view of rationality reflects an underlying metaphysical assumption. Liberals assume that human individuals are ontologically prior to society. That is, human individuals are the basic constituents of social groups, in the sense that social groups are composed of individuals. Liberals believe that logically, if not empirically, human individuals can exist outside a social context; and that their essential characteristics, their needs and interests, their capacities and desires, not only are given independently of their social context, but also are not created or fundamentally altered by their social context. This metaphysical assumption is sometimes referred to as "abstract individualism," because its conception of individuals abstracts them from their social circumstances. The assumption of abstract individualism influences the liberal conception of rationality, which liberals regard as an essential characteristic of human individuals. Liberals find the assumption of abstract individualism to be compatible with the idea that the presence of a social group may be an empirical prerequisite for an individual's learning to exercise his or her capacity to reason, insofar as an individual's ability to reason is primarily inferred from one's ability to speak, and that speech develops only in groups. But, liberals find the assumption of abstract individualism to be incompatible with the idea that rationality is constituted by or defined by group norms, let alone as being a property of social structures. Instead, liberals identify as rational only those individuals who have the capacity to act in quite specific ways, ways which will be described shortly.

Third, liberals consider rationality to be a capacity that is possessed in approximately equal measure at least by all men. Descartes—who was not a political liberal, but his radically dualistic metaphysics and individualistic epistemology had a formative influence on the foundations of liberal theory—described rationality as a good sense, which is a good thing, and which is the most equally distributed among all individuals, and everybody thinks they are so abundantly provided with it that even those who are most difficult to please in other matters do not commonly desire more of it than they already possess. It does not seem that such individuals are making a mistake; it seems rather to be evidence in support of the view that the capacity of living a good life and of distinguishing the true from the false, which is called good sense or reason, is by nature equal in all men.

The human capacity to reason is described differently by different groups of liberals. Some liberals advocate the classical conception of reason as the guide to morality and values. However, they are often dominated by other liberals who advocate the more instrumental conception of reason, which began to develop with the rise of the new science in the seventeenth century.

In other words, there are two liberal conceptions of rationality: moral and prudential. Some liberal theorists emphasize one of those aspects, some other liberal theorists emphasize the other one, and still other liberals try to hold both in balance. For instance, Rousseau and Kant considered the essence of reason to be the ability to grasp the rational principles of morality, which is the distinguishing characteristic of humans from animals, and gave humans their special worth. On the other hand, Hobbes and Bentham considered rationality in instrumental terms and as the capacity to calculate the best means to an individual's ends, which were taken as given and were insusceptible to rational evaluation. Locke and some contemporary liberal theorists such as John Rawls and Robert Nozick advocate the maintenance of a balance between the moral and the instrumental aspects of rationality, arguing, for instance, that the establishment of the liberal state, is rational both because it is morally acceptable and because it is in the self-interest of the people who are subject to it. Rawls succeeds in striking an uneasy balance between the two aspects; but Nozick, who stresses the prudential justification of the state, the instrumental aspect of rationality dominates. Certainly, it is the instrumental conception of rationality that dominates in orthodox economics and in game theory.

It is also possible to differentiate between various liberal interpretations of rationality by distinguishing between the ends of human action and the means for achieving those ends. Some liberals believe that the ends of human action can be subjected to rational evaluation; some other liberals believe that reason can be used only in determining the most efficient means for achieving human ends. The ends/means distinction corresponds to the moral/prudential distinction because the rational evaluation of ends is typically made by liberals on moral grounds. In other words, those liberals who believe that reason has a moral dimension use their preferred moral theory to criticize the irrationality of immoral desires. Other liberals view each individual as the expert in following his or her own interest; and they refrain from criticizing the rationality of an individual's desires, except on formal grounds, for example, consistency. For instance, if an individual has several desires, a liberal theorist may criticize the rationality of that individual's desire to become a drug addict because addiction, for most people except the very wealthy, means that the individual's other desires are unlikely to be fulfilled. But, if an individual has no desires other than to become a drug addict, there is no grounds, except for moral ones, on which the liberal theorist can criticize the rationality of that desire. Thus, for many liberal theorists the specific content of each individual's desires cannot be subjected to rationality. Liberal theorists consider reason as instrumental, and they are concerned with means rather than ends. In other words, for liberals, reason has a perfectly clear and precise meaning. It is the choice of the right means to achieve a desired end. In this way, reason is not in any way related to the choice of ends.

Liberal theorists acknowledge the possible variety of individual desire, but they often attempt to identify desires that they believe are universal. Attempts by different liberal theorists have produced different results. For instance, Hobbes and Locke give high priority to the desire for "reputation," or the esteem of others; Rawls, in contrast, places high priority on the desire for self-respect, which he regards as the most important primary social good. Despite their differences, liberals tend to generally agree on the probable objects of most people's desire. This agreement is based on two assumptions that underlie liberal thought. The first one is the metaphysical assumption of abstract individualism, which was discussed earlier in this section. According to the assumption of abstract individualism, the desires and interests of each human individual can be fulfilled separately from the desires and interests of other people. The second assumption is more about the world rather than about human nature. It concerns the limited availability of resources necessary to sustain human life. That is, humans always face relative scarcity. Based on these two assumptions, liberal theorists tend to suppose that the desires of each human individual will motivate him or her to secure the largest individual share of the available limited resources. Hobbes explicitly states that humans are motivated by the desire for gain. Locke almost identifies rationality with the desire for unlimited accumulation, which he regards as rational not just in the prudential sense but also in the moral sense of being in accordance with the law of nature or reason. Rawls, too, in his formulation of principles of justice, considers that it is rational for any human individual to desire the largest possible share of what he calls the "primary social goods," which include "rights and liberties, opportunities and powers, income and wealth." Rawls adds that rational individuals balance the chance of receiving a large share of these goods against the risk of receiving a small share of such goods such that the risk of loss is minimized.

The liberal theorists' assumption that, in general, people seek to maximize their individual self-interest is one way of expressing their assumption of universal egoism. This assumption underlies liberal thinking, although liberals do not often explicitly refer to it as a motivational postulate. Only a few liberal philosophers, for example, Hobbes and Bentham, state that people always act on the basis of their perceived self-interest. Most of the other major liberal philosophers, for example, Locke, Kant, Mill, and Rawls, state that people are able to act on a moral principle of impartiality, which means that they are able to refrain from placing their own selfish interests before the interests of others. Therefore, these philosophers cannot be viewed as confirming the thesis of universal egoism. However, most of these philosophers believe that people naturally tend toward egoism, even though they are sometimes able to refrain from self-interested behavior. For instance, Mill believes that only "cultivated" adults have the capacity to act on moral principle. More specifically, Mill believes that such moral capacity emanates from an innate propensity to what he calls "sympathetic selfishness," that is, the ability to take pleasure in the pleasure of other people and to be saddened by their grief. In addition, Mill believes that people have such sympathy only with a relatively few other people, and not with all humanity. Consequently, Mill calls his postulated "innate capacity for sympathy."

John Rawls, compared to the other major liberal theorists, is committed less obviously to an assumption of universal egoism. Rawls bases his theory on the assumption that human individuals are mutually disinterested, that is, they tend to take no interest in each other's interest. Simultaneously, Rawls explicitly denies that this assumption commits him to universal egoism. He claims that the assumption of mutual disinterest, together with the fact that no human individual in the original position can know in advance his or her own position in the society which is being planned, results in the formulation of principles of justice that are identical to those that result from an assumption of universal benevolence. Rawls adds that the assumption of mutual disinterestedness is used only for the purposes of simplicity and clarity. He tries very hard to show that his theory of justice is compatible with a non-egoistic assumption about human nature. Rawls ultimately attempts to justify his theory based on the criterion that it adequately maximinimizes each individual's share of what he calls the "primary social goods." But, his use of the criterion of adequacy assumes that actual individuals in ordinary life, as well as hypothetical individuals in the contract situation, actually desire for the largest individual share. In general, even those liberal philosophers who believe that individual humans have the capacity for altruism or benevolence note that individual humans are, in general, confronted with a conflict between duty and inclination, and when there is scarcity, an individual human is often forced to choose between furthering his or her own interests or furthering the interests of others, and an individual human's natural inclination is invariably to favor what he or she perceives to be his or her own interests.

The preceding discussion makes it evident that liberal theory rests on the assumption that all individuals, at all times, and in all places, have a common essence or nature. Of course, this assumption is not unique to liberalism, and it is shared by any positive account of human nature. But, the liberal account of human motivation and rationality makes the universal truths about human nature quite specific. Human beings, no matter where or when they live, are viewed as tending naturally toward egoism or the maximization of their own individual utility, even though sometimes they may be constrained by moral principles. Liberalism assumes that human nature is essentially changeless, and therefore, liberalism is said to be "ahistorical," that is, liberalism does not account for such "accidental" differences among human individuals which result from living in different historical periods, occupying different rank or class positions, and belonging to different race or sex categories. Liberals define human beings in the abstract by their universal and "essential" capacity for reason.

Although liberal theorists consider human nature as essentially changeless, they acknowledge that certain psychological differences exist among individuals, and that those differences may be the result of individuals' different social experiences. Liberals also acknowledge that different individuals have different wants; that different individuals have different degrees of concern about the interests of others; that different individuals are different as to the extent they are receptive with respect to moral principles; and that different individuals vary in how far and by which emotions they are influenced. Liberals agree that many of these variations among individuals are likely to be the result of differences in individual social experience. Whereas Descartes postulates innate mental structures, Locke develops the empiricist conception of the mind as a "tabula rasa" which is inscribed by experience.

Liberals do not believe that by acknowledging individual differences they are contradicting their basic assumption of a universal human nature. Their argument is that they view rationality, that is, the human essence, as a potential rather than as an empirically-observable characteristic. They add that for different individuals this potentiality may be actualized to different degrees, such that rational individuals may behave irrationally in certain situations. Consequently, although all individuals may have an equal capacity for rationality, actual individuals may not be equally rational. It should be noted that the liberal conception of reason is both normative and descriptive. This means that individuals who have failed to develop their capacity for reason are not only different from those who have succeeded but also they are deficient because they have failed to fulfill their uniquely human potential.

INTERPRETIVE VIEW

The Enlightenment viewed man as wholly of a piece with nature and complying with the general uniformity of composition which Baconian and Newtonian natural science had discovered there. That is, there is a human nature which is regularly organized, thoroughly invariant, and marvelously simple as Newton's universe. Some of its laws may be different, but there are laws; some of its regularities may be obscured by the trappings of local fashion, but it is regular. Men are men under any guise and against any backdrop.[2]

According to the Enlightenment view, all the differences among men, in beliefs and values, in customs and institutions, both over time and across place, do not play any role in defining human nature. These differences are nothing but mere accretions, distortions, overlaying, and obscuring the true in human nature: the constant, the general, and the universal. In general, anything of which the intelligibility, verifiability, or actual affirmation is limited to men of a special age, race, temperament, tradition, or condition lacks truth, value, or importance to a reasonable man.

In contrast to the Enlightenment type of view, a constant human nature independent of time; place; circumstance; studies and professions; transient fashions and temporary opinions, does not exist. What man is, indeed, depends on where he is, who he is, and what he believes, because man is so entangled with them and so is inseparable from them. These considerations have given rise to the cultural view of man, which stands in contrast to the uniformitarian view of man. The former strongly believes that men unmodified by the customs of their particular places do not exist, have never existed, and cannot exist. To use the metaphor of performing actors, there is, and there can be, no backstage where one can go to see the "real persons" who are relaxing in their casual clothes, and are disengaged from their profession, displaying their spontaneous desires and unprompted passions. This is because they only change their roles, their styles of acting, and their play's drama; that is, they are always performing.

This makes the distinction between what is natural, universal, and constant in man and what is conventional, local, and variable extraordinarily difficult. Any attempt to make such distinction falsifies the human situation. What can one conclude about human nature from thousand peculiar things that people in different cultures do, which anthropologists discover, investigate, and describe. That people living in a specific culture are peculiar? That they are just the same as other people living in totally different cultures, but with some peculiar and incidental customs? That they are innately different or instinctively led in certain directions rather than others? Or, that human nature does not exist; and men are pure and they are simply what their culture makes them?

All of these interpretations are unsatisfactory. A more viable concept of man would account for not only culture and the variability of culture but also the basic unity of mankind. This more viable concept of man would not totally leave the uniformitarian view of human nature. It, at the same time, would not adhere to the idea that the diversity of custom across time and space is not a mere matter of garb and appearance, of stage settings and comedic masques, because such adherence would mean that human nature is as various in its essence as it is in its expression.

Attempts to locate man within his customs have taken several directions and have followed diverse tactics. But, almost all of them, have proceeded along a single overall intellectual strategy, which may be called the "stratigraphic" conception of the relations between biological, psychological, social, and cultural factors in human life. In this conception, man is composed of several "levels," each of which is superimposed upon those beneath it, and, at the same time, is underpinning those above it. In the analysis of man, these layers are peeled off one after another. Each of these layers is complete and irreducible in itself. After one layer is peeled off, underneath it is another layer, which is of a quite different type. Beneath the layer designated for the motley forms of culture, there is the layer designated for structural and functional regularities of social organization. After these two layers are peeled off, there is the layer designated for the underlying psychological factors—that is, "basic needs"—that support them and make them possible. After the layer for psychological factors is peeled off, there is the layer designated for the biological foundations—that is, anatomical, physiological, and neurological—of the whole edifice of human life.

This type of conceptualization not only has guaranteed the independence and sovereignty of established academic disciplines, but also has avoided stating that man's culture is all there is to him, and has stated that culture is an essential, irreducible, and paramount ingredient in his nature. According to this type of conceptualization, cultural facts can be interpreted against the background of non-cultural facts, such that without either dissolving cultural facts into that background, or dissolving that background into the cultural facts. In this conceptualization, man is a hierarchically stratified being and at each of his various levels—organic, psychological, social, and cultural—he has an assigned and incontestable place. In order to see what he really is, it is necessary to superimpose findings from the various relevant sciences— anthropology, sociology, psychology, biology—upon one another. When this is done, the cultural level, which is distinctive to man, would contribute, in its own right, to the understanding of what man really is. In this way, the eighteenth-century image of man as pure "reasoner"—that is, when he took off his cultural costumes—was replaced, in the late nineteenth and early twentieth centuries—by the image of man as the stratified being—that is, when he put on his cultural costumes.

This grand strategy, at the level of concrete research and specific analysis, translates into two steps. First, a search for universals in culture, that is, for empirical uniformities that, despite the diversity of customs across time and space, can be found everywhere in almost the same form. Second, relating such universals in culture to the established constants of human biology, psychology, and social organization. If some customs can be found as common to all local variants of it, and if these can then be related in a determinate manner with certain invariant points of reference on the subcultural levels, then progress can be made toward specifying which cultural traits are essential to human existence and which are merely adventitious, peripheral, or ornamental. In this way, cultural dimensions of a concept of man can be determined such that they are commensurate with dimensions similarly determined by biology, psychology, and sociology.

Of course, this is not a new idea. It is the notion of a "consensus gentium" (a consensus of all mankind), which states that there are some things that all men agree upon as right, real, just, or attractive, and, therefore, in fact, these things are right, real, just, or attractive. This notion was present in the Enlightenment and perhaps, some form of it has been present in all ages. The question is whether this research project would work?

The answer depends on whether it is possible to establish and sustain the dualism between empirically universal aspects of culture rooted in subcultural realities, on the one hand, and empirically variable aspects of culture not rooted in subcultural realities, on the other hand. This requires: (1) that the universals can be found and that they be substantial; (2) that they be closely and directly intertwined with particular biological, psychological, or sociological processes; and (3) that they can be defended as core elements in the characterization of human nature such that the much more numerous cultural particularities be of secondary importance. On all of these three counts the "consensus gentium" approach fails. That is, rather than moving closer to the essentials of human nature, it moves away from it.

The major reason for the search for universals, and shying away from cultural particularities, in defining human nature is that the enormous variation in human behavior haunts them by a fear of historicism, of becoming lost in cultural relativism that deprives them of any fixed bearings at all. The notion that only an empirically universal cultural phenomenon can reflect something about the nature of man is not logical. This is because this notion has the same logic as the notion that because sickle-cell anemia is, fortunately, not universal it cannot tell us anything about human genetic processes. In science, what is critically important is not whether phenomena are empirically common, but, whether phenomena can reveal the enduring natural processes that underlie them. For instance, this is why Becquerel had been so interested in the peculiar behavior of uranium.

Therefore, there should be a search for systematic relationships among diverse phenomena, instead of a search for substantive identities among similar ones. For this purpose, the "stratigraphic" conception of the relationships among the various aspects of human existence should be replaced with a synthetic one. In this one, biological, psychological, sociological, and cultural factors are treated as variables within unitary systems of analysis. This does not mean that the establishment of a common language in the social sciences is either a matter of coordination of terminologies or of creating new ones; or it is a matter of imposing one set of categories upon the whole area. But, it is a matter of integrating different types of theories and concepts in order to formulate meaningful propositions embodying findings which are now compartmentalized in separate fields of study.

In order for such an integration to provide a more accurate image of man, it would be useful to account for the following two ideas. The first idea is that culture should be viewed not as complexes of concrete behavior patterns—customs, usages, traditions, habit clusters—as has been done up to now, but as a set of control mechanisms—plans, recipes, rules, instructions (or "programs," as in parlance of computer engineers)—for the governing of behavior. The second idea is that man is most desperately dependent upon such cultural programs that would act as extra-genetic, outside-the-skin control mechanisms for ordering his behavior.

The "control mechanism" view of culture assumes that the foundation of human thought is both social and public. That is, the natural habitat of human thought is the house yard, the marketplace, and the town square. Thinking does not consist of "happenings in the head," although what happens in the head and elsewhere are necessary for thinking to occur. Thinking consists of traffic in "significant symbols"—that is, words (for the most part), gestures, drawings, musical sounds, mechanical devices (e.g., clocks), or natural objects (e.g., jewels). These significant symbols are, indeed, composed of anything that is disengaged from its mere actuality and used to impose meaning upon experience. Each individual takes such symbols as given. When the individual is born, he finds such symbols already current in the community. During his life, some of the existing symbols remain in place, some of the existing symbols are partially altered, some of the existing symbols are discarded, and some new symbols are added. The individual may or may not have had a role in these changes. After the individual dies, these symbols remain in circulation with their relevant changes. During his life, the individual uses some or all of the symbols either deliberately and with care, or spontaneously and with ease. The individual always uses the symbols to put a construction upon the events of his life, and to orient himself with respect to his life experiences.

Man needs these symbolic sources of illumination in order to find his bearings in the world. This is because the non-symbolic sources, which are constituted in his body, provide only a diffused light. For lower animals, their behavior patterns, to a much larger extent, is given to them by their physical structure. Their genetic sources of information order their behavior within much limited ranges of variation. The narrower and more completely their behavior are determined by the genetic sources, the lower the animal. For man, on the other hand, genetic sources provide only extremely general response capacities. Although, these innately given capacities allow for far greater plasticity, complexity, and effectiveness of behavior (under certain perfect conditions), they leave human behavior much less precisely regulated. Therefore, if man's behavior is undirected by culture patterns—that is, organized systems of significant symbols—it would be virtually ungovernable. There will be a mere chaos of pointless acts and exploding emotions, such that man's experience will be virtually shapeless. Culture, the accumulated totality of such symbolic patterns, is not merely an ornament of human existence, but the principal basis of the specificity of human existence, that is, culture is an essential condition for human existence.

The most crucial support for such cultural position comes from recent advances in knowledge and evidence with respect to the emergence of "Homo sapiens" out of his general primate background. Of these advances three are most important: (1) the replacement of a sequential view of the relations between the physical evolution and the cultural development of man with an overlap or interactive view; (2) the discovery that the major biological changes that produced modern man out of his most immediate progenitors took place in his central nervous system and most especially in his brain; (3) the understanding that, in physical terms, man is an incomplete and an unfinished animal; that what distinguishes him most graphically from non-men is not so much his sheer ability to learn (great as that is), but how much and what specifically he has to learn before he is enabled to function. Let me take each of these points in turn.

The traditional view of the relations between the biological and the cultural advance of man was that at some point in time the biological development was completed and exactly at that time the cultural development began. According to the evidence, such a moment in time did not exist. The transition to the cultural mode of life took the genus *Homo* more than one million years to accomplish. Over such a long period of time, complex and closely ordered sequence of genetic changes took place.

In the current view, the evolution of "Homo sapiens"—that is, modern man—from his immediate pre-sapiens counterpart started nearly two million years ago with the emergence of Australopithecines—that is, the ape men of southern and eastern Africa—and culminated with the appearance of *sapiens* himself one to two hundred thousand years ago. Thus, as at least basic forms of cultural, or proto-cultural, activity (e.g., simple tool-making, hunting, etc.) were present among some of the Australopithecines. There was an overlap of more than one million years between the beginning of culture and the appearance of the current man. This overlap was an extended one. The final phases (i.e., final as of today) of the phylogenetic development of man took place in the same grand geological era—that is, Ice Age—as the initial phases of his cultural development.

This means that culture was not added on to a finished animal, but was a crucial ingredient in the production process of that animal itself. The slow and steady growth of culture through the Ice Age played a major directive role in man's evolution. The development of tools, the adoption of organized hunting and gathering practices, the beginnings of true family organization, the discovery of fire, and the increasing use of systems of significant symbols (language, art, myth, ritual) for orientation, communication, and self-control, all created a new environment for man, who had to adapt to them. As culture slowly accumulated and developed, an advantage was given to those individuals in the community who were most able to benefit from it—that is, the effective hunter, the persistent gatherer, the adept toolmaker, and the resourceful leader—until the small-brained, proto-human "Homo Australopithecus" became the large-brained fully human "Homo sapiens." Among the cultural pattern, the body, and the brain, a feedback system came to being such that each shaped the progress of the other. For instance, in this system, the interaction among increasing tool use, the changing anatomy of the hand, and the expanding representation of the thumb on the cortex represents how the feedback system worked. By adopting symbolically mediated programs for producing artifacts, organizing social life, or expressing emotions, man determined, perhaps unknowingly, the final stages of his own biological development. Quite literally, but quite inadvertently, man created himself.

This suggests that human nature is not independent of culture. As man's central nervous system—and most particularly its crowning curse and glory, the neocortex—developed in great part in interaction with culture, it cannot direct man's behavior or organizing his experience without the guidance generated by systems of significant symbols. In the Ice Age, man was obliged to replace the regularity and precision of detailed genetic control over his conduct with the flexibility and adaptability of a more generalized genetic control over his conduct. To receive the additional information which was necessary to be enabled to act, man was forced to increasingly rely on cultural sources—that is, the accumulated significant symbols. Thus, such symbols are not mere expressions, instrumentalities, or correlates of man's biological, psychological, and social existence; but, they are prerequisites for it. Without men, there is no culture; and without culture, there are no men. Men are incomplete animals who complete themselves through culture, and they complete themselves not through culture in general but through highly particular forms of it. Men's ideas, values, acts, emotions, and nervous system are cultural products, products which are manufactured out of tendencies, capacities, and dispositions with which men were born, but manufactured nonetheless.

RADICAL HUMANIST VIEW

Socialist feminism was born in the 1970s. The central project of socialist feminism is the synthesis of the best insights of radical feminism and of the Marxist tradition. It is not easy to clearly define socialist feminism in the same way that it is not easy to define liberal feminism, radical feminism, or Marxist feminism. This is because feminist theorists and activists do not always specify their group membership, and, even if they do, they do not always agree on who should belong to which group, and those who belong to the same group do not always agree with each other. For instance, most Marxists are placing much emphasis on the oppression of women; while radical feminists are paying increasing attention to class, ethnic, and national differences among women. As a result, it is getting more difficult to draw a line between socialist feminism and other feminist theories. However, it is still possible to identify socialist feminism, as with other brands of feminism, based on its underlying conception of human nature.[3]

One way to draw the outline of socialist feminism is to compare and contrast it with the other feminist theories, especially with radical feminism and Marxist feminism, to which it is most closely related. In general, all feminists are concerned with the following problems: what constitutes the oppression of women, and how that oppression can be ended? Both liberal feminists and Marxist feminists believe that such problems can be dealt with in terms of the categories and principles which were originally formulated to deal with other problems. That is, these feminists treat the oppression of women as just another problem among many other problems. Socialist feminists, similarly to radical feminists, believe that older established theories are incapable, in principle, of giving a sufficiently adequate consideration to women's oppression, and therefore, it is necessary to develop new analytical categories.

Socialist feminists, similarly to radical feminists, believe that such new analytical categories must reconceptualize both the so-called "public sphere" and the "private sphere" of human life. Such new analytical categories must provide a way of understanding sexuality, childbearing, childrearing, and personal maintenance in political and economic terms. Socialist feminists, in contrast to many American radical feminists, attempt to deliberately conceptualize such activities in an historical, in contrast to a universal and sometimes biological, way. A defining characteristic goal of socialist feminists is to reinterpret the historical materialist method of Marxist feminists, and to apply it to the issues raised by radical feminists. That is, socialist feminists intend to use a feminist version of the Marxist method to provide feminist answers to feminist questions.

The relationship between feminism and Marxism has been in a chronic dispute ever since the inception of the women's liberation movement in the mid-1960s. One of the main forms of this dispute is most commonly interpreted in terms of political priorities. The political analysis of Marxism has implied that the struggle for feminism should be subordinated to the class struggle; whereas the political analysis of radical feminism has implied that the struggle for women's liberation should take priority over the struggle for all other forms of liberation. Socialist feminism does not view this situation as a dilemma. It refuses either to compromise socialism for the sake of feminism, or to compromise feminism for the sake of socialism. It argues that either of these two compromises would ultimately be self-defeating. Socialist feminists believe that capitalism, male dominance, racism, and imperialism are so inextricably intertwined and inseparable such that the abolition of any one of these systems of domination requires the end of all of them. Socialist feminists are concerned with a full understanding of the following two relationships: (1) the ways in which the capitalist system is structured by male dominance; and (2) the ways in which contemporary male dominance is organized by the capitalist division of labor. Socialist feminists believe that an adequate understanding of "capitalist patriarchy" requires the application of the historical materialist method of Marxism after it has been made more precise by feminist consciousness.

The conception of human nature to which socialist feminism is committed is the basic Marxist conception of human nature. As the Marxist conception of human nature will be explained under the radical structuralist section, human nature is created historically through the dialectical interaction between human biology, human society, and the physical environment. This interaction is mediated through human labor or praxis. The prevailing dominant form of praxis in a specific society creates the distinctive physical and psychological human-type characteristic of that society.

Liberals recognize only a very limited number of human types. They acknowledge individual human variation and utilize it as their argument for a firm limitation on the extent of state power. Some liberals, such as Locke and Mill, explain the reasons for some of the variations among individuals in terms of the social opportunities available to different classes; and liberal feminists explain psychological differences between the sexes in terms of sex-role socialization. Liberals, however, ultimately view the differences among individuals as relatively superficial, as they believe what underlies these superficial individual differences is a certain fixed human nature, which is only modified, but not fundamentally created, by social circumstances.

Marxists, in contrast, view human nature as constituted in society. They believe that particular historical circumstances create distinctive human types. They believe that, in contemporary capitalism, and based on class analyses, there are two human types: the capitalist and the proletariat. They have a conception of human nature that only recognizes difference in social class, but neglects differences in sex, age, race, ethnicity, and national backgrounds. Contemporary society consists of these groups, which differ markedly from each other, both physically and psychologically.

Liberals have tended to either ignore or minimize all these differences. Marxists have tended to recognize only differences in class. Radical feminists have tended to recognize only differences in age and sex, which are understood in universal terms, and are determined biologically. Socialist feminists, in contrast, recognize all these differences as constituent components of contemporary human nature, and seek to understand them in a way that is not only materialist but also historical. Socialist feminists, in particular, have emphasized theoretical progress in understanding the differences between women and men. Socialist feminists, in applying Marxist methodology, seek to enhance such understanding through an examination of what is called "the sexual division of labor." Socialist feminists, in other words, focus on the different types of praxis undertaken by women, in contrast to men, in order to develop a fully historical materialist explanation of the social construction of sex and gender.

According to socialist feminists, the differences between women and men are both physical and psychological, as they have investigated both of these aspects of human nature. For instance, studies have found that variations in menstruation and menopause are often socially determined. Another study has investigated the ways in which society influences women's sporting achievements, as well as their menstrual patterns. Still another study has explored some of the socially determined ways in which men and women move differently from each other; and experience space, objects, and even their own bodies differently; and also that women in sexist societies are "physically handicapped." In yet another study, differences between men's and women's body language have been the focus. Socialist feminists, in undertaking such investigations, focus on the dialectical relationship between sex and society, which emerges through activity organized by gender norms. In this way, the methodological approach of socialist feminists clearly illustrates that they have abandoned an ahistorical conception of human biology. Socialist feminists, instead, believe that human biology is, in part, socially constructed, that is, biology is "gendered" as well as sexed.

Socialist feminists, as well as other contemporary feminists, have been far more concerned with psychological differences between women and men, than physical differences between women and men. Their main focus has been on the social construction of masculine and feminine character types, rather than on masculine and feminine physical types. They have found that very early in life masculine and feminine character structures are established; and that once established, these structures are very rigid. They have utilized, in their analysis, some version of psychoanalysis to explain the mechanism by which psychological masculinity and femininity are imposed on infants and young children. They believe psychoanalytic theory provides the most plausible and systematic explanation of how the individual's psyche is structured by gender. Socialist feminists—unlike Freud, the father of psychoanalysis—do not believe that psychological masculinity and femininity is the child's inevitable response to a fixed and universal biological endowment. They believe, instead, that the acquisition of gendered character types is the result of specific social practices, particularly procreative practices, which are not determined by biology, and therefore, are alterable. They intend to debiologize Freud, and to reinterpret him in terms of historical materialism.

Socialist feminism's utilization of psychoanalytic theory should not be taken as its defining characteristic. This is because not only various feminist and non-feminist theorists utilize certain insights of psychoanalysis, but also that socialist feminists may ultimately reject all versions of Freudian theory—perhaps either in favor of a more elegant theory, or in the belief that Freud's fundamental assumptions about human nature are incompatible with historical materialism.

Socialist feminism's recognition of the social determination of human beings' "inner" lives should not be taken as its distinguishing character. The recognition of such determination has been growing since the start of the twentieth century, partly because of the general popularization of Freudian theory, and partly because of the help it provided to the left movement in explaining political phenomena such as the occurrence of fascism rather than socialist revolution in Western Europe. For instance, in the 1930s, Wilhelm Reich and the members of the Frankfurt School found out that the sexually repressive German family created the so-called authoritarian character structure, which in turn, easily accepted Nazism. These explorations on the left have enriched the nineteenth-century Marxist view of "man," whom was treated as having been born at the time of applying for "his" first job.

The distinctive aspect of the socialist feminism is that it approaches human psychology by synthesizing insights from various sources. Socialist feminism claims all of the following: (1) human beings' "inner" lives, bodies, and behavior are structured by gender; (2) gender structuring is not innate, but is socially imposed; (3) particular characteristics that are imposed are intimately related to the particular system of the organization of the social production that historically prevails in society; (4) gender structuring of human beings' "inner" lives occurs when human beings are very young, and it is reinforced not only throughout their lives but also in various spheres of their lives; and (5) such relatively rigid masculine and feminine character structures play a very important role in maintaining male dominance. Socialist feminism uses this conception of human psychology to provide a historical materialist analysis of the relationship between human beings' "inner" lives and their social praxis. It seeks to relate the masculine and feminine psychology to the sexual division of labor.

Socialist feminism believes that human beings constantly recreate themselves through historically-specific forms of praxis. Accordingly, socialist feminism's conception of human nature is inseparable from its social theory. Consequently, the socialist feminist explanation of the social construction of women and men is based on not only its views about human psychology and physiology but also its views about social institutions and ways of organizing social life.

It is generally accepted, by both feminists and non-feminists, that in contemporary society, the most common manifestation of the sexual division of labor is between the so-called public and private spheres of human life. The line between these two spheres of life has been variously drawn historically. For instance, in ancient Greece, "the economy" was associated with the private sphere, but in contemporary society, "the economy" is considered to be part of the public realm. Wherever the distinction between the two spheres of life has existed, the private realm has always: (1) included sexuality and procreation; (2) been viewed as more "natural," and therefore, less "human" than the public realm; and (3) been viewed as the realm of women. Although, throughout history, women have always done various types of work, they have been primarily defined by their sexual and procreative labor, that is, women have been defined as "sex objects" and as mothers.

Socialist feminist theory has mostly focused on sexuality and procreation, partly because they believe that an individual's gender identity is established very early in life, and partly because women are primarily defined in terms of their sexual and procreative labor. Their theory has conceptualized sexuality and procreation while remaining historical, rather than biological; as well as remaining specific, rather than universal. Socialist feminism has drawn on the radical feminist insight that sexual activity, childbearing, and childrearing are social practices that involve power relations, and therefore, should be treated as subjects of political analysis. Socialist feminism, however, rejects biological determinism of radical feminism, and therefore, denies the radical feminism's belief that such practices are fundamentally invariant. Socialist feminists, in contrast, have stressed historical variations both in such practices, and in the categories by which they are understood.

According to socialist feminism, all of the processes in which a woman engages should be understood in connection with the society in which she lives, and with the ideology of that society. For instance, the act of a woman giving birth to a child is called an act of "motherhood," if it reflects the relations of marriage and the family. Otherwise, the very same act is called "adultery," and the child is called "illegitimate" or "bastard." The term "mother" may have a totally different meaning when different relations are involved, such as "unwed mother." The meaning depends on what relations are embodied in the act. Similarly, fatherhood is a social invention which is located in a series of functions rather than in biology. Likewise, being a child is a fairly variable social relation.

Socialist feminists believe that there is no trans-historical definition of marriage that encompasses the marital institutions of different cultures. Even within a class-divided society, the working-class family unit not only is defined very differently from the upper-class family unit, but also it performs very different social functions. In general, socialist feminists believe that human nature is constructed, in part, through the historically-specific ways in which human beings have organized their sexual, childbearing, and childrearing activities. The organization of such activities both affects and is affected by class and ethnic differences, but it is regarded as playing a very important role in creating the masculine and feminine physiques and character structures which are considered appropriate in a specific society.

The socialist feminist theory emphasizes the importance of the so-called private sphere of procreation in constructing the historically-specific types of masculinity and femininity, but it does not ignore the so-called public sphere. It recognizes that women have always worked besides procreation, and have provided goods and services not only for their families, but also for society at large. Socialist feminists argue that the conception of women as primarily sexual beings and/or as mothers is an ideological mystification that misrepresents the facts, for example, in the world, more than half the farmers are women; and in the United States, about half the paid labor force are women.

Socialist feminists believe that women's, just as much as men's, labor transforms the non-human world. Socialist feminists see the slogan "A women's place is everywhere" as more than a call for change, because they see it as already constituting a partial description of existing reality. Socialist feminists recognize that women perform productive work, but they also recognize that women's work has rarely, if ever, been the same as men's work. Socialist feminists recognize that even in contemporary market society, the paid labor force is almost completely segregated by sex, that is, there are "women's specialities." Moreover, within the contemporary labor force, women's work is invariably regarded as less prestigious, lower paid, and defined as less skilled than men's, even when it involves such socially valuable and complex skills as dealing with children or sick people. Socialist feminists, therefore, recognize that the sexual division of labor is not only a division between procreation and "production," but also a division within procreation and within "production." Socialist feminists, in addition, recognize that contemporary masculinity and femininity are not only constructed through the social organization of procreation, but also are elaborated and reinforced in nonprocreative labor. Socialist feminists not only stress the historical variation in women's procreative work but also stress the historical variation in women's non-procreative work. They not only consider the consequences of changes in the mode of procreation but also in the mode of "production."

RADICAL STRUCTURALIST VIEW

Marxist theory was formulated in the middle of nineteenth century, that is, when the worst of the Industrial Revolution was becoming apparent, and when most of the liberal democratic, or "bourgeois," revolutions had taken place or were taking place in Europe. Marxist theory stands in contrast to liberal theory. Liberal theory is historically associated with capitalism and provides a rationale for it. Marxism, on the other hand, provides a devastating critique of the capitalist system. According to Marxism, the liberal theory, which was employed to justify the bourgeois revolutions, is only an egalitarian rhetoric which is used to disguise the deep-seated inequalities that characterize all class-divided societies. In Marxism, the notion of class plays a foundational role in understanding all social phenomena. In Marxism, the classless society is the good society.[4]

Marx and Engels, who was Marx's friend and collaborator, produced a huge amount of writings, which include: (1) their early exploratory essays in the 1840s; (2) their main ideas as reflected in The Communist Manifesto of 1848 (the "year of revolutions"); (3) Marx's vast, but unfinished technical treatise Capital; and (4) Engels' attempts to develop and popularize his and Marx's ideas after Marx's death in 1883. Overall, Marx and Engels produced their writings during a period of half a century, and therefore, inevitably there are changes, and perhaps inconsistency, in their ideas. After the death of Marx and Engels, many authors have attempted to interpret, revise, and extend Marxist theory; however, they have strongly disagreed not only about what Marx meant, but also about what he actually said, as well as what he would have said if he were currently alive. Of course, there is no certain way to resolve the continuing controversy over how to characterize Marxist theory. Marx's writings, as those of any other writer, are open to various interpretations; and he did not get the chance to fully address a number of issues, including the status of women. Engels, after Marx's death, undertook a systematic analysis of women's oppression in "The Origin of the Family, Private Property and the State," which has been accepted as the classic statement on women by generations of Marxists.

In general, Marxist theory can be regarded as a developing science, that is, the century-old writings of Marx and Engels should not be regarded as the final word on anything, especially in the light of the enormous social changes that have taken place since their writings. Nonetheless, it is possible to identify an interpretation of Marxism that has been the most widely accepted interpretation of Marxist theory.

Marxism refutes liberalism. It rejects liberalism's conception of rationality and philosophical method. It follows an approach which is founded on a conception of human nature, which is directly opposed to the liberal conception of human nature. Marx's explicit discussions of human nature mostly occur in his earlier and unpublished writings, which have been found only in relatively recent years. Marx's later and published work stress the scientific status of his social analysis, but, infrequently discuss the philosophical foundations of his scientific analysis, and ridicule his earlier use of such terminology as "human essence." There has been a considerable controversy regarding the continuity between Marx's earlier and later work. Some scholars argue that the old Marx made a sharp break with the young Marx. Some other scholars argue that the differences between Marx's earlier and later work should be seen as differences of emphasis rather than differences of content. Still other scholars argue that Marx chose to place emphasis on a "scientific" approach in his published work, but for his own clarification established the philosophical foundations of that analysis, which therefore he decided not to publish. According to this last argument, a conception of human nature underlies all Marx's work. In any case, in order to stay away from this controversy as far as possible, the rest of this section draws chiefly, though not entirely, on Marx's later work.

The Marxist conceptions of human nature are in fundamental contrast to the liberal conception of human nature because it rejects metaphysical dualism. Marxists do not believe that the human essence is a capacity for rationality that may be embodied in various forms. In contrast, Marxists believe that human beings are one biological species among others. Marxists also believe that it is a necessary, rather than an accidental, fact that humans have a specific kind of biological constitution, which has profound consequences for human social life.

Marxists believe that the survival of the physical structure of the human body requires humans to draw on the resources of the non-human world. Humans need food, water, shelter, clothing, and so on, which are obtainable from non-human nature. Based on their biology, human beings have many needs, and therefore, humans can be conceived only in relation to a world in which these needs may be satisfied. This partly explains why Marxists reject the possibility of making a sharp conceptual distinction between human and non-human nature, because they are two internally related aspects of a larger whole.

So far, no distinction is made between humans and other biological species. This is because both humans and animals, for their physical survival, must draw on the non-human world. Marxists believe that human beings differ from animals because when human beings attempt to fulfill their needs, they do not simply utilize what the world provides, they transform the world. Human beings do not simply graze or find ready-made shelter, they grow food and prepare it, and they construct their own shelters. Of course, this is different from what some animals do when they produce their means of subsistence by building nests, webs, and so on. More specifically, a spider's operations resemble those of a weaver, and a bee's operations resemble those of an architect. But, what distinguishes the worst architect from the best of bees is that the architect constructs his or her structure in imagination before he or she constructs it in reality. In other words, at the end of every labor process, human beings obtain an outcome that already existed in the imagination of the laborer at the start of that process. The laborer not only changes the form of the material on which he works, but also he realizes a purpose of his own that gives the law to his modus operandi, and to which he must subordinate his will. Although the way humans and animals utilize the world's resources look similar, they are fundamentally different. This is because the activity of humans, in contrast to the activity of animals, is conscious and purposeful, which is what Marx calls it "praxis."

The history of the word "praxis" can be traced back to the time of Homer. It is a noun which is derived from a Greek verb which means "to do" or "to act." So, the earliest meaning of "praxis" is "conscious action or achievement," rather than "making an object." Afterward, "praxis" was used in association with economic activity, and meant "a transaction; a business; or even the exaction of money, or the recovery of debt." Marx used "praxis" to mean "conscious physical labor that transforms the material world in order to satisfy human needs." For Marx, praxis, rather than pure rational thought, constitutes the essential human activity. An adequate understanding of the Marxist notion of praxis provides an adequate understanding of the Marxist conception of human nature.

Praxis is essentially a social activity. This does not rule out the possibility that individuals sometimes plan their own labor, or work alone. It emphasizes that no individual can live an entirely solitary life. Indeed, a solitary human individual cannot survive physically, as the human biological constitution requires human interdependence for simple survival. Even if an individual, through some unique circumstances, were able to survive in isolation, that individual would lack not only language but also any of the accumulated experience of the human species. Furthermore, his or her survival efforts would resemble the instinctive efforts of animals. Human praxis, in contrast, is cooperative as it invariably involves division of labor, and is based on the knowledge, skills, and experience of previous workers. As a result, the worker's frame of reference regarding what needs to be done, how it should be done, and when it has been done correctly have all been determined by previous social experience and within the social context of the worker. This explains why praxis is a fundamentally social phenomenon.

Praxis involves satisfying human needs, which are based on human biology. Human beings must be alive in order to "make history." Being alive, first and foremost, involves eating, drinking, habitation, clothing, and many other things. Thus, "the first historical act" is the production of the means to satisfy such needs, that is, the production of material life. But, praxis involves more. This is because the satisfaction of the first set of needs (i.e., the action of satisfying and the instrument of satisfactions which have been acquired) leads to new needs. The production of such new needs is "the first historical act." Therefore, "the first historical act" has two aspects: (1) it provides the means of satisfying the existing needs; and (2) it also, at the same time, creates new needs. In other words, praxis involves: (1) changing of the non-human world; and (2) changing of the human beings who produce. With the emergence of the new needs, human beings develop new means to satisfy such needs; and, in turn, the new products give rise to still other needs, such that, at some point, the original human nature is completely transformed. That is, human beings, through productive activity, create and change their own nature.

The notion that human beings create and change their own nature allows infinite possibilities for humans to control their own destiny. It may seem paradoxical that these possibilities are offered to humans by a theory that places so much emphasis on the biological basis of human nature. Often, a philosophical emphasis on human biology is used to show biologically imposed limits to social possibility. But, Marxism conceptualizes the relation between human biology and human society in such a way that it rules out the biological determination of human nature. According to Marxism, human nature is not conceptually separate from non-human nature. Similarly, Marxism does not separate the biological and the social components of human nature. Marxism believes that human biology and human society are "dialectically" related. In other words, biology and society are not separate from each other; instead, they are related such that each partially constitutes the other. More specifically, human biology allows the development of particular types of social organization, and at the same time, those particular types of social organization allow and encouraged a certain direction in biological evolution. For instance, the use of tools is a cause as well as an effect of bipedal locomotion. A limited bipedalism partially freed the hands, with which sticks and stones could be picked up; and the use of these objects allowed an evolutionary advantage toward more bipedalism and more developed tool use. On this basis, it can be noted that the hands are not only the organs of labor, but also the product of that labor. The mutual interaction between human biology and human society has been continuing as humans have been continuing, through praxis, to modify and develop human nature. For instance, science has been expanding human beings conceptions of what is biologically possible, such as: sporting achievements, test-tube babies, and flights to the moon. In turn, the expansion of biological possibility, resulting from social developments, expands the possibilities of social organization.

In Marxism, the notion of praxis plays the key role in the general conception of human nature. More specifically, the specific form of praxis adopted in a given society determines the fundamental features of that society and of the nature of its inhabitants. The "peculiar, distinctive character" of every society is ultimately determined by its "mode of production," that is, by the way in which the members of that society organize their productive activity. In other words, in the social production of their life, human beings enter into definite relations which are indispensable and independent of their will. Such relations can be called the "relations of production," which correspond to a definite stage in the development of their material productive forces. The totality of these relations of production constitutes the economic structure of society, that is, the society's real foundation, on which rises the society's legal and political superstructure, and to which correspond the society's forms of social consciousness. In general, the mode of production of material life conditions the processes of the social, political, and intellectual life. It is not the consciousness of men that determines their being, but, it is their social being that determines their consciousness.

It should be noted that the previous paragraph expresses a sharp contrast with the liberal view of rationality. Marxism believes not only that praxis, rather than pure rational thought, is the characteristic human activity, but also that rational thought itself as inseparable from praxis. This is because Marxism believes not only that thought is typically expressed in productive activity, but also that the very parameters of rational thought are ultimately determined by the dominant mode of production. In contrast to liberalism, Marxism does not believe that rationality is the universal or transcultural standard of thought. Instead, Marxism believes that rationality is expressed in action, and what counts as rational action is defined within a given society.

In general, in its analysis, Marxism adheres to an historical approach; and therefore, it adheres to an active and historical conception of rationality in order to understand human nature. In contrast to liberalism, Marxism does not believe that human nature as changeless, but Marxism believes that human beings' capacities, needs, and interests are ultimately determined by the mode of production that characterizes the society which they inhabit. Therefore, human nature is a historical product. Marxism rejects liberalism's notion of the abstract individual, because Marxism believes that human beings realize their human potentialities only in a specific historical context, that is, it is even impossible to conceive of a human being outside any such context.

Marxism believes that human nature is necessarily historical, and therefore, human nature cannot be investigated by any method that abstracts from particular circumstances. According to Marxism, human nature is precisely the particular circumstances that prevail in any given society; and therefore, any method that abstracts from those circumstances, it abstracts precisely what is human. Instead, human nature must be investigated empirically within specific historical circumstances, and, in particular, in view of the prevailing mode of organizing productive activity. This is called the "historical materialist" method of investigation.

Marxism's historical materialist investigation of human nature takes account of the division of society into classes. It notes that the history of all existing societies has been the history of class struggles. Consequent to the institution of private property, societies have been divided into two main opposing classes, and the members of each class have shared a common relation to the means of production and, as a result, shared similar economic conditions, interests, and cultural preferences. Under capitalism, the two main classes are the proletariat, or the working class; and the bourgeoisie, or the capitalist class. Members of each class participate in similar productive activity and experience similar social conditions; therefore, they develop certain physical and personality characteristics, but are denied developing others. For instance, the material conditions of capitalism result in the members of the capitalist class being, on average, taller and healthier, as well as having a longer life expectancy than the members of the working class. Similarly, the social circumstances of the capitalist class will encourage the members of the capitalist class to be greedy, insensitive, and hypocritical; while the circumstances of the working class will block the working class from developing their capacities for poetry or for intellectual work. In this way, a class society creates broad social types of human beings. Therefore, the nature of human beings is determined not only by the mode of production that prevails in their society, but also by their place within the class system of that society. Human beings are likely to develop a character structure that is shared by other members of their class. In other words, human beings who belong to the same class are likely to share a relatively permanent set of attitudes that generally determine the way in which they think about and react to the world.

According to Marxism, the specific character structures that prevail in a class society are reinforced both by the dominant ideology and, more substantively, by the structure of daily life. The dominant ideology of a society is the framework of beliefs and values which is generally used to explain and justify actual social experience. The dominant ideology is expressed in various ways, such as: systematic theories, the legal system, the prevailing religion, arts, and cultural artifacts. According to Marxism, in every class-divided society, there is a dialectical relationship between the dominant ideology and the mode of production, that is, each influences the other. However, the mode of production ultimately determines the ideology, and it does it by way of setting limits to the type of ideas which will be accepted within a given society.

According to Marxism, in a class society, the ruling class ultimately dominates the production and distribution of scientific, religious, and artistic ideas. That is, the ruling class exerts direct control over the concepts and values that are generated and disseminated. It is noteworthy that the mode of production ultimately determines the prevailing ideology through the structuring of daily life. Thus, in class societies, the prevailing mode of production generates specific forms of "false consciousness," that is, distorted perceptions of human nature and reality that present the status quo as inevitable or "natural," and serve the interests of the ruling class. The notion of false consciousness has been used to explain, among other things, the absence of working-class revolutions in the advanced capitalist societies.

CONCLUSION

This chapter briefly discussed four views expressed with respect to human nature. The functionalist paradigm regards human beings as essentially rational agents. The interpretive paradigm believes that what man is depends on where he is, who he is, and what he believes. The radical humanist paradigm believes that the differences between women and men are both physical and psychological. The radical structuralist paradigm believes that human nature is created historically through the dialectical interaction between human biology, human society, and the physical environment.

Each paradigm is logically coherent—in terms of its underlying assumptions—and conceptualizes and studies the phenomenon in a certain way, and generates distinctive kinds of insight and understanding. Therefore, different paradigms in combination provide a broader understanding of the phenomenon under consideration. An understanding of different paradigms leads to a better understanding of the multifaceted nature of the phenomenon.

NOTES

1. For this literature, see Alhadeff (1982), Becker (1976), Crouch (1979), Doucouliagos (1994), Friedman (1953), Kaufman (1989), Simon (1957), Steen (1996), Thaler (2000), Vyverberg (1989), and Wilson (1978). This section is based on Jaggar (1983).

2. For this literature, see Brown (1988), Cooley (1992), Coutu (1949), Dewey (1957), Granovetter (1985), Jensen (1987), Midgley (2002), Montagu (1957), Sperry (1965), and Thomas (1997). This section is based on Geertz (1973). See, for example,

Brown (1988), Cooley (1992), Coutu (1949), Dewey (1957), Granovetter (1985), Jensen (1987), Midgley (2002), Montagu (1957), Sperry (1965), and Thomas (1997). This section is based on Geertz (1973).

3. For this literature, see Habermas (2003), Held (2004), Horkheimer (1974), Jaggar (1983), Kellner (1977), Lewontin, Rose, and Kamin (1984), Sayers (1998), and Williams (1999). This section is based on Fromm (2004).

4. For this literature, see Berry (1986), Fromm (1968), Geras (1983), Jaggar (1983), Kupperman (2010), Marx (1969), Plamenatz (1975), Stevenson (1981), Stevenson and Haberman (2008), and Venable (1966). This section is based on Mitin (1966).

REFERENCES

Alhadeff, David A. 1982. *Microeconomics and Human Behavior: Toward a New Synthesis of Economics and Psychology.* Berkeley, CA: University of California Press.

Becker, Gary S. 1976. *The Economic Approach to Human Behavior.* Chicago, IL: University of Chicago Press.

Berry, Christopher J. 1986. *Human Nature.* Atlantic Highlands, NJ: Humanities Press International.

Brown, Donald E. 1988. *Hierarchy, History, and Human Nature: The Social Origins of Historical Consciousness.* Tucson, AZ: University of Arizona Press.

Cooley, Charles Horton. 1992. *Human Nature and the Social Order.* New Brunswick, NJ: Transaction Publishers.

Coutu, Walter. 1949. *Emergent Human Nature: A Symbolic Field Interpretation.* New York, NY: A.A. Knopf.

Crouch, Robert L. 1979. *Human Behavior: An Economic Approach.* North Scituate, MA: Duxbury Press.

Dewey, John. 1957. *Human Nature and Conduct: An Introduction to Social Psychology.* New York, NY: Random House.

Doucouliagos, Chris. 1994. "A Note on the Evolution of Homo Economicus." *Journal of Economic Issues* 28(3): 877–883.

Friedman, Milton. 1953. *Essays in Positive Economics.* Chicago, IL: University of Chicago Press.

Fromm, Erich. 2004. *Marx's Concept of Man.* New York, NY: Continuum.

Fromm, Erich, and Ramon Xirau, ed. 1968. *The Nature of Man.* New York, NY: Macmillan.

Geertz, Clifford. 1973. "The Impact of the Concept of Culture on the Concept of Man." In *The Interpretation of Cultures*, edited by Geertz, Clifford, 33–54. New York, NY: Basic Books, Inc., Publishers.

Geras, Norman. 1983. *Marx and Human Nature: Refutation of a Legend.* London, England: NLB and Verso.

Granovetter, Mark. 1985. "Economic Action and Social Structure: The Problem of Embeddedness." *American Journal of Sociology* 91(3): 481–510.

Habermas, Jurgen. 2003. *The Future of Human Nature.* Cambridge, England: Polity.

Held, David. 2004. *Introduction to Critical Theory: Horkheimer to Habermas.* Cambridge, England: Polity Press.

Horkheimer, Max. 1974. *Critique of Instrumental Reason: Lectures and Essays since the End of World War II.* New York, NY: Continuum.

Kupperman, Joel J. 2010. *Theories of Human Nature.* Indianapolis, IN: Hackett Publishing Company, Inc.

Jaggar, Alison M. 1983. *Feminist Politics and Human Nature.* Totowa, NJ: Rowman and Allanheld Publishers.

Jensen, Hans E. 1987. "The Theory of Human Nature." *Journal of Economic Issues* 21(3): 1039–1073.

Kaufman, Bruce E. 1989. "Models of Man in Industrial Relations Research." *Industrial and Labor Relations Review* 43(1): 72–88.

Kellner, Douglas. 1977. "Human Nature and Capitalism in Adam Smith and Karl Marx." In *The Subtle Anatomy of Capitalism*, edited by Jesse Schwartz. Santa Monica, 66–85. CA: Goodyear Publishing Company, Inc.

Lewontin, Richard C., Steven Rose, and Leon J. Kamin. 1984. *Not in Our Genes: Biology, Ideology, and Human Nature.* New York, NY: Pantheon Books.

Marx, Karl. 1969. "Theses on Feuerbach." In *Marx and Engels Selected Works*, Volume One, 13–15. Moscow, USSR: Progress Publishers.

Midgley, Mary. 2002. *Beast and Man: The Roots of Human Nature.* New York, NY: Routledge.

Mitin, Mark. 1966. "The Concept of Man in Marxist Thought." In *The Concept of Man*, edited by S. Radhakrishnan and P.T. Raju, 476–535. Lincoln, NE: Johnsen Publishing Co.

Montagu, Ashley. 1957. *Anthropology and Human Nature.* Boston, MA: Porter Sargent Publishers.

Plamenatz, John. 1975. *Karl Marx's Philosophy of Man.* New York, NY: Oxford University Press.

Sayers, Sean. 1998. *Marxism and Human Nature.* New York, NY: Routledge.

Simon, Herbert A. 1957. *Models of Man: Social and Rational.* New York, NY: John Wiley and Sons.

Sperry, Roger W. 1965. "Mind, Brain and Humanist Values." In *New Views of the Nature of Man*, edited by John Rader Platt, 71–92. Chicago, IL: University of Chicago Press.

Steen, R. Grant. 1996. *DNA and Destiny: Nature and Nurture in Human Behavior.* New York, NY: Plenum Press.

Stevenson, Leslie, ed. 1981. *The Study of Human Nature.* New York, NY: Oxford University Press.

Stevenson, Leslie, and David L. Haberman. 2008. *Ten Theories of Human Nature.* Oxford, England: Oxford University Press.

Thaler, Richard H. 2000. "From Homo Economicus to Homo Sapiens." *Journal of Economic Perspectives* 14(1): 133–141.

Thomas, Robert Murray. 1997. *Moral Development Theories—Secular and Religious: A Comparative Study.* Westport, CT: Greenwood Press.

Venable, Vernon. 1966. *Human Nature: The Marxian View.* Cleveland, OH: Meridian Books.

Vyverberg, Henry. 1989. *Human Nature, Cultural Diversity, and the French Enlightenment.* New York, NY: Oxford University Press.

Williams, David. 1999. "Constructing the Economic Space: The World Bank and the Making of Homo Oeconomicus." *Millennium: Journal of International Studies* 28(1): 79–99.

Wilson, Edward O. 1978. *On Human Nature.* Cambridge, MA: Harvard University Press.

Chapter 3

Feminist Theories
Four Paradigmatic Views

Any explanation of feminism is based on a worldview. The premise of this book is that any worldview can be associated with one of the four broad paradigms: functionalist, interpretive, radical humanist, and radical structuralist. This chapter takes the case of feminism and discusses it from the four different viewpoints. It emphasizes that the four views expressed are equally scientific and informative; they look at the phenomenon from their certain paradigmatic viewpoint; and together they provide a more balanced understanding of the phenomenon under consideration. In this chapter, the first four sections present the four perspectives, and the fifth section concludes the chapter.

FUNCTIONALIST VIEW

Liberal feminists follow an equal rights tradition which predates modern feminism and is based on a very different ideology. Although most forms of secular feminism may be considered as sharing a similar point of departure, the direction chosen by the liberal feminists is somewhat different from that chosen by other feminists, such as the Women's Liberation Movement.[1]

Liberal feminists have been historically concerned with political rights, as defined in the eighteenth- and nineteenth-century liberalism. This is in contrast to the historical concerns of socialist feminists with economic rights, as defined by the nineteenth- and twentieth-century socialist theory; and is also in contrast to the concerns of radical feminists with sexual rights, as outlined in the twentieth-century sexual liberation theory. As a consequence to this broad distinction, liberal feminists, in contrast to radical feminists, have been actively supporting legal reforms as an important part of their strategy.

Furthermore, liberal feminists, in contrast to Marxist feminists, have been content to work within the existing system with the hope that a sounder non-sexist educational program, together with new legislation, eventually brings about a new era that provides women more freedom. This reflects the fact that liberal feminists share an optimism which some other feminists do not share.

Liberal feminists' thinking can be said to go back to the work of John Stuart Mill (1806–1873). Harriet Taylor, after the death of her husband, married John Stuart Mill. She influenced the feminism of Mill, and together they wrote a series of essays and pamphlets that demanded a reappraisal of the position of women. However, Mill's main work in this area was written by himself alone, and after Harriet Taylor's death. His work, which was entitled "On the Subjection of Women," was published in 1869, and within a year it became available in twelve countries and in eight languages. It soon became the center of attention of feminists such that educated women throughout the world read and discussed it. It became the focal point of women's discussion groups all over Europe as they found it irresistible.

It is instructive to examine Mill's position as it well spells out the difference between liberal feminists and radical feminists. Mill was a prominent liberal theorist and was committed to Enlightenment, which emphasized the autonomy of the individual and the faith in human reason. He, then, combined this individualism with the nineteenth-century admiration of self-help, self-discipline, laissez-faire, and morality. Liberalism was against the "divine right" of monarchs or aristocrats to rule, although it was not in favor of the rule of masses. Mill believed that majority was mediocre, and that social collectivities would enforce conformity and mediocrity on the whole society and on the individual. He, therefore, disliked social collectivities. He preferred the activities of the state to be reduced to a minimum so that the sovereignty of the individual would receive full political and economic recognition. In this way, all artificial inequalities and all barriers to the free competition of free individuals would be destroyed. In consequence, the leaders who emerge would have a good foundation in justice, ability, and morality, who would use their power not to usurp or dictate but in the interests of all the people. Mill's Utilitarian maxim can be summarized in his dictum: "The greatest happiness of the greatest number."

Mill had some reservation about the possibility of combining the sovereignty of the individual with the maximization of happiness for all the people. This was because happiness for the majority of people means their freedom from poverty, their good health, and their sound diet. Indeed, liberals believe in laissez-faire in the sense that they contest state interference; they endorse private property and inheritance; and they advocate unregulated freedom of production and exchange. Mill was hesitant on this point, and through his reading of Saint-Simon he became appreciative of socialism, but, of course, a socialism within liberalism. That is, Mill advocated limitations on the system of distribution, but left almost all other aspects of capitalist society intact, that is, he did not challenge the fundamental capitalist system. This is inherited as the hallmark of liberal feminism.

Mill believed that in a society individuals should be free, citizens should have fundamental rights, and exceptional people should have the opportunity to transcend mediocrity and provide strong and firm leadership. Mill found Victorian England as the society that came closest to his liberal utopia. However, Mill recognized that even in Victorian England the liberal utopia was not realized. This was because he noticed that there was one major exception to the freedom of the individual. He noticed that the higher social functions are closed to women who constitute half of the human race, that is, women were subjected to a fatality by birth which no exception and no change in circumstances can overcome. Women were denied access to the higher social functions without regard to their merit or ability. Mill believed that the transition of women from subjection to full equality would constitute the final stage in the development of a perfectly liberal and reasonable society.

It is interesting to note that the Victorian England which Mill so greatly endorsed with his one exception, was the same Victorian England which earlier Engels had described in his "Condition of the Working Classes." Mill viewed and judged society from the position of an able, educated, and affluent gentleman. Even the women whom Mill envisioned were similarly middle-class, privileged women who would profit from education, entry into the professions, the right to retain an inheritance, and so on. Mill's concept of equality would not affect the working-class women who provide domestic service or perform factory work.

Mill believed that legal constraints handicapped women. He concluded that with the removal of legal constraints women would begin to experience freedom, would become self-sufficient, and would gain the ability to direct their own lives. Thus, the emancipation or liberation of women required changing the law, providing women with employment opportunities, allowing women to own property after marriage, and granting women suffrage and full citizenship. This did not involve the discussion of social classes. However, Mill believed that it was not individual women who were denied true citizenship and its consequent equality, but it was women as a social group or, as later feminists have claimed, a "sexual" class. His belief in structural inequality separates him from traditional liberals and brings his radical stance more in line with Engels or Saint-Simon. Of course, as noted earlier, his radicalism did not involve any challenge to capitalism or of patriarchy—two systems that underlie and define liberalism. Mill thoroughly believed in patriarchy, in terms of women's "natural" role. He thought, in the end, women were more likely to be happiest at home with children and domestic life. He held such beliefs even though he denied that women had any "innate nature," and even though he made reference to the "legal slavery of marriage." He believed that a woman should not actually support herself because she would be able to do so, and that as a matter of practice she would not decide to support herself. Ideally, the husband should be able to earn enough for the whole family such that there would be no need for the wife to take part in providing what is merely needed to support life. It would be for the happiness of both that wife's occupation should be to adorn and beautify it. Mill did not believe that men and women were the same. He noted that perhaps women had quite different psychological needs and faculties from men, although he believed their mental and creative powers are equal. However, this was not Mill's main concern. It was that women should be given the choice of developing all their abilities and discovering for themselves their limitations. In the end, it would be left to her, and in the context of the free play of market forces (the liberal dream), to do what she is best fitted for. If women wished to work then the law should not hinder it. Indeed, the free play of competition provides strongest incentives for women to perform those services which are most wanted from women.

Mill was more than a theorist. He was a Member of Parliament and he was active in reforms which reflected his liberal faith and commitment, especially the legal equality of women. He started fighting for women's suffrage in 1865, which was sixty-four years before it was fully granted. He even joined the Christian campaigner Josephine Butler in 1871 with the hope of repealing the Contagious Diseases Act that fully endorsed the Victorian "double standard" of sexual morality. Mill, of course, joined the campaign based on his response to the threat against individual liberty rather than based on the Christian position of the campaign leader.

Mill's attitude toward Christianity was interesting. He generally approved of Protestantism, but he stayed distanced from Christianity and stayed close to the Unitarian circles in which he was active. He endorsed the vital importance of religion and conscience in the development of morality, which would be socially and theologically tolerant of all others. Therefore, the "repressive" tendencies of some creeds and churches must be kept at bay. He brought Calvinism into sharp focus as a repressive and harsh system that limits human options and threatens individuality. This is because the emphasis on obedience, even to God, stifles human character. Mill's harsh comments on Calvinism indicate that his own tolerant liberal faith was not tolerant enough toward those with whom he did not agree.

Although Mill's liberal theoretical contributions to feminism and his legal reformer activities on behalf of women have had a long-lasting effect on liberal feminists, his particularly Victorian liberal emphasis has not endured.

Nowadays, few, if any, feminists accept liberalism as laissez-faire, self-help, and self-determination. In other words, liberal feminist politics have outlived their own theory. The "freedom of the individual" loses its original meaning when it is removed from its original context which was the well-tuned nineteenth-century liberal philosophy. As a result, today, liberal feminism does not have any theory to use as a basis for its political strategy and policies. Liberal feminists have maintained the basic tenets: freedom of choice, equality of opportunity, freedom of competition, and the rights of the individual. But, nowadays, this has become the status quo, as liberal values are so comprehensively embedded in our Western societies. In other words, nowadays, since liberalism has become the establishment ideology, it is difficult to be reflective and self-conscious about it. Consequently, liberal values have lost their original identity, and currently they constitute the neutral starting-point, and are the hidden assumptions behind much political strategy. For this reason, these days, liberal feminists seldom discuss a theory of individuality, and they most likely take for granted the ideology of individualism and competition. Liberal feminists today believe that emancipation can be fully achieved without any major change to the economic structures of contemporary capitalist democracies. They do not challenge in any major way the patriarchal system either. They do not see any problem with systems per se—neither class nor patriarchy. They are deeply committed to the individual freedom. They believe that freedom can be denied in any economic or political system, and therefore, measures need to be introduced to counter it. The fact that liberalism has not yet produced a "society of equals," as envisioned by Mill, does not mean that liberalism has failed, but it means that liberalism has not yet been fully implemented.

Customarily, the historically-recent feminist activity is divided into two periods. By the 1920s, strong efforts by women's pressure groups produced enormous changes in the legal, political, and educational status of women. Most people regard this period as the heyday of liberal feminism. In a two-year period, from 1918 to 1920, women were enfranchised in Britain, Germany, Austria, Netherlands, Poland, the United States, and the USSR.

By 1925, in Britain and the United States, women were admitted to jury and magistrate service, joined the police force, entered the British parliament, were admitted to the professions, formed part of the delegation at the League of Nations, were granted degrees at Oxford University, and were given maintenance after divorce as well as equal guardianship of infants. In 1922, a woman was elected to the judiciary of the Ohio State Supreme Court. In 1923, for the first time, the ERA was introduced into the American Congress, and the British Trade Union Congress was chaired by a woman. Women made a lot of progress and the liberal dream seemed realizable.

However, from 1930 to 1960 the activities of liberal feminists with respect to the campaign for women's equality were lean. This period started with the Great Depression, which was not a suitable time for women to focus on their rights. Then, World War II erupted, which complicated women's issue. Suddenly, there was an increasing demand for women's work. Massive propaganda campaigns, in both Britain and the United States, encouraged women to prioritize their country over themselves. The home was no longer regarded as the only place to raise a family. Government-sponsored day nurseries were viewed as happy environment for a small child as any living room or kitchen. Women were thought to be able to adapt themselves to munitions work as easily as to a sewing machine. Thus, many women joined the war effort and started to experience the advantages of earning a wage and contributing to their nation's security. However, these newly-developed work roles for women abruptly vanished when men returned home at the end of the war. The propaganda was reversed that blamed the neglectful working mother who overlooked the fact that her place was in the home. Day nurseries were closed, and women's skills were no longer found desirable. Of course, for many women, who had been required to work for their country, liberation meant having the freedom to stay home to enjoy their domestic role. However, other women felt that they had been used by the government machinery. That is, the government dragged them into the labor force when the country needed them, but discarded them without compensation as soon as those needs no longer existed. Then, in the 1950s, many feminists became complacent, as it was the decade of the domestic woman, the decade of rebuilding, the decade of population growth, and the decade of affluence.

In the 1960s, after the calmness of the 1950s, during which a massive sea-swell of anger was slowly developing, came the next wave of feminism that had gathered so much pent up force and energy that it threatened to wash away the patriarchal structures which resisted it. This new feminism, that is, "radical feminism," held strong opposing views with respect to liberal feminism. The radical feminism dismissed the liberal feminism outright as "bourgeois feminism," because it focused on superficial symptoms of sexism—such as legal inequalities, employment discrimination, and so on.

It is often claimed that liberal feminism withered away by the end of the 1960s such that it did not emerge significantly ever since. It is further claimed that the utopia of individual freedom, attempted through changes in legislation to ensure a more egalitarian system, is not and cannot be realized. Thus, the claimants conclude that it was necessary for the radical stance of radical feminism of the 1960s and the 1970s to sweep away the reformist ideas of liberal feminism in order for the feminist movement to make further progress. However, it is quite misleading to suggest that the advent of the radical feminism meant the demise of the liberal feminism and the equal rights tradition. In fact, throughout this period, liberal feminists were as active as radical feminists. Indeed, during this period, the high publicity of the demands for women's liberation gave additional support to the old liberals, not to the new radicals. Furthermore, the deeper feminist fervor brought new members into the liberal camp and invigorated many stronger campaigns. Moreover, many of the laws which were enacted in the 1960s were directly related to the historical activities of liberal feminists, that is, even before the radicals came to the scene. Many of these new enacted legislative issues were rejected a decade ago as too demanding, but, through the protracted efforts of liberals, general consciousness were raised to the level such that the suggestions of the liberals no longer seemed as far-fetched as they were thought to be. Liberal feminist activities led to definite products such as: The American Equal Pay Act of 1963, the British Equal Pay Act of 1970, and the Sex Discrimination Act of 1975. That is, the sixties and seventies saw consolidation and development of many liberal programs. The old generation of liberal feminists who remained at work in Congress and in Parliament gathered more grassroots support with a larger movement behind them.

While in the United States the distinction between radical and liberal stayed quite pronounced during this period, in Britain there was much blurring of the edges. Although three positions could be found they were not always represented by different groupings. Women's groups in the Labour Party, for example, although in many senses still in the liberal feminist tradition with accent on legislation, would also include women much further to the left and those who adopted a more radical stance. Single campaigns tended to draw feminists of all perspectives together. The pro-abortion campaign of the 1960s was one such issue culminating in the Abortion Law of 1968. Yet the support was still not unanimous, even here. Many of the older generation of liberal feminists argued that abortion was not part of the feminist case. Edith Summerskill, the Labour MP, was one such example. As a public supporter of birth control since 1935 when she had faced hostility from many in her constituency, she felt abortion was a retrogressive step in the women's program. A long-term champion of the rights of housewives she also vehemently opposed the changes in the divorce laws which became effective in 1971, on the grounds that they were a "Casanova's charter." They would give a green light to male desertion and leave many women undefended and unsupported.

Many people regard Betty Friedan as the most influential contemporary liberal feminist. She wrote a famous book entitled "The Feminine Mystique" in 1963, and organized the "National Organization for Women (NOW)" in 1966 with a mass audience. She focused on the traditional roles of woman, that is, the housewife and the mother. She came up with the following diagnosis: the reason women were discontent was not due to the lack of enough training as housewives and mothers, but was due to the fact that being a housewife was intrinsically boring. In this way, women lost their individual identity. Women's potential was limited to the roles of wife and mother. Women's individuality was stifled, their real personhood denied, and their true choice was absent. Women should be as the (male) culture defines femininity, that is, the "feminine mystique." Betty Friedan's ambition, then, was to free women from destructive dependence which the patriarchal culture produced in them.

INTERPRETIVE VIEW

The women's movement in the United States has changed the way of thinking about both gender and politics. In this context, gender—which is different from sex—is viewed as a socially constructed "role." This means that gender is the outcome of political arrangements and, therefore, it is to be treated as a subject of social and political analysis. For this purpose, "roles" need to be thought about the way it is thought about by social scientists, not as determined by God or nature. That is, how and with what rationale a particular culture distributes among its members certain tasks, certain privileges, and certain responsibilities.[2]

This radical idea was originally formulated by the anthropologist Margaret Mead. In her study of three primitive societies in New Guinea, she noticed that although in each of the three different cultures certain tasks, responsibilities, and privileges were assigned by gender, those assignments were not identical. For example, in one culture, males were assigned the military task of protecting the village, but in another culture both sexes were assigned the task of defending the village in case of a war. As for another example, in one of the three cultures, agricultural food production was assigned to women, and hunting and gathering was assigned to men. In this social arrangement, men had much more free time, and when they were not away, they were home with ample time and energy, and indeed, they were expected to sit around and indulge in what is nowadays, in the United States, called "gossip." Whereas in that society, at that time, gossiping was viewed to be a male privilege; in the United States, currently, that type of conversation is considered to be a frivolous female pleasure.

Mead's analysis demonstrated that, although each culture defined certain activities as either male or female, different cultures had different gender designation of those activities. That is, there was no role which was universally defined as either male or female. Mead noted that among the three cultures she studied, there was almost no contact, such that each culture had invented its own gender arrangements almost independently. Nonetheless, in all three cultures there was a gender definition, and in all three cultures one pattern held true: People valued more highly whatever men did compared to whatever women did. Stated in modern terminology, males were assigned tasks that portrayed higher status. Thus, the discussion of sexual politics in the United States needs to face the challenge of the universality of socially constructed gender differences and, despite myths about matriarchies, the challenge of the universality of socially constructed superiority of men over women.

It is important to ask why this has been the case? Indeed, this has been the question which ethnologists, anthropologists, sociologists, and political scientists have been trying to answer during the past several decades. Some analysts believe that it is due to the physical strength of males over females, and that males have physically threatened women in order to maintain their superior status. Some other analysts believe that it is due to the childbearing and childrearing functions of females that so debilitate females such that they become unwilling or unable to compete with men for positions of leadership and power. These analysts emphasize that, in a world without contraception, a healthy female will be pregnant throughout her adult life; and that the only contraceptive is mother's malnutrition.

Although finding a definite answer to the above question is difficult, the reason for women's inferior status has to be addressed. If biology is not the answer, then some other explanation of how women's status, in culture after culture, came to be defined as inferior must be provided.

Feminists not only have reconceptualized gender but also have expanded the concept of politics. Politics, in its narrowest sense, is defined as participation in government, party politics, and elective or appointed office. Politics, somewhat more broadly, is related to power: getting people to do what you want them to do. This definition is contested by academics, and feminists refuse to limit politics to formal roles. Politics, according to feminists, includes relations in the world of work—for instance, who is hired, who is fired, who is always boss, and who is never boss. Kate Millett, in her book entitled "Sexual Politics," even more broadly defines sexual politics as the power relationship between men and women in formal groups and in the family.

Accordingly, sexual politics includes the politics of motherhood. Although one point of view may regard contraception and abortion to pertain only to a woman and her pregnancy; in most countries today, it is the society that determines whether a woman is legally obligated to carry her fetus to term. In some countries, it is forbidden to end a pregnancy, even if it is medically possible. In some other countries, it is the husband and the father who is entitled to make such a decision because the fetus is considered to be his property. In the United States, since 1973, the decision may be made only by the person who is pregnant, in consultation with her medical adviser—neither the father of the child nor the state are entitled to make such a decision. It should be emphasized that these issues are political, which are not determined by nature.

Similarly, this broader definition of politics considers child care today as a political issue, but in a different society it might be considered a family or a private matter, or, likewise, at another time it might have been considered a family or a private matter. According to this broader definition, politics impinges on various rights—such as the right to work, marriage and divorce, participation in the military, pornography, and even advertising—that affects both people's view of women and women's view of themselves.

Feminists have not always defined politics in this broader sense. Indeed, in the nineteenth century, at the beginning of the women's rights movement, women activists aimed at equal rights (both civil and political, in the narrow sense) of men and women, and focused on a complex, protracted struggle for the right to vote. They realized that they needed to form strong organizations that could concurrently work across the nation for their common goal. This was not an accident of history, and therefore, many questions arise, including: Under what conditions, and through what kind of local struggles, did this first wave of feminism emerge? What led to the mobilization of so many women activists in such a concentrated and comprehensive suffrage effort?

Such questions about the women's movement—about political expediency, the quirks of fate and circumstance, and individual leadership as well as theory—help to understand how these fundamental changes in women's thinking have occurred. The new feminism (i.e., the second wave of feminism) in the United States started sometime between 1967 and 1968 without prior awareness of the general newspaper-reading public. Suddenly, as if they were brought through a burst of extraterrestrial force, the words sexism, male chauvinism, and patriarchy were in common usage. The movement was closely related to the civil rights struggle of African Americans and the 1960s counter-culturalism. Nonetheless, it was Millett who sketched the theory of patriarchy in her book "Sexual Politics," which led to the emergence of the new feminism.

Patriarchy is often defined as a society whose ethos appreciates the characteristics of masculine gender. Kate Millett used this term to characterize a society which is not only dominated by masculinity but also by men whose primary purpose is to construct and maintain their power relationship over women. In such a society, much of what people actually believe to be traditional or even "true" is really an extended political ploy to maintain the superior power relationship of males over females. This does not necessarily imply that all men have conspired and colluded with each other to keep women out of power, which means that men have malevolent intention. Rather, feminists believe that men enjoy the privileges and advantages of the system which is in place, and all (or most) men have no particular interest in changing it.

Kate Millett was the first who outlined this theory. She observed that, in her society, males and females are traditionally differentiated on three dimensions: temperament, role, and status. People, no matter what their profession, hold certain beliefs about sex differences. They believe that: (a) women are more passive, while men are more active; (b) women are more dependent, while men are more independent; and (c) women are more emotional, while men are more rational. The consequences of these temperamental differences are that: (a) women, in contrast to men, are less apt to and less likely to seek a life of their own; and (b) women are more likely to rely on their feelings when in search of truth, while men tend to concentrate on what is demonstrably true when in search of truth. Clearly, these sex differences—real or perceived—significantly impact women who intend to succeed in a world whose values are set by men.

Next, Millett examined people's views about adult roles. Patriarchs lead people to believe that adult role differentiation is natural and that it is the outcome of temperamental differences. That is, by their very nature, females desire to marry, to mother, and to make a home, while, by their very nature, males need to make their mark on the outside world. Woman is a private entity, while man is a public one. Millett also observed that as a consequence of role differentiation men enjoy higher status than women because what men like and do are socially more valued than what women like and do.

As for status, Virginia Woolf, who is an early-twentieth-century British novelist and one who has inspired many feminists, in her book "Three Guineas" wrote that Leo Tolstoy was considered a greater writer than Jane Austen because he wrote about war and peace, while she wrote about the drama of interpersonal relationships. But, Woolf provocatively asked: Who decides that war is more important than interpersonal relationships? She replied: Of course, society, the particular society in which the novelists write and are read. Since men gain status based on what they do, the argument soon becomes cyclical. That is, what men do is of higher stature because men do it.

People believe that the causality runs as follows: temperament, then role, then status, that is, the causality begins with temperament and ends with status. They believe that temperamental differences are present at birth such that they automatically (without the need to plan and enforce anything) lead to role and status differences. More specifically, since, in an industrial society, the most crucial years of professional advancement are between the ages of twenty-five and forty—that is, the period in which "normal" women are attending to their home and motherhood tendencies—men, without conspiracy, end up in higher status positions than women.

However, Millett informs feminists that the order of causal chain is the reverse of what people believe it is. That is, in patriarchy, status really comes first. This is because the most important goal of patriarchy is to maintain the superiority of males over females. Therefore, patriarchy reduces competition from women by assigning women roles that isolate them from men and busy them in caretaking.

Millett realized the way these roles are assigned, and found out the reason women accept such roles without engaging in rebellion. Millett explained that professionals—such as social and behavioral scientists, therapists, and educators—promote patriarchy when they define what is normal and what is not normal. As a consequence of such definitions, when a woman states that the mother role is constricting, or when a woman asks for the kind of economic power which is usually enjoyed by men, she is immediately judged as needing "professional help." Millett showed that it is in this way that women in her society are made to accept their social roles.

Millett's analysis was unsettling because it shook so many previously accepted traditions and because it shook so many women. Millett's contribution was similar to the Copernican revolution that, in contrast to the ancients who thought the earth was the center of the solar system, placed the earth in an orbit around the sun. That is, Millett turned upside down the conventional assumptions about women's temperament, roles, and status. Women, in the early 1970s, who read Millett or heard her theories secondhand, began to look in new light at what they had arranged in their lives, particularly in their relationships with men, and had the "click!" experience, that is, a sudden awareness of the intensity of the political character of those relationships.

Millet explained how heavily sexual politics bears on women in the culture of her society. Currently, it is antithetical to what is defined normal behavior for a female to apply intense temperament which is required for dedicated, original work—such as the staying up all night, and I can't think about anything else darling not even you tonight because I've got those things growing in the petri dish. So there is a double bind in which the American female finds herself. To the extent that she has career ambitions, she is not considered feminine; and to the extent that she follows to the needs of her feminine nature, she is not considered a serious professional. As mentioned earlier, the childbearing years not only constitute the period during which a woman is healthiest and has the most energy for childrearing, but also constitute the peak opportunity years in any profession. Therefore, the longer the woman spends time as caretaker at home the heavier would be the cost to her career, given the dominance of the male model. Indeed, the underlying reason women leave their careers and the underlying reason men encourage them to leave their career involves this double bind.

Millett's model incorporates the three roles which have traditionally been appropriate for women in her society: the mother role, the wife-like role, and the decorative role (which is a possibility only for young women). Any woman who does not naturally fit into any of these roles is placed in a different category: the witch-bitch trough. Those careers are considered most appropriate for women that are considered as natural extensions of women's three approved roles. Careers in which women work in some nurturing capacity with either children, the handicapped, or the old are an obvious extension of the mother role. Careers in which women work as either research associates, secretaries, lab technicians, or assistants require women to perform a wife-like role for the men they serve. Careers in which women strongly use their femininity correspond to their decorative role.

There is another bias within the ideology of patriarchy that prevents women from seeking work in the intellectual professions and the arts. This bias is the embedded idea that any really good work has to begin in the young age. If a woman, at the age of thirty-five, decides to continue her university training in science, even if she intends to spend the thirty years after her graduation in full-time research, most likely her colleagues are apt to believe that she is not likely to make a major contribution. This is because, currently it is widely believed that science and many other intellectual and artistic professions are young people's fields. This myth about science, the arts, and the professions is based on the data gathered from the eighteenth and nineteenth centuries when young men did not live as long as their counterparts live today. This myth ignores an important variable, that is, newness to the field, which is at work besides the number of brain cells in youth.

In the final analysis, knowledge is power. This is why any dominant group applies its utmost efforts to keep subordinate groups away from knowledge. For example, during slavery and even afterward, African Americans were not allowed to learn to read, which is considered the first tool of knowledge. As for a second example, in earlier centuries, women were formally forbidden to study art, for the reason that the presence of nude models was thought to compromise women's purity. As for a third example, historically, every colonial power has limited the education of its colony's native-born citizens. Increased knowledge leads not only to higher status, but also increased power, which is exactly what the patriarchal structure is totally against.

There is an important role that a political movement can play in order to change ideology. Similar to the differences of opinion with respect to religion, it is difficult to convince people to leave their current beliefs, especially those beliefs from which they have derived status and power. On the other hand, theory can act as the glue that holds a movement together because theory offers a sense of shared identity among the members of the movement. Moreover, theory can give the movement proper direction because theory can revise history such that it can give a movement the knowledge of its past, and that it can envision the possibility of a future that would be different from that past. Furthermore, theory provides a political agenda by which the movement can get from its past to that possible future.

Accordingly, a feminist strategy should involve the proper interpretation of the past and current events. Millett offered one new way of interpreting the past and the present events. Indeed, it was by sharing such views that feminists rapidly achieved their first set of political goals. But, of course, politics, in general, and feminist politics, in particular, are affected not only by gender but also by other factors: race and class. These factors have led to differences in prioritization of various goals among women, and those differences in turn need to be dealt with both in feminist theory and feminist practice.

RADICAL HUMANIST VIEW

Socialist feminism views human nature as partly defined by biological, that is, both physiological and psychological, characteristics of the human beings. These characteristics, however, are subject to change because human beings continuously transform themselves through their conscious and cooperative productive activity. Thus, human nature changes in a historical sense.[3]

Socialist feminism recognizes that productive activity involves not only the production of goods and services, but also the production of people; and that such production is historically determined and changing. Socialist feminism believes that productive activity not only includes the economy, in which money in exchanged; but also, procreative and sexual work, which is done by women in the home. Socialist feminism analyzes productive activity not only with the analytic tool of class but also with the conceptual tool of gender. Socialist feminism believes that productive activity is organized based on a sexual division of labor, and that the specific historical form taken by the sexual division of labor is basic in determining the historically prevailing constitution of human nature. Socialist feminism claims that the differences between women and men are not pre-social givens, but are socially constructed, and therefore, socially alterable.

Socialist feminism views human nature in relation to productive activity, that is, work. It, accordingly, believes human fulfillment is to be found in free productive activity. Socialist feminism highly values work because not only it has direct products, which fulfill specific and historically determined human needs; but also it offers the possibility of developing the potentialities of the workers. Socialist feminism regards sexuality and procreation as important avenues for possible human development because they are viewed as historically changing forms of productive activity. Of course, socialist feminism cannot specify what the full flowering of human procreative and sexual capacities would be like, but attempts to identify the material preconditions for such a flowering. For this purpose, the distinction between the "realm of freedom" and the "realm of necessity" needs to be made.

The realm of necessity has boundaries which are determined by two inter-related conditions: the level of development of the forces of production, and the type of organization of the social relations of production. When the level of development of the productive forces is low, or when exploitation or forced labor exists, then the realm of necessity is relatively large, and most of the people spend most of their life in that realm. When the level of development of the productive forces is high, and when exploitation is reduced or eliminated, then the realm of necessity is relatively small, and all of the people spend most of their life in the realm of freedom. There is a dialectical relationship between the technical and social boundaries of the realm of necessity. On the one hand, certain forms of technological development have shaped certain social relations of production; that is, those certain forms of technology have set limits to the ways in which people can organize themselves when they have decided to utilize those forms of technology. On the other hand, exploitative class relations have allowed the development of only specific types of productive techniques, which are primarily designed to maximize productivity regardless of their adverse effects on the workers. Thus, the historical development of modes of sexual and procreative activity has been subject to constraints that are simultaneously social and technological.

Women have primarily performed the sexual and procreative labor of most societies. Men, of course, have had a role in conceiving children, but they have had no role in giving birth to children and they have had minimal role in rearing children. Men's work has been defined as primarily belonging to the public sphere consisting of "politics," "culture," government, and war. Women's work, on the other hand, has been defined as belonging to the private sphere, and women have mostly performed what society has defined as necessary sexual and procreative labor.

Women's energy has been mostly spent on sexual and procreative labor, and most of this labor has been forced rather than free. Women's sexual and procreative activity have been limited to the realm of necessity by both technological and social conditions. For instance, low levels of development in the productive forces have often resulted in high infant mortality rate, and the consequent need for a high birth rate. Furthermore, primitive contraceptive techniques have sometimes resulted in higher birth rates than desired. These technological factors, however, have been inseparable from their contemporary system of social relations. For instance, the infant mortality rate has often been related to the class, race and sex of the infants. Furthermore, the desired birth rate has largely depended on social factors: a high birth rate has been desired primarily when the dominant class has needed more labor power in order to exploit. In primitive hunting and gathering societies, with little opportunity for surplus creation and exploitation, a low birth rate was desired, which was generally achieved, but sometimes partly through infanticide.

A high birth rate became desirable only when the development of agriculture and later the Industrial Revolution made possible the accumulation of surplus wealth and offered new opportunities for the exploitation of labor. Consequently, women were forced to give birth to more children, partly by denying knowledge and availability of the contraceptive and abortion techniques which already existed. For these reasons, the historical engagement of women in procreative labor is viewed more accurately as resulting from "social" rather than from "natural" necessity, insofar as these two categories can be given some distinct meaning. Women's sexual labor is even more clearly a result of "social" rather than of "natural" necessity, as in male-dominant societies, women have always been compelled to engage in more and varied types of sexual activity than were required for conceiving children.

Since sexual and procreative activity is constrained by both technological and social conditions, then sexual and procreative freedom hinges on developments in both technology and social organization. One of the basic technological requirements for free sexual and procreative activity is the availability of means for controlling fertility, that is, avoiding babies when procreation is not desired, and having babies when they are desired. Procreative freedom also requires the material resources for raising children to adulthood in a certain fashion.

Social and technological preconditions exist for the free development of human sexual and procreative potentialities. That is, it must be possible for those who engage in any type of sexual or procreative activity to do so freely rather than out of coercion. In general, in any society, a certain level of sexual and procreative activity is always needed, in the same way that there is always a need for a certain level of other types of productive activity. Socialist feminism does not believe that one can specify exactly how this socially necessary work should be assigned, in the same way that it does not believe that one can specify exactly how other types of socially necessary work should be assigned. Socialist feminism does not believe that one can anticipate in any detail exactly what freely creative, rather than coerced, sexual and procreative activity would be like. However, socialist feminism emphasizes that free sexual and procreative activity requires the abolition of exploitation. In the context of political economy, this means not only the abolition of capitalism, but also the abolition of male dominance. That is, without the elimination of both of these forms of exploitation, the full development of human sexual and procreative potentialities is impossible.

Socialist feminism has a conception of freedom which is rooted in the orthodox Marxism conception of freedom, but its actual vision of the realm of freedom differs from that of both orthodox Marxism and liberalism. Liberal feminism believes that freedom primarily lies in the private realm outside the scope of state regulation, although paradoxically liberal feminism expects the state to guarantee that freedom. Marxist feminism, in contrast, believes that freedom can exist only in the public realm, where citizens engage in conscious political action to change the course of history. Socialist feminism has a view of freedom, which is different from these two other views, and which is based on its conception of human nature and of human productive activity. Socialist feminism conceives sexuality and procreation as any other human activities, which are partly biologically determined, and equally partly capable of social development. Socialist feminism, thus, on the one hand, disagrees with the liberal feminism's belief that sexuality and procreation are matters purely of individual or "personal" concern; and on the other hand, socialist feminism disagrees with the Marxist feminism's belief that sexuality and procreation are not possible arenas of human development, and are subject to small variation from one society to the next. Socialist feminism's conception of freedom is defined neither in terms of the Marxist feminism, nor in terms of the liberal feminism versions of the public/private distinction. The socialist feminism's conception of freedom is, indeed, incompatible with the public/private distinction of both Marxist feminism and liberal feminism. Socialist feminism believes that freedom is constituted by transcending the realm of necessity in every area of human life, including sexuality and procreation. Furthermore, freedom is a social achievement, in the sense that it cannot be achieved by isolated individuals in the absence of a general reordering of society.

Socialist feminism rejects the public/private distinction based on its vision of the good society, which is closest to the vision of radical feminism. All other theories have devalued the daily work of bodily maintenance, particularly the care of children, and have viewed human freedom and fulfillment as constituted by transcending this work. Only socialist feminism and radical feminism have believed that human nature and human society are shaped by prevailing modes of organizing sexuality and procreation, and have speculated about the way human history may be changed through conscious political activity directed toward transforming existing modes of organizing such activities. Radical feminists, among themselves, of course, hold widely diverse views about the desirable, or even possible, changes in procreation, and the future modes of procreation. In contrast, socialist feminists, who adhere to historical materialism, do not believe that the future modes of procreation can be determined in much detail and far in advance. Socialist feminists and radical feminists have a common concern for ecology. Radical feminists have always had respect for nonhuman nature. They have linked feminism and ecology, and have grounded feminist ecological concern in women's spiritual experience of communion with nonhuman nature. Socialist feminists share the radical feminists' concern for the environment, but their Marxist conception of human nature enables them to provide a materialist, as opposed to a spiritual, grounding for that concern. Socialist feminists, on the basis of Marxism, recognize that human and nonhuman nature cannot be conceived separately from each other. That is, socialist feminists believe that human beings depend on nonhuman nature for their sustenance, and they also shape and transform that nature by their labor. The socialist feminists' conception of the dialectical unity between human and nonhuman nature constitutes their theoretical approach to their ecological concerns, and their approach is not incompatible with the radical feminists' intuition of a spiritual unity between human and nonhuman nature. Marxist feminists could have conceptualized the relation between human and nonhuman nature in the same way that socialist feminists have done it, but Marxist feminists have tended to stress the domination, rather than the balance, of nature. Indeed, some socialist feminists believe that the Marxist feminists' dominating attitude toward nature is the psychological result of a certain mode of organizing procreation.

The basic values of socialist feminism, when applied to the issue of women's oppression in contemporary society, lead to a distinctive analysis, which, in turn, implies a set of distinctive political proposals for overcoming that oppression. Socialist feminism uses its concept of "alienation" as the point of entry to the analysis of women's oppression.

The concept of alienation has been used, since the latter part of the twentieth century, by orthodox Marxists to analyze the oppression of the working class under capitalism. The concept of alienation can also be used as a theoretical framework for the socialist feminists' critique of women's contemporary oppression. Socialist feminists utilize the concept of alienation but not in its religious interpretation, which considers the separation of the individual from God, nor in its psychological interpretation, which considers an individual's feelings of being an outsider, lonely, or unwanted. Instead, socialist feminist utilize the concept of alienation, which is based on Marxism, that describes the structure of social relations that define the typical human condition in capitalist society.

The Marxist conception of alienation has been primarily developed in the explanation of the condition of wage workers, but it has also been applied to capitalists, who suffer their own special form of alienation. According to the Marxist view, alienation is a specific human condition under capitalism; although certain features of capitalism may exist in other modes of production, and therefore, humans who do not directly participate in those social relations that characterize the capitalist mode of production are not alienated. For instance, peasants and servants are not alienated, although they are certainly exploited. Women are alienated if they participate in the capitalist relations of production either as wage laborers or, very rarely, as capitalists. According to the Marxist interpretation of alienation, women are not alienated if they are excluded from the capitalist relations of production. That is, not all women are alienated, and those who are alienated do not suffer any gender-specific forms of alienation. These are the main features of the Marxist conception of alienation, which socialist feminism intend to revise and to show that, in contemporary society, women are alienated in all aspects of their lives, and that such alienation takes special, gender-specific forms.

The central feature of Marxist conception of alienation is that things or people which are, in fact, dialectically related to each other are seen as alien, separated from, and even opposed to, each other. At the core of the concept of alienation is the situation of the wage laborer under capitalism. Marxists believe that labor is the essential human activity which connects each human being to not only the nonhuman world but also each other; and which paves the way for the development of human capacities. Under capitalism, however, the way in which labor is organized makes these connections disguised; makes it appear as if individuals must always be separate or alienated from the nonhuman world, from their own products, from the process of their work, and from their coworkers; and makes it seem as if labor (i.e., work) must always prevent human beings from fulfilling their potentialities. These apparent separations are experienced because, under capitalism, human beings are deprived of control over their own labor power; and they are forced to work according to the dictates of the capitalist class. Consequently, workers' products are taken from them to be used against them, their fellow workers are turned into their competitors, and the work process in relation to their "real" lives becomes an exhausting interruption, which forces them to overdevelop a few primitive skills but prevents them from developing more complex and "global" capacities. In this way, alienation fragments not only the human community, but also the human individual.

A few socialist feminist authors have built on radical feminist insights to argue that women's experience in contemporary society is the exact representation of alienation. Socialist feminists' explorations illustrate the ways in which women are alienated as sexual beings, as mothers, and as wives. Indeed, one socialist feminist has stated that femininity itself is alienation.

Socialist feminists analyze the contemporary oppression of women in terms of the concept of alienation, which is inevitably related to capitalism. Socialist feminists deny that "patriarchy" is an unchanging trans-historical and cross-cultural universal; and in contrast, they assert that the subordination of women takes different forms in different historical periods. Currently, the alienation of women is a historically specific product of the capitalist mode of production. More specifically, at the present time, the alienation of women results from historically specific features of capitalism such as the fetishism of commodities, the rise of positive science, separation of home from workplace, split between emotion and reason, and distinction between personal and political.

Socialist feminists neither say that women's oppression stems only from capitalism, nor do they say that the abolition of capitalism would eliminate women's oppression. Socialist feminists say that the abolition of capitalism would end only the specifically capitalist form of women's oppression, and they add that there is no reason to suppose that after capitalism there could not be a new form of "patriarchy," or male dominance, and perhaps new modes of alienation. The socialist feminist analysis of women's oppression points out that women's liberation requires totally different modes of organizing all forms of production, and the final abolition of "femininity." In contrast to Marxism, that has specified its goal as the abolition of class, but not the abolition of gender, socialist feminism has specified its goal as the abolition of both class and gender. Socialist feminists, as everyone else, do not determine how male dominance and capitalism will be overthrown. What socialist feminists have determined, however, is a conception of the material base of society, which includes the mode of producing sexuality and children, as well as the mode of producing what are customarily called goods and services. Therefore, several of their proposals for social change, like many of the proposals of radical feminists, involve the transformation of sexuality and procreation.

RADICAL STRUCTURALIST VIEW

Engels analyzed women's social position relative to that of men, and provided an explanation based on a materialist theory, in which women's position varies from society to society, or epoch to epoch, according to the economic and political relationships that prevail in society. His ideas best explain the ethnographic and historical data showing that women's social position has not always, everywhere, or in most respects been subordinate to that of men.[4]

Engels recognized that in order to understand the present state of affairs and to help shape the future it is useful to look to the past through ethnographic and historical reconstruction. On the one hand, capitalism has dominated and transformed the social orders of most of the world's people; and on the other hand, non-capitalist ways of organizing economic and political relations have affected the relative positions of men and women in various societies. Such ethnographical and historical analyses provide an answer to why women were subordinate to men in capitalist society, and what political and economic changes are needed to end sexual inequality.

Engels provided an analysis that went well beyond the consideration of women's status. His analysis contrasted non-class and class societies. He used a historical approach to show how private property originated; and, after its establishment, how it undermined an egalitarian tribal order, created families as economic units, brought about inequality of property ownership, and resulted in exploitative class societies. Within this wide-ranging explanation, Engels explained how women's social position declined as private property gained strength and became the organizing principle for society. His analyses provided the reasons why private property had such effects; showed specifically, how private property transformed women's work organization; and showed generally, how private property was related to class and sex.

As is discussed in the rest of this section, the sexual egalitarianism of pre-class societies was undermined by class societies through changes in women's work, and through the growth of families as important economic units. Certain terminology and framework is used in the analysis of non-class societies; and, then, emphasis is placed not only on the importance of public labor in determining women's social status, but also on the distinction between the role of women as social adults or as wifely dependents. Finally, reasons are provided for why class societies have used the family to circumscribe and subordinate women.

It is through a historical dynamic that the role of women is changed from free and equal productive members of society to subordinate and dependent wives and wards. This change is caused by the spread of male-owned private properly, which is appropriated and perpetuated by the institution of family.

In early societies, clans or tribes communally owned productive resources. They collected and cooked food on a daily basis. Their aim in production was only for use, that is, to meet people's subsistence needs, as there was no surplus produced for exchange. The group consisting of husband, wife, and dependent children was not considered a productive unit, was not intended to perform housework, and did not own property. This group was not an economic unit, as it had not precipitated out of the larger household. Since economic functions are of crucial importance, the family did not exist in early societies. The household was the basic social and economic unit. The household was communistic because all food stores were held in common, and all work was performed for the good of the common, rather than for the benefit of individuals or couples. The household was run by women, who performed the housework. That is, a communistic household embraced numerous couples and their children. In a communistic household, the administration of the household was entrusted to women. The administration of the household by women was as much a public and a socially necessary activity as the providing of food by the men.

In early societies, the family—as a productive, consuming, and property-owning group—did not exist. The tribe or clan, instead, constituted the context of men's and women's life and labor. The tribe or clan was a communal property-owning group. Although members of both sexes owned tools and personal effects, upon their death their belongings passed to their tribe or clan, which in turn distributed such belongings to the members of the same sex, not necessarily to the children of the deceased. Men and women equally participated in economic and political decision-making. Men and women were equal members of the group because both of them crucially contributed to the economic life of the group.

It was the absence of private property that brought into equality the social significance of men's productive work and women's household work. In early societies, men and women participated in different stages of the production of the same goods, that is, the production of subsistence. All production was for the same purpose, that is, production for use. People worked for the communal household, that is, for the tribe or clan, rather than for themselves or other specific individuals. Since all work was for social use, and since all adults were social producers, all adults (i.e., men and women) were equal members of the group (i.e., the tribe or clan).

In early societies, the public rights of men and women—for example, the individual right to participate in political decision-making, and the collective right to depose a chief—depended on the membership in the clan, which in turn depended on the performance of public, or social, labor. Wives, relative to their husbands, held a higher status, which was attributable to the solidarity and kinship among the women, who formed the core of the household.

The material base for the change in the role of women from equal members of society to subordinate wives lay in the development of private property, that is, the development of valuable productive resources, initially the domestication of large animals. The term "private property" has a special meaning. It refers to goods or resources that have productive potential. Although individuals held personal goods, which were "private," they were not "property" in the sense of "private property." In non-industrial societies, domesticated animals and cultivated land are the most important types of private property, that is, productive resources. In this context, tools, that is, productive means, do not play an important role because the skills and materials for their manufacture are equally available to everyone. "Property" has productive potential. Other goods, which are used for conspicuous consumption or display, are not private property. They are a result of economic and political inequality rather than a cause of it.

In human history, for the first time, private property became possible only when technological development and its application to natural resources resulted in the development of the skills needed for the domestication of animals, or for the investment of labor in land for the extension of the productivity of land over an appreciable length of time. In this way, enduring productivity led to enduring private ownership.

"Private" as used here has a broader meaning than when it is used under capitalism, where the owner can do almost anything with the property.

"Private," as used here, means property owned by an individual, or by a family, such that rights to manage it stay with one of the owners. It also means that the owner can dispose of these goods with some leeway. That is, the owner can acquire wives, clients, or services from others. Here, "gaining a livelihood" is men's work, and the means of production are owned by the user, but the inheritance remained within the clan. In this way, the earliest private productive property, that is, domestic animals, were owned by men.

Domesticated animals fell into the older category of tool ownership. That is, they were privately owned. However, these animals were of a qualitatively different kind. This is because they satisfied subsistence needs, and also, they reproduced themselves. In this way, they constituted the first form of private property. With the growth of private property, the communal political economy of the clan was shattered. The egalitarianism of the clan had been founded on collective ownership of productive property. With the growth of private ownership of property (by men), the family gained importance, soon overshadowed the clan, and became the main economic and decision-making group. In sharp contrast to the clan, the internal structure of the family was not egalitarian. Families had propertyless members: all women and children, and some men.

Private property changed the relations between men and women within the family only because it also radically changed the economic and political relations in society at large. Now, a surplus of goods was produced for exchange between productive units. Over time, men were increasingly involved in the development and expansion of production for exchange, which overshadowed the household's production for use. In the era of industrial capitalism, production became almost exclusively social, was performed outside the household, and was undertaken for exchange. Industrial capitalist production left women's work as private maintenance for family use.

As production for exchange overshadowed production for use, it changed the nature of the household, it changed the significance of women's work within the household, and, consequently, it changed women's position. Women, as a result, worked for their husbands and families, instead of working for society. Their labor played a necessary, but socially subordinate, role in the production of an exchangeable surplus. Women were changed to wards, wives, and daughters from what they used to be: adult members of society.

Private property turned its owner to the ruler of the household. Women and other propertyless dependent members of the household worked to maintain, and to help increase, the property of the head of the household. This was because the head of the household was engaged in competitive production and exchange with other heads of households.

Over time, families perpetuated themselves through the inheritance of property. This changed the definition of children. They changed from the new members of a society to either private heirs or subordinate, dependent workers. The consequence of this change was that women's reproductive labor, similarly to their productive work, changed from social to private. People and property became intertwined, and each one partly defined the other.

As technology was further developed and it made the further accumulation of wealth a reality, the property owners distanced themselves away from their subordinate kinsmen, and moved closer to other property owners in order to preserve and defend their wealth against the claims of the non-propertied. It is at this time that the kinship-based productive group ended, and the class society and the state started.

To illuminate the ideas which have been discussed in this section, the approach of ethnographical reconstruction and comparison can be used to analyze some of the variety in women's status in non-capitalist societies—non-class as well as class. The rest of this section illustrates an ethnographical reconstruction of women's position in four African societies before their domination by imperialists.

The four African societies are as follows. The Mbuti is located in Zaire and can be considered as a band society, and its subsistence is based on communal net hunting and gathering of vegetables. Lovedu is located in South Africa and is primarily hoe agriculturalists. Pondo is also located in South Africa and is involved in a combination of agriculture and livestock. Ganda is located in Uganda and is a class society with subsistence based on hoe agriculture.

These societies can be placed on a continuum from egalitarian society to class society, based on three principal respects. First, type of production: the Mbuti and Lovedu are involved in economies of production for use; the Pondo are involved in the initial stages of production for exchange in cattle; and Ganda is quite extensively involved in production for exchange. Second, type of labor: the Mbuti and Lovedu involve the social labor of both sexes in a use economy; the Pondo involves the social labor of women, and the social labor of men is at least in part performed in an exchange economy; and Ganda involves women's work in individual domestic production for household use, and men work in groups almost entirely in production for exchange. Third, type of productive ownership: the Mbuti band owns the productive resources; in Lovedu and Pondo productive resources are largely patrilineal family estates; in Ganda the productive resources are in control of males, and bear almost no relationship with family obligations.

In Mbuti, Lovedu, and Pondo, women perform productive activities that are social, and women have an adult social status. However, in Ganda women perform productive activities that are domestic, and the status of women is only wife and ward—even though women produce most of the food. This confirms the earlier discussion in this section that public or social labor is the basis for social adulthood.

Of course, the data also suggest that women do not have to be characterized as either social adults or wifely wards, and that women can be both simultaneously. Women's status in a marital relationship varies somewhat independently of their status in the larger society. As discussed earlier in this section, the relative status of wife to husband is dependent on their relative ownership of the property of the household. That is, the spouse who owns the property rules the household. The data show that the Mbuti and Lovedu women are the equals to men, in Ganda women are subordinate to men, and the Pondo women belong somewhere in between the two poles.

Women self-representation in legal proceedings can be used as an indicator of whether a woman is able to be wronged or to do wrong. In the Mbuti, Lovedu, and Pondo, women can represent themselves in the court of law. However, in Ganda, a woman needs a male guardian (generally husband or father) to represent her case in the court of law; and, in addition, the guardian is held responsible for her wrongdoing, and receives compensation for wrongs done to her.

Participation in social activities can be used to see the relative position of women to men. In the Mbuti, Lovedu, and Pondo, both men and women participate in most social activities. Although, in the latter two societies, young wives are kept busy with domestic work, and their ability to participate in social events is significantly reduced. It is the older wives, the sisters visiting their own kinsmen, and the diviners, who attend social events as freely as men do. In Ganda, many of the social activities are patron-oriented, or state-oriented and women are excluded from these social activities.

Divorce can be used as another indicator of the relative position of women to men. The divorce for men versus women is an indicator of their relative importance for each. In the Mbuti, Lovedu, and Pondo, both men and women are entitled to divorce each other. In Ganda, a husband can effectively get a divorce simply by ignoring his wife. However, a woman must contend not only with her husband but also with her brother, who generally acts, as partial guardian, to preserve the marriage.

Another indicator of the relative position of women to men in a society is the ability to give and receive food and items of social exchange as it act as the material basis for exercising political power. In general, real power develops only as a result of production for exchange and private property. In societies where there is no production for exchange and there is no private property— that is, in societies based on production for use—a person who performs social labor has the right to join other adults to make political decisions and settle disputes. This is because in an egalitarian society, adult members are responsible for making political decisions and settling disputes. In the Mbuti and Lovedu, both women and men give and receive food. In Lovedu, women give and receive cattle, hold political positions, and enter the decision-making processes. In Pondo, although women are social producers, they cannot dispose of livestock, which is the most important exchange item. This might be explained with reference to the nature of production for exchange in Pondo. Women's agricultural work, over the short run and the long run, is directed toward the needs of the household, that is, it is for use. On the other hand, men participate in livestock raiding, which involves them in production for exchange. The livestock raiding, over the short run, is more closely connected with the power need of a chief than to household needs. That is, over the short run, a chief keeps a following by having cattle to distribute. Over the long run, a chief's power is based on the actual distribution of cattle more widely. Since Pondo women are not involved in production for exchange, that is, raiding, they cannot dispose of the property that establishes power relationships, and thus, they lack overt political power. In Ganda, peasant women cannot even have a minimal access to political positions which are available to peasant men. Although the mother and the sister of the king hold important official positions, their exercise of power is based on their relationship to the king.

CONCLUSION

This chapter briefly discussed four views expressed with respect to feminism. The functionalist feminists have been historically concerned with political rights, as defined in the eighteenth- and nineteenth-century liberalism. The interpretive paradigm believes that gender—which is different from sex—can be viewed as a socially constructed "role." The radical humanist paradigm believes that productive activity should not only be analyzed with the analytic tool of class but also with the conceptual tool of gender. The radical structuralist paradigm believes that women's position varies from society to society, or epoch to epoch, according to the economic and political relationships that prevail in society.

Each paradigm is logically coherent—in terms of its underlying assumptions—and conceptualizes and studies the phenomenon in a certain way, and generates distinctive kinds of insight and understanding. Therefore, different paradigms in combination provide a broader understanding of the phenomenon under consideration. An understanding of different paradigms leads to a better understanding of the multifaceted nature of the phenomenon.

NOTES

1. For this literature, see Assiter (1996), Banks (1993), Catt and Shuler (1923), Chunn, Boyd, and Lessard (2007), Derr, MacNair, and Naranjo-Huebl (2005),

DuBois (1978), Evans (1979), Flexner (1968), Gabin (1990), Gerhard (2001), Gilmore (2008), Grimes (1967), Harlan (1998), Kraditor (1965), O'Neill (1969), Osborne (2001), Paulson (1973), Rymph (2006), Scott and Scott (1975), Stanton, Anthony, Gage, et al. (1881), Storkey (1985), and Walters (2005). This section is based on Storkey (1985).

2. For this literature, see Bem (1993), Brooks (1997), Butler (1986), Clark and Lange (1979), Davis (2007), Dicker and Piepmeier (2003), Dow (1996), Duran (2006), Farrell (2008), Ferree (2012), Ferree and Tripp (2006), Fisanick (2008), Gelb (1989), Gottfried (1996), Gross (1996), Hirsch and Keller (1990), Jacoby (1994), Koedt, Levine, and Rapone (1973), Lerner (1986), Mead (1935), Millet (1970), Mitchell and Oakley (1986), Mudgal (2007), Murphy (2004), Nicholson (1990), Oakley (1972), Ore (2010), Ortner and Whitehead (1981), Rosaldo and Lamphere (1974), Roth (2004), Seigfried (1996), Sharma and Young (1999), Shiach (1999), Vetterling-Braggin, Elliston, and English (1977), Wekesser (1995), and Zeisler (2008). This section is based on Tobias (1997).

3. For this literature, see Bartky (1979, 1982), Benhabib and Cornell (1987), Blum (1991), Bowden and Mummery (2009), Butler and Weed (2011), De Beauvoir (1952), Diamond and Quinby (1988), Ehrenreich (1984), Eisenstein (1979), Eisenstein (1993), Elliot (1991), Ferguson (1980), Ferguson (1989), Ferguson and Folbre (1981), Foreman (1977), Gatens (1991), Gottlieb (1989), Greer (1970), Hartsock (1979), Hartsock (1985), Hewitt (2010), Jacoby (1976), Johnson (2007), MacKinnon (1982), McRobbie (2009), Morgan (1976), Morgan (1977), Narayan (1997), Oliver and Walsh (2004), Ore (2010), Phelps (1971), Redstockings (1975), Sargent (1981), Taylor (1983), Walker (1995), and Wing and Davis (2000). This section is based on Jaggar (1983).

4. For this literature, see Atkinson (1974), Bebel (1904), Delmar (1976), Delphy (1977, 1984), Donovan (2006), Draper (1970), Engels (1948), Ferguson and Folbre (1981), Firestone (1970), Griffin (1978), Hartmann (1981), Kuhn and Wolpe (1978), Marx, Engels, Lenin, and Stalin (1951), Phillips (1987), Sacks (1974), Sargent (1981), Slaughter and Kern (1981), Storkey (1985), Wallerstein (2000), and Zetkin (1934). This section is based on Sacks (1974).

REFERENCES

Assiter, Alison. 1996. *Enlightened Women: Modernist Feminism in a Postmodern Age.* New York, NY: Routledge.

Atkinson, Ti-Grace. 1974. *Amazon Odyssey.* New York, NY: Links Books.

Banks, Olive. 1993. *Faces of Feminism: A Study of Feminism as a Social Movement.* New York, NY: Basil Blackwell.

Bartky, Sandra L. 1979. "On Psychological Oppression." In *Philosophy and Women*, edited by Sharon Bishop, and Marjorie Weinzweig, 34–41. Belmont, CA: Wadsworth.

Bartky, Sandra L. 1982. "Narcissism, Femininity and Alienation." *Social Theory and Practice* 8(2): 127–143.

Bebel, August. 1904. *Woman under Socialism.* New York, NY: Source Book Press.

Bem, Sandra Lipsitz. 1993. *The Lenses of Gender: Transforming the Debate of Sexual Inequality.* New Haven, CT: Yale University Press.

Benhabib, Seyla, and Drucilla Cornell, eds. 1987. *Feminism as Critique: On the Politics of Gender.* Minneapolis, MN: University of Minnesota Press.

Blum, Linda M. 1991. *Between Feminism and Labor: The Significance of the Comparative-Worth Movement.* Berkley, CA: University of California press.

Bowden, Peta, and Jane Mummery. 2009. *Understanding Feminism.* Durham, England: Acumen.

Brooks, Ann. 1997. *Postfeminisms: Feminism, Cultural Theory, Cultural Forms.* New York, NY: Routledge.

Butler, Judith. 1990. *Gender Trouble.* New York, NY: Routledge.

Butler, Judith, and Elizabeth Weed, eds. 2011. *Question of Gender: Joan W. Scott's Critical Feminism.* Bloomington, IN: Indiana University Press.

Catt, Carrie Chapman, and Nettie Rogers Shuler. 1923. *Woman Suffrage and Politics.* New York, NY: Charles Scribner's Sons.

Chunn, Dorothy E., Susan B. Boyd, and Hester Lessard, eds. 2007. *Reaction and Resistance: Feminism, Law, and Social Change.* Vancouver, Canada: UBC Press.

Clark, Lorenne M.G., and Lynda Lange, eds. 1979. *The Sexism of Social and Political Theory: Women and Reproduction from Plato to Nietzsche.* Toronto, Canada: University of Toronto Press.

Davis, Kathy. 2007. *The Making of Our Bodies, Ourselves: How Feminism Travels Across Borders.* Durham, NC: Duke University Press.

De Beauvoir, Simone. 1952. *The Second Sex.* New York, NY: Bantam.

Delphy, Christine. 1977. *The Main Enemy: A Materialist Analysis of Women's Oppression.* London, England: Women's Research and Resources Center Publications.

Delphy, Christine. 1984. *Close to Home: A Materialist Analysis of Women's Oppression.* Amherst, MA: University of Massachusetts Press.

Delmar, Rosalind. 1976. "Looking Again at Engels' Origin of Family, Private Property and the State." In *The Rights and Wrongs of Women*, edited by Juliet Mitchell, and Ann Oakley, 271–287. Hamondsworth, Middlesex: Penguin Books.

Derr, Mary Krane, Rachel MacNair, and Linda Naranjo-Huebl, eds. 2005. *Prolife Feminism: Yesterday and Today.* Kansas City, MO: Feminism and Nonviolence Studies Association.

Diamond, Irene, and Lee Quinby, eds. 1988. *Feminism and Foucault: Reflections on Resistance.* Boston, MA: Northeastern University Press.

Dicker, Rory, and Alison Piepmeier, eds. 2003. *Catching a Wave: Reclaiming Feminism for the 21ˢᵗ Century.* Boston, MA: Northeastern University Press.

Donovan, Josephine. 2006. *Feminist Theory: The Intellectual Traditions of American Feminism.* New York, NY: Continuum International Publishing Group Inc.

Dow, Bonnie J. 1996. *Prime-Time Feminism: Television, Media Culture, and the Women's Movement Since 1970.* Philadelphia, PA: University of Pennsylvania Press.

Draper, Hal. 1970. "Marx and Engels on Woman's Liberation." *International Socialism* 57: 20–29.

DuBois, Ellen Carol. 1978. *Feminism and Suffrage: The Emergence of an Independent Women's Movement in America, 1848–1869.* Ithaca, NY: Cornell University Press.

Duran, Jane. 2006. *Eight Women Philosophers: Theory, Politics, and Feminism.* Urbana, IL: University of Illinois Press.

Ehrenreich, Barbara. 1984. "Life without Father: Reconsidering Socialist-Feminist Theory." *Socialist Review* 68(3): 48–57.

Eisenstein, Zillah R., ed. 1979a. *Capitalist Patriarchy and the Case for Socialist Feminism.* New York, NY: Monthly Review Press.

Eisenstein, Zillah R. 1979b. "Developing a Theory of Capitalist Patriarchy and Socialist Feminism." In *Capitalist Patriarchy and the Case for Socialist Feminism*, edited by Zillah R. Eisenstein, 5–40. New York, NY: Monthly Review Press.

Eisenstein, Zillah R. 1993. *The Radical Future of Liberal Feminism.* Boston, MA: Northeastern University Press.

Elliot, Patricia. 1991. *From Mastery to Analysis: Theories of Gender in Psychoanalytic Feminism.* Ithaca, NY: Cornell University Press.

Engels, Friedrich. 1948. *The Origin of the Family, Private Property, and the State.* Moscow, USSR: Progress Publishers.

Evans, Sara M. 1979. *Personal Politics: The Roots of Women's Liberation in the Civil Rights Movement and the New Left.* New York, NY: Alfred A. Knopf, Inc.

Farrell, Warren. 2008. *Does Feminism Discriminate against Men?: A Debate.* Oxford, England: Oxford University Press.

Ferguson, Ann. 1989. "Sex and Work: Women as a New Revolutionary Class in the United States." In *An Anthology of Western Marxism: From Lukacs and Gramsci to Socialist-Feminism*, edited by Roger S. Gottlieb, Oxford, 348–380. England: Oxford University Press.

Ferguson, Ann, and Nancy Folbre. 1981. "The Unhappy Marriage of Patriarchy and Capitalism." In *Women and Revolution: A Discussion of the Unhappy Marriage of Marxism and Feminism*, edited by Lydia Sargent, 313–337. Boston, MA: South End Press.

Ferguson, Andy. 1980. "Childbirth as Alienated Labor." *Breaking Ground* 1 (Spring) 4–6.

Ferree, Myra Marx. 2012. *Varieties of Feminism: German Gender Politics in Global Perspective.* Stanford, CA: Stanford University Press.

Ferree, Myra Marx, and Aili Mari Tripp, eds. 2006. *Global Feminism: Transnational Women's Activism, Organizing, and Human Rights.* New York, NY: University Press.

Firestone, Shulamith. 1970. *The Dialectic of Sex: The Case for Feminist Revolution.* New York, NY: Bantam Books.

Fisanick, Christina, ed. 2008. *Feminism.* Detroit, MI: Greenhaven Press.

Flexner, Eleanor. 1968. *A Century of Struggle: The Women's Rights Movement in the United States.* Cambridge, Massachusetts: Belknap Press of Harvard University Press.

Foreman, Ann. 1977. *Femininity as Alienation: Women and the Family in Marxism and Psychoanalysis.* London, England: Pluto Press.

Gabin, Nancy Felice. 1990. *Feminism in the Labor Movement: Women and the United Auto Workers, 1935–1975.* Ithaca, NY: Cornell University Press.

Gatens, Moira. 1991. *Feminism and Philosophy: Perspectives on Difference and Equality.* Bloomington, IN: Indiana University Press.

Gelb, Joyce. 1989. *Feminism and Politics: A Comparative Perspective.* Berkley, CA: University of California Press.

Gerhard, Jane F. 2001. *Desiring Revolution: Second-Wave Feminism and the Rewriting of American Sexual Thought, 1920 to 1982.* New York, NY: Columbia University Press.

Gilmore, Stephanie, ed. 2008. *Feminist Coalitions: Historical Perspectives on Second-Wave Feminism in the United States.* Urbana, IL: University of Illinois Press.

Gottfried, Heidi, ed. 1996. *Feminism and Social Change: Bridging Theory and Practice.* Urbana, IL: University of Illinois Press.

Gottlieb, Roger S., ed. 1989. *An Anthology of Western Marxism: From Lukacs and Gramsci to Socialist-Feminism.* Oxford, England: Oxford University Press.

Greer, Germaine. 1970. *The Female Eunuch.* New York, NY: McGraw-Hill Book Company.

Griffin, Susan. 1978. *Woman and Nature: The Roaring inside Her.* New York, NY: Harper and Row, Publishers.

Grimes, Alan. 1967. *The Puritan Ethics and Woman Suffrage.* Westport, Connecticut: Praeger.

Gross, Rita M. 1996. *Feminism and Religion: An Introduction.* Boston, MA: Beacon Press.

Harlan, Judith. 1998. *Feminism: A Reference Handbook.* Santa Barbara, CA: ABC-CLIO.

Hartmann, Heidi. 1981. "The Unhappy Marriage of Marxism and Feminism: Toward a More Progressive Union." In *Women and Revolution: A Discussion of the Unhappy Marriage of Marxism and Feminism*, edited by Lydia Sargent, 1–41. Boston, MA: South End Press.

Hartsock, Nancy C. 1979. "Feminist Theory and the Development of Revolutionary Strategy." In *Capitalist Patriarchy and the Case for Socialist Feminism*, edited by Zillah R. Eisenstein, 56–82. New York, NY: Monthly Review Press.

Hartsock, Nancy C. 1985. *Money, Sex, and Power: Toward a Feminist Historical Materialism.* Boston, MA: Northeastern University Press.

Hewitt, Nancy A., ed. 2010. *No Permanent Waves: Recasting Histories of U.S. Feminism.* New Brunswick, NJ: Rutgers University Press.

Hirsch, Marianne, and Evelyn Fox Keller, eds. 1990. *Conflicts in Feminism.* New York, NY: Routledge.

Jacoby, Robin Miller. 1976. "Feminism and Class Consciousness in the British and American Women's Trade Union Leagues, 1890–1925." In *Liberating Women's History: Theoretical and Critical Essays*, edited by Berenice A. Carroll, 137–160. Urbana, IL: University of Illinois Press.

Jacoby, Robin Miller. 1994. *The British and American Women's Trade Union Leagues, 1890–1925: A Case Study of Feminism and Class.* Brooklyn, NY: Carlson Publishing, Inc.

Jaggar, Alison M. 1983. *Feminist Politics and Human Nature.* Totowa, NJ: Rowman and Allanheld Publishers.

Johnson, Merri Lisa, ed. 2007. *Third Wave Feminism and Television: Jane Puts It in a Box.* New York, NY: Palgrave Macmillan.

Koedt, Anne, Ellen Levine, and Anita Rapone, eds. 1973. *Radical Feminism.* New York, NY: Quadrangle Books.

Kraditor, Aileen S. 1965. *The Ideas of the Woman Suffrage Movement, 1890–1920.* New York, NY: Norton.

Kuhn, Annette, and AnnMarie Wolpe, eds. 1978. *Feminism and Materialism: Women and Modes of Production.* London, England: Routledge and Kegan Paul.

Lerner, Gerda. 1986. *The Creation of Patriarchy.* Oxford, England: Oxford University Press.

MacKinnon, Catherine A. 1982. "Feminism, Marxism, Method, and the State: An Agenda for Theory." *Signs* 7(3): 515–544.

Marx, Karl, Friedrich Engels, V.I. Lenin, and Joseph Stalin. 1951. *The Woman Question: Selections from the Writings of Karl Marx, Friedrich Engels, V.I. Lenin, and Joseph Stalin.* New York, NY: International Publishers.

McRobbie, Angela. 2009. *The Aftermath of Feminism: Gender, Culture and Social Change.* Thousand Oakes, CA: Sage Publications.

Mead, Margaret. 1935. *Sex and Temperament in Three Primitive Societies.* New York, NY: William Morrow and Company.

Millet, Kate. 1970. *Sexual Politics.* New York, NY: Doubleday and Company, Inc.

Mitchell, Juliet, and Ann Oakley, eds. 1986. *What is Feminism: A Re-Examination.* New York, NY: Pantheon Books.

Morgan, Robin. 1976. *Papers on Patriarchy, Patriarchy Conference, London, 1976.* Brighton, England: Women's Publishing Collective.

Morgan, Robin. 1977. *Going Too Far: The Personal Chronicle of a Feminist.* New York, NY: Random House.

Mudgal, S.D. 2007. *Feminism and Status of Women.* Jaipur, India: Book Enclave.

Murphy, Peter F., ed. 2004. *Feminism and Masculinities.* Oxford, England: Oxford University Press.

Narayan, Uma. 1997. *Dislocating Cultures: Identities, Traditions, and Third-World Feminism.* New York, NY: Routledge.

Nicholson, Linda J., ed. 1990. *Feminism/Postmodernism.* New York, NY: Routledge.

Oakley, Ann. 1972. *Sex, Gender, and Society.* London, England: Maurice Temple Smith Ltd.

Oliver, Kelly, and Lisa Walsh, eds. 2004. *Contemporary French Feminism.* Oxford, England: Oxford University Press.

O'Neill, William. 1969. *Everyone Was Brave: The Rise and Fall of Feminism in America.* New York, NY: HarperCollins.

Ore, Tracy E. 2010. *The Social Construction of Difference and Inequality: Race, Class, Gender, and Sexuality.* New York, NY: McGraw-Hill.

Ortner, Sherry B., and Harriet Whitehead, eds. 1981. *Sexual Meanings: The Cultural Construction of Gender and Sexuality.* Cambridge, England: Cambridge University Press.

Osborne, Susan. 2001. *Feminism.* Harpenden, Herts, England: Pocket Essentials.

Paulson, Ross Evans. 1973. *Women's Suffrage and Prohibition: A Comparative Study of Equality and Social Control.* Glenview, IL: Scott, Foresman.

Phelps, Linda. 1971. "Death in the Spectacle: Female Sexual Alienation." *Liberation* (May).

Phillips, Anne, ed. 1987. *Feminism and Equality.* New York, NY: New York University Press.

Redstockings. 1975. *Feminist Revolution.* New Paltz, NY: Random House.

Rosaldo, Michelle Zimbalist, and Louise Lamphere, eds. 1974. *Women, Culture, and Society.* Stanford, CA: Stanford University Press.

Roth, Benita. 2004. *Separate Roads to Feminism: Black, Chicana, and White Feminist Movements in America's Second Wave.* Cambridge, England: Cambridge University Press.

Rymph, Catherine E. 2006. *Republican Women: Feminism and Conservatism from Suffrage through the Rise of the New Right.* Chapel Hill, NC: University of North Carolina Press.

Sacks, Karen. 1974. "Engels Revisited: Women, the Organization of Production and Private Property." In *Women, Culture, and Society*, edited by Michelle Zimbalist Rosaldo, and Louise Lamphere, 207–222. Stanford, CA: Stanford University Press.

Sargent, Lydia, ed. 1981. *Women and Revolution: A Discussion of the Unhappy Marriage of Marxism and Feminism.* Boston, MA: South End Press.

Scott, Anne F., and Andrew M. Scott. 1975. *One Half the People: The Fight for Women Suffrage.* Philadelphia, PA.

Seigfried, Charlene Haddock. 1996. *Pragmatism and Feminism: Reweaving the Social Fabric.* Chicago, IL: University of Chicago Press.

Sharma, Arvind and Katherine K. Young, eds. 1999. *Feminism and World Religions.* Albany, NY: State University of New York Press.

Shiach, Morag, ed. 1999. *Feminism and Cultural Studies.* Oxford, England: Oxford University Press.

Slaughter, Jane and Robert Kern, eds. 1981. *European Women on the Left: Socialism, Feminism, and the Problems Faced by Political Women, 1880 to the Present.* Westport, CT: Greenwood Press.

Stanton, Elizabeth Cady, Susan B. Anthony, Matilda Joslyn Gage, et al., eds. 1881. *History of Women Suffrage*, Rochester, NY: Project Gutenberg.

Storkey, Elaine. 1985. *What's Right with Feminism.* Grand Rapids, MI: William B. Eerdmans Publishing Company.

Taylor, Barbara. 1983. *Eve and the New Jerusalem: Socialism and Feminism in the Nineteen Century.* New York, NY: Pantheon Books.

Tobias, Sheila. 1997. *Faces of Feminism: An Activist's Reflections on the Women's Movement.* Boulder, CO: Westview Press.

Vetterling-Braggin, Marry, Frederick A. Elliston, and Jane English, eds. 1977. *Feminism and Philosophy.* Totowa, NJ: Littlefield, Adams and Company.

Walker, Rebecca, ed. 1995. *To Be Real: Telling the Truth and Changing the Face of Feminism.* New York, NY: Anchor Books.

Wallerstein, Immanuel. 2000. *The Essential Wallerstein.* New York, NY: New Press.

Walters, Margaret. 2005. *Feminism: A Very Short Introduction.* Oxford, England: Oxford University Press.

Wekesser, Carol, ed. 1995. *Feminism: Opposing Viewpoints.* San Diego, CA: Greenhaven Press.

Wing, Adrien Katherine, and Angela Y. Davis. 2000. *Global Critical Race Feminism: An International Reader.* New York, NY: New York University Press.

Zeisler, Andi. 2008. *Feminism and Pop Culture.* Berkley, CA: Seal Press.

Zetkin, Clara. 1934. *Lenin on the Woman Question.* New York, NY: International Publishers Co., Inc.

Chapter 4

Family

Four Paradigmatic Views

Any explanation of the family is based on a worldview. The premise of this book is that any worldview can be associated with one of the four broad paradigms: functionalist, interpretive, radical humanist, and radical structuralist. This chapter takes the case of the family and discusses it from the four different viewpoints. It emphasizes that the four views expressed are equally scientific and informative; they look at the phenomenon from their certain paradigmatic viewpoint; and together they provide a more balanced understanding of the phenomenon under consideration. In this chapter, the first four sections present the four perspectives, and the fifth section concludes the chapter.

FUNCTIONALIST VIEW

Many aspects of the organization and behavior of families, such as divorce rates, fertility, the labor force participation of married women, have changed dramatically during recent decades. The magnitude and speed of these changes, and the considerable attention they have received, should not leave one with the impression that the family had been a stagnant phenomenon prior to the recent era. The family was an entirely different institution in primitive and peasant societies, and it has undergone a considerable transformation in the West during the last few centuries. The economic approach to the analysis of the family illustrates the main factors that have been responsible both for the long-term evolution of the family, and for the more recent developments of the family.[1]

Traditional Societies: All traditional societies have many difficulties in dealing with uncertainty and limited information. Belief in witchcraft, sorcery, and superstition emanate from ignorance of the material world. The majority of children die before they reach the age of ten, and many women become widowed before the tenth year of their marriage. Bad weather and pests can destroy a harvest, and predators or disease can destroy herds and prey. Ordinary transactions, let alone the complicated ones, are fraught with uncertainty about the quality of merchandise, and the honesty and reliability of buyers and sellers. In peasant market systems, information is poor, scarce, maldistributed, inefficiently communicated, and highly valued, and therefore, people constantly search for the information which they need, and then, protect the information which they obtain.

Traditional societies, for example, primitive and peasant societies, generally do not experience much progress in techniques which are used for farming, hunting, fishing, or other activities. As a result, the economy and social life tend to be static and stationary, even though families rise and fall due to the unequal incidence of luck and ability, as well as the fact that plagues and unusual weather may last for many years.

Traditional societies deal with uncertainty and ignorance in various ways. Since they lack formal insurance programs, persons who have a good harvest, catch, or kill are encouraged (even required) to share such fortunes with others. Although open fields with physically scattered plots of land are a primitive and costly method of reducing fluctuations in income from crops, they are commonly used in peasant societies as protection against the possible harm of weather and pests.

The family—or more accurately, the kinship group—plays an important role in traditional societies because the family protects its members against uncertainty. In many primitive societies, gifts are commonly given to kin; and people assist their relatives who are in distress. A kinship group acts as a reasonably effective "insurance company," because even an extended kinship group is sufficiently small to allow its members to monitor each other in terms of preventing each other from becoming lazy or careless, as well as preventing each other from taking advantage of the protection provided by their kin. Moreover, because they live together, or live close by to each other, the behavior of the members of the kinship are easily observed, and their characteristics known.

In traditional societies, altruism more commonly prevails in families than in other organizations. In the family, even selfish members are encouraged, by the expectation of altruistic members, to account for the interests of other members before taking any action. Otherwise, selfish members, acting based on their selfish interest, would have to bear the consequences of such behavior, because altruistic members would reduce the amount of time and other resources which they would spend on them. Therefore, even selfish members are induced to act as if they were altruistic.

The important role that kin plays in providing protection against uncertainty also reconcile the following two views: (1) that plots are scattered because of partible inheritances; and (2) that plots are scattered to provide protection against fluctuations in income. This is because, scattered plots of family members based on partible inheritances reduce fluctuations in family income, which reduces fluctuations in the income of each member due to family insurance.

In traditional societies, older persons are held in high respect because of their accumulated knowledge, which is especially valuable to younger persons in such stationary environments. Knowledge is passed from older to younger generations in the family and mainly through the culture, which is inherited by the children in the family. Specialized knowledge and skills of the elderly—with respect to their jobs, land, and so on—are more directly conveyed to younger persons with similar family backgrounds.

In traditional societies, members monitor each other in order to prevent shirking and other "moral hazards" of insurance by kin, and in this way, they encourage families to monitor their members to prevent crimes against other families, including nonpayment of debts. Such encouragement is often conveyed through the possibility of the punishment of whole families for antisocial acts by their members.

Younger members tend to join the same occupations, for example, till the same land, as their parents and other relatives because younger members learn the specific knowledge and skills from their elder parent and relatives. Indeed, families can be regarded as small schools that train specialized graduates for particular occupations, for example, land or firms, and bear the responsibility of the qualifications of their graduates when qualifications are not readily ascertained. In traditional societies, the family "schools" play an important role to the extent that peasant farms remain in the same family for many generations, and that families specialize in producing soldiers (samurai), clergymen (Brahmins), merchants (bazari), farmers (peasants), servants, and other types of workers.

In general, families are expected to produce graduates only for specified occupations, or other activities, and are held responsible for the quality of their graduates, especially badly prepared or dishonest graduates. For instance, Ando Hiroshige, who is a highly regarded Japanese artist, inherited his occupation, that is, fire warden in Tokyo, from his father, and passed it first to his cousin, then to his son, and later to his grandson, during the nineteenth century. From this discussion, one conclusion which can be drawn is that in the caste and feudal systems wealth is distributed to upper-class families based on the expectation that such families train and certify their graduate members for particular occupations. The caste and feudal systems used this system, because to them better methods for distributing persons among occupations were not available.

Since families are held accountable for the performance of their members, families would then guide, and even force, their members toward activities in which they would contribute most to the reputation and opportunities of the whole family. Even in seventeenth-century England, which was an individualistic society in comparison with other countries, upper-class fathers chose the occupations for their sons.

In traditional societies, marriages are among the most important events, because families do not want to be affiliated with dishonorable or badly managed families that will either damage the family's own reputation or frequently ask for help. Therefore, families seriously get involved in the process of choosing a mate for their members. For instance, in a fourteenth-century French village, marriages often were arranged by either the family or family friends without much consideration of the feelings of the couple involved. In primitive societies, two families sometimes maintained their alliance by multiple marriages between their members. In a cast of Indian civil servants, during the nineteenth century, multiple marriages occurred among members of a few families. In some societies, marriage of cousins and other kin was common partly because it reduced the risk of bad affiliation. Under these circumstances, families do not support marriage for love, unless it also contributes to the family's interests. Furthermore, the families of an unhappily married couple discourage their divorce, if their union continues to benefit the families.

In traditional societies, kin plays a very important role, as indicated by the emphasis they place on kinship and descent, as well as by the various terms they use for different kinds of kin. Upper-class families protect their family names, as seriously as well-known companies protect their business trademarks, because their family name is a valuable asset or, "trademark." Such families respect, and even worship, their ancestors for their accomplishments, and are, therefore, exempt from being criticized.

Members of poor and unsuccessful families usually have greater autonomy in their economic and social choices than members of successful families do. This is because his family has little to lose as a result of his choice of spouse and economic activity. Indeed, an ambitious poor person may decide to move away from his family in order to prevent his progress from being subjected to his family's low status.

Modern Societies: In modern societies, markets organize trade and production, and dynamic economic environments quickly change technologies, incomes, and opportunities. In addition, the knowledge which older members have accumulated is much less useful to younger members than in traditional societies because the younger members live in a different economic condition. Moreover, small family "schools," which, in traditional societies, provide family members with specialized training for traditional activities, are not as efficient as modern societies' large schools that teach students from many families general knowledge, which is adaptable to changing environments. Furthermore, whereas in traditional societies families are held responsible for the quality of the training which they provide to their family members; in the modern societies, schools provide "certification," which is based on examination. Moreover, in modern societies, contracts and the hope for receiving repeat business reduce the role of certification. This is because individuals know that if they violate their contracts, then they will be punished by the legal system, and that if they misrepresent themselves or are incompetent they will not receive repeat business.

Whereas in traditional societies, family insurance was provided through gifts and loans to members in distress, in modern societies, they are less needed, as individuals can "self-insure" either by borrowing in the capital market during bad times, or by saving during good times. Moreover, in modern societies, market insurance provides more effective protection against various hazards—such as fire, death, old age, and ill health—than any single family can do in traditional societies.

Whereas, kinship plays an important role in traditional societies, it plays a less important role in modern societies, whether in terms of insurance, schooling, or certification. In modern societies, not only kin are less involved in monitoring and controlling other members but also they are less able to do so because such members scatter in pursuit of their best opportunities. Furthermore, as kinship plays a less important role in modern societies, elder members and ancestors receive less respect and attention; they receive less defense against criticism by others; and they receive more criticism in public, or in the privacy of a psychiatrist's office.

In modern societies, the importance of the family is reduced, which means that members of middle-class and upper-class families gain the freedom and privacy of action which is available only to poor families in traditional societies. In addition, children gain independence from their parents in choosing their own spouse, that is, they can date and search in marriage markets in order to find mates with their desired characteristics, based on personal compatibility and love, rather than family compatibility.

Unfortunately, love and desired personal characteristics are more difficult to recognize before actual marriage than family reputation and position, which are the important considerations in traditional societies. It is after marriage that many people find out that they are either no longer in love, or no longer happy with their marital experience, and therefore may divorce to reenter the marriage market. This explains the paradoxical combination of many love-marriages and divorces in modern societies.

In modern societies, compared to traditional societies, parents have fewer children and invest more in their children. In further comparison, in traditional societies, a good deal of the investment of time and other resources in children is made by grandparents, aunts, and other kin because they are concerned with the children's well-being and behavior. As a consequence, modern parents are at a greater loss by the death of each one of their children; and generally, are more concerned about the well-being of each one of their children, because of the amount of time, money, and energy they have invested in each of them.

The members of nuclear families of modern societies are more affectionate and closer than the members of families in traditional societies, but in contrast, cousins and more distant kin are closer in traditional societies than in modern societies. The reason that modern spouses are closer is that love plays a more important role in the selection of mates; and the reason that modern parents and children are closer is that quality, rather than quantity, of children plays a more important role in modern societies. The reason cousins and other kin are closer in traditional societies is that kin groups insure and train members and are more broadly concerned about them.

The modern society evolved from the traditional society, which means that the individualism and nuclear familialism of modern society evolved from the extended families and kinship groups of traditional society. The reason individualism replaced familialism is that many functions of family in traditional societies are more effectively performed by markets and other organizations of modern societies, whether it is the insurance, training, or certification.

The Family in the Last Few Decades in the United States: In the United States, the historical trends since 1950 show that the family has changed dramatically after World War II. For instance, from 1950 to 1977 the birth rate declined by about one-third, the divorce rate more than doubled, the labor force participation rate of married women with young children more than tripled, and the percent of households headed by women with dependent children almost tripled. This shows that, in the United States, during this period, the family has changed more rapidly than during any similar-length period since the founding of the colonies.

All these changes emanate from the growth in the earning power of women in the American economy. The growth in the earning power of women raised the labor force participation of married women, because it raised the foregone value of (i.e., opportunity cost of) their time spent on nonmarket activities. It also raised the relative cost of children, which reduced the demand for children, because children require much of their mothers' time.

The gain from marriage went down because: (a) women's earnings and labor force participation rose; and (b) fertility decreased, as a result of which a sexual division of labor became less advantageous. Since the gain from marriage went down, divorce became more attractive. Furthermore, the decline in the gain from marriage and the increase in divorce increased the number of unmarried couples who lived together, and the percent of families which was headed by women, and partially explain the large growth in the illegitimate birth rate relative to the legitimate birth rate.

Greater labor force participation of women tended to further increase the earning power of women because women invested more in their skills when they noticed that they spent a larger fraction of their time on market activities. This, in turn, enhanced economic development.

There were further interactions among divorce rates, fertility levels, and labor force participation of women. For instance, when the probability of divorce increased it caused fertility to go down, because children became more difficult to take care of, and children provided less pleasure after a marriage was dissolved. In addition, when the probability of divorce increased it also caused the labor force participation of women to increase, because market experience becomes useful when a marriage is dissolved and a woman becomes the main financial supporter of her dependent children.

INTERPRETIVE VIEW

The diversity that exists in families, even within the United States, calls for the provision of family professional services that are sensitive to such diversity. Unfortunately, the diversity in families is often insufficiently addressed in traditional professional educational environments, for example, undergraduate and graduate curricula.[2]

The existence of family diversity encourages a focus on issues or programs that promote the understanding of various types of families (e.g., ethnic or racial minority, gay/lesbian, single-parent, stepparent), or that examine diversity in family processes (e.g., parenting styles, division of family labor, communication). The foci of such ideas are represented in such topics as values regarding families; definitions of families; single-parent families; step families; gay stepfathers; lesbian mothers; African American families; family structure differences in division of household labor; parenting behaviors and their relations to child adjustment in different family structures; family diversity education; and the translation of assessment instruments into another language. Despite the wide variation among such topics, they share a common theme: families vary in many important ways; and family professionals need to be sensitive to and promote the understanding of both the similarities and differences of families. In what follows, some of the important aspects of family diversity are briefly discussed.

In the United States, the continuation of demographic changes will make family more diverse. On the one hand, the traditional family (i.e., white, two biological parents, and children) has been, and will be, losing its extent of prevalence. On the other hand, there has been, and there is expected to be, an increase in variety in families, such as African American, Hispanic, single-parent, and stepparent families. In addition, gay and lesbian families have been receiving an increasing societal recognition.

Different definitions of family are based on different values and have different implications. There is no single correct definition of family. Rather, there are several definitions of family in the literature, and these definitions are, by necessity, based on the values of those who have supplied such definitions. The choice of a particular definition is an important matter, because such a decision greatly impacts the lives of many individuals. For instance, the definition of family (and marriage) affects various matters, such as who can be covered by health insurance, who can have access to children's school records, who can file joint tax returns, and who is eligible for certain public programs. Since there is no single correct definition of family, it is better to advocate quite inclusive and broad definitions of family.

For instance, grounded theorizing can help in understanding culturally diverse families. This is because grounded theorizing collects data and draws culturally relevant conclusions from such data based on the meanings that respondents assign to the issues being studied. This grounded understanding can be achieved through a careful review of both the humanities and clinical literatures.

Alternatively, one can adopt a "pedi-focal" definition of family, whose members include all individuals who are involved in the nurturance and support of a child, regardless of where the child lives. This inclusive definition suggests that families can include nonrelatives and can have flexible boundaries.

Each of different types of families is itself heterogeneous. In the initial stage of research about a new type of family, there is often a tendency to treat individuals in this new type of family as homogeneous. As research about this new type of family advances, the heterogeneity that is inevitably present in any large grouping of people emerges and becomes the subject of study. This notion is demonstrated, for instance, in the study of the relationship between lesbian mothers and children. That is, these women can have different experiences depending on how the child had been conceived. Similarly, in the study of gay stepfathers, it has been found that both gay men and stepfathers have varying experiences.

A commitment to family diversity requires attention not only to differences but to similarities among families. In other words, family diversity not only directs attention to how importantly and meaningfully families differ but also directs attention to similarities across different types of families. Without examining such similarities, the researcher may mistakenly arrive at the conclusion that different types of families are more distinct than they actually are.

For instance, one of the studies that has also given importance to examining similarities of processes in different family forms has arrived at the conclusion that relationship satisfaction among partners in white American and African American dating couples could be predicted by the same set of variables. That is, although previous studies have documented the existence of racial differences, this study suggests that the processes that are linked to relationship satisfaction are similar between these two racial groups.

Social institutions find it difficult to adapt to different types of families. Demographic changes in families affect many of the social institutions that interact with families. Even those social institutions that attempt to adapt to family diversity, find it difficult to adapt to increases in the prevalence of some types of families. For instance, in assessing the experiences of single-parent families in the U.S. Army, a study found that single parents, particularly fathers, adapted more strongly with the availability of family, community, and army resources than to the presence of work stressors. This leads to the recommendation that the army should develop policies that are more supportive of single parents.

An appreciation of the existence of different types of families helps families in their effective encounter with adversity. For instance, divorced individuals of European descent can learn from the experiences of those individuals who are of African descent. More specifically, in adjusting to the stressful circumstances that follow divorce, white families can benefit from an understanding of how African American families have adapted to oppression and adversity, particularly with respect to the way they took care of their children.

Empirical research helps to test professionals' theories and popular beliefs. There are many untested, unsubstantiated "truths" which are believed by individuals in both the professional community and the general population. For instance, although some people believe that men are assuming more housework responsibilities than they previously were, women still undertake the vast amount of household activities across multiple family structures.

Family diversity is better understood when the researcher studies multiple generations within families. As a result of the increase in life expectancy, families are more commonly having more than two generations that interact regularly with each other. Consequently, family professionals will have a better understanding of such families when they consider different experiences of members of the multiple generations. For instance, the study of three-generation African American families found that members of these three generations had different experiences and perceptions in areas such as family cohesion, help received, and help given. Therefore, the members of each generation have their own specific needs; and in the provision of assistance to them, their specific type of intervention should be followed.

Training individuals to appreciate family diversity can be a challenging task. This is because the values of educators who respect family diversity may come into conflict with the values of some of their students, who may believe that some types of families lead to better outcomes for their members than do others. Teachers can attempt to convey their value that different kinds of families need to be respected and appreciated, but they need to be attentive to the possibility that their students hold different beliefs. Teachers need to remind themselves that students have the right to hold different beliefs, and that students should be provided with an educational environment that helps students feel comfortable expressing their opinions and feelings. The process of reflexivity can be used as a means to help implement these goals.

Understanding family diversity requires attention to, and characterization of, processes that are followed within families. Unfortunately, some people use diversity to refer to differences in family structure, rather than differences in the way families function and operate both within and outside of their homes. For instance, in comparing traditional and nontraditional families, it has been found that there is no difference between them in terms of effective parenting, but that nontraditional families engaged in more ineffective parenting. Despite these differences, processes in different family structures had similar relations to child well-being.

Concepts and techniques which are used with respect to white, English-speaking American families may not be applicable to other types of families. More specifically, research techniques, assessment instruments, and therapeutic interventions which have been developed through studying white, middle-class families may not be applicable to other types of families. This is partly because some important family constructs may have very different meanings in different families. Similarly, there is the difficult challenge of translating assessment instruments from one language to another, because translating an instrument from one language to another does not necessarily retain the original meaning of the items, and therefore, translation must be performed with utmost care.

Knowledge about diverse families is enhanced by understanding family members' perceptions of their own experiences. That is, it is important to understand the phenomenological experiences of members of diverse families. Generally, researchers have values which are different from the values of the family members whom they study; therefore, there is the risk that investigators may reach erroneous conclusions about the experiences of diverse families. Consequently, researchers who attempt to understand culturally diverse families should use the meanings that family members assign to their experiences. The importance of acquiring the perspective of the family members themselves, in addition to the perspectives of the researcher, is promoted through qualitative research methods and studies, such as interviews with noncustodial single mothers, single parents, and lesbian mothers.

Values play a very important role in the study of culturally diverse families. Researchers hold values and make assumptions that impact their approaches to understanding families. Researchers need to examine their own values before they conduct the study of culturally diverse families. Such examination may lead to understanding the limitations of various paradigms and canons, which are founded on cultural values and assumptions. Therefore, researchers and practitioners, in creating and using relevant knowledge about diverse families, need to account for the role of values.

Researchers' values shape the approaches and conceptual ideas which they use to study culturally diverse families. When researchers' values are placed within a larger cultural space, which may be called "cultural landscape," researchers are challenged to recognize that there are multiple world perspectives which are accompanied by many value orientations. In addition, researchers are challenged to recognize the limitations of their own value orientations, and to broaden their views in order to include a larger value orientation in the study of culturally diverse families. This means that researchers should use processes that develop broader perspectives and approaches on the study of culturally diverse families. Otherwise, researchers' values would limit, rather than expand, knowledge and the application of knowledge.

Every individual or group holds a value orientation. A value orientation is a conceptualization that is both generalized and organized; and greatly influences one's perceptions of time, nature, humankind's relationship to nature, and how humans relate to one another, as well as how groups and individuals regard the world and interact with it.

Values can be defined as a temporal abstraction of generalized principles which are emotionally adhered to by most individuals of a particular subgroup. They can be generalized and defined as values systems that serve as frameworks based on which individuals approach their lives. They form standards against which actions and goals are judged.

Researchers' value orientations regarding the family affect the way they conceptualize and study the family. All the content areas of family science—such as marital stability, parent-child socialization, gender relations, and family violence—are entirely imbued with researchers' personal, cultural, and religious values. Value plays an important role in forming the scientific questions researchers ask, as well as the way they interpret the information which they gather on families. The values of researchers also reflect their society's mainstream value orientations that prevail at particular socio-historical time, which is closely related to the value vocabulary that underlies their views. In addition, in studying ethnic families, researchers must recognize their objective reality based on their socioeconomic and political status, as well as the subjective reality of value frameworks or paradigms that underlie their scientific investigations.

In order to uncover and understand the impact that researchers' values have on their empirical investigations of the family, it is a good idea to look at some studies, as examples, and focus on the relationship between the researcher's own values (or conformity to existing norms) and the data which have been gathered. This exercise will also allow the assessment of the belief that scientists search for "facts" which can be assimilated into their world-views. That is, humans are biased by their tendency to search for "facts" that support their prior beliefs.

Example 1: In performing research on black families in the United States, one researcher suggested that the black culture had little, if any, African characteristics. But, another researcher identified a set of African cultural characteristics among blacks.

Example 2: Two scientists using the same U.S. Census data and similar methodology, arrived at contrasting conclusions about black families and made different recommendations for black families. One scientist, who was white, described the deterioration and dysfunctionality of black families, and recommended social policies that would encourage changes toward more mainstream ways of functioning. Another scientist, who was black, observed resilience and strength in black families, and recommended social policies that would build on such strengths. These two contrasting interpretations of black families show that the two scientists used different value orientations and frames of reference to interpret the data on black families. The former scientist's views reflected assumptions from the pathological or order model, while the latter scientist's views reflected assumptions from the cultural variant or cultural relativity models.

Example 3: In studying the contextual strengths in the lives of black women, one researcher viewed them as reflective of their culture's ability to absorb and address the needs of its members. But, another researcher focused on the women's weaknesses, and did not view their cultural context as having any important role in helping them to address such weaknesses.

Without passing judgment on the scientific validity of the foregoing contrasting studies, it is clear that researchers' different value orientations and worldviews have framed their research on the family. This also supports the idea that scientific knowledge is a construction of the human mind, and that the mind is constructed in a social context, which is in part how individuals come to know the world.

When researchers become aware that their experiences and their consequent value orientations are limited, they are more likely to realize that there is a larger cultural landscape. This realization would then facilitate the promotion of the understanding of different cultural realities that go beyond the researchers' limited experience. Incorporating this understanding into a research agenda on the family encourages what is described as "a new cultural hegemony." A new cultural hegemony in the United States reflects a larger landscape of the American society that includes diverse groups with their own cultural realities. This larger cultural landscape paves the way for researchers to be aware of, to gain knowledge about, and to encourage understanding of the variety in values, norms, beliefs, and behaviors of different peoples. Recognizing and understanding the larger cultural landscape in the United States can also enhance researchers' abilities to see the need to include ethnic/racial minority families in their research on family, and to study them in a culturally sensitive framework.

RADICAL HUMANIST VIEW

Current theories about the nature and consequences of relationship within the family, use "family" as their analytical concept. However, the focus should not be placed on the family as a unit, but on the working lives of individual family members and on the patriarchal and capitalist nature of the relationships that shape family life.[3]

The extant research on families has significantly contributed to the understanding of the diverse structures of family, and the relationship of family, as a unit, to various constituents of social life. The extant research on families, however, has generally neglected to identify and discuss the sources of conflict within family life. It, accordingly, has been of limited use for understanding women's situation.

The persistence and resilience of family forms, in spite of general social change, have certainly prompted feminists to consider whether any of women's interests will be served with the maintenance of a type of family life which feminists have often viewed as a primary source of women's oppression. Historical, anthropological, and sociological studies of families have discussed various ways in which women and men have defended the family unit, despite the unequal responsibilities and rewards of the two sexes in family life. Such studies, however, have not sufficiently paid attention to the differences between women's and men's experiences and interests within families. Such studies, in this way, have overlooked potentially decisive sources of change in families and society. This is because people struggle both within and outside families to advance their own interests. Such studies commit this oversight because they view the family as a unified interest group, and as an agent of change in its own right.

For instance, family historians have considered the role of the family in wealth accumulation; in population change; in labor supply to a new industrial system; and in social values transmission to new generations. Family historians have consistently placed the family in the larger social context. Their findings are very diverse and their interpretations are very wide, such as: the size of the household has stayed constant before, during, and after industrialization; it has decreased because capitalism reduced household production; it has varied, depending on the processes of rural-to-urban migration and wage levels in the new industries, but has often increased in practice; industrialization liberated both sexuality and women; capitalism replaced the extended family with the nuclear family; capitalist industrialization destroyed the nuclear family; the nuclear family helped industrialization; the family and industrialization cooperated in modernization. Family historians, despite their diversity, consistently focused on the relationship between family and society, and in this way, they viewed family as a unit. They viewed family as either a social unit that is a source of dynamic change, an actor, or an agent, that interacts with other "social forces" such as economic change, modernization, or individualism. Their view treats the family as a unit, and assumes that family members share the same set of interests. Their view, in this way, tends to neglect conflicts, or differences of interest, among family members.

Indeed, the concept of the family as an active agent with unified interests should be replaced with an alternative concept of the family as a locus of struggle. For a better understanding of the family, instead of viewing it solely, or primarily, as a unit shaped by affect or kinship, it must be viewed as a location where production and redistribution take place. In this location, people with different involvements and interests in the processes of production and redistribution often come into conflict with one another. This view does not intend to deny that families also involve strong emotional ties, play an extremely important role in our psychic life, and establish ideological norms, but the intention is to identify and explore the underlying material aspects of gender relations within family units. Therefore, the focus is placed on the nature of the work which people do in the family, and their control over the products of their labor.

In modern Western societies, patriarchy and capitalism shape the organization of production, both within and outside the family. The resulting social structure is based on an unequal division of labor by gender and by class, which is the source of tension, conflict, and change. The patriarchal and capitalist relations among people, rather than familial relations themselves, underlie the dynamism of society, including familial relations. For instance, the patriarchal and capitalistic organization of production, through its particular division of labor, leads to its specific redistribution that occurs within the family between wage earners and non-wage earners. This model can explain the prevailing form of the family—that is, the heterosexual nuclear family living together in one household—and can address the various ways in which people of different periods, regions, races, or ethnicities have structured and experienced their family life. For the purposes at hand, the model will be used to show the potential for differing, rather than harmonious, interests among family members, especially between women and men.

In what follows, the case of housework is used to illustrate that patriarchy and capitalism cause different family members to have different material interests. This is in contrast to the view held by family historians who believe that "the family" as a unit resists or embraces capitalism, industrialization, or the state. In what follows, it is emphasized that people—whether men and women, or adults and children—use familial forms in various ways. When they use their "familial" connections and their locations in families to do a project—such as to find jobs, to build labor unions, to wage community struggles, to buy houses, to borrow cars, or to share child care—they act not only as family members but also as members of gender categories, which are related to the division of labor, which are, in turn, organized by capitalism and patriarchy.

As documented by family historians and others, there exist tensions between families and the world outside of families, which means that families indeed act as entities with unified interests against other entities. At first sight, this may seem as a paradox, but family members have relations to production and redistribution that not only ensure family members' mutual dependence but also their distinct interests. For instance, in a family, both the wife who does not work for wages and the husband who works for wages have mutual interest in the size of the husband's paycheck, the efficiency of the wife's cooking facilities, and the quality of their children's education. However, the same historical processes that created families in opposition to (but also in cooperation with) the state, also increased the power of men in families (by making men heads of their families), and magnified tensions within families.

The tensions and conflicts that involve the family can be divided into four categories, as follows. The family can be a site for internal struggle regarding issues related to production (i.e., housework) or redistribution (i.e., paychecks). It can also be a site for external struggle by its members against larger institutions, such as corporations or the state, on issues related to production or redistribution. Some examples for each of the four categories are provided, as follows:

1. Internal struggle related to production (i.e., housework) can be regarding issues such as: Who does it? How? According to which standards? Should women work for wages outside the home or for money inside the home?
2. Internal struggle related to redistribution (i.e., paychecks) can be regarding issues such as: How should the money be spent? Who decides?

Should the husband's paycheck be spent on luxuries for him or on household needs?

3. External struggle related to production (i.e., household production versus
   production organized by capital and the state) can be regarding issues
   such as: Who should do the cooking? Parents or fast-food chains? Who
   should take care of children? Parents or the state?
4. External struggle related to redistribution (i.e., taxes) can be regarding
   issues such as: Who should make decisions about the redistribution
   of family resources? Family members or representatives of the state
   apparatus?

Similar to most other typologies, the categories offered here are in reality
not as rigidly bounded or easily separable. Rather, they represent different
aspects of the same phenomena. That is, not only production and redistribution are interrelated but also struggles within and outside families are inter-
related. In what follows, the focus will be placed on one source of conflict,
that is, the housework, and other issues raised by tensions in other arenas will
be discussed tangentially.

Some observers believe that the family is no longer a place where men
exercise their power, and if any patriarchy exists for men, it exists only on
the impersonal, institutional levels. For some other analysts, whose work
falls in the Marxist traditions, the ceaseless progress of capitalism has
eliminated patriarchy within the family and has given rise to the women's
movement, that is, capitalism weakened patriarchal power to the extent that
women were enabled to confront patriarchy directly. However, in what follows, it is argued that although capitalism has somewhat changed the boundary of men's control, the family still remains a primary arena in which men
exercise their patriarchal power over women's labor. The support for such
argument is provided through a review of some of the empirical findings on
time spent on housework by husbands and wives. Of course, the implicit
assumption is that the time spent on housework, as well as other indicators
of household labor, can be fruitfully used as a measure of power relations
in the family.

Several time-budget studies have measured the amount of time people
spend on housework, as well as other activities, such as paid work and leisure.
Such studies have generally asked people to record their activities for specified time intervals, for example, every fifteen minutes, for one or two days.
Although such studies differ in terms of their data-collection procedures, such
as sampling (national v. local, husband-and-wife families v. individuals), and
reporting (interview v. self-report, contemporaneous v. retrospective reporting), their findings are extremely consistent and their conclusions are firmly
united in term of who does how much housework.

Women, who were not employed for pay outside the home, and who are called, alternatively as "house-workers," "homemakers," or "housewives," worked about fifty-five hours per week on household chores, such as: preparing and cleaning up after meals; doing laundry; cleaning the house; taking care of children and other family members; and shopping and keeping records. These women report that their husbands spent about eleven hours per week on housework, and that their children also spent about eleven hours per week on housework. These time-budget studies show that household production has clearly been more than a full-time job.

The way that the amount of time spent on housework changes as housewives join the work force outside the house, and therefore, the demand on family members' time increases, is a good indicator of the extent to which patriarchy operates in the home, at least with respect to housework. Many people have expressed high expectations about the potentially equalizing effects of women's increased labor-force participation, in the sense that, as women earn wages they may become capable of exercising more power in various activities both within and outside the family. However, time-budget studies have shown that husbands of those wives who work for wages outside the house do not spend more time on housework than those husbands whose wives do not work for wages outside the house. Such studies have also shown that the more a woman spends time on earning wages outside the house, the fewer hours she spends on housework, but the longer is her total hours of work per week. More specifically, women who spent thirty or more hours per week on outside paid employment, had, on average, a total work week of seventy-six hours, which included an average of thirty-three hours per week of housework. Moreover, those women who had the longest work weeks, their husbands had the shortest work weeks. The lack of responsiveness of men's housework time to women's increased outside paid-work time was also evident in time-budget data gathered from cities in various industrialized countries. More specifically, in all countries studied, those women who had a wage-work outside the house, worked substantially more hours every day than their husbands or their full-time house-working counterparts. Moreover, those women who had a wage-work outside the house, on their days off, spent substantially more time on housework (about double their weekday time), whereas their husbands, and even their full-time house-working partners, used such days for increased leisure.

In addition to the time spent by husbands and wives, it is informative and instructive to look at the tasks performed by husbands and wives in order to better understand their relative burden of housework. In examining participation rates of husbands and wives in various household tasks, it has been found that only 26 percent of the husbands spent some time cleaning the house (on either of two days: one day during the week and one day during weekend), while 86 percent of the wives spent some time cleaning the house on either of those two days; and that 27 percent of the husbands contributed 2.5 hours per week to cooking, while 93 percent of the wives contributed 8.5 hours per week to cooking. Only 2 percent of the husbands did some laundry, but 50 percent of the wives did some laundry. These data indicate that most married women perform the regular, necessary, and most time-consuming tasks in the household every day. In addition, since their husbands' contribution is small and selective, married women can expect doing such tasks for the rest of their lives.

Similar data, regarding the percentage of days that wives and husbands, as well as the other members of the household, participated in various household tasks, similarly indicate that while the husbands of wage-working wives participated more often than the husbands of non-wage-working wives in almost all household tasks, they contributed only a small amount to the time required to complete the tasks. In other words, the husbands of wage-working wives did more housework by participating more often, but the substance of their contributions was insignificant. Wage-working women, for the most part, are not able to balance their wages with reduced work weeks, either by buying sufficient substitute products, or labor, or alternatively, by getting their husbands to do appreciably more housework. In the absence of patriarchy, there should be equal sharing of wage work and housework between husband and wives, but there is no such thing in current life.

The amount of housework substantially increases when there are either very young children or many children in the household. The household time-budget data indicate that under such circumstances, the wife's hours of work expanded to meet the consequent requirements of the family, but the husband's hours of work did not change. In families with a child under one year old, the full-time wage-earner wife spent about seventy hours per week on housework, of which about thirty hours per week was spent on family (primarily child) care. In the same families, the husband spent five hours per week on family care, but reduced the amount of time he spent on other housework, such that his total housework stayed the same. When the wife was employed for fifteen or more hours per week, she spent over fifty hours on housework, of which twenty hours were spent on child care. The husband spent two hours more per week on child care, and his time spent on housework increased to twenty hours (compared to twelve for the husband whose wife did less wage work). Overall, when there were very young children in the household, the wage-worker wife's total housework time substantially expanded, but the husband's housework time only moderately increased.

The rather small, selective, and unresponsive contribution of the husband to housework points to the idea that the husband may be a net drain on the family's resources in terms of housework time, that is, husbands may require more housework than they contribute. Indeed, this idea is implied by a materialist definition of patriarchy, according to which men directly benefit from women's labor power.

These studies illustrate the patriarchal benefits reaped in housework. First, the wife spends the vast majority of required time on housework, that is, wife spends about 70 percent, while both the husband and the children spend about 15 percent each. Second, the wife is mostly responsible for child care. More specifically, in those families where there are very young or very many children, the wife accepts the excess burden of housework, but the husband's contribution to housework remains about the same. That is, the wife, at least with respect to housework, does all of the adjusting to the family life cycle. Third, the wife who works for wages (of course, she does so usually due to economic necessity) finds out that her husband spends very little additional time on housework than the husband whose wife is not a wage-worker. Fourth, the wife spends an additional eight hours of housework for taking care of the husband. And fifth, the wife spends at least forty hours per week to maintain the house and husband if she does not have outside employment, and at least thirty hours per week if she has outside employment.

RADICAL STRUCTURALIST VIEW

The monogamous patriarchal family—like capitalism—is not a fixed characteristic of human societies in all ages, but the product of historical development. The stages in the evolution of the family begin with primitive communism and continue through human history, that is, the sequence of slavery, feudalism, and capitalism. The history of the family, and the changing power relationships between the sexes within it, has a special importance in the Marxian materialistic concept of history. This is based on the idea that the production and reproduction of human beings, that is, the propagation of the human species, play as important a role as the production of the means of subsistence, such as food, clothing, and shelter as well as the required tools.[4]

The study of the history of the family started around 1860s. Before this, historical science was entirely under the influence of the Five Books of Moses. These described the patriarchal form of the family in greater detail than anywhere else, accepted it as the oldest form of the family, and identified it with the present-day bourgeois family, as if the family had really undergone no historical development at all.

The study of the history of the family started in 1861, when it was found that: (a) in the beginning, human beings lived in a community with sexual promiscuity, which may be called "hetaerism"; (b) such promiscuity excludes all certainty regarding paternity, and therefore, lineage could be considered only through the female line (according to mother right), and that originally this pattern prevailed among all the peoples of antiquity; (c) consequently, women, as mothers, were the only detectable parents of the younger generation, and therefore, were given a high degree of consideration and respect, which was elevated to the complete rule of women (gynaecocracy); (d) the transition to monogamy (i.e., the woman belongs exclusively to one man) meant the violation of a primeval religious injunction (i.e., the violation of the right of the other men to the same woman), a violation which had to be paid for, or the toleration of which had to be purchased, by surrendering the woman for a limited period of time.

Another study, in 1871, found that: (a) the American Indian system of kinship also prevailed among many tribes in Asia, and, in a somewhat different form, in Africa and Australia; (b) it was entirely explained by a form of group marriage, which is now approaching extinction, in Hawaii and in other Australian islands; and (c) in these same islands, however, beside group marriage, a system of kinship prevailed which could only be explained by a still earlier but now extinct form of group marriage.

The 1871 study was further developed in 1877, according to which endogamy did not constitute an antithesis to exogamy, which had not been seen in any "tribes" anywhere up to that time. More specifically, at the time when group marriage still prevailed (and in all likelihood it prevailed everywhere at one time or other), the tribe consisted of a number of groups which were related by blood on the mother's side (gentes), within which marriage was strictly prohibited. Accordingly, the men of a gens took their wives from outside their gens, but within their tribe. Thus, the gens itself was strictly exogamous, but the tribe, which consisted of all the gentes, was strictly endogamous.

The 1877 study was further performed to discover that the gens, which was organized based on mother right, was the original form from which developed the later gens, organized based on father right, which is the gens found among the civilized peoples of antiquity. The Greek and Roman gens, which puzzled all previous historians, is now explained by the Indian gens. In this way, a new basis was found for the entire history of primitive society.

The aforementioned studies, of the three main epochs of human history (i.e., savagery, barbarism, and civilization), was concerned only with the first two, and with the transition to the third one. They subdivide each of the first two epochs into lower, middle, and upper stages, based on the progress made in the production of the means of subsistence. They reason that it is the development of humans' skill in this direction on which the human supremacy on the earth depend. Human beings are the only beings who may be considered to have gained an absolute control over the production of food. The main epochs of human progress have been identified based on the enlargement of the sources of subsistence. Moreover, the evolution of the family proceeds concurrently.

It is possible, now, to generalize the above-mentioned periodization as follows. (a) Savagery: the period in which the appropriation of natural products, which were ready for use, predominated; and the main things which man produced consisted of instruments that facilitated such appropriation. (b) Barbarism: the period in which knowledge of cattle breeding and land cultivation was gained, and the methods of increasing the productivity of nature through human activity were learned. (c) Civilization: the period in which knowledge of the further increasing the efficiency of natural products, of industry proper, and of art was acquired.

According to previously mentioned studies, out of the original condition of promiscuous intercourse, there developed the following stages in the family.

The Consanguine Family: In this first stage of the family, the marriage groups are formed according to generations. That is, all the grandfathers and grandmothers within the limits of the family are all mutual husbands and wives. The same relationship holds true with respect to their children, that is, the fathers and mothers, whose children, in turn, form a third circle of common husbands and wives, whose children, that is, the great-grandchildren of the first generation, in turn, form a fourth circle of husbands and wives. In the Consanguine form of the family, ancestors and descendants, for example, parents and children, are prevented from becoming husbands and wives. Brothers and sisters, male and female cousins of the first, second, and more remote degrees are all considered mutually brothers and sisters, and therefore, all of them are mutually husbands and wives. In this form of the family, the relation of brother and sister includes the exercise of sexual intercourse with one another. The consanguine family is almost extinct, except for the Hawaiian system of consanguinity, which still prevails in Polynesia.

The Punaluan Family: Whereas the first advance in the organization of the family was the exclusion of parents and children from mutual sexual relations, the second advance was the exclusion of brothers and sisters. This second advance was more important and more difficult than the first advance, because of the similarity in the ages of the participants. The second advance was accomplished gradually, and most probably it commenced with the gradual exclusion of natural brothers and sisters (which was considered on the maternal side) from sexual relations, which was implemented first in isolated cases, then gradually became the rule (in Hawaii exceptions to this rule still existed in the present century), and ended with the prohibition of marriage between collateral brothers and sisters, that is, between first, second, and third cousins. The tribes that restricted inbreeding by this advance were bound to develop more rapidly and more fully than the tribes that followed the rules of intermarriage between brothers and sisters. The powerful effect of this advance was felt through the institution of the gens, which arose directly from it and had far-reaching consequences. The gens was the foundation of the social order of almost all the barbarian peoples of the world; and Greece and Rome pass directly from it into civilization.

Every primeval family was bound up to break up after a couple of generations, at the latest. According to the Hawaiian custom, a few sisters, whether natural or collateral (i.e., first, second, or more distant cousins), were the common wives of their common husbands, which excluded their brothers. These husbands no longer addressed each other as brothers (which indeed they no longer had to be), but as punalua, which means, intimate companion or partner, as it were. Similarly, a group of natural or collateral brothers held in common marriage a few women, who were not their sisters, and these women addressed one another as punalua. This is the classical form of family structure (which was later modified in a series of variations), and its essential characteristic feature was as follows: mutual community of husbands and wives within a specific family circle, from which the brothers of the wives (first the natural brothers, and then the collateral brothers as well) were excluded, and the same applying to the sisters of the husbands. This form of the family actually existed in Hawaii, and was demonstrable throughout Polynesia.

The Pairing Family: Pairing took place for some time during group marriage, or even earlier. The man, among his several wives, had a principal wife (whom cannot be said to have been his favorite wife) and he was her principal husband, among her several husbands. Pairing became increasingly established as the gens developed and as the numbers of classes of "brothers" and "sisters" between which marriage was prohibited increased. Gens played an important role in this matter because they prevented marriage between blood relatives. Indeed, this is found among the Iroquois and most other Indian tribes (who are in the lower stage of barbarism), in which marriage is prohibited between all relatives, according to their system, which are of several hundred types. This growing complexity of marriage prohibitions made increasingly impossible the continuation of group marriages, which were replaced by the pairing family. In the pairing family, one man lives with one woman, but polygamy and occasional infidelity remain as men's privileges, even though polygamy is seldom practiced for economic reasons. From the woman, the strictest fidelity is demanded during the period of cohabitation, and her involvement in adultery is cruelly punished. However, the marriage tie can be easily broken by either side, and the children belong solely to the mother, as it was the case previously.

Before we deal with monogamy, a few words should be spent on polygamy and polyandry, which developed rapidly following the overthrow of mother right. Both of these marriage forms are only exceptions. They did not appear side by side in any country. Since the number of men and women, without regard to social institutions having been fairly equal, it is clear that neither polygamy nor polyandry could rise to general prevalence. Actually, polygamy, on the part of a man, was evidently a product of slavery, and was limited to a few exceptional cases. In the Semitic patriarchal family, only the patriarch himself and, at most, a couple of his sons lived in polygamy; and each of the other members of the family had to be content with one wife only. It remains true today throughout the entire Orient. Polygamy is a privilege of the rich and the grandees, and the wives are recruited mainly through the purchase of female slaves; and the mass of the people live in monogamy.

The Monogamian Family: This type of family arises out of the pairing family during the transition period from the middle to the upper stage of barbarism, and becomes established at the beginning of civilization. It is based on the supremacy of the man, and its aim is to have children with undisputed paternity, which is required for these children in order to inherit their father's wealth as his natural heirs. The monogamian family when compared to the pairing marriage, is far more rigid in terms of the marriage tie, because the family can no longer be dissolved at the pleasure of either party. Under the rules of the monogamian family, only the man can dissolve the marriage and divorce his wife. Furthermore, man have the right of conjugal infidelity, which is sanctioned, at least, by custom (e.g., the Code Napoleon gives this right to the husband so long as he does not bring his concubine into the conjugal home), and is exercised more and more with the growing development of society. However, if the wife attempts to revive the ancient sexual practice, she is punished more severely than ever before. This new form of the family, in all its severity, is found among the Greeks. The monogamian family, however, did not appear everywhere and always in the classically harsh form which prevailed among the Greeks. Among the Romans and Germans, woman was more free and respected.

The origin of monogamy, as far as it can be traced among the most civilized and highly developed people of antiquity, was not in individual sex love. This is because, as before, the marriages remained marriages of convenience. It was the first form of the family which was based, not on natural, but, on economic conditions. That is, the victory of private property over common ownership, which was naturally developed. The rule of the man in the family, the reproduction of children who could only be his, and the children who could be the heirs of his wealth, were the only reasons which Greeks frankly avowed as the exclusive aims of monogamy. For the rest of the people, it was a burden, as well as a duty to the gods, to the state, and to their ancestors, which just had to be fulfilled. In Athens, by law, the marriage was not only compulsory but also the fulfillment by the man of a minimum of the so-called conjugal duties.

Thus, monogamy is not a reconciliation of man and woman, let alone the highest form of such a reconciliation. On the contrary, monogamy is the subjection of woman by man, and it is the proclamation of a conflict between the sexes which was completely unknown in prehistoric times. The first division of labor was between man and woman for child bearing. The first class antagonism which appeared in history not only coincided with the development of the antagonism between man and woman in monogamian marriage but also coincided with the first class oppression of the female sex by the male. Monogamy was a great historical advance, but at the same time it inaugurated (together with slavery and private wealth) that epoch (which has been lasting until today), in which every advance is likewise a relative regression. That is, the development of well-being of the one group is obtained at the expense of the misery and repression of the other group.

The old relative freedom of sexual intercourse did not disappear with the victory of the pairing family, or even the emergence of monogamy. The old conjugal system, which was reduced to narrower limits by the gradual disappearance of the punaluan groups, finally disappeared in the new form of hetaerism, which is the extramarital sexual intercourse between men and unmarried women, which exists beside monogamy, and has flourished in the most diverse forms during the whole period of civilization and is steadily developing into open prostitution.

In the old communistic household, which consisted of numerous couples and their children, the administration of the household, which was entrusted to the women, was as much a public and socially necessary activity as the providing of food by the men. This situation changed with the patriarchal family, and changed even more with the monogamian individual family. The administration of the household lost its public character, it was no longer of society's concern, and turned into a private service. The wife, who was pushed out of participation in social production, became the first domestic servant. Only modern large-scale industry made it possible for her (and only for the proletarian woman) to participate in social production. However, such possibility was provided with the provision that, when she fulfills her duties in the private service of her family, she remains excluded from public production and cannot earn anything; and when she participates in public industry and earn her living independently, she cannot fulfill her family duties. What applies to the woman in the factory applies to her in all the professions, even to professions in medicine and law. The modern individual family is founded on the open or disguised domestic enslavement of the woman; and modern society is a mass consisting of individual families as its molecules. Today, in most cases, the man has to be the breadwinner of the family, at least among the propertied classes, and this puts him in the dominant position, which does not require any special legal privileges. In the family, the husband is the bourgeois, and the wife is the proletariat. In the industrial world, the specific character of the economic oppression of the proletariat stands out after complete juridical equality of both classes is established. Then, it will be seen that the democratic republic does not abolish the antagonism between the two classes, but, it provides the environment for their fight. Similarly, special character of man's domination over woman in the modern family will be brought out only when both are completely equal before the law. Then, it will be seen that the first requirement for the emancipation of women is their reintroduction into public industry; and that this again demands that the individual family as the economic unit of society must be abolished.

In summary, the three chief forms of marriage conform to the three main stages of human development. In savagery, there was group marriage; in barbarism, there was pairing marriage; and for civilization, there was monogamy, which was supplemented by adultery and prostitution. In the upper stage of barbarism, that is, between pairing marriage and monogamy, there was the control of men over female slaves, and polygamy.

The individual family would no longer be the economic unit of society, when the means of production become common property. Private housekeeping becomes a social industry. The care and education of the children is turned into a public matter. Society takes care of all children equally, whether or not they are born in wedlock. Therefore, a girl's anxiety, about the "consequences" that hinders her from giving herself freely to the man she loves, disappears. Such consequences are today important social factors, both moral and economic. This will cause a gradual rise in unrestrained sexual intercourse, and a more lenient public opinion regarding virginal honor and feminine shame. Prostitution disappears, and there will be monogamy with individual sex love.

CONCLUSION

This chapter briefly discussed four views expressed with respect to the family. The functionalist paradigm believes that the economic approach should be used to analyze the main factors that have been responsible both for the long-term evolution of the family and for the more recent developments of the family. The interpretive paradigm believes that the existence of family diversity should encourage a focus on issues or programs that promote the understanding of various types of families or that examine diversity in family processes. The radical humanist paradigm believes that in the analysis of the family, the focus should not be placed on the family as a unit, but on the working lives of individual family members and on the patriarchal and capitalist nature of the relationships that shape family life. The radical structuralist paradigm believes that the stages in the evolution of the family begin with primitive communism and continue through human history, that is, the sequence of slavery, feudalism, and capitalism.

Each paradigm is logically coherent—in terms of its underlying assumptions—and conceptualizes and studies the phenomenon in a certain way, and generates distinctive kinds of insight and understanding. Therefore, different paradigms in combination provide a broader understanding of the phenomenon under consideration. An understanding of different paradigms leads to a better understanding of the multifaceted nature of the phenomenon.

NOTES

1. For this literature, see Becker (1981a, b), Becker and Murphy (1988), Ben-Porath (1982), Brodsky, Troyer, and Vance (1984), Hareven (1976), Morgan (1975), Parsons (1964), Parsons and Bales (1955), Pollak (1985), and Schultz (1974). This section is based on Becker (1981a).

2. For this literature, see Blau, Ferber, and Winkler (1986), Brabant and Mooney (1999), Byrd (2009), Cheal (2008), DeGenova (1997), Demo and Acock (1993), Dilworth-Anderson, Burton, and Turner (1993), Dolfsma and Hoppe (2003), Fine (1993), Freud (1999), Humphries (1995), Hutter (1991), Julian, McKenry, and McKelvey (1994), Levi-Strauss (1960), Maines (2000), Moxnes (1997), Nelson (1996), Smith and Hamon (2012), Strong and Cohen (2014), Swidler (2001), Taylor, Chatters, and Jackson (1993), Tilly and Scott (1978), Trask and Hamon (2007), White and Klein (2002), and Wooley (1993). This section is based on Fine (1993) and Dilworth-Anderson, Burton, and Turner (1993).

3. For this literature, see Barker and Feiner (2004), Frankfurt Institute for Social Research (1972), Hartmann (1981), Held (1980), Horkheimer (1972), Morgan (1975), Poster (1978), Young (1990), and Zaretsky (1986). This section is based on Hartmann (1981).

4. For this literature, see Brown (2013), Ciscel and Heath (2001), Delphy and Leonard (2004), Engels (1970, 1988), Hutter (1988), Reiter (1975), Selsam (1943), Smith and Wallerstein (1992), and Vogel (2014). This section is based on Engels (1988).

REFERENCES

Barker, Drucilla K., and Susan F. Feiner. 2004. *Liberating Economics: Feminist Perspectives on Families, Work, and Globalization.* London, England: Routledge.

Becker, Gary Stanley. 1981a. *A Treatise on the Family.* Cambridge, MA: Harvard University Press.

Becker, Gary Stanley. 1981b. "Altruism in the Family and Selfishness in the Market Place." *Economica* 48(189): 1–15.

Becker, Gary Stanley, and Kevin M. Murphy. 1988. "The Family and the State." *Journal of Law and Economics* 31(1): 1–18.

Ben-Porath, Yoram. 1982. "Economics and the Family—Match or Mismatch? A Review of Becker's A Treatise on the Family." *Journal of Economic Literature* 20(1): 52–64.

Blau, Francine D., Marianne A. Ferber, and Anne E. Winkler. 1986. *The Economics of Women, Men, and Work.* Englewood Cliffs, NJ: Prentice Hall.

Brabant, Sarah, and Linda Mooney. 1999. "The Social Construction of Family Life in the Sunday Comics: Race as a Consideration." *Journal of Comparative Family Studies* 30(1): 113–133.

Brodsky, Garry, John Troyer, and David Vance. 1984. *Contemporary Readings in Social and Political Ethics.* Buffalo, NY: Prometheus Books.

Brown, Heather. 2013. *Marx on Gender and the Family.* Chicago, IL: Haymarket Books.

Byrd, Stephanie Ellen. 2009. "The Social Construction of Marital Commitment." *Journal of Marriage and Family* 71(2): 318–336.

Cheal, David. 2008. *Families in Today's World: A Comparative Approach.* New York, NY: Routledge.

Ciscel, David H., and Julia A. Heath. 2001. "To Market, to Market: Imperial Capitalism's Destruction of Social Capital and the Family." *Review of Radical Political Economy* 33: 401–414. DeGenova, Mary Kay. 1997. *Families in Cultural Context: Strengths and Challenges in Diversity.* Mountain View, CA: Mayfield Publishing Company.

Delphy, Christine, and Diana Leonard. 2004. *Familiar Exploitation: A New Analysis of Marriage in Contemporary Western Societies.* Cambridge, England: Polity Press.

Demo, David H., and Alan C. Acock. 1993. "Family Diversity and the Division of Domestic Labor: How Much Have Things Really Changed?" *Family Relations* 42(3): 323–331.

Dilworth-Anderson, Peggye, Linda Burton, and William L. Turner. 1993. "The Importance of Values in the Study of Culturally Diverse Families." *Family Relations* 42(3): 238–242.

Dolfsma, Wilfred, and Hella Hoppe. 2003. "On Feminist Economics." *Feminist Review* 75: 118–128.

Engels, Friederich. 1970. *The Origin of the Family, Private Property and the State.* Harmondsworth, England: Penguin Books.

Engels, Friederich. 1988. "Engels on the Origin and Evolution of the Family." *Population and Development Review* 14(4): 705–729.

Fine, Mark A. 1993. "Current Approached to Understanding Family Diversity: An Overview of the Special Issue." *Family Relations* 42(3): 235–237.

Frankfurt Institute for Social Research. 1972. "The Family." In *Aspects of Sociology*, edited by Frankfurt Institute for Social Research, 129–147. Boston, MA: Beacon Press.

Freud, Sophie. 1999. "The Social Construction of Normality." *Families in Society* 80(4): 333–339.

Hareven, Tamara K. 1976. "Modernization and Family History: Perspectives on Social Change." *Signs* 2(1): 190–206.

Hartmann, Heidi I. 1981. "The Family as the Locus of Gender, Class, and Political Struggle: The Example of Housework." *Journal of Women in Culture and Society* 6(3): 366–394.

Held, David. 1980. *Introduction to Critical Theory.* Berkeley, CA: University of California Press.

Horkheimer, Max. 1972. "Authority and the Family." In *Critical Theory*, edited by Max Horkheimer, 47–128. New York, NY: Herder and Herder.

Humphries, Jane, ed. 1995. *Gender and Economics.* Aldershot, Hants, England: Edward Elgar.

Hutter, Mark. 1991. *The Family Experience: A Reader in Cultural Diversity.* New York, NY: Macmillan Publishing Company.

Julian, T.W., P.C. McKenry, and M.W. McKelvey. 1994. "Cultural Variations in Parenting: Perceptions of Caucasian, African-American, Hispanic, and Asian-American Parents." *Family Relations* 43(1): 30–37.

Levi-Strauss, Claude. 1960. "The Family." In *Man, Culture and Society*, edited by Harry L. Shapiro, 261–285. New York, NY: Oxford University Press.

Maines, D.R. 2000. "The Social Construction of Meaning." *Contemporary Sociology* 29: 577–584.

Morgan, D.H.J. 1975. *Social Theory and the Family.* London, England: Routlege and Kegan Paul.

Moxnes, Halvor. 1997. *Constructing Early Christian Families: Family as Social Reality and Metaphor.* New York, NY: Routledge.

Nelson, Julie A. 1996. *Feminism, Objectivity and Economics.* New York, NY: Routledge.

Parsons, Talcott. 1964. *Social Structure and Personality.* New York, NY: Routledge.

Parsons, Talcott, and Robert F. Bales. 1955. *Family, Socialization and Interaction Process.* Glencoe, IL: Free Press.

Pollak, Robert A. 1985. "A Transaction Cost Approach to Families and Households." *Journal of Economic Literature* 23(2): 581–608.

Poster, Mark. 1978. *Critical Theory of the Family.* New York, NY: Seabury Press.

Reiter, Rayna R., ed. 1975. *Toward an Anthropology of Women.* New York, NY: Monthly Review Press.

Schultz, Theodore W., ed. 1974. *Economics of the Family: Marriage, Children and Human Capital.* Chicago, IL: University of Chicago Press.

Selsam, Howard. 1943. *Socialism and Ethics.* New York, NY: International Publishers Co., Inc.

Smith, Joan, and Immanuel Wallerstein. 1992. *Creating and Transforming Households: The Constraints of the World-Economy.* Cambridge, England: Cambridge University Press.

Smith, Suzanne R., and Raeann R. Hamon. 2012. *Exploring Family Theories.* Oxford, England: Oxford University Press.

Strong, Bryan, and Theodore F. Cohen. 2014. *The Marriage and Family Experience: Intimate Relationships in a Changing Society.* Belmont, CA: Wadsworth.

Swidler, A. 2001. *Talk of Love: How Culture Matters.* Chicago, IL: University of Chicago Press.

Taylor, Robert Joseph, Linda M. Chatters, and James S. Jackson. 1993. "A Profile of Familial Relations among Three-Generation Black Families." *Family Relations* 42(3): 332–341.

Tilly, Louise A., and Joan W. Scott. 1978. *Women, Work and Family.* London, England: Holt, Rinehart and Winston.

Trask, Bahira Sherif, and Raeann R. Hamon, eds. 2007. *Cultural Diversity and Families: Expanding Perspectives.* Thousand Oaks, CA: Sage Publications.

Vogel, Lise. 1983/2014. *Marxism and the Oppression of Women: Toward a Unitary Theory.* New Brunswick, NJ: Rutgers University Press.

White, James M., and David M. Klein. 2002. *Family Theories: Understanding Families.* Thousand Oaks, CA: Sage Publications, Inc.

Wooley, Frances R. 1993. "The Feminist Challenge to Neoclassical Economics." *Cambridge Journal of Economics* 17: 485–500.

Young, Iris Marion. 1990. *Justice and the Politics of Difference.* Princeton, NJ: Princeton University Press.

Zaretsky, Eli. 1986. *Capitalism, the Family, and Personal Life.* New York, NY: Harper and Row, Publishers.

Chapter 5

Patriarchy

Four Paradigmatic Views

Any explanation of the origin of the patriarchy is based on a worldview. The premise of this book is that any worldview can be associated with one of the four broad paradigms: functionalist, interpretive, radical humanist, and radical structuralist. This chapter takes the case of the origin of the patriarchy and discusses it from the four different viewpoints. It emphasizes that the four views expressed are equally scientific and informative; they look at the phenomenon from their certain paradigmatic viewpoint; and together they provide a more balanced understanding of the phenomenon under consideration. In this chapter, the first four sections present the four perspectives, and the fifth section concludes the chapter.

FUNCTIONALIST VIEW

The analyses of patriarchy should address the evolutionary basis of male motivation to control female sexuality. Evidence from other primates, with respect to male sexual coercion and female resistance to it, indicates that the sexual conflicts of interest that underlie patriarchy predate the coming to existence of the human species. Humans, however, more extensively get involved with both male dominance and male control of female sexuality than most other primates do. The way in which this unusual degree of gender inequality came about over the course of human evolution can be explained through six hypotheses.[1]

The explanation of the origins of patriarchy in the human species is based on an evolutionary perspective, which is, in turn, based on biology. An evolutionary approach to understanding the origins of patriarchy explains why male power over women so often revolves around female sexuality.

Evolutionary theory explains the origins of male desire for control of female sexuality, and in this way, it adds a new and important dimension to the analysis of patriarchy.

The central thesis of this evolutionary theory is that the origins of patriarchy go very far back in history, even long before the development of agriculture, civilization, capitalism, or other similar phenomena which are used by various scholars to explain patriarchy. The explanation of this evolutionary theory rests on several interrelated concepts. First, there are the basic aspects of evolutionary theory, including reproductive differences between the sexes. Second, there is the evolutionary basis of conflicts of interest between females and males. Finally, there are the six interrelated factors that underlie the origins of patriarchy in the human species. The conclusion is that patriarchy is the product of the reproductive strategies which are typically followed by men.

Evolutionary Theory: Natural selection favors individuals' behaviors that promote reproductive success; however, evolutionary theory is distinct from genetic determinism. Evolutionary theory is based on Darwin's well-known concept of natural selection, which, in modern form, means that genes that are associated with phenotypic characteristics (i.e., physical or behavioral traits) that increase individual reproductive success will tend to increase over many generations, because individuals who have such genes will leave more descendants (i.e., more of their genes) than those who do not. Natural selection is the process of evolution by way of adaptations (i.e., phenotypic characteristics that help organisms to survive and reproduce).

It should be noted that, in the Darwinian theory of evolution, although selection takes place through the gene, it does not mean that the development of phenotypic characteristics in individuals is determined by genes, with little possibility for environmental effect. Evolutionary processes are dependent on differential selection of genes. But, it should be noted that, the selection of particular genes during evolution takes place within the context of a particular environment (where "environment" encompasses everything that affects development, i.e., both inside and outside the organism). Thus, specific gene-environment complexes determine the development of adaptive traits, and complex, gene-environment interaction determines all phenotypic characteristics.

Evolution of Conflict between Sexes: Female and male mammals have different reproductive interests, which often result in conflict. Males tend to employ coercion in order to resolve such conflicts in their favor. Female and male mammals have different sexual behavior because they are differently involved in the ways they reproduce. Female mammals have a physiological commitment to internal gestation and lactation, and therefore, must invest a great deal of time and energy in each offspring. In contrast, a male's role in reproduction is simply the fertilization of a female. The male, after fertilizing the female, can proceed to fertilize additional females, without having any commitment, in terms of time or energy, to the offspring of the first female. Thus, for males, rather than females, reproductive success is measured by the number of times mating that can take place with fertile partners. For females, rather than males, on the other hand, reproductive success is measured by the time and effort which is required to garner and transfer energy to offspring as well as to protect and care for them. Therefore, males, more than females, are generally willing to mate at any time with any partner who may be fertile; whereas females, more than males, are generally careful to choose mates who seem more likely to provide good genes, protection, parental care, or resources.

The widespread conflict of interest between the sexes arises from the fact that male interest is in mate quantity, but female interest is in mate quality. The conflict is mitigated when males offer females desirable support, such as food, protection, or help in rearing children. However, to males, the provision of such support is often costly in terms of time and energy. Consequently, males can lower such costs to themselves, and overcome female resistance to mating, using either force or the threat of force, that is, by sexual coercion.

Male sexual coercion and female resistance to it are studies in nonhuman primates. Such studies have examined male's ability to use force and other means in order to control and constrain female sexuality, and have shown clear manifestations of conflicts between male and female interests. For instance, in a variety of monkeys and apes, a female who is going through her period of estrus (i.e., when she is fertile and sexually receptive) is the subject of significantly more aggression exerted by males, and is wounded more often, than when she is not in estrus. This is an evidence that suggests a relation between sex and aggression in nonhuman primates. This and other examples of male sexual coercion should not leave one with the impression that the male always gets his way. Indeed, very often, he does not.

Female Resistance to Male Coercion: Female primates can use several means in order to resist and thwart male coercion. By doing so, in many primate societies, male control over female sexuality has been limited; and in some primates, females look totally free from male sexual control.

Some examples of the means which female primates use in order to resist male coercion are as follows. In rhesus monkeys, females form strong, lifelong bonds with their female kin, and together they protect their female relatives against male aggression. Furthermore, in female-bonded species, females hold considerable "king-making" power. That is, a male's attempt to achieve and maintain high dominance status is strongly dependent on the support of high-ranking females. Therefore, the males avoid challenging the dominant females. In the olive baboons, in Kenya, female primates reduce their vulnerability to male aggression by forming long-term, friendly relationships with particular males. These examples indicate that female primates are not helpless victims of male control because they typically have several means of resisting males' interests and asserting their own interests. Females use these means to balance the male's larger size.

Origins of Patriarchy: Compared to nonhuman primate societies, many human societies appear to involve greater male control over female sexuality; and in contrast, human males tend to control both resources and political power. The "origins of patriarchy" deals with such issues.

Although there is disagreement among anthropologists regarding whether male dominance over women characterizes all human societies (which partly stems from their definitions of male dominance), many feminist anthropologists believe that male dominance is universal. Among nonhuman primates, males are not universally dominant; and even in species that individual males dominate individual females, male control over female behavior (including female sexuality) is usually quite limited. For instance, it is only in very exceptional cases that male nonhuman primates control either female movements or the resources on which females depend for survival and reproduction. Why, in many human societies, there is a more extreme pattern of male domination of females than is characteristic of most other primates?

To respond to this question, it is necessary to find out under what conditions female nonhuman primates are most vulnerable to male coercion. One underlying important factor, as suggested by a survey of the primate literature, is reduced availability of social support from relatives and friends. Some of this evidence is based on humans' closest living relatives, that is, the great apes: the orangutan, gorilla, and chimpanzees. Among chimpanzees, male sexual coercion is common. Among gorillas, male infanticide is common. Among orangutans, forced copulations is the rule, rather than a very rare exception.

The vulnerability of these great ape females to male coercion is related to the combination of two particularly important factors. First, in contrast to most other primates, female apes depart from their birthplace such that in their adulthood they usually do not have relatives around them to help protect them. Second, in contrast to most other primates, who travel in tightly knit groups in which females are almost always accompanied by several other members of the same species, female apes sometimes travel completely alone, except for carrying their dependent young. The degree of females' solitude varies among ape species. Orangutan females almost always travel alone with their most recent infant, and consequently, they are most vulnerable to sexual coercion. Female chimpanzees spend up to 75 percent of their time alone with their young offspring, and accordingly, during such periods they are more vulnerable to male sexual coercion because there are no other males around to protect them. Gorilla females spend most of their time in groups, and as a result they are protected by the silverback male. But, when the silverback male either dies or is killed by another male, the females depart and travel alone with their offspring, and in consequence, they become most vulnerable to infanticide.

Such evidence from nonhuman primates leads to the first of four hypotheses regarding the factors that can account for the evolution of patriarchy:

Hypothesis 1: Among ancestral hominids, female's ability to resist male aggression was reduced because social support from kin and female allies was reduced.

Ethnographic surveys have documented that the majority of traditional human societies follow patrilocal residence, that is, modern humans follow the same pattern as great ape females do by way of departing from their kin (although there are important exceptions). This pattern of female dispersal is especially important because the opposite pattern generally holds in many other primates and mammals. In addition, among humans (similar to chimpanzees, gorillas, and orangutans), female-female coalitions are relatively weak compared with such coalitions formed in many female-bonded primates. Such female human coalitions tend to be weak even when women do not disperse from their natal groups. To sum up, both in nonhuman primates and in human species, female dispersal away from kin, and weak female-female coalitions have reduced female's ability to resist male aggression.

Hypothesis 2: Over the course of human evolution, males have increasingly developed sophisticated alliances. Such alliances have often been directed against females, and they have increased male power over females.

During human social evolution, male reproductive strategies have increasingly been based on alliances with other males. This idea is derived from the following two observations. First, humans' close relative, the chimpanzee, has the most elaborate male-male alliances in comparison to any other nonhuman primate. Second, in most modern human societies, male-male alliances play the central political role.

The chimpanzee pattern of male alliances is strikingly similar to what happens in many human societies. In chimpanzees, males always stay in their natal communities and grow up among male relatives. Male adults, among themselves, form long-term alliances, which they use to compete for status and privileges within the group. They engage in prolonged power struggles over the alpha position. These power struggles involve complex and shifting alliances that are strikingly similar to human political maneuvering. The male who wins and maintains the alpha status does it with the aid of alliances with other males. Chimpanzees form male alliances in their own community against males from other communities. They organize male raids from one community against another. During these raids, solitary males and mature mothers from other communities are brutally attacked, and sometimes killed.

Such attacks by males on females from other communities typically involve members of a male alliance cooperating against a single female. Similarly, within their community, chimpanzee males sometimes use their alliance against their females. Male bottlenose dolphins and lions also follow the same pattern of cooperative aggression against their females. Observations of these three species suggest that, when males form alliances among themselves and against other males, they also use such alliances in order to coerce females. Under such circumstances, female resistance to male coercion is much more limited, because the female faces the aggression of several allied males rather than a single one.

Hypothesis 3: Over the course of human evolution, and especially since the start of agriculture and animal husbandry, males have gained control over resources which females need to survive and reproduce. In this way, males' ability to control and coerce females increased.

In all other primates, when individuals are weaned, they take full responsibility for feeding themselves. Accordingly, females are totally responsible to obtain food for themselves and do not depend on males for resources. However, during human evolution, humans shifted from an omnivorous diet based on individual foraging to a more meat-based diet, more extensive food-sharing, and a sexual division of labor. It seems very likely that from the beginning, males have been doing most of the hunting, as male chimpanzees and male human foragers do today. With the shift toward meat-eating and food-sharing, the stage was set for increased male control over females, based on male's control over meat. This may not have been inevitable, but the prior cooperation among males for political and reproductive goals perhaps facilitated male cooperation in hunting and in controlling the hunted meat. Males' control over resources increased males' benefits, which in turn, led to the formation of stronger alliances among males.

Hypothesis 4: Over the course of human evolution, the sociopolitical arrangements of males increased their differences in terms of wealth and power, and perpetuated such differences across families over generations. The consequence of increasingly unequal relationships among men was that women became increasingly vulnerable to the desires of the few most powerful men, and that women had increasingly less control over their own sexuality.

Studies have found that the more male-male relations are organized along hierarchical principles, the more women are controlled and dominated by men. In any gregarious species, the extent to which males can dominate and control females depends on the extent to which males can also dominate and control other males. If no male can dominate any other male, then no male can coerce females into mating because other males will intervene in order to reduce a rival's reproductive success and increase the intervener's own chances of gaining sexual access to the female. Among humans, as difference in male power increases, the males at the very top not only use their power to exclude other males but also monopolize control over females and form polygyny among the elites.

Hypothesis 5: When women pursue their material and reproductive interests, their behaviors promote males' control over both resources and female sexuality. In this way, not only men but also women contribute to the perpetuation of patriarchy.

For instance, when women express a preference for marrying men with more resources, they not only reflect the importance of resources to female reproductive success but also they reinforce male-male competition for resources, and therefore, they contribute to male resource control.

Hypothesis 6: Over the course of human evolution, the capacity for language enabled males to consolidate and increase their control over females through the creation and propagation of ideologies of male dominance/female subordination and male supremacy/female inferiority.

Language greatly facilitated further development of male-male alliances, male control of resources, and the development of hierarchical relationships among men. This is because language made it easier for men to communicate more directly and clearly about such activities. In addition, with further evolution of language, men began to develop and promulgate views of society that supported their own interests, that is, ideologies were born.

To summarize, the roots of patriarchy lie in our prehuman past, but many of its forms reflect human behaviors. This evolutionary analysis does not imply that patriarchy is inevitable, because humans have evolved the capacity to behave in a wide range of possible ways.

INTERPRETIVE VIEW

In order to understand the origin of patriarchy it is necessary to understand the social construction of gender, which is better understood when it is compared with essentialism, that is, constructionist versus essentialist. Some people mistakenly think that essentialists argue for the biological determination of gender. The essentialist and constructionist views of gender differ in the location of gender qualities, but not in their origin.[2]

Essentialist views consider gender as resident within the individual. In other words, gender is a quality or trait that describes one's personality, cognitive process, moral judgment, and so on. For instance, an essentialist stance argues that "relationality" or a "morality of justice" is a quality which is possessed by the individual. Essentialist views regard gender as fundamental attributes of the individual that are internal, persistent, and generally separate from the individual's ongoing experience of interaction with the daily socio-political contexts of his or her life.

In the same way that essentialism is often confused with biological determinism, the social construction of gender is often confused with the socialization of gender. When constructionists state that gender is socially constructed, they do not simply refer to the environmental origin of gender traits. Rather, the constructionists refer to the idea that gender is certainly not a trait of an individual, but simply a construct that identifies particular transactions which are understood to be appropriate to one sex.

According to constructionists, gender is not resident in the person, but prevails in those interactions that are socially construed as gendered. Moreover, "relationality" or "morality" is a quality of interactions, not a quality of individuals, and not a quality which is essentially connected with sex. When a transaction is termed feminine or masculine, it means that such transaction is socially agreed upon, and it is reproduced by the very process of participating in that transaction.

It is instructive to compare and contrast essentialism and constructionism. Consider the metaphor of "friendly" and see the difference between when it is used to describe an individual as "friendly," and when it is used to describe a conversation as "friendly." In the former case, "friendly" is viewed as a trait of the individual, that is, an "essential" component of her or his personality. In the latter case, "friendly" is viewed as the quality of the interaction taking place between or among individuals. In this case, "friendly" has a particular meaning which is agreed upon by the participants, which is compatible with meanings of their social reference groups, and which is confirmed by the process of engaging in this interaction. In the metaphor of "friendly," the essentialist view of gender regards it as "friendly person," but the constructionist view of gender regards it as "friendly conversation."

Essentialists and constructionists have different views with respect to the relationship between "friendly" and "gender." Essentialists would argue that women are friendlier than men. That is, "friendly" is a trait of women, no matter if this quality has come from biological imperatives, from socialization, or from a combination of both. Constructionists would argue that the gendering of friendly transactions is the outcome of social agreements about the appropriateness of certain behavior. Accordingly, the differential engagement of men and women in those contexts that elicit friendly behavior results in a differential linkage between sex and friendliness, and friendliness becomes gendered.

Social constructionism (including the social construction of gender) is founded on the premise that we have no way of knowing with certainty the nature of reality. According to social constructionism, the so-called knowledge does not involve the discovery of a freestanding reality, existing apart from the knower, and revealed by careful application of procedures and methods. Rather, what we claim to know, and what we regard as truth, is indeed a construction, and a best understanding, which is based on, and inextricably intertwined with, the contexts in which it is created. Among the most influential factors that shape the way we construct our knowledge are the modes of discourse by which we exchange our perceptions and descriptions of reality. In this way, our knowledge is a product of our social interchange. More specifically, what we call knowledge is what we agree to call truth.

In the process of socially agreeing on the reality of a particular phenomenon, we construct exactly the reality of that phenomenon. For instance, "gender" does not exist inside individuals as an actual, freestanding phenomenon which is to be discovered and measured by social scientists. Rather, "gender" is the outcome of an agreement which is arrived at through social interchange. In other words, "gender" is exactly what we agree it to be.

According to social constructionism, gender is the meaning which we have agreed to give to a specific set of transactions between individuals and their environmental contexts. That is, one does not have gender, but one does gender. What defines a specific transaction as feminine or masculine is not the sex of the actors, but the agreed-upon situational parameters within which the actors perform. Thus, none of us is either feminine, masculine, or incapable of being either feminine or masculine. In some specific contexts, we do feminine; and in some other specific contexts, we do masculine.

Indeed, there has been scholarly research that supports this interpretation. For instance, research on nonverbal communication has shown that women who hold powerful positions follow a pattern of behavior toward their subordinates which is usually described as "masculine." Similarly, it has been found that women and men who have comparable status at work adhere to similar values and behaviors, which is in contrast to the common assumption of sex differences in workplace values. In both instances, individuals' behavior is determined not by their sex, but by the context of their work relationships, that is, power and status.

In addition, scholarly research has shown that women behave in a more gender-traditional manner when interacting with a man whose attitudes toward gender are conservative than when interacting with a man who holds more liberal attitudes. Moreover, research has also found that single fathers act more like mothers than married fathers, that is, they behave in a more "feminine" manner when it is demanded by their particular context. In both of these two research studies, gendered actions are shaped by the social location of the individual, not by the sex.

Such pieces of research show that there is a disjunction between sex and gender; and that "gender" is not a trait inherent in an individual, rather, "gender" refers to qualities which are usually seen as sex-related, but are in fact contextually determined. "Gender" is a term that refers to a set of behavior-environment interactions which we have agreed to characterize members of one sex.

We come to view certain interactions as being either feminine or masculine through the differential contexts of our experience. It is far more likely for women to encounter situations that elicit feminine transactions (e.g., subordination), and for men to encounter circumstances that elicit masculine transactions (e.g., dominance). This partitioning is the outcome of the self-sustaining nature of the socially constructed knowledge.

The vast majority of circumstances in which we live involve gendered prescriptions and proscriptions. As we accordingly do gender "correctly," we in fact legitimize the prescriptive quality of that circumstance for members of our sex, and thus reinforce and reproduce the gendering of those situations. Selective exposure of women and men to gendering contexts elicits behavior such that sex is compatible with gender, and therefore, perpetuating the perception that gender is both sex-differentiated and sex-defined. Thus, by continuing the process of doing gender, we re-create the construction of gender.

Women are different, because they have become women, not because they are women. The demands of social context act as the primary determinants of our gendered behavior. Women experience life differently from men, because, to a large extent, life situations are differentially gendered, which is a circular and self-sustaining process. Furthermore, even when men and women seem to encounter a similar situation, women face a different prescription than men. Even though a woman might free herself from the gendered demands of her social world by occasionally or frequently doing masculine, her experience would be different from that of a man. This is because, in such situations, the woman has to face the discrepancy between her actions and those socially expected of her, whereas the man does not.

Gendering of experience is so prevalent in our lives that we regularly learn lessons in doing gender and bear the consequences of failing to appropriately participate in gender transactions. We become so familiar with this process that it becomes ingrained in our makeup. Gender so thoroughly suffuses our experience that we perceive ourselves as intrinsically gendered.

The socially constructed gender guides our behavior, and generally leads us to conform to socially expected gendered interaction, that is, to do gender in a manner which is compatible with its construction in a specific social context. Furthermore, the experience of gender as an aspect of our internal identity, and a "natural" quality of ourselves, supports the social construction of gender as an intrapsychic trait intrinsically connected to sex.

Moreover, the fundamental attribution error enhances our overestimation of the role of personal factors and underestimation of situational forces that form the gendered behavior of ourselves and others. In this way, the social construction of gender, which involves both agreements about sex-specific transactions and a belief in the intrapsychic nature of gender, underlies both our own behavior and our assessment of others. We take this construction as reality, while failing to see that it is socio-historically situated.

A constructionist position recognizes the diversity among women. Being a universal woman by itself does not shape and gender one's experience. Different circumstances generate different meanings of "gender," which elicit different gender transactions, in the same way that those meanings order other aspects of the individual's realities. Sex is only one of the several dimensions that frame women's lives. Focusing on sex as the only factor that defines women's experience is tantamount not only to homogenizing all women but also to presenting a unidimensional picture of a multidimensional reality. Essentialism risks denying that multidimensionality; but in contrast, constructionism, with its focus on the centrality of context, embraces multidimensionality.

Constructionist views prepare us against the insidious and unacknowledged shaping forces of sociopolitical context, which have haunted essentialist positions. Constructionists' stance is sensitive to context, and is active in persuading against the idea that prescribed spheres are natural, enduring, or independent of their socio-historical circumstances.

Constructionists focus on social context, and therefore, they do not blame women for their own troubles. Furthermore, constructionists are aware of the reciprocal consequences of knowledge production, and are self-consciously value oriented in their theory and practice. Constructionists are cognizant that their approach has a reciprocal relationship with social beliefs and systems. Constructionists warn against ideas that risk further victimizing victims of oppression, for example, women.

However, constructionism has been criticized based on the argument that it is an extremely risky position for feminist politics. Critiques argue that if constructionists believe that knowledge is always situational, and that there is no freestanding truth to be discovered by some disinterested means, then all views are equally "true." Critiques, therefore, conclude that constructionism is irredeemably apolitical. More specifically, if one truth is as good as another, then there will be justification for political action. Furthermore, if misogynist bigotry is as valid a position as is feminist consciousness, then it is not possible to take a political stance in favor of feminism.

In response, constructionists emphasize ethical responsibility. They say that knowledge is not only situational but also explicitly value laden. Truth is not absolute and cannot escape from values issues. Feminist consciousness should be privileged, not because it has more adequate access to an absolute and freestanding truth, but because it has its foundation in humanity-enhancing values.

In addition to this philosophical argument for the possibility of a political position of constructionism, research has shown that constructionist views and political positions are not inconsistent. More specifically, research has shown that politically active feminists tend to hold a constructionist epistemological position. Such research, furthermore, has shown that politically active feminists are able to take a position that supports both individual change and social action. Such a position, indeed, realistically recognizes both the socially defined assumptions about gender (a constructionist interpretation) and the need for personal action (a feminist political commitment).

Constructionism believes that the designation "women's ways" prevents women from alternative ways of being. The constructionist position is that there are no "women's ways," but there are modes of being that we have agreed to see as gendered. Furthermore, all modes of being are, in principle, available to people of either sex, if there is a context that elicits and supports them.

In general, a constructionist perspective does not expect sex differences, but instead would look into the context. A constructionist would expect to find no empirical support for sex differences. Scholarly research that has aimed at exploring sex differences, has in fact found the centrality of context, rather than sex.

Constructionism believes that gender resides in context, rather than in individual, and consequently, its focus shifts from the individual to the situation. In this way, the issue of power, which is the reality underlying women's oppression, is revealed in full light. Constructionism's focus on power, allows them to recognize the role of power in the construction, activation, and perpetuation of gender.

The difference between the perspectives of constructionists and essentialists leads to different change strategies. Consider the case for relationality as a worthy human quality. Constructionists locate relationality in context, but constructionists locate it in individual psyches. Accordingly, with respect to change strategy, constructionists prescribe the enhancement of contexts that elicit doing relationality, but essentialists prescribe encouraging women to lay satisfied claim to relationality as a trait of their sex.

Indeed, essentialism has troubling implications for collective feminist action. Essentialism locates responsibility for a woman's experience and behavior within herself. It construes gender as one of the aspects of the individual's personality structure. It leads to victim blaming. That is, women's experience, including their marginalization and oppression, is a result of qualities that exist within women themselves, rather than a reflection of the social systems that shape their lives.

Therefore, essentialism, in order to improve women's lot, prescribes changing women themselves, not the system. Essentialism, for instance, prescribes that we encourage women to take assertiveness training, rather than changing the contextual forces that shape and interpret assertive interactions. Furthermore, essentialism might prescribe that we develop self-defense classes for women, rather than working to change the beliefs that make women vulnerable and that condone violence against them. Essentialism prescribes that we attribute women's gendered behavior in relationships to women's own codependence, not to patriarchal structures.

It is doubtless easier to attribute failures to individual inadequacies, and to work for individual change, rather than to confront vast and rigid social institutions. However, such person-blame prescriptions ignore the omnipresent role of power and its differential distribution in society, that is, ignore the painful reality of the abuse of power against women. The prescriptions offered by essentialism places feminism at the risk of becoming a mental health rather than a social change movement.

RADICAL HUMANIST VIEW

It is a good idea to begin the discussion with a well-known quote from Engels: "According to the materialistic conception, the determining factor in history is, in the final instance, the production and reproduction of immediate life. This, again, is of a twofold character: on the one side, the production of the means of existence, of food, clothing and shelter and the tools necessary for that production; on the other side, the production of human beings themselves, the propagation of the species. The social organization under which the people of a particular historical epoch live is determined by both kinds of production."[3]

However, Engels and later Marxists did not continue with this dual project. Indeed, the concept of production consists of both the production of "things," or material needs, and the "production" of people, or more specifically, the production of people with particular attributes, such as gender. However, for Marxists the concept of production consists primarily of the production of things. The concept of the production of people requires an understanding of the way people are produced by a set of arrangement, called the "sex/gender system," which a society uses not only to transform biological sexuality into products of human activity but also to make sure that these transformed sexual needs are satisfied. Such a set of arrangements, which reproduces the species, including gender, is basically social. The biological aspect of sex differences is interpreted in various ways by various people. In other words, biology is mediated by society.

In the context of economics, the creation of gender can be regarded as the creation of a division of labor between the sexes, that is, the creation of two categories of workers who need each other. In Western societies, the division of labor between the sexes directs men primarily to wage labor outside the household, and women primarily to production within the household; and men and women, who live together as a family, pool their resources. The commonly known form of the family, in which men are in a more advantageous position than women in its gender hierarchy, is only one of many possible structures of this human activity that creates gender.

Although feminist psychoanalytic theory, in a typical nuclear family, emphasizes the relations among children, mother, and father, and the way these relations shape the child's personality along gender lines, and perpetuate hierarchical gender relations; that theory neglects to emphasize the pervasiveness of gender relations in all aspects of social life. This is because, the creation and perpetuation of hierarchical gender relations emanates not only from family life but also from the organization of economic production, that is, the production of the material needs of human beings. A child's personality is partly formed by the personality of that child's mother and the mother's relations to others, but the mother's relations to others are reflections of the prevailing social arrangements, not simply those prevailing within the household. Such social arrangements are collectively generated and collectively maintained by the people in society. "Dependence," at the same time, is both a psychological and a political-economic relationship. For instance, male-dominated trade unions and professional associations have excluded women from taking skilled jobs, and have reduced women's opportunities in gaining the ability to support themselves. Similarly, the denial of abortions to women deepens women's dependence on men. In these and other ways, which are mostly institutionalized, men, as a group, have been able to maintain control over women's labor power, and thus, perpetuate men's dominance over women. Men's control of women's labor power is the lever which men use in order to benefit from women's provision of personal and household services, so that men would be relieved from not only child rearing but also many unpleasant tasks both within and outside households. In this context, the nuclear family arrangement, which is based on monogamous and heterosexual marriage, is an institutional form that can enhance such control. Patriarchy's material base is men's control of women's labor, both inside and the outside of the household. The division of labor by gender tends to benefit men, because it enables men to gain control over women's labor power.

In a capitalist system, the production of material needs is performed mostly outside households, that is, in large-scale enterprises whose productive resources are owned by capitalists. Most people who do not have their own productive resources, offer their labor power in exchange for wages, because this is the only alternative available to them. Capitalists appropriate the surplus value, which is the value the workers create above and beyond the value of their wages. This production process leads to one of the fundamental dynamics in Western societies: on the one hand, workers try to retain control, to the extent possible, over both the conditions and products of their labor; and on the other hand, capitalists, who are driven by competition and the requirements of the accumulation process, try to take control away from the workers in order to increase the amount of surplus value. Workers receive wages and spend them on commodities which they need for their survival. These commodities are then taken home, and are transformed in order to become usable in producing and reproducing people. In Western societies, which are organized by both patriarchy and capitalism, the sexual division of labor by gender assigns men primarily to wage labor and women primarily to household production. That portion which involves household production, and is called "housework," largely consists of purchasing commodities and transforming them into usable forms. For instance, sheets must be purchased, spread on beds, tidied after every sleep, and washed. Similarly, food must be purchased, cleaned, cooked, and served to be called a meal. Household production, moreover, includes the biological reproduction of family members and the shaping of their gender, as well as their maintenance. In Western societies, the household production, in the labor process of producing and reproducing people, gives rise to another fundamental dynamics of such societies: The system of production, in which people live, cannot be understood without reference to the production and reproduction of both commodities (in factories, service centers, or offices) and of people (in households). Although neither type of production can self-reproduce, together they create and re-create themselves and people's existence.

This patriarchal and capitalist arrangement of production needs a means of redistribution. Because of the class and gender division of labor some people do not have direct access to the economic means of survival. An overall view of the development of capitalism in Western societies indicates that, in general, capitalism originated in societies whose production and redistribution had been taking place mostly in households and villages. Although capitalism moved much of production outside the household, it did not destroy all the traditional ways of organizing production and redistribution. In preindustrial households, people not only got involved in production but also shared their output among themselves (of course, after external obligations, such as feudal dues, were met), according to prevailing patriarchal relations of authority. In the period of primitive accumulation of capitalism, capitalists had to alienate the productive resources which were under the control of the people who were previously attached to the land, in order to establish the capitalist mode of production, which is based on "free" wage labor. Accordingly, laborers became "free" to work for capitalists, because they had no other means of subsistence, and therefore, needed to work for wages in order to buy from the capitalists what they used to produce in households and villages and exchanged with each other.

With the development of the capitalist mode of production, those who were old, young, or women of childbearing age, were less active in economic production, and therefore, became dependent on those who actively participated in economic production and earned wages, which increasingly consisted of adult men. People continued to live in households for the purposes of reproducing the species and redistributing resources. Households as units were used primarily for income pooling rather than income producing. Capitalist setting perpetuated the previously established patriarchal division of labor, in which men benefited from women's labor, because men became primarily wage laborers and retained the personal services of their wives, and women became primarily "housewives." In the capitalist setting, the interdependence of men and women, which had arisen as a consequence of the division of labor by gender, was also maintained. In capitalism, the need for the household to be an income-pooling unit, that is, a place where redistribution between men and women occurs, arises fundamentally due to the patriarchal division of labor. Indeed, it is this income pooling that makes the household seen as a unit with unitary interests, despite disunity which is inherent in the "unity" of the family. This disunity is based on both the division of labor among family members, and the different relationships that different family members have to production.

Anthropological and historical research, whose focus is on the development of households and their role in political arenas, suggests that women's status has declined as political institutions have been appended to the state apparatus. This occurred because the process of state formation elevated the power of men as they were made "heads" of "their" households. The state promoted households as political units because the state needed to undermine the prior political apparatus, which was based on kinship. In pre-state societies, kinship groups made fundamental political and economic decisions, such as: how to share resources in order to provide for everyone's welfare, how to redistribute land periodically, how to settle disputes, how to build new settlements. In the development of the state, such functions were gradually absorbed by the state.

For instance, in the process of state formation in England and Wales, which took place approximately between the eighth and fifteenth centuries, emerging state rulers consolidated their power against kin groups by gaining the allegiance of men at the expense of their kin. States gained the allegiance of men partly by allowing men to usurp some of the kin group's authority, specifically over land as well as women and children. Indeed, the household and its male "head" can be seen as a "creation" of the state. In mid-thirteenth century, the household was the basis of taxation everywhere in Western society. The state's interests were served by an authoritarian household structure, because the hierachy at the household level was expected to be mentally transferred to the national level, that is, from the head of household to the king. Indeed, the power of kings and the power of heads of households grew in tandem in the sixteenth century. The state was very supportive of the patriarchal nuclear family, and was very hostile to the kin-oriented family. The former was a support for the state power, and the latter was a threat to the state power.

However, the authoritarianism of the new nation-state was inconsistent with developing capitalism. The state, therefore, was legitimated based on a new ideology that related authority to the individual, that is, the state serves with the consent of the propertied individuals. For this ideology to have logical coherence, it had to assert the authority of all individuals, including women and children. But, then, the elevation of women to the status of individuals was in contradiction to patriarchal authority in the household. To solve this contradiction, the family was removed, ideologically at least, from the political sphere. That is, women were elevated to the status of individuals and patriarchal authority was maintained. The family became private, that is, had no role in conducting the politics of social interchange, and man became the head of the family, that is, to represent family's interests in the world. The ideology of individualism, which increased the political importance of men outside their households, not only strengthened patriarchy at home but also completed the legitimation of male public power which had begun during the process of the development of the state.

Even though the household, and particularly the man as the head of the household, became an agent of the state and confronted collectivities, which were organized by kinship, the household also remained the last repository of kin ties. For instance, the nuclear household continues to tie its members to other households through the processes of marriage, childbirth, and the establishment of kinship. These ties to other households beyond one's household (though much more limited than in the past), together with the interdependence of household members (which emanates from their different relations to production), continue to give members of households a basis for common interests against the state or other outside forces. Household members continue to make decisions about pooling incomes, caring for dependent members, engaging in wage work, and having children, but it is important to keep in mind that both within the household and outside the household men have more power than women. Therefore, viewing the household as a unit which jointly chooses, for instance, to use its available labor power to maximize the interests of all its members (which is the view of those who discuss family strategies and adaptations) ignores the reality of both the capitalist and patriarchal relations of production in which households are embedded. Mutual dependence does not preclude the possibility of coercion. Women and men mutually are dependent in the household, in the same way that workers and capitalists, or slaves and slave-owners, are dependent. In fundamentally coercive environments (such as patriarchy and capitalism) concepts of choice and adaptation are inevitably flawed, in the same way that the belief that workers and capitalists or men and women have unified interests is flawed. This does not mean that such unity can never exist.

When the members of the households work within the capitalist organization of production, households enter into class relations with each other and realize the extent of their access to commodities. However, with respect to women's work in the home—that is, the rearing of children, the maintenance of the home, the serving of men, and so on—patriarchy is a more salient feature than class. Women of all classes are subject to patriarchal power because they all perform household labor for men.

The literature related to the women's movement has attempted to document women's oppression so that women may recognize exploitation when they experience it in their daily lives. The sexual division of labor is an example of such oppression, but it is so ancient that its unfairness is often accepted as normal. The women's liberation movement has changed the perceptions of many women about patriarchy. In a struggle, the first step is awareness, and the second is recognition that the situation can change.

What is the prospect of the decline in patriarchal power in the home, as measured by the relative amount of housework which is performed by women compared to men? The prospects for the decline in housework time performed by women compared to men, while dependent on economic and political changes at the societal level, is most directly related to the strength of the women's movement. This is because the amount and quality of housework services provided by women, like the amount of effort and pay for wage work, result from historical processes of struggle. Such struggle helps to establish norms that form the expected standard of living. Time spent on housework by both full-time house-workers and employed house-workers has remained stable. The data gathered in the United States indicate that total time spent on housework has not declined significantly. Although the time spent on some tasks—such as preparing and cleaning up after meals—has declined, the time spent on other tasks—such as shopping, recordkeeping, and child care—has increased. The time spent on laundry has increased, despite the introduction of new easy-care fabrics and the prevalent use of automatic washing machines. The failure of housework time to decline is partly due to the rising standards of cleanliness, child care, and emotional support, as well as in the limitation of technology applied to small decentralized units, such as homes.

A reduction in housework time may be due to gender struggle around housework or may be due to changing boundaries between home and market production. This means that production which was formerly undertaken by women at home may be increasingly performed in capitalist production sites. In such transfer of production, the products change as well, for example, home-cooked meals are replaced by fast food. Historically, the boundary between home production and market production has been flexible, rather than fixed, and such boundary has been determined by the requirements of patriarchy and capitalism in reproducing themselves and by the corresponding gender and class struggles that arise from these processes.

While women's struggles, together perhaps with capital's interests, may be successfully improving standards for housework and transferring some production outside the home, prospects for transferring some of the household work to men within the home do not appear to be as good. This is indicated by time-budget studies data that show men whose wives work for wages do not spend more time than other married men on housework. This means that, as more women increase their wage-labor employment and share the financial burden of supporting families with men, men in all likelihood will not share the burden of housework with women. Historically, there has been an ongoing increase in women's labor-force participation. Studies have shown that husbands' work time may have increased at most about a half hour per week, but the work time of women, whether employed outside the home or full-time house-workers, may have increased by five hours per week. Furthermore, women's housework time has somewhat decreased, men's housework time has not increased, women still spend more than twice as much time on housework than do men, and women have a total work week that is still seventeen hours longer than men's. The conclusion is clear that the increase in women's wage-labor employment will not by itself bring about any increase in sharing of housework by men; therefore, continued struggle is necessary.

RADICAL STRUCTURALIST VIEW

According to historical materialism, the determining factor in the history of human beings is, in the last resort, the production and reproduction of immediate life. This consists of two components. The first component is the production of the means of subsistence, such as food, clothing, and shelter as well as the required tools. The second component is the production of human beings themselves, that is, the propagation of the species. These two types of production (i.e., the stage of the development of labor, and the stage of the development of the family) condition the social institutions under which men of a specific historical era and of a specific country live. When the development of labor is lower, and therefore, the society's volume of production and wealth is lower, the social order is more dominated by ties of sex. However, when the structure of society is based on ties of sex, the following takes place: the productivity of labor grows, private property emerges, exchange prevails, differences in wealth develop, possibility of utilizing the labor power of others becomes a reality, which is the basis of class antagonisms. New social elements, which in the course of generations strive to adapt the old structure of society to the new conditions, encounter the incompatibility of the two, which leads to a complete revolution. The old society, which was built on groups based on ties of sex, after collision with the newly developed social classes breaks apart, and in its place a new society appears that has the following characteristics: it is constituted in a state built on territorial groups, rather on ties of sex; its family system is entirely dominated by the property system; and within it the class antagonisms and class struggles freely develop, which has been prevailing ever since.[4]

The three main epochs of human history are as follows: savagery, barbarism, and civilization. According to research studies, out of the original condition of promiscuous intercourse, there developed the following stages in the family.

The Consanguine Family: In this first stage of the family, the marriage groups are formed according to generations. That is, all the grandfathers and grandmothers within the limits of the family are all mutual husbands and wives. The same relationship holds true with respect to their children, and then their grandchildren, and so on.

The Punaluan Family: Whereas the first advance in the organization of the family was the exclusion of parents and children from mutual sexual relations, the second advance was the exclusion of brothers and sisters. This second advance was more important and more difficult than the first advance, because of the similarity in the ages of the participants.

The Pairing Family: Pairing took place for some time during group marriage, or even earlier. The man, among his several wives, had a principal wife (whom cannot be said to have been his favorite wife) and he was her principal husband, among her several husbands. Pairing became increasingly established as the gens developed and as the numbers of classes of "brothers" and "sisters" between which marriage was prohibited increased. This ever-widening exclusion of blood relatives from marriage enjoys the benefits of natural selection, according to which, marriage between non-consanguineous gentes tends to create generations which are more physically and mentally fit. Metaphorically, after two tribes are blended together, the skull and brain of new generation would widen and lengthen to the sum of the capabilities of both tribes. Thus, tribes which are formed according to gentes tend either to gain the upper hand over the more backward ones, or to carry them along by force of the precedent they have set.

In this way, the evolution of the family in prehistoric times involved the progressive narrowing of the circle within which marital community between the two sexes was possible. Originally, such circle included the whole tribe. Then, there came successive exclusions: first of closer relatives, second of ever remoter relatives, and finally of those related by marriage. Accordingly, every kind of group marriage was made impossible; and in the end there remained only the one couple (the molecule), who were loosely united, with the dissolution of which marriage itself completely disappears. This fact shows that individual sex love, in the modern sense of the word, played no role as the origin of monogamy. Whereas, under previous forms of the family, men not only were never in want of women but also had a surfeit of them; now under new circumstances, women became scarce and were sought after. Consequently, with the advent of pairing marriage, there came the abduction and purchase of women, which are widespread symptoms of a much more deeply rooted change that had started.

The pairing family, was too weak and unstable such that it could not be used as an independent or desirable form of household. For this reason, it did not dissolve the communistic household which was inherited from earlier periods. The communistic household implies the supremacy of women in the house. This is because of the exclusive recognition of a natural mother. In other words, it is because of the impossibility of determining the natural father with certainty. Therefore, the communistic household signifies high esteem for the mothers, that is, for the women. Woman was free and highly respected among all savages; and all barbarians of the lower, and middle stages, as well as even part of the upper stage. In the communistic household, most of the women, or even all the women, belong to the same gens, while the men come from various other gentes. The communistic household is the material foundation of the predominancy of women in primitive times. It should be noted that the reports of travelers and missionaries about savages' and barbarians' women, who were burdened with excessive toil, does not conflict with what has been said earlier. What determine the division of labor between the two sexes is entirely different from those that determine the status of women in society. Peoples whose women have to work much harder than what current Europeans would consider proper, often have far more real respect for women than current Europeans have for theirs. In barbarism, the social status of the lady of civilization, who is surrounded by sham homage and who is estranged from all real work, is socially very much lower than that of the hard-working woman of barbarism, who was regarded among her people as a real lady, and was such due to the nature of her position.

The transition from hetaerism to monogamy was brought about essentially by the women. The development of the economic conditions of life undermined the old communism and led to the growing density of the population. As a result, the old traditional sexual relations increasingly lost their naive, primitive jungle character, which appeared degrading and oppressive to the women, who longed for the right to chastity, to temporary or permanent marriage with one man only. The advance from hetaerism to monogamy could not have originated from the men. This is because men have never thought of renouncing the pleasures of group marriage. It was only after the transition to pairing marriage, which had been effected by the women, that men introduced strict monogamy, which was for the women only, of course.

The pairing family arose in between savagery and barbarism. More specifically, it arose mainly at the upper stage of savagery, and to some extent only at the lower stage of barbarism. The pairing family is the form of the family which is characteristic of barbarism; in the same way that group marriage is characteristic of savagery, and monogamy is characteristic of civilization. In the pairing family, the group was already reduced to its smallest unit consisting of one man and one woman, that is, two-atom molecule. Natural selection had been constantly reducing the circle of community marriage; and it had completed its work because there was nothing more left for it to do in this direction. However, new social driving forces came into operation that led to the rise of a new form of the family out of the pairing family.

In the Old World, the domestication of animals and the breeding of herds became a source of wealth, and created totally new social relationships. Until the lower stage of barbarism, fixed wealth consisted almost entirely of the house, clothing, crude ornaments, and the means which were used for procuring and preparing food, such as boats, weapons, and household utensils of the simplest kind. Food had to be obtained on a daily basis. Now, the advancing pastoral peoples possessed herds of horses, camels, donkeys, oxen, sheep, goats, and pigs. The advancing pastoral peoples consisted of the Aryans in the Indian land of the five rivers and the Ganges area, as well as in the then much more richly watered steppes of the Oxus and the Jaxartes, and the Semites on the Euphrates and the Tigris. The advancing pastoral peoples had possessions which required only supervision, together with most elementary care, in order to propagate in ever-increasing numbers and to provide the richest nourishment in milk and meat. All previous means of procuring food now became part of the background; and hunting, which was once a necessity, now became a luxury.

But, who was considered the owner of this new wealth? Originally, it is known that the gens was considered to be the owner. But, perhaps, private property in herds developed at a very early stage. It is not known whether Father Abraham was regarded by the author of the so-called First Book of Moses as the owner of his herds and flocks as the head of a family community or as the actual hereditary chief of a gens. However, it is known with certainty that we must not regard him as a property owner in the modern sense of the term. It is also known with certainty that on the threshold of authenticated history, everywhere the herds were the property of the family chiefs, in exactly the same way as were the artistic products of barbarism, metal utensils, articles of luxury, and, finally, human cattle, that is, the slaves.

For now, slavery was invented. The slave was of no use to the barbarian of the lower stage. This is why the American Indians treated their defeated enemies quite differently from the way defeated enemies were treated in the upper stage. The men among defeated enemies were either killed or adopted as brothers by the tribe of the victors. The women among defeated enemies were either taken in marriage or adopted along with their surviving children. At this stage, human labor power did not yield any noticeable surplus above the cost of its maintenance. However, this situation changed with the introduction of cattle breeding, of the working up of metals, of weaving, and of field cultivation. In the same way that wives who were so easily obtainable had now acquired an exchange value and were bought, the labor power now acquired an exchange value and was bought and sold, especially after the herds had become family possessions. The family did not increase as rapidly as the cattle. As a result, more people were required to take care of them. Defeated enemies, who were taken as captives in war, were useful for just this purpose, and furthermore, they could be bred like the cattle itself.

When such a huge amount of wealth passed into the private possession of families, who could rapidly multiply that wealth, it was inconsistent with a society which was founded on pairing marriage and mother-right gens. Pairing marriage had incorporated a new feature into the family. The paring family, next to the natural mother, placed the authenticated natural father, who was perhaps better authenticated than many fathers of the present day. According to the division of labor, which prevailed in the pairing family, man was responsible for the procuring of food and the means necessary thereto, as well as the ownership of the means, because the man took them with him in case of separation, in the same way that the woman retained the household goods. Thus, according to the custom of society at the time, the man was also the owner of the new sources of food, that is, the cattle, and later, of the new means of labor, that is, the slaves.

The increase in wealth, on the one hand, increased the status of the man above the woman in the family; and, on the other hand, spurred the man to utilize this strengthened position in order to overthrow the traditional order of inheritance in favor of his children. But, this was against the prevailing tradition of descent according to mother right. Nevertheless, the prevailing tradition was overthrown; and it was not as difficult a task as it appears to us now. This revolution, which was one of the most decisive revolutions ever experienced by mankind, did not have to disturb any member of a gens. All the members could maintain their previous positions. The simple decision was only that in the future the descendants of the male members were to remain in the gens, but that the descendants of the females were to be excluded from the gens and were to be transferred to the gens of their father. The descent through the female line and the right of inheritance through the mother were overthrown and replaced by male lineage and the right of inheritance through the father. We do not know how and when this revolution was effected among the civilized peoples, but it falls entirely within prehistoric times.

The man's overthrow of mother right was his world-historic defeat of the female sex. The man seized the reins in the house; and the woman became degraded, enthralled, the slave of the man's lust, and a mere instrument for breeding children. This lowered position of women, especially manifest among the Greeks of the Heroic and still more of the Classical Age, has gradually become embellished, but by no means abolished.

The first effect of the newly established sole rule of the men is the patriarchal family. Its chief characteristic is not polygamy, but it is the organization of a few persons into a family, and under the paternal power of the head of the family. In its Semitic form, the family chief lives in polygamy, the bondsman has a wife and children, and the purpose of the organization of the family is to take care of flocks and herds over a limited area. The important features are the incorporation of bondsmen and the paternal power. The Roman family constitutes the ideal type of this form of the family. The word "familia" did not originally signify a compound of sentimentality and domestic discord. It was used by Romans, in the beginning, to refer to the slaves, not the married couple and their children. "Famulus" means a household slave, and "familia" means all of slaves who belong to one individual. Romans used the term to describe a new social organism, in which the man was the head, and under him he had his wife and children as well as several slaves, under Roman paternal power, with power of life and death over all of them. The term is not older than the ironclad family system of the Latin tribes, which came in after field agriculture, legalized servitude, and the separation of the Greeks and (Aryan) Latins. The modern family contains in embryo not only slavery but also serfdom, because from the very beginning it is related to agricultural services. The modern family contains all the antagonisms which later develop on a large scale within society and its state.

This form of the family is the intermediate type between the pairing family and monogamy. It aims to guarantee the fidelity of the wife, that is, the paternity of the children, and places the woman in the man's absolute power, such that if he kills her, he is only exercising his right. Patriarchal family prevailed around the time of the start of the written history, and the science of comparative law has provided us with important confirmation. The patriarchal household community constituted the transition stage between the mother-right family, which evolved out of group marriage, and the individual family, as is known to the modern world. The patriarchal household community (Hausgenossenschaft), is found among the Serbs and the Bulgars under the designations of Zadruga (meaning something like fraternity) or Bratstvo (brotherhood), and among the Oriental peoples in a modified form. The aforementioned confirmation has been proved at least as far as the civilized peoples of the Old World, that is, the Aryans and Semites, are concerned.

The South-Slavic Zadruga provides the best existing example of such a family community. It consists of several generations of the descendants of one father and their wives. All the members of the family live together in one household, till their fields with cooperation, feed and clothe themselves from the common store, and own all surplus products communally. The community has a master of the house (domacin), who supremely manages the community, represents the community in its external affairs, may dispose of smaller objects, and manages the business as well as its finances. He is elected and does not need to be the eldest. The women and their work are managed by the mistress of the house (domacica), who is usually the master's (domacin's) wife. She has an important, often the decisive voice, in the choice of husbands for the girls. However, supreme power is vested in the Family Council, which is the assembly of all adult members, including women and men. The Family Council monitors the performance of the master, makes all the important decisions, administers justice among the members, decides on purchases and sales of important items, especially of landed property, and so on.

The existence of such large family communities in Russia has also been proved. They are now firmly rooted in the popular customs of the Russians, and are known as the "obscina," or village community. They appear in the most ancient Russian law code, that is, the Pravda of Yaroslav, under the same name (verv) as in the Dalmatian Laws, and references to them can be found also in Polish and Czech historical sources.

The patriarchal household community, with common land ownership and common tillage, now gains special significance than it had previously. We should certainly appreciate the important transitional role which it played among the civilized and many other peoples of the Old World, and between the mother-right family and the monogamian family.

The Monogamian Family: This type of family arises out of the pairing family during the transition period from the middle to the upper stage of barbarism, and becomes established at the beginning of civilization. It is based on the supremacy of the man, and its aim is to have children with undisputed paternity, which is required for these children in order to inherit their father's wealth as his natural heirs.

CONCLUSION

This chapter briefly discussed four views expressed with respect to the origin of the patriarchy. The functionalist paradigm believes that the explanation of the origins of patriarchy in the human species is based on an evolutionary perspective, which is, in turn, based on biology, which explains the origins of male desire for control of female sexuality. The interpretive paradigm believes that in order to understand the origin of patriarchy it is necessary to understand the social construction of gender, that is, gender is not resident in the person, but prevails in those interactions that are socially construed as gendered. The radical humanist paradigm believes that the creation and perpetuation of hierarchical gender relations emanates not only from family life but also from the organization of economic production. The radical structuralist paradigm believes that two types of production (i.e., the stage of the development of labor, and the stage of the development of the family) condition the social institutions under which men of a specific historical era and of a specific country live.

Each paradigm is logically coherent—in terms of its underlying assumptions—and conceptualizes and studies the phenomenon in a certain way, and generates distinctive kinds of insight and understanding. Therefore, different paradigms in combination provide a broader understanding of the phenomenon under consideration. An understanding of different paradigms leads to a better understanding of the multifaceted nature of the phenomenon.

NOTES

1. For this literature, see Becker (1981), Boehm (1999), Buss (1989, 1995, 1996, 1998), Buss and Kenrick (1998), Buss and Schmitt (1993), Caporael (2001), Chagnon (1988), Chodorow (1994), Ehrenberg (1989), Ember (1983), Gangestad and Simpson (2000), Geary (1996, 1998), Goldberg (1984, 1993), Harris (1993), Hrdy (1997), Kenrick, Ackerman, and Ledlow (2006), Kenrick and Keefe (1992), Low (1990), Manson and Wrangham (1991), Mealey (2000), Parsons and Bales (1955), Ridgeway (1991), Smuts (1995), Trivers (1972), and Wilson and Daly (1992). This section is based on Smuts (1995).

2. For this literature, see Adams (2010), Bakan (1979), Bohan (1993), Eagly and Wood (1999), Epstein (1991), Geertz (1973, 1974), Gergen (2001a, b), Goldstein (2001), Hare-Mustin and Marecek (1990), Hester (1992), Lerner (1986), Levi-Strauss

(1969), Lorber (1994), Marecek (1995), Martin (1987), Mead (1935), Moore (1994), Oyama (1997), Sanday (1981), Scott (1986), Sered (1999), Stein (1996), Stockard and Johnson (1979), West and Zimmerman (1987), and Wood and Eagly (2002). This section is based on Bohan (1993).

3. For this literature, see Barker and Feiner (2004), Cockburn (1985), Connell (1994), Coward (1983), Eisenstein (1979), Frankfurt Friedl (1975), Institute for Social Research (1972), Hartmann (1976, 1979, 1981), Held (1980), Horkheimer (1972), Kuhn (1978), Leibowitz (1979), Lipman-Blumen (1984), Majstorovic and Lassen (2011), Morgan (1975), Poster (1978), Quick (1977), Rubin (1975), Walby (1991), Young (1990), and Zaretsky (1986). This section is based on Hartmann (1981).

4. For this literature, see Engels (1970, 1977, 1988), Farrelly (2011), Figes (1987), Fluehr-Lobban (1979), Godelier (1981), Hutter (1988), Leacock (1978), Reiter (1975), Schlegel (1977), and Walby (1994). This section is based on Engels (1988).

REFERENCES

Adams, Carol J. 2010. *The Sexual Politics of Meat: A Feminist-Vegetarian Critical Theory*. New York, NY: Continuum.

Bakan, David. 1979. *And They Took Themselves Wives: The Emergence of Patriarchy in Western Civilization*. New York, NY: Harper and Row.

Barker, Drucilla K., and Susan F. Feiner. 2004. *Liberating Economics: Feminist Perspectives on Families, Work, and Globalization*. London, England: Routledge.

Becker, Gary Stanley. 1981. *A Treatise on the Family*. Cambridge, MA: Harvard University Press.

Boehm, C. 1999. *Hierarchy in the Forest: The Evolution of Egalitarian Behavior*. Cambridge, MA: Harvard University Press.

Bohan, Janis S. 1993. "Regarding Gender: Essentialism, Constructionism and Feminist Psychology." *Psychology of Women Quarterly* 17(1): 5–21.

Buss, David M. 1989. "Sex Differences in Human Mate Preferences: Evolutionary Hypotheses Tested in 37 Cultures." *Behavioral and Brain Sciences* 12: 1–49.

Buss, David M. 1995 "Evolutionary Psychology: A New Paradigm for Psychological Science." *Psychological Inquiry* 6: 1–30.

Buss, David M. 1996. "Sexual Conflict: Evolutionary Insights into Feminism and the 'Battle of the Sexes'." In *Sex, Power, and Conflict: Evolutionary and Feminist Perspectives*, edited by D.M. Buss, and N.M. Malamuth, 296–318. New York, NY: Oxford University Press.

Buss, David M. 1998. "The Psychology of Human Mate Selection: Exploring the Complexity of the Strategic Repertoire." In *Handbook of Evolutionary Psychology: Ideas, Issues, and Applications*, edited by C. Crawford, and D.L. Krebs, 405–429. Mahwah, NJ: Erlbaum.

Buss, D.M., and D.T. Kenrick. 1998. "Evolutionary Social Psychology." In *The Handbook of Social Psychology*, Volume 2, 4th edition, edited by D.T. Gilbert, S.T. Fiske, and G. Lindzey, 982–1026. Boston, MA: McGraw-Hill.

Buss, D.M., and D.P. Schmitt. 1993. "Sexual Strategies Theory: An Evolutionary Perspective on Human Mating." *Psychological Review* 100: 204–232.

Caporael, L.R. 2001. "Evolutionary Psychology: Toward a Unifying Theory and a Hybrid Science." *Annual Review of Psychology* 52: 607–628.

Chagnon, N.A. 1988. "Life Histories, Blood Revenge, and Warfare in a Tribal Population." *Science* 239 (February): 985–992.

Chodorow, Nancy. 1994. "Gender, Relation and Difference in Psychoanalytic Perspective." In *The Polity Reader in Gender Studies*, edited by David Held, Dan Hillman, Don Hubert, Debbie Seymour, Michelle Stannorth, and John Thompson, 41–49. Cambridge, England: Polity Press.

Cockburn, Cynthia. 1985. *Machinery of Dominance: Women, Men and Technical Know-How.* London, England: Pluto Press.

Connell, R.W. 1994. "Gender Regimes and the Gender Order." In *The Polity Reader in Gender Studies*, edited by David Held, Dan Hillman, Don Hubert, Debbie Seymour, Michelle Stannorth, and John Thompson, John, 29–40. Cambridge, England: Polity Press.

Coward, Rosalind. 1983. *Patriarchal Precedents.* London, England: Routledge and Kegan Paul.

Eagly, Alice H., and Wendy Wood. 1999. "The Origins of Sex Differences in Human Behavior: Evolved Dispositions versus Social Roles." *American Psychologist* 54(6): 408–423.

Ehrenberg, M.R. 1989. *Women in Prehistory.* London, England: British Museum.

Eisenstein, Zillah, ed. 1979. *Capitalist Patriarchy and the Case for Socialist Feminism.* New York, NY: Monthly Review Press.

Ember, Carol R. 1983. "The Relative Decline in Women's Contribution to Agriculture with Intensification." *American Anthropologist* 85(2): 285–304.

Engels, Friederich. 1970. *The Origin of the Family, Private Property and the State.* Harmondsworth, England: Penguin Books.

Engels, Friedrich. 1977. "The Origin of the Oppression of Women." In *History of Ideas on Woman: A Source Book*, edited by Rosemary Agonito, 273–288. New York, NY: Capricorn Books.

Engels, Friederich. 1988. "Engels on the Origin and Evolution of the Family." *Population and Development Review* 14(4): 705–729.

Epstein, Cynthia Fuchs. 1991. "Inevitabilities of Prejudice." In *The Family Experience: A Reader in Cultural Diversity*, edited by Mark Hutter, 14–26. New York, NY: Macmillan Publishing Company.

Farrelly, Colin. 2011. "Patriarchy and Historical Materialism." *Hypatia* 26(1): 1–21.

Figes, Eva. 1987. *Patriarchal Attitudes: Women in Society.* London, England: Faber and Faver.

Fluehr-Lobban, Carolyn. 1979. "A Marxist Reappraisal of the Matriarchate." *Current Anthropologist* 20(2): 341–348.

Frankfurt Institute for Social Research. 1972. "The Family." In *Aspects of Sociology*, edited by Frankfurt Institute for Social Research, 129–147. Boston, MA: Beacon Press.

Friedl, Ernestine. 1975. *Women and Men: An Anthropologist's View*. New York, NY: Holt, Rinehart and Winston.

Gangestad, S.W., and J.A. Simpson. 2000. "The Evolution of Human Mating: Trade-Offs and Strategic Pluralism." *Behavioral and Brain Sciences* 23: 573–587.

Geary, David C. 1996. "Sexual Selection and Sex Differences in Mathematical Abilities." *Behavioral and Brain Sciences* 19: 229–247.

Geary, David C. 1998. *Male, Female: The Evolution of Human Sex Differences*. Washington, DC: American Psychological Association.

Geertz, C. 1973. *Interpretations of Cultures: Selected Essays*. New York, NY: Basic Books.

Geertz, C. 1974. "Deep Play: Notes on the Balinese Cockfight." In *Myth, Symbol, and Culture*, edited by C. Geertz, 1–37. New York, NY: Norton.

Gergen, Mary M. 2001a. *Feminist Reconstructions in Psychology: Narrative, Gender, and Performance*. Thousand Oaks, CA: Sage Publications.

Gergen, Mary M. 2001b. "Social Constructionist Theory." In *Encyclopedia of Women and Gender: Sex Similarities and Differences and the Impact of Society on Gender*, edited by J. Worrell. San Diego, CA: Academic Press, https://marist.idm.oclc.org/login?url=https://search.credoreference.com/content/entry/estwomen/social_constructionist_theory/0?institutionId=7655. Accessed 28 Aug. 2021.

Godelier, Maurice. 1981. "The Origins of Male Dominance." *New Left Review* 127: 3–17.

Goldberg, Steven. 1984. "The Inevitability of Patriarchy." In *Contemporary Readings in Social and Political Ethics*, edited by Garry Brodsky, John Troyer, and David Vance, 131–145. New York, NY: Prometheus Books.

Goldberg, Steven. 1993. *Why Men Rule: A Theory of Male Dominance*. Chicago, IL: Open Court.

Goldstein, J.S. 2001. *War and Gender: How Gender Shapes the War System and Vice Versa*. Cambridge, MA: Cambridge University Press.

Hare-Mustin, Rachel T., and Jeanne Marecek, eds. 1990. *Making a Difference: Psychology and the Construction of Gender*. New Haven, CT: Yale University Press.

Harris, Marvin. 1993. "The Evolution of Human Gender Hierarchies: A Trial Formulation." In *Sex and Gender Hierarchies*, edited by Barbara Diane Miller, 57–79. New York, NY: Cambridge University Press.

Hartmann, Heidi I. 1976. "Capitalism, Patriarchy, and Job Segregation by Sex." *Signs* 1 (Spring): 168.

Hartmann, Heidi I. 1979. "The Unhappy Marriage of Marxism and Feminism: Towards a More Progressive Union." *Capital and Class* 8 (Summer): 1–33.

Hartmann, Heidi I. 1981. "The Family as the Locus of Gender, Class, and Political Struggle: The Example of Housework." *Journal of Women in Culture and Society* 6(3): 366–394.

Held, David. 1980. *Introduction to Critical Theory*. Berkeley, CA: University of California Press.

Hester, Marianne. 1992. *Lewd Women and Wicked Witches: A Study of the Dynamics of Male Domination*. New York, NY: Routledge.

Horkheimer, Max. 1972. "Authority and the Family." In *Critical Theory*, edited by Max Horkheimer, 47–128. New York, NY: Herder and Herder.

Hrdy, Sarah Blaffer. 1997. "Raising Darwin's Consciousness: Female Sexuality and the Prehominid Origins of Patriarchy." *Human Nature* 8(1): 1–49.

Hutter, Mark. 1988. *The Changing Family: Comparative Perspectives.* New York, NY: Macmillan Publishing Company.

Kenrick, Douglas, Josh Ackerman, and Sudan Ledlow. 2006. "Evolutionary Social Psychology: Adaptive Predispositions and Human Culture." In *Handbook of Social Psychology*, edited by John Delamater, 103–122. New York, NY: Springer.

Kenrick, D.T., and R.C. Keefe. 1992. "Age Preferences in Mates Reflect Sex Differences in Reproductive Strategies." *Behavioral and Brain Sciences* 15: 75–91.

Kuhn, A. 1978. "Structures of Patriarchy and Capital in the Family." In *Feminism and Materialism*, edited by A. Kuhn, and A. Wolpe. London, England: Routledge and Paul.

Leacock, Eleanor. 1978. "Women's Status in Egalitarian Society: Implications for Social Evolution." *Current Anthropology* 19(2): 247–275.

Leibowitz, Lila. 1979. *Females, Males, Families: A Biosocial Approach.* North Scituate, MA: Duxbury Press.

Lerner, Gerda. 1986. *The Creation of Patriarchy.* New York, NY: Oxford University Press.

Levi-Strauss, Claude. 1969. *The Elementary Structures of Kinship.* Boston, MA: Beacon Press.

Lipman-Blumen, Jean. 1984. *Gender Roles and Power.* Englewood Cliffs, NJ: Prentice-Hall.

Lorber, Judith. 1994. *Paradoxes of Gender.* New Havens, CT: Yale University Press.

Low, B.S. 1990. "Sex, Power, and Resources: Ecological and Social Correlates of Sex Differences." *International Journal of Contemporary Sociology* 27: 49–73.

Manson, J.H., and R.W. Wrangham. 1991. "Intergroup Aggression in Chimpanzees and Humans." *Current Anthropology* 32: 369–377.

Marecek, J. 1995. "Gender, Politics, and Psychology's Way of Knowing." *American Psychologist* 50: 162–163.

Martin, E. 1987. *The Woman in the Body.* Boston, MA: Beacon.

Majstorovic, Danijela, and Inger Lassen, eds. 2011. *Living with Patriarchy: Discursive Constructions of Gendered Subjects across Cultures.* Philadelphia, PA: John Benjamins Publishing Company.

Mead, M. 1935. *Sex and Temperament in Three Primitive Societies.* New York, NY: Morrow.

Mealey, L. 2000. *Sex Differences: Developmental and Evolutionary Strategies.* San Diego, CA: Academic Press.

Moore, Henrietta. 1994. "The Cultural Constitution of Gender." In *The Polity Reader in Gender Studies*, edited by David Held, Dan Hillman, Don Hubert, Debbie Seymour, Michelle Stannorth, and John Thompson, 14–21. Cambridge, England: Polity Press.

Morgan, D.H.J. 1975. *Social Theory and the Family.* London, England: Routlege and Kegan Paul.

Oyama, S. 1997. "Essentialism, Women, and War: Protesting Too Much, Protesting Too Little." In *Toward a New Psychology of Gender*, edited by M.M. Gergen, and S.N. Davis, 521–532. New York, NY: Routledge.

Parsons, Talcott, and Robert F. Bales. 1955. *Family, Socialization and Interaction Process*. Glencoe, IL: Free Press.

Poster, Mark. 1978. *Critical Theory of the Family*. New York, NY: Seabury Press.

Quick, Paddy. 1977. "The Class Nature of Women's Oppression." *Review of Radical Political Economics* 9(3): 42–53.

Reiter, Rayna R., ed. 1975. *Toward an Anthropology of Women*. New York, NY: Monthly Review Press.

Ridgeway, Cecilia L. 1991. "The Social Construction of Status Value: Gendered and Other Nominal Characteristics." *Social Forces* 70(2): 367–386.

Rubin, Gayle. 1975. "The Traffic in Women: Notes on the 'Political Economy' of Sex." In *Toward an Anthropology of Women*, edited by Rayna Rapp Reiter, 157–210. New York, NY: Monthly Review Press.

Sanday, Peggy Reeves. 1981. *Female Power and Male Dominance: On the Origins of Sexual Inequality*. Cambridge, England: Cambridge University Press.

Schlegel, Alice. 1977. "Toward a Theory of Sexual Stratification." In *Sexual Stratification: A Cross-Cultural View*, edited by Alice Schlegel, 1–40. New York, NY: Columbia University Press.

Scott, Joan Wallach. 1986. "Gender: A Useful Category of Historical Analysis." *American Historical Review* 91(5): 1053–1075.

Sered, S.S. 1999. "'Woman' as Symbol and Women as Agents." In *Revisioning Gender*, edited by M.M. Ferree, and J. Lorber, 193–221. Thousand Oaks, CA: Sage.

Smuts, Barbara. 1995. "The Evolutionary Origins of Patriarchy." *Human Nature* 6(1): 1–32.

Stein, H.F. 1996. "Cultural Relativism." In *Encyclopedia of Cultural Anthropology*, Volume 1, edited by D. Levinson, and M. Ember, 281–285. New York, NY: Holt.

Stockard, Jean, and Miriam M. Johnson. 1979. "The Social Origins of Male Dominance." *Sex Roles* 5(2): 199–218.

Trivers, R. 1972. "Parental Investment and Sexual Selection." In *Sexual Selection and the Descent of Man: 1871–1971*, edited by B. Campbell, 136–179. Chicago, IL: Aldine.

Walby, Sylvia. 1991. *Theorizing Patriarchy*. Oxford, England: Blackwell.

Walby, Sylvia. 1994. "Towards a Theory of Patriarchy." In *The Polity Reader in Gender Studies*, edited by David Held, Dan Hillman, Don Hubert, Debbie Seymour, Michelle Stannorth, and John Thompson, 22–28. Cambridge, England: Polity Press.

West, Candace, and Don H. Zimmerman. 1987. "Doing Gender." *Gender and Society* 1(2): 125–151.

Wilson, M., and M. Daly. 1992. "The Man Who Mistook His Wife for a Chattel." In *The Adapted Mind: Evolutionary Psychology and the Generation of Culture*, edited by J.H. Barkow, L. Cosmides, and J. Tooby, 289–322. New York, NY: Oxford University Press.

Wood, Wendy, and Alice H. Eagly. 2002. "A Cross-Cultural Analysis of the Behavior of Women and Men: Implications for the Origins of Sex Differences." *Psychological Bulletin* 128(5): 699–727.

Young, Iris Marion. 1990. *Justice and the Politics of Difference.* Princeton, NJ: Princeton University Press.

Zaretsky, Eli. 1986. *Capitalism, the Family, and Personal Life.* New York, NY: Harper and Row, Publishers.

Chapter 6

Discrimination

Four Paradigmatic Views

Any explanation of discrimination is based on a worldview. The premise of this book is that any worldview can be associated with one of the four broad paradigms: functionalist, interpretive, radical humanist, and radical structuralist. This chapter takes the case of discrimination and discusses it from the four different viewpoints. It emphasizes that the four views expressed are equally scientific and informative; they look at the phenomenon from their certain paradigmatic viewpoint; and together they provide a more balanced understanding of the phenomenon under consideration. In this chapter, the first four sections present the four perspectives, and the fifth section concludes the chapter.

FUNCTIONALIST VIEW

There is empirical evidence that there are pay and occupational differences between men and women, and that such differences are not accounted for by productivity differences. Economists have shown how discrimination produces such sex-related differences in economic outcomes, and why this inequality has persisted over time. Economists have developed various models for the analyses of these issues. These models usually assume that male and female labor are perfect substitutes in production. That is, they assume that male and female workers have equal qualifications and, in the absence of discrimination, are equally productive such that they should receive the same pay. This assumption is not an accurate description of reality, because there are sex-related differences in qualifications that explain some of the pay gap. Nevertheless, this assumption is made because models of discrimination are intended to explain the portion of the pay gap which is not due to differences in qualifications. That is, models of discrimination are intended to explain pay differences between men and women who are (potentially) equally productive.[1]

Tastes for Discrimination: Gary Becker laid the foundation for the modern neoclassical analysis of labor-market discrimination. Becker conceptualized discrimination as a personal prejudice, that is, as a taste against being with a particular group. More specifically, employers, coworkers, and/or customers may have such discriminatory tastes. This specific conceptualization may seem more appropriate for the case of racial discrimination (which Becker initially analyzed), than the case of women, with whom men generally live in families. This issue can be regarded as being more closely related to socially appropriate roles than as a desire to maintain social distance, which was considered in the case of race by Becker.

Some examples that show the meaning of socially appropriate roles are as follows. Employers may not hesitate to hire women as secretaries, but may resist to employ them as pipefitters. Men may be willing to work with women who hold complementary or subordinate positions, but may dislike to interact with them when they hold equal or superior positions. Customers may be delighted to purchase nylons from female clerks, but may avoid women who are car dealers or attorneys. These are examples of discriminatory tastes, which may be held independently of the belief that women are less qualified than men for nontraditional pursuits. This latter possibility is discussed later under the notion of "statistical discrimination."

Such discriminatory tastes actually influence people's behavior which have important consequences for women's earnings and employment. In his model, Becker conceptualized individuals who have tastes for discrimination against women acting as if there are nonpecuniary costs of associating with women, who are performing socially inappropriate roles. Becker measured the extent of the individual's discriminatory taste, which is called "discrimination coefficient," by the monetary size of such costs. With this background, it is now possible to examine the consequences of discrimination based on employer, employee, and customer preferences, respectively.

Employer Discrimination: Discriminating employers, that is, those employers who have tastes for discrimination against women, act as if there is a nonpecuniary cost associated with employing women and that, in dollar terms, this cost is equal to d_r (the discrimination coefficient). To discriminating employers, the cost of employing a man is his wage, w_m, but the full cost of employing a woman is her wage plus the discrimination coefficient $(w_f + d_r)$. This means that discriminating employers hire women at a lower wage than men $(w_m - d_r = w_f)$. Furthermore, if men are paid in accordance with their productivity, then women are hired and paid less than their productivity.

The extent of the impact of this situation on female workers depends on the prevalence and severity of discriminatory tastes among employers, as well as on the number of women seeking employment. Nondiscriminatory employers are willing to hire men and women at the same wage rate, as their discrimination coefficient is equal to zero. If there are relatively many such nondiscriminatory employers and/or there are relatively few women seeking employment, then all of them may be hired by the nondiscriminatory firms. In this case, there is no sex-based discriminatory pay differential, even though there are some employers who have tastes for discrimination against women.

However, if there are relatively many discriminatory employers and/or there are relatively many women seeking employment, some women necessarily find jobs at discriminatory firms. These women, as was discussed before, obtain such employment at a wage rate of w_f, which is less than w_m. Under the assumption of competitive labor market, all employers pay the same going wage rate for hiring labor of a particular sex. This means that, in equilibrium, the market wage rate differential between men and women is large enough such that all the women find employment, including those women who necessarily find work at the discriminatory firms. Thus, the more prevalent and the more severe are employers' discriminatory tastes against women, and/or the more numerous are women seeking employment, the more sizable is the aggregate wage gap between men and women ($w_m - w_f$).

This model, which is based on the employer taste for discrimination, is consistent with the observed labor-market wage inequalities between men and women. This model explains the possibility that there is a wage differential between equally qualified male and female workers due to discriminatory employers hiring women workers only at a wage discount. This model, furthermore, explains that since less discriminatory employers hire more women workers than more discriminatory employers, male and female workers may be segregated by the firm, as it is observed in labor market. This model, finally, explains that if employer taste for discrimination vary across occupations, then occupational segregation by sex can also occur, which is a likely scenario.

This model, however, has been identified with one problem. In this model, discrimination is not costless to the employer who foregoes the opportunity to substitute the lower-wage female labor for the higher-wage male labor. Consequently, less discriminatory firms have lower production costs, and their competitive advantage enables them to expand their production and drive the more discriminatory firms out of business in the long run. With the expansion of the less discriminatory firms, the demand for female labor increases, and the male-female wage gap reduces. In the extreme case, where there are enough entirely nondiscriminatory firms to hire all the women workers, then the male-female wage gap is eliminated. Hence, the question for this model is: how discrimination, which represents a departure from profit-maximizing behavior, can survive competitive pressures.

Several answers have been given to this question. One answer to this question is that discrimination is related to the lack of competitive pressures in the economy. Becker hypothesized that, on average, employer discrimination is less severe in competitive than in monopolistic industries; and his hypothesis has received some empirical support. Furthermore, women have less representation in unionized employment, and thus, do not benefit from the monopoly wage advantage of unionism to the same extent as men do.

Moreover, the monopsony power by employers in the labor market may produce and perpetuate the male-female pay differential. Recall that a firm has monopsony power when it is a large buyer of labor relative to the size of the particular labor market. An example of this case is the university hiring of a couple who both have a PhD and would like to be hired by the university located in a university town. In this situation, the employer enjoys a degree of monopsony power and lowers the pay of both members of the couple, but the wife's salary may be more adversely affected.

Another reason for the persistence of discrimination in the labor market is as follows. It is possible that the employers' discrimination against women is not based on personal prejudice, but it is based on the actual or perceived differences between male and female workers in productivity or behavior. This model is called "statistical discrimination," which is discussed later in this section.

Another reason for the persistence of discrimination in the labor market is put forth by Becker, which is as follows. Even if employers do not have taste for discrimination against women, their profit-maximizing behavior may result in sex-related discrimination in the labor market if their employees or customers have discriminatory tastes against women. Since this situation does not conflict with the profit-maximization behavior of employers, there is no economic reason why this type of discrimination cannot continue. With this background, it is time now to consider the possibility of discriminating employees and customers.

Employee Discrimination: A male employee who has tastes for discrimination against women, acts as if he incurs nonpecuniary costs for working with women, as measured by his discrimination coefficient, d_e. This is the premium he must be paid in order to be enticed to work with women. Under such circumstances, a profit-maximizing employer hires a sex-segregated work force, as this eliminates the payment of the premium to male workers for associating with female workers. When all employers follow this policy, then male and female workers are paid the same wage rate, but they are segregated.

Complete segregation, however, may not be profitable when there are substantial costs associated with adjustment from the previous situation. For instance, in hiring new workers, the firm incurs recruitment and screening costs, as well as firm-specific training costs. These adjustment costs together with employee tastes for discrimination perpetuate segregation and result in market-wide wage differences between male and female workers. As in the case of employer discrimination against women, the size of the wage differential depends on the prevalence and intensity of employees' discriminatory tastes, as well as the relative number of women seeking employment. If a relatively large proportion of employees have no taste for discrimination against women, and/or relatively few women seek employment, then it is possible for all the women to work with nondiscriminatory men, and there is no pay differential. In the opposite situation, both segregation and wage differential would be more severe.

If the employees' tastes for discrimination against women not only exist but also vary across occupations, then there is occupational segregation as well as pay differentials. For instance, women are not usually hired for supervisory and managerial positions because male employees who do not mind working with women, but, do not like being supervised by them. Furthermore, male and female employees may not like to have women supervisors.

Furthermore, employee discrimination may adversely affect the morale and productivity of discriminating male workers who are expected to work with women. This makes employers reluctant to hire women, especially when their male employees have considerable firm-specific training and, therefore, are very costly to replace. If employers decide to hire women under such circumstances, then employers pay them less in order to offset the reduction in the productivity of the discriminating male employees.

Employee discrimination can reduce the productivity of women in comparison to men. This may happen in traditionally male fields. For instance, on-the-job training frequently takes place informally as supervisors and/or coworkers demonstrate how things are done, as well as provide advice and assistance. When male employees have tastes for discrimination against women, they tend to be reluctant to teach women these important skills, and consequently, women learn less, become less productive, and receive lower pay.

Customer Discrimination: Customers or clients, whether male or female, who have tastes for discrimination against women act as if there is a nonpecuniary cost associated with purchasing a good or a service from a woman, and such cost equals to their discrimination coefficient, d_c. This means that if a woman wants to sell as much as a comparable man does, then she would have to charge a lower price. Women are, therefore, less desirable employees and receive a lower pay. If customer discrimination is not spread uniformly, then occupational segregation may also occur.

Statistical Discrimination: As noted earlier, models of statistical discrimination are based on a different employers' motivation for discrimination, which is consistent with profit maximization and discrimination persistence in the long run. In models of statistical discrimination, employers need to make decisions under conditions of incomplete information or uncertainty. Even if employers carefully study all available information about the qualifications of the job applicants, they never certainly know how individuals will perform on the job or how long they will stay with the company after they are hired. Any mistakes on the part of the employer can be costly to the company, especially where hiring and training costs are substantial. Employers' decisions with respect to the promotion of their employees involve similar risks, even though employers have additional firsthand information based on the past job performance of employees within their company.

Employers who need to make personnel decisions under conditions of risk and uncertainty, often use any readily available information which may be related to the productivity or job stability of the employee. If employers believe that, on average, women are less productive or less stable employees, they commit statistical discrimination against the individual woman. That is, employers commit statistical discrimination when employers judge the individual woman on the basis of their beliefs about group averages. This results in discrimination against women in hiring, pay, and/or promotion.

Employers commonly hold beliefs regarding differences in average ability or behavior by sex. Male managers and administrators, when comparing men and women with respect to a variety of traits that are likely to be related to productivity, generally hold the following beliefs. Men as a group are rated more highly on understanding the "big picture" of the organization; approaching problems rationally; getting people to work together; understanding financial matters; sizing up situations accurately; administrative capability; leadership potential; setting long-range goals and working toward them; wanting to get ahead; standing up under fire; keeping cool in emergencies; independence and self-sufficiency; and aggressiveness. Women as a group are rated more highly on clerical aptitude; being good at detail work; enjoyment of routine tasks; crying easily; being sensitive to criticism; timid; jealous; being excessively emotional regarding their jobs; being more likely to be absent and to quit; and putting family matters ahead of their job.

If such employer beliefs are incorrect, exaggerated, or reflect time lags in adjusting to a new reality, and if the employer takes actions based on them, then their actions are unfair and constitute labor-market discrimination. This is because such actions result in wage and occupation differences between men and women which are not based on (potential) productivity differences.

For an individual women, the consequences are far from satisfactory. This is because the individual woman who is as productive and as stable an employee as a male employee is denied employment or is paid a lower wage. From a normative perspective, the employment decision which is based on a characteristic like sex—a characteristic that the individual cannot change—is unfair. Indeed, when an individual is judged on the basis of his or her group characteristics, rather than upon his or her own individual merits, constitutes stereotyping and discrimination. Such behavior is illegal under the antidiscrimination laws and regulations.

Statistical discrimination can have very harmful consequences, particularly where there are feedback effects. For instance, if employers believe that females have job instability, and therefore, the employers give women less firm-specific training, and assign them to jobs with minimized turnover costs, then women have little incentive to stay with the company and may respond by exhibiting exactly the unstable behavior that employers expect, that is, self-fulfilling prophecy. Employers note that their perceptions are confirmed in practice, and therefore, they see no reason to change their discriminatory behavior. In contrast, if employers had believed that women are stable workers and had assigned them to positions that rewarded such stability, then women might have performed as stable workers. Thus, when statistical discrimination has feedback effects, an employer behavior, which is initially based on incorrect assessments of average sex differences, may persist in the long run and be fairly resistant to competitive pressures.

INTERPRETIVE VIEW

In the United States, the Census Bureau is responsible to gather data on all residents every ten years. Such data are very important, because they form the basis for the determination of the distribution of federal funds to support housing assistance, highway construction, employment services, schools, hospital services, programs for the elderly, and other funding targets. In the last census, for the first time, persons with mixed racial heritage were given the unique opportunity of selecting more than one racial category; that is, as a result of the new government policy, the category "multiracial" became a reality in the United States.[2]

This, of course, does not mean that multiracial people have never before lived in the United States, because multiracial people have been present throughout the history of the United States. However, until recently, the U.S. government policies had not allowed for the recognition of a multiracial identity. Instead, the U.S. government policies had enforced the rule of "hypodescent"—according to which one drop of black blood makes you black—in order to define and maintain distinct racial categories.

The preceding example was intended to show that not only we use categories to describe ourselves and those around us, but more importantly, the categories we use are the products of social, rather than biological, factors. Biologically multiracial people have certainly lived throughout the U.S. history, and it is unlikely that anyone has been "racially pure." Therefore, it is in our social setting that our recognition, definition, and grouping of these factors make them culturally significant in our daily interactions. We rely so much on such distinct categories that, for instance, when we encounter someone, whose race is not immediately discernible to us, we ask: "What are you?"

The significant characteristic of these culturally defined classifications is that they are structured as categories that are fundamentally different and separate from one another. For instance, we expect people to be either black or white, but never in between. It is important to note that difference is not a negative quality. On the contrary, the existence of categories of difference makes our lives much richer. More specifically, the existence of different cultural traditions, types of food, forms of music, and styles of dance make our life experience more interesting. Whereas differences by themselves do not cause inequality in our culture, the meanings and values which we apply to these differences make differences harmful. For instance, in the United States, not only people of color are defined as different from whites, but in addition, that whites are viewed as superior and as the cultural standard against which all others are judged. They are such meanings and values that transform different categories of race into a system of racial inequality.

Generally, the categories of difference with regard to race/ethnicity, social class, sex/gender, and sexuality are socially constructed and socially transformed into systems of inequality. Through social processes, people simultaneously create categories of difference and construct structures of social stratification—that is, a system based on which society ranks categories of people in a hierarchy—and social stratification results in systems of inequality. The categories of difference and inequality affect the lives of all the members of our society, and therefore, such inequalities need to be addressed.

Essentialism and Social Construction: As noted earlier, in the United States, there is a system of stratification which is based on various categories of difference, such as race/ethnicity, social class, sex/gender, and sexuality. Those people who believe in essentialism tend to view this stratification system as fixed because they assume that these categories are unchangeable. Essentialism is the idea that human behavior is "natural," predetermined by genetic, biological, or physiological mechanisms, and thus, not subject to change. Human behaviors that are somewhat similar are assumed to be reflections of an underlying human drive or tendency. In the United States, people rarely call into question the natural or biological status of gender and sexuality. Essentialism informs the way most people in the United States think about such things as gender, and remains the hegemonic or culturally dominant belief in the U.S. culture. Essentialism guides the way people in the United States order their social world, and determines what people value as well as what people devalue.

Social construction theory offers a different perspective. Social construction theory is based on the premise that categories such as race/ethnicity, social class, sex/gender, and sexuality are socially constructed. According to this theory, social order is neither part of the "nature of things," nor it can be derived from the "laws of nature," because social order is a product of human activity. Social construction theory believes that what we see as "real" (e.g., cultural categories of difference and systems of inequality) is the result of our (i.e., human) interaction. Through our interaction, we not only create various aspects of our culture but also objectify them, internalize them, and take them (i.e., the cultural products) for granted.

When we adopt a social construction theory framework, we understand that we are not born with a sense of what it means to be male, female, or intersexual; with a disability, or not; black, Latina/o, Asian, white, or Native American; gay, straight, asexual, or bisexual; or rich, working class, poor, or middle class. This is because we learn about all these categories through social interaction. That is, we are given the meanings and values for all these categories by our social institutions, peers, families, and so on. This means that what we learn depends on both the culture in which we live, and our place in that culture.

It is important to recognize the effect of such cultural definitions. This is because, cultural definitions often determine how we experience our social world. In other words, cultures define situations as real, and as such they have real consequences. For example, when we define one group as inferior to another, although this does not make that group inferior, it may cause them to have an inferior experience. For a more detailed example, consider the vicious cycle that results from the allocation of substandard resources to people who are considered to be poor. Low-income housing is generally located in geographic areas with low-quality resources, such as low-quality public schools and low-quality health care. Such low-quality resources further deepens their social disadvantage, that is, perpetuates the poverty of this group. Thus, although reality is "soft" when it is initially constructed, it can become "hard" when it takes effect.

According to the social construction theory, reality is socially constructed in three stages: (1) externalization, (2), objectivation, and (3) internalization.

Externalization is the first stage in which we create cultural products through social interaction. These cultural products may be in the form of material artifacts, social institutions, or values and beliefs regarding a particular group. After these cultural products are created, they become "external" to those who have produced them. As an example, let us take the case of the social construction of gender. The construction of gender identity begins at birth when the child is placed within a sex category, either male or female. Child's culturally defined dress and adornment inform people of the sex of the child, and people treat the child according to the culturally defined gendered expectations for that particular sex. The child then behaves differently because of the different treatment he or she receives. Therefore, a situation which is initially defined as real, becomes real in its consequences. Different behaviors are defined for boys and girls, and as a consequence, they do behave differently, and boys and girls are seen as being different from each other.

As a second example of externalization can be racial formation, which is the process through which social, economic, and political forces interact to shape not only the content and importance of racial categories but also racial meanings. In this context, the recognition of a multiracial identity involves more than individuals being identified as biologically multiracial. Instead, interactions that take place at the social, economic, and political levels lead to the construction of such categories of race.

Objectivation is the second stage in which the products created by people in the first stage take on a reality of their own, and become independent of the people who created them. People lose awareness that they themselves are the authors of their cultural products, that is, their social and cultural environment and their interpretations of reality. Consequently, people feel as if such cultural products have an objective existence, and that such cultural products are another part of reality to be taken for granted. For example, as was noted earlier, most people in the United States take race categories for granted, because they believe in essentialism, which views race categories as the result of biological or genetic factors. However, as was also noted earlier, various social, economic, and political forces interact to construct race categories. When people forget their part in the social construction of race, or lose sight of the social forces that operate to construct race categories and their meanings, these categories take on objective realities. In the recent census conducted by the U.S. Census Bureau, the objective realities that many people attribute to racial categories can be inferred. According to the census data, only 2.5 percent of respondents identified themselves as multiracial. Such a low response rate can be attributed to (1) lack of knowledge of the available options; and (2) identification with one race, without regard to one's multiracial heritage. These findings demonstrate that most respondents believe in the objective reality of clear and mutually exclusive race categories.

Internalization is the third and final stage in which we learn the so-called "objective facts" about the cultural products which have already been created. This learning primarily occurs through socialization. That is, through the process of social interaction one learns the norms of the society and their implications with respect to one's specific roles—that is, the sets of rules and expectations associated with a social position (or status) in that society. In this stage, we absorb these "facts" in our subjective consciousness. It is through the process of internalization that members of a culture share the same understanding of reality, and rarely question the origins of their beliefs or the processes by which their beliefs came to being. For instance, the mass media acts as a very powerful tool in shaping the way we think. Mass media constitutes a significant part of our culture, and operates as a very important socialization mechanism. The phenomena which are selected and presented in the mass media, as well as the way they are presented in the mass media, convey important messages about the extent to which who and what is or is not valued. More specifically, mass media join forces in the internalization of certain constructs about class in our society. Mass media not only convey the message that poverty is not a significant problem in this country but also that those who are poor should blame themselves, and that we are a middle-class society, and that blue-collar and union workers should be blamed for the declining economic security. When we are presented with these images by the mass media, we develop a particular view of the class structure in our country. Accordingly, we internalize beliefs about the members of each specific class (e.g., the poor are lazy) as if they are "objective facts." In this way, the media play a significant role in maintaining constructions of difference and the resulting systems of inequality.

The discussion of the three stages through which cultural products are generated does not imply that the creation of reality occurs in a neat and overt progression. In some cases, such as the invention of heterosexual identity, the process of externalization in the creation of a social category is clear. In general, the construction of reality does not always involve such a clear process. However, the discussion of the three stages through which cultural products are generated provides a general understanding of how the knowledge that guides our behavior is established, and how it becomes a part of our culture and our common sense. In addition, it is important to be aware that the categories of difference are not only constructed and transformed into systems of inequality but also they are often maintained by the same social forces and practices. To clearly understand these phenomena, it is necessary to examine the processes that construct them.

The categories of race, class, gender, and sexuality are socially constructed and transformed into systems of inequality. The preceding explanation of social construction theory provided an understanding of how these categories are socially constructed. A more detailed understanding of this process requires an understanding of social factors that are involved in creating these categories.

The social categories of difference which we use are the result of our social activities, which are guided by the values of our culture. We engage in the process of creating categories of difference when we, as parents, teach our child how to behave like a "lady" or act like a "gentleman;" when one child labels another child a "sissy" or a "fag;" or when a girl under pressure stops playing "rough" in order to avoid being called a "tomboy." We take these everyday actions for granted, but they reflect our fundamental view of the world. The kinds of categories we create, as well as the meanings we attach to them, are based on our cultural values regarding the extent to which who or what is important.

These categories are created through processes which we encounter every day in various contexts. Institutional context is one of the most significant of them. An institution is the set of rules and relationships that govern the social activities in which we get involved in order to meet our basic needs. The major social institutions are as follows:

The family: responsible for reproducing, socializing, and protecting the young, regulating sexual behavior, and providing emotional comfort and support to the family members.

Education: responsible for teaching members of society the knowledge, skills, and values which are considered most important for the survival of the individual as well as society.

The economy: responsible for creating, controlling, and distributing the human and material resources of a society.

The state: responsible for using the legal power to regulate the behavior of members of that society, and in addition, it is responsible for regulating the relationship of that society to other societies.

The media: responsible for providing information to members of society, for reinforcing the policies of other institutions, and for socializing members of society with the norms of proper behavior and accepted cultural values.

These institutions follow policies and practices, which are based on our cultural values, and create categories of difference. For instance, when we, as parents, teach our child how to behave like a "lady" or act like a "gentleman," we create categories of difference within the institutional context of the family.

Interpersonal context, which refers to our daily interactions with others, provides us with a context in which we create categories of difference. During these interactions, we follow common guidelines for behavior (norms) to define situations and create categories of difference. For instance, in the United States, when an American, operating on stereotypes based on race and ethnicity, labels a person "foreigner," she or he is following the commonly assumed images of what is an "American." In this way, she or he creates categories of difference within an interpersonal context.

Finally, in internal contexts, we create categories of difference by internalizing the values and beliefs which are established in institutional and interpersonal contexts. For instance, when a girl decides to stop playing "rough" to avoid being called a "tomboy," she is internalizing the socially constructed criteria of being a girl which she had learned from her family as well as her peers.

People create these categories of difference based on their beliefs. For instance, European explorers created separate categories for reference to the people who were indigenous to the lands which the European explorers "discovered." When the European explorers encountered people who looked different from them, their assumptions regarding the origin of the human species became questionable. As a result, religious debates about creation, and creation of a single species of humanity, led to questions about the possibility of the natives of the New World to be "saved," and how they should be treated. European settlers deemed themselves as children of God, and indigenous people as "other," accordingly the European settlers maintained their worldview.

RADICAL HUMANIST VIEW

Any mode of inequality involves a social process through which a powerful group of humans (top dogs) reaps benefits for itself at the expense of a less powerful group (underdogs). The process is constituted by an institutionalized struggle over power, status, and wealth. The four most important and most common modes of inequality are as follows: (1) gender, (2) race, (3) class, and (4) nation. These four modes of inequality overlap and reinforce each other.[3]

Inequality, more specifically, is a whole complex of "modes," "practices," "enabling myths," "focal points," and "antidotes." To each mode of inequality, corresponds a set of "practices" in which the top dogs take advantage of the underdogs, that is, such "practices" ensure that the top dogs win. To each mode of inequality, also corresponds a set of "enabling myths" that culturally enforce the "practices" by making the game seem fair to both the top dogs and the underdogs. To each mode of inequality, also corresponds a "focal point," which is a particular institution wherein the inequality resides—that is, where the myths justifying the mode of inequality are learned, and the practices realizing it actually take place. The "focal point" of a mode of inequality changes as the mode of inequality evolves. To each mode of inequality, also corresponds an "antidote," which is a set of values, meanings, and beliefs, that can debunk the "enabling myths." Inequality—as a whole complex of "modes," "practices," "enabling myths," "focal points," and "antidotes"—does not reach a balance of forces, that is, equilibrium, because it involves an interacting process of cumulative causation in which inequality either gets better or worse, that is, it seldom, if ever, stays the same.

Values play a central role in inequality. Values either rationalize inequality by making it seem fair and true, or values debunk inequality by exposing its injustice and falsehood. People may pretend to be value neutral about inequality, but they never are. Table 6.1 classifies all the modes, practices, myths, and antidotes of the four inequalities.

Four Modes of Inequality: Mode of inequality refers to the way in which one group gives offense and another group receives the offense. Individuals do not choose to join one group or the other, but they are assigned to one group by the operation of law, tradition, and myth. Culture and coercion are the operative factors, not the individual preference and choice.

Gender inequality: is the practice of the domination of one gender by another. Nowadays, men dominate women through various gendered practices. These practices are justified and supported by myths regarding female inferiority and male superiority. These myths constitute the substance of sexism. Sexist myths not only enable men to dominate women without having guilt conscious but also numb women so that they can be dominated without mass rebellion or suicide. Those who transcend sexist myths, form the antidote to gender inequality, which is called "feminism."

Females are taught by their culture to behave like women; and males are taught by their culture to behave like men. Nowadays, the males are expected to be superior to the females, and the females are expected to be inferior to the males.

Race inequality: is the practice of one race discriminating against another race. Nowadays, its most significant crystallization is white Europeans discriminating against either black Africans or other people of color. It is justified by myths regarding African, Asian, and Latin American inferiority and white European superiority. These myths constitute the substance of prevailing racism. Racist myths not only enable white Europeans to discriminate against non-European people of color without having guilt conscious but also

Table 6.1 The Whole Complex of Inequality

Modes Practices	Myths	Antidotes
Gender Domination	Sexism	Feminism
Race Discrimination	Racism	Civil Rights
Class Exploitation	Classism	Economic Democracy
Nation Predation	Jingoism	Internationalism

Source: Dugger (1996).

numb such people of color so that they can take their unfair treatment without fully realizing that it is unfair. Those who transcend racist myths, form the antidote to discrimination, which is called "civil rights."

Race, like gender, is as much cultural as it is biological. For instance, in the United States, "African American" is as much a cultural as a biological grouping. It does not, on the one hand, include all people whose skin is black, such as people from India, Melanesia, Sri Lanka, and Native Australians, who have their own problems and suffer from their own injustices. The group of "African Americans," on the other hand, includes some people whose skin is white, that is, the white skin people whose ancestors were seized for slaves in Africa and forcibly transported to the Americas. It has been miscegenation and a whole set of laws, traditions, and myths that has forced generations of "African Americans" into an inferior position relative to "white" Europeans. It should be noted that cultural learning, not genetics, has been the principal factor operating throughout their history.

Class inequality: in capitalism, is the practice of the exploitation of the workers by the capitalists. In Soviet communism, the exploitation of workers took place by the nomenklatura. Class exploitation is justified and supported, in the West, by the myths about market efficiency, while in the East, it was done by the myth about the dictatorship of the proletariat. Class myths not only enable a powerful class to exploit a powerless class without having the guilt conscious but also numb the powerless class to bear with the hardship of the exploitation. Those who transcend class myths, form the antidote to exploitation, which is called "economic democracy."

Individuals are grouped into classes based on how they appropriate their incomes, and how large their incomes are. The upper class is composed of capitalists and those who have appropriated large incomes for themselves, and have prevented the lower classes from doing the same. The middle class is composed of those who want to appropriate large incomes but lack the differential advantage needed to do so. Members of the lower class are far from having the desires of the middle class. Among classes, there is a limited opportunity for individual choice, merit, and luck. Notwithstanding, an individual's membership in a particular class is determined primarily by the class in which the individual is born into, rather than that individual's rise or fall.

Although class is an economic category, it is also strongly affected by cultural factors. Youth learning about beliefs, values, and meanings takes place through school, family, and religion, and it varies by class. In this way, the youth learn and accept the appropriate class role, and grow up as a well-adjusted person.

Nation inequality: is the practice of the predation of powerful nations on weak nations. It is justified and supported by jingoistic myths regarding national honor and foreign treachery. Jingoistic myths not only enable the members of powerful nations to take pride in the preying of the members of weak nations without having the guilt conscious but also numb the members of the weak nations to bear the hardship of being preyed on. Those who transcend jingoistic myths, form the antidote to national predation, which is called "internationalism."

People are grouped into separate nations based on arbitrary geopolitical boundaries that divide people into nationals and foreigners. A nation is an area controlled by one state; and allegiance is made to that state and against others. Cultural, educational, ethnic, religious, and language differences may further differentiate the people in one state from those in another. When these differences are combined with the power and propaganda of the nation-state, they result in a very effective mode of inequality. For instance, individuals who find themselves identified as French, German, Italian, or Russian are not so by nature; rather, they have been taught these identities. People are taught that foreigners are untrustworthy, ignorant, brutal, and inferior. Based on this propaganda, state leaders use their jingoism either for gaining support for attacks against other nations, or for mounting a defense against (imagined) attacks. States create formidable security agencies to implement the group-ings. Security agencies such as the former Soviet State Security Committee (KGB), as well as the U.S. Central Intelligence Agency (CIA) and Federal Bureau of Investigation (FBI) serve as the focal points of nationalism.

Four Practices of Inequality: Each of the four practices of inequality is multifaceted, and therefore, each practice is discussed separately.

Domination: The institutionalized focal point of the domination of women by men in patriarchal societies is the family. An institution, for example, the family, consists of a group of people who perform their activities according to a set of rules which are justified by a common set of values, beliefs, and meanings. As the members of the group perform their activities according to such rules, they internalize the values, beliefs, and meanings that justify the rules. Domination within the patriarchal family involves the male parent, that is, the patriarch, exercising power over the other family members, and appro-priating most of the family status, wealth, and power. All the members of the family, including the female parent, accept the rules that support the male parent's practices because they accept the values, beliefs, and meanings that support such practices. All the members of the family come to believe that family means the patriarchal family only, and that no other types of family are possible. This mind-set—which consists of values, beliefs, and meanings that support male domination within the family—also spreads to other social institutions.

Discrimination: In the United States, the focal point for discrimination against African Americans was slavery and the process of production. Despite its variation, slavery was always supported by a racist culture, according to which Europeans were considered to be the superiors and Africans to be the inferiors. The racist culture dehumanized Africans, and turned them into property, which could be bought and sold. Slavery was always coercive. Racism did not end with the abolition of slavery. Racism supports various discriminatory practices which are diffused throughout the economy, society, and polity. The practice of discrimination has become institutionalized in various bureaucracies of modern society, has been joined by male domination over females, upper class exploitation of the lower class, and the predation of the chosen people on foreigners.

Exploitation: The focal point in capitalism is the hierarchical workplace, in which owners hire workers to produce commodities, which will be sold for as high a profit as possible. They seek a differential economic advantage that will allow them to appropriate more income at the expense of those who do not have such advantages. Such advantages are usually obtained through property ownership. Owners increase their incomes by lowering wages and increasing the prices of their products.

Predation: The nation state is the focal point for predation, which is practiced by war and diplomacy. Nation states seek favorable treatment for their elite groups of capitalist corporations and state bureaucracies (military or civilian). The most successful predator nations build empires by forming alliances with other predators, and deal with opposing nations by either occupying them, subjecting them to unfavorable trade relations, or setting up puppet regimes within them. Predation enables the predatory apparatus of each state to extract status, power, and wealth from the population of that state in the name of defending the homeland and national security, even though these occur at the expense of the reduction of the liberties of citizens and the increase in their taxes.

Myths as the Cultural Support of Inequality: Myths are primarily stereotypes which are believed by the beneficiaries of inequality, such as what men believe about women, European Americans believe about African Americans, the upper class believes about the lower class, and the chosen people believe about foreigners. In addition, myths justify the inequality in the minds of both its victims and its beneficiaries. In order to prevent the victims from unrest, they must be taught that their treatment is not unfair. In order to prevent the beneficiaries from having guilt conscience they must be taught that their advantages are due for them. Teaching the victims is much harder than teaching the beneficiaries. This is because it is easy to convince the beneficiaries that they deserve all the good things that come their way. It is much harder to convince the victims that they deserve all the bad things that come their way. Teaching the victims is much more important than teaching the beneficiaries, and therefore, it is the primary function of myths.

Myths not only instill superiority in the top dogs and inferiority in the underdogs but also create "otherness," that is, centrality and marginality. That is, in order for one to be superior, an "other" must be inferior. Similarly, in order for one to be at the center of things, an "other" must be on the margin. For instance, the myths of sexism put males at the center of humanity and females on the margin.

Sexism as the Myths that Support Gender Inequality: Sexist myths begin with "otherness," in which males are the center, and females, as the "others," are the margin. Thus, "mankind" or "man" is used to refer to human species, but "womankind" or "woman" is used to refer to women, the margin. This forms the foundation of the justification for males dominating females. Public activities—which yield wealth, status, and power—are for men. Private activities—which do not yield wealth, status, and power—are for women. Men can speak better in public; are more intelligent and articulate; are better bosses; are less emotional; and more straightforward and honest in the pursuit of goals. Women are too emotional and intuitive; and less straightforward. Women who internalize these myths find it easier to put up with their narrowed role in life. Men who internalize these myths find it easier to exclude women and have no guilt conscience.

Racism as the Myths that Support Race Discrimination: Racist myths also begin with "otherness," in which, in the United States, the European is the one, and the African American is the other. In the United States, culture, for example, literature and art, refers to the culture of white Europeans. Racial myths exist in the realm of magic and superstition, not that of fact and experience. They emanate from the otherness of the African American in the mind of the European American. Racial myths enable "whites" to take advantage of "blacks." However, they are psychologically grounded in magic and in superstitions.

Classism as the Myths that Support Class Exploitation: Classist myths consist of a set of components: (a) the free market system is neutral in regards to class, and therefore, it involves no class exploitation; (b) the capitalist/Western world operates on a free market system; (c) the free market system involves individual competition, which results in benefits for all. According to these myths, the free market system through market competition, not differential economic advantage, distributes income. The underdogs can improve their position by working harder, being smarter, and saving more. If they do not succeed, it is their own fault. When the victims of inequality actually believe in these myths, then the top dogs are safe.

Jingoism as the Myths that Support National Predation: In the United States, jingoism is used to mean that "Americans" are "the one," and foreigners are "the other." Jingoism involves denial and projection, and is used to justify attack on foreign nations. More specifically, when the predatory apparatus of the United States attacks another nation, the attack is accompanied by: (a) the denial of the United States' own hostile intentions, and (b) the projection of hostile intentions onto the nation being attacked.

Myths simultaneously do four related things: (a) they provide a rationalization of privilege; (b) they create the "otherness" of the victim; (c) they create a superstitious apprehension of the unknown, "other," in the minds of the top dogs; and (d) they encouraging the underdogs to blame themselves for injustices.

Antidotes for Inequality: Inequality must be attacked through its myths and practices. The myths of inequality must be debunked by the churches, the schools, the sciences, the arts, and the social movements. The actual practices of inequality must be transformed through collective action by the unions, the professional associations, the corporate boards, the courts, the legislatures, and the social movements.

RADICAL STRUCTURALIST VIEW

A large amount of empirical research has documented that there is persistent divisions among American workers. They are divided by race, sex, educational credentials, industry grouping, and so forth. These groups practically operate in different labor markets that have different working conditions, different promotional opportunities, different wages, and different market institutions.[4]

The continuing divisions in labor market are anomalous to neoclassical economists. The orthodox theory assumes that profit-maximizing behavior of employers leads to the evaluation of workers in terms of their individual characteristics, and therefore, predicts that labor market differences among various groups will decline over time due to the competitive mechanisms. However, by most measures, the labor market differences among various groups have not been declining. Thus, the continuing importance of the existence of various groups in the labor market is neither explained nor predicted by the orthodox theory.

A radical theory of labor-market segmentation can explain the reason that the labor force is, generally, still so fragmented; and that group characteristics are, repeatedly, so important in the labor market. This radical theory of labor-market segmentation argues that economic forces within American capitalism have not only given rise to but also perpetuated segmented labor markets. It further argues that it is incorrect to view the sources of segmented labor markets as exogenous to the economic system.

Prevalence of Labor-Market Segmentation: Labor-market segmentation can be considered as the historical process through which economic and political forces lead the division of the labor market into separate submarkets, or segments, which have different labor-market characteristics and behavioral rules. That is, segmented labor markets are the outcome of a segmentation process. Segments may cut vertically as well as horizontally, that is, across the occupational hierarchy. The prevailing labor market conditions can most usefully be understood as the outcome of four segmentation processes, as follows.

Segmentation into Primary and Secondary Markets: The primary and secondary segments—which is the terminology used in the dual labor market theory—are distinguished primarily by stability characteristics of the job. Primary jobs share common characteristics as follows: (a) they require and develop stable working habits; (b) they provide extensive on-the-job skill training; (c) they pay relatively higher wages; and (d) they offer the opportunity for climbing the job ladder. Secondary jobs share common characteristics as follows: (a) they do not require and often discourage stable working habits; (b) they provide minimal on-the-job skill training; (c) they pay relatively much lower wages; (d) they offer very few opportunities for climbing the job ladder; (e) they experience high turnover rate; and (f) they are filled mainly, though not exclusively, by minority workers, women, and youth.

Segmentation within the Primary Sector: Within the primary sector there is a segmentation between what can be called "subordinate" primary jobs and "independent" primary jobs. Subordinate primary jobs share common characteristics as follows: (a) they are routinized; (b) they encourage personality characteristics of dependability, discipline, responsiveness to rules and authority, and acceptance of the firm's goals. Examples of subordinate primary jobs are factory and office jobs. In contrast, independent primary jobs share common characteristics as follows: (a) they encourage and require personality characteristics of creativity, problem-solving, and self-initiating; (b) they often have professional standards for work; (c) they have relatively high voluntary turnover; and (d) they highly reward individual motivation and achievement.

Segmentation by Race: Although minority workers have jobs in secondary segment, subordinate primary segment, and independent primary segment, they are often led to distinct subsegments within those labor-market segments. There are certain jobs which are "race-typed," that is, they are segregated by prejudice and by labor-market institutions. In these cases, the divisions between race-segments are often maintained by geographic separation.

Segmentation by Sex: Particular jobs have generally been reserved for men, and others for women. Female segments share common characteristics as follows: (a) they usually offer lower wages than offered in comparable male jobs; and (b) they often require and encourage a "serving mentality," that is, having an orientation toward providing services to other people and especially to men. These characteristics are encouraged during upbringing in institutions such as family and school.

The Historical Origins of Labor-Market Segmentation: The prevailing divisions in the labor market are best understood through an historical analysis of their development from their origins. As will be noted, these labor-market segmentations have arisen during the economic transition from competitive capitalism to monopoly capitalism. For this purpose, the historical analysis focuses on the era of monopoly capitalism, that is, from around 1890 to the present, and places special emphasis on the earlier years of such transition.

During the preceding period, that is, competitive capitalism, labor-market developments had an orientation toward the increasing homogenization of the labor force, not toward segmentation. The factory system eliminated many skill-crafted occupations, and created a large number of semiskilled jobs. Production was made for a mass market; and increased mechanization led to standardized work requirements. Large establishments housed large numbers of workers in common working environments.

With the emergence of monopoly capitalism, the labor force—which was characterized by having become increasingly homogeneous and proletarian—generated tensions which were manifest in the tremendous upsurge in labor conflicts: in railroads dating back to 1877, in steel before 1901 and again in 1919, in coal mining during and after World War I, in textile mills throughout the same period, and in countless other plants and industries around the United States. The success of the Industrial Workers of the World (IWW), the emergence of a strong Socialist party, the general (as opposed to industry-specific) strikes in Seattle and New Orleans, the mass labor revolts in 1919 and 1920, and the increasingly national character of the labor movement throughout this period were based on a general, widespread, and growing opposition to capitalist hegemony. Increasingly, strikes which begun just over wage issues gained momentum and moved toward much more general issues.

While the workforce was becoming more homogeneous, oligopolistic corporations, which still dominate the economy today, began not only to emerge but also to consolidate their power. The leaders in the new era of monopoly capitalism, who had been released from short-run competitive pressures, were in search of long-run stability, and therefore, planned for the capture of strategic control over product and factor markets. That is, their new concerns became the creation and implementation of monopolistic control, rather than their old concern regarding allocation based on the calculus of short-run profit maximization.

Monopoly capitalism's new needs for control were threatened by the consequences of the changes in the characters of the labor force, which was becoming increasingly homogeneous and proletarian. There is a large body of evidence which shows that the owners of large corporations were at pains when they became aware of the potentially revolutionary character of labor force movements. Indeed, the employers' mass offensive on unions, between 1903 and 1908, was more geared toward ideology than specific demands. At the same time, the formation of the National Civic Federation (NCF)—which consisted of a group dominated by large "progressive" capitalists—was another observable manifestation of the fundamental crises which the capitalist class was facing. Employers, to meet this threat, actively and consciously promoted and supported the implementation of labor-market segmentation in order to "divide and conquer" the labor force. Moreover, the efforts of monopolistic corporations, which was aimed at gaining greater control over their product markets, led to a dichotomization of the industrial structure which unintentionally, but indirectly and desirably, reinforced their conscious strategies. Thus, labor-market segmentation was the result of both conscious strategies and systemic forces. Although in this historical analysis, more space is allocated to employers' conscious efforts, it should not be interpreted as if systemic forces are not active as underlying forces.

Conscious Efforts: Monopoly capitalist corporations deliberately planned strategies in order to advantageously resolve the contradictions between the work force's increased proletarianization and the corporate's growth, consolidation, and concentration. At the core of the new corporate strategy was the plan to break down the increasingly unified workers' interests which arose out of the proletarianization of work and the concentration of workers in urban areas. Several aspects of these large firms' operations exhibited that their new strategy aimed at dividing the labor force into various segments so that the actual experiences of different groups of workers were different and therefore, the basis of workers' common opposition to capitalists were undermined.

Large corporation's efforts were "conscious" in the sense that, as capitalists, they faced immediate major problematic events and in response they devised strategies to meet them. However, capitalists' strategies were not "conscious" in the sense that the capitalists who devised them understood fully the historical forces acting upon them, or understood all the ramifications of their strategies. In certain cases, capitalists acted based on a broader class consciousness. Those strategies which were successful, as a result were copied.

In corporate strategy, the first component was related to the internal relations of the corporation. Because of the tremendous growth in the size of monopoly capitalist workforces, and because of the demise of craft-governed production, there arose the need for a change in the authority relations in the corporation which underlay the control relations in the corporation. One of the changes in this area was Taylorism, that is, Scientific Management, which involved the establishment of personnel departments, experimentation with different organizational structures, and the use of the services of industrial psychologists, that is, "human relations experts," in order to devise proper "motivating" incentives, and so forth. The implementation of Taylorism led to the intensification of hierarchical control, especially the "bureaucratic form" of modern corporations. For instance, in the steel industry, shortly after the formation of U.S. Steel, an entirely new system of stratified jobs was introduced. In practice, bureaucratization established a rigidly graded hierarchy of jobs and power, based on which "top-down" authority could be exercised.

In restructuring the internal relations of the firm, capitalist corporations created segmented "internal labor markets," and in this way, enhanced labor-market segmentation. They created job ladders, which had specific "entry-level" jobs and defined patterns of promotion. White-collar workers joined the firm's workforce and then they were promoted within this segment of the firm's workers. This was in contrast to the treatment which was received by the blue-collar production workforce. More specifically, workers who did not have the qualifications for specific entry-level jobs were excluded from having access to the entirety of the corresponding job ladder. In response, labor unions often demanded a seniority criterion for promotion so that they could gain freedom from the arbitrary discretionary power of supervisors. Unions who succeeded in such endeavors, essentially took over the management of the internal labor markets. That is, they allocated workers and disciplined recalcitrant workers. Unions, thus, helped to legitimize the internal market, in exchange for some degree of control over the operation of the internal market.

The emphasis on the efforts which were directed at the internal control eventually resulted in labor-market segmentation by industry. Firms initially set policies to raise the cost to workers for leaving their company, but not the cost of entering their company. Such policies were based on firms granting certain benefits only to those employees who continued their employment in their company. Part of this strategy was "welfare capitalism," which emerged, in particular, from the National Civic Federation (NCF), and became most pronounced in the advanced industries. For instance, at Ford, only those workers who continued their employment at Ford, were able to receive benefits, including benefits such as education for the workers' children, and credit. In this way, workers were more securely tied to the firm. This is because the worker's loss of job meant a complete disruption in all aspects of his family's life. In addition, worker's seniority benefits were lost when a worker switched companies. Later, when industrial unions gained power, they were able to transform some of such firm-specific benefits to industry-wide privileges. However, the net effect of all of these efforts was an intensification of labor-market segmentation not only internally but also industry-wide, which, as will be discussed next, had other origins as well.

While capitalist corporations were segmenting their internal labor markets, similarly they were active with respect to their external relations. More specifically, employers quite consciously took advantage of existing race, ethnic, and sex antagonisms in order to counter unionism and break strikes. During the consolidation of monopoly capitalism, many times, employers manipulated the mechanisms of labor supply by importing blacks as strikebreakers; and employers stirred up racial hostility in order to divert attention from class conflicts to race conflicts. For instance, during the steel strike of 1919, which has been one of the critical points in U.S. history, in a short few weeks, many black (30,000 to 40,000) were imported as strikebreakers. Employers also often designated some jobs as "female jobs" in order to make such jobs less susceptible to unionization.

Employers also consciously took advantage of ethnic antagonisms in order to achieve labor-market segmentation. For this purpose, employers often hired workers from rival nationalities whether in the same plant or in different plants. During labor unrest, the companies sent spies and rumormongers to each ethnic group in order to stir up fears and antagonisms of other ethnic groups. Their strategy was most effective when many groups of immigrant workers had little command of English language.

Employers also turned to educational "credentials" as a relatively new divisive means. They used educational credentials to regulate job skill requirements. Employers played an active role in changing educational institutions to fit these channeling functions. The new educational requirements performed the following two tasks: (a) they perpetuated the distinctions between factory workers and the workers in routinized office jobs; and (b) they generated some strong divisions among the office workers, that is, between semiskilled white-collar workers and the more highly skilled office workers.

Systemic Forces: The rise of giant corporations and the emergence of a monopolistic core reinforced segmentation. As different firms and industries grew at different rates, a dichotomy within the industrial structure developed. The larger, more capital-intensive firms were sheltered by barriers to entry; and enjoyed economies of scale in technology, market power, and finance; and enjoyed higher rates of profit and growth than their smaller, labor-intensive competitive counterparts. Large monopolistic corporations, with their large capital investments, required stable market demand and stable planning horizons to ensure that their investments would not go unutilized. Where demand was unstable, production was subcontracted or "exported" to small, more competitive and less capital-intensive firms on the industrial periphery. The dualism in the industrial structure led to the development of a dualism of working environments, wages, and mobility patterns. Monopoly corporations developed stable job structures and internal relations that reflected the stability in their production and sales. Peripheral firms developed unstable job structures that reflected the instability in their production and sales. The result of such systemic forces was the dichotomization of the urban labor market into "primary" and "secondary" sectors.

The Social Functions of Labor-Market Segmentation: As the preceding historical analysis has shown, labor-market segmentation is inherently related to the dynamics of monopoly capitalism. The labor-market segmentation was initiated and perpetuated because it facilitates the operation of capitalist institutions. Segmentation helps to reproduce capitalist hegemony. First, segmentation divides workers and prevents their unity against employers. Second, segmentation establishes "fire trails" across vertical job ladders, and workers tend to perceive separate segments with different criteria for access, and therefore limit their own aspirations for mobility. As a result, less pressure is placed on other social institutions, such as family and school, which reproduce the class structure. Third, segmentation legitimizes inequalities in authority and control between superiors and subordinates. In this context, for instance, institutional sexism and racism reinforce the industrial authority of white male foremen.

Political Implications: Labor-market segmentation is one of the principal barriers to the united anti-capitalist opposition among workers. This segmentation has penetrated into the class consciousness of workers. A better understanding of the endogenous nature of labor-market segmentation helps to explain the difficulties involved in overcoming divisions among workers.

CONCLUSION

This chapter briefly discussed four views expressed with respect to discrimination. The functionalist paradigm conceptualize discrimination as a personal prejudice based on socially appropriate roles. The interpretive paradigm believes the categories of difference with regard to race/ethnicity, social class, sex/gender, and sexuality are socially constructed and socially transformed into systems of inequality. The radical humanist paradigm believes that any mode of inequality involves a social process through which a powerful group of humans (top dogs) reaps benefits for itself at the expense of a less powerful group (underdogs). The radical structuralist paradigm believes that economic forces within capitalism have not only given rise to but also perpetuated segmented labor markets.

Each paradigm is logically coherent—in terms of its underlying assumptions—and conceptualizes and studies the phenomenon in a certain way, and generates distinctive kinds of insight and understanding. Therefore, different paradigms in combination provide a broader understanding of the phenomenon under consideration. An understanding of different paradigms leads to a better understanding of the multifaceted nature of the phenomenon.

NOTES

1. For this literature, see Aguirre and Turner (2010), Aigner and Cain (1977), Altonji and Blank (1999), Arrow (1973), Ayres (1991), Ayres and Siegelman (1995), Becker (1971, 1976, 1985, 1995), Benabou (1996), Bertrand, Chugh, and Mullainathan (2005), Bertrand and Mullainathan (2004), Black (1995), Blau and Ferber (1992), Blecker and Seguino (2007), Borjas and Bronars (1989), Cain (1999), Crouch (1979), England (1992), Fershtman and Gneezy (2001), Friedman (2002), Fuchs (1986), Gronau (1988), Gunderson (1989), Heckman (1998), Hoffman (1991), Kahne and Kohen (1975), Lang (2007), Levy and Hughes (2009), List (2004), Loury (1977), Loury (1981), Lundberg and Startz (1998), Marshall (1974), Medina (2010), Nelson (2009), Phelps (1972), Polachek (1995), Reagan (1975), Riach and Rich (2002), Rodgers (2006), Schiller (2012), Stangor (2009), Thurow (1969, 1975), Williams (2011), Wolfson, Palumbo, Lindgren, and Taub (2011), Wooley (1993), and Zarate (2009). This section is based on Blau and Ferber (1992).

2. For this literature, see Allport (1955), Back and Solomos (2000), Berger and Luckmann (1966), Bergmann (1989), Better (2008), Bettio (2008), Bettio and Verashchagina (2008), Bonilla-Silva (2006), Duckitt (1992), Figart (2005), Greenwood (1984), Hellman (2008), Humphries (1995), Kennedy (2013), Montagu (1957), Myrdal (1944), Ore (2010), Piore (1970), Rose (1951), Rutherglen and Donohue (2009), Saenger (1953), Warnke (2007), and Wooley (1993). This section is based on Ore (2010).

3. For this literature, see Abdela, Drago, and Shulman (2004), Barker and Feiner (2004), Burrell (2010), Chakrabarty, Roberts and Preston (2013), Coates (2011), Crenshaw, Gotanda, Peller and Thomas (1995), Delgado (2012), Dugger (1996), Ehrlich (1973), Essed and Goldberg (2002), Feagin (2006), Feiner and Morgan (1987), Feiner and Roberts (1990), Frankfurt Institute for Social Research (1972), Held (1980), Johnson (2006), Ladson-Billings (2009), Lynn and Dixson (2013), Miles (2000), Mills (1997), Ore (2010), Parker and Lynn (2009), Saunders and Darity (2003), Sherman (1996), Sidanius and Pratto (2001), Stefancic and Delgado (2013), Taylor (2009), Taylor, Gillborn and Ladson-Billings (2009), Valdes, Culp and Harris (2002), Young (1990), and Zamudio, Russell, Rios and Bridgeman (2011). This section is based on Dugger (1996).

4. For this literature, see Aptheker (1948), Bonacich (1972, 1976), Bowles and Gintis (1947), Braverman (1974), Cox (2000), Edwards, Reich, and Gordon (1975), Edwards, Reich, and Weisskopf (1978), Fanon (2008), Foster and McChesney (2004), Gordon (1972), Gorz (1978), Humphries (1976), Longhi (2013), Marglin (1978), Reich (1978, 1981), Reich, Gordon, and Edwards (1973), Rose (1951), Smith, Collins, Hopkins, and Muhammad (1988), Sokoloff (1988), Stevenson (1988),

Wallerstein (2000), Wright (1978), and Wright, Costello, and Sprague (1982). This section is based on Reich, Gordon, and Edwards (1973).

REFERENCES

Abdela, Randy, Robert W. Drago, and Steven Shulman. 2004. *Unlevel Playing Fields: Understanding Wage Inequality and Discrimination.* Boston, MA: Economic Affairs Bureau, Inc.

Aguirre, Jr. Adalberto, and Jonathan H. Turner. 2010. *American Ethnicity: The Dynamics and Consequences of Discrimination.* New York, NY: McGraw-Hill.

Aigner, Dennis J., and Glen G. Cain. 1977. "Statistical Theories of Discrimination in Labor Markets." *Industrial and Labor Relations Review* 30(2): 175–187.

Allport, Gordon Willard. 1955. *The Nature of Prejudice.* Cambridge, MA: Addison-Wesley Publishing Company, Inc.

Altonji, Joseph G., and Rebecca M. Blank. 1999. "Race and Gender in the Labor Market." In *Handbook of Labor Economics,* Vol. 3C, edited by Orley Ashenfelter, and David Card, 3143–3259. Amsterdam, the Netherlands: Elsevier Science B.V.

Aptheker, Herbert. 1948. *The Negro People in America: A Critique of Gunnar Myrdal's an American Dilemma.* New York, NY: International Publishers.

Arrow, Kenneth J. 1973. "The Theory of Discrimination." In *Discrimination in Labor Markets*, Princeton, edited by Orley Ashenfelter, and Albert Rees, 3–33. Princeton, NJ: Princeton University Press.

Ayres, Ian. 1991. "Fair Driving: Gender and Race Discrimination in Retail Car Negotiations." *Harvard Law Review* 104(4): 817–872.

Ayres, Ian, and Peter Siegelman. 1995. "Gender and Race Discrimination in Bargaining for a New Car." *American Economic Review* 85(3): 304–321.

Back, Les, and John Solomos, eds. 2000. *Theories of Race and Racism: A Reader.* New York, NY: Routledge.

Barker, Drucilla K., and Susan F. Feiner. 2004. *Liberating Economics: Feminist Perspectives on Families, Work, and Globalization.* London, England: Routledge.

Becker, Gary Stanley. 1971. *The Economics of Discrimination.* Chicago, IL: University of Chicago Press.

Becker, Gary Stanley. 1976. *The Economic Approach to Human Behavior.* Chicago, IL: University of Chicago Press.

Becker, Gary Stanley. 1985. "Human Capital, Effort, and the Sexual Division of Labor." *Journal of Labor Economics* 3(S): 33–58.

Becker, Gary Stanley. 1995. "Discrimination, Economics." In *Gender and Economics*, edited by Jan Humphries, 385–387. Aldershot, Hants, England: Edward Elgar.

Benabou, Roland. 1996. "Equity and Efficiency in Human Capital Investment: The Local Connection." *Review of Economic Studies* 63(2): 237–264.

Berger, Peter L., and Thomas Luckmann. 1966. *The Social Construction of Reality: A Treatise in the Sociology of Knowledge.* New York, NY: Doubleday.

Bergmann, Barbara R. 1989. "Does the Market for Women's Labor Need Fixing?" *Journal of Economic Perspectives* 3(1): 43–60.

Bertrand, Marianne, Dolly Chugh, and Sendhil Mullainathan. 2005. "Implicit Discrimination." *American Economic Review* 95(2): 94–98.

Bertrand, Marianne, and Sendhil Mullainathan. 2004. "Are Emily and Greg More Employable than Lakisha and Jamal? A Field Experiment on Labor Market Discrimination." *American Economic Review* 94(4): 991–1013.

Better, Shirley. 2008. *Institutional Racism: A Primer on Theory and Strategies for Social Change.* New York, NY: Rowman and Littlefield Publishers, Inc.

Bettio, Francesca. 2008. "Occupational Segregation and Gender Wage Disparities in Developed Economies." In *Frontiers in the Economics of Gender*, edited by Francesca Bettio, and Alina Verashchagina, 167–191. New York, NY: Routledge.

Bettio, Francesca and Alina Verashchagina, eds. 2008. *Frontiers in the Economics of Gender.* New York, NY: Routledge.

Black, Dan A. 1995. "Discrimination in an Equilibrium Search Model." *Journal of Labor Economics* 13(2): 309–334.

Blau, Rrancine D., and Marianne A. Ferber. 1992. *The Economics of Women, Men, and Work,* 2nd edition. Englewood Cliffs, NJ: Prentice-Hall.

Blecker, Robert A. and Stephanie Seguino. 2007. "Macroeconomic Effects of Reducing Gender Wage Inequality in an Export-Oriented, Semi-Industrialized Economy." In *The Feminist Economics of Trade*, edited by Irene Van Staveren, Diane Elson, Caren Grown, and Nilufer Cagatay, 91–114. New York, NY: Routledge.

Bonacich, Edna. 1972. "A Theory of Ethnic Antagonism: The Split Labor Market." *American Sociological Review* 37: 547–549.

Bonacich, Edna. 1976. "Advanced Capitalism and Black-White Relations in the U.S.: A Split Labor Market Interpretations." *American Sociological Review* 41(1): 34–51.

Bonilla-Silva, Eduardo. 2006. *Racism without Racists: Color-Blind Racism and the Persistence of Racial Inequality in the United States.* Lanham, MD: Rowman and Littlefield Publishers, Inc.

Borjas, G.J., and S.G. Bronars. 1989. "Consumer Discrimination and Self-Employment." *Journal of Political Economy* 97(3): 581–606.

Bowles, Samuel, and Herbert Gintis. 1947. *Schooling in Capitalist America: Educational Reform and the Contradictions of Economic Life.* New York, NY: Basic Books, Inc., Publishers.

Braverman, Harry. 1974. *Labor and Monopoly Capital: The Degradation of Work in the Twentieth Century.* New York, NY: Monthly Review Press.

Burrell, Tom. 2010. *Brainwashed: Challenging the Myth of Black Inferiority.* New York, NY: Smiley Books.

Cain, Glen G. 1999. "The Economic Analysis of Labor Market Discrimination: A Survey." In *Handbook of Labor Economics,* Vol. 1, edited by Orley Ashenfelter, and David Card, 693–785. Amsterdam, the Netherlands: North-Holland.

Chakrabarty, Namita, Lorna Roberts, and John Preston, eds. 2013. *Critical Race Theory in England.* New York, NY: Routledge.

Coates, Rodney D., ed. 2011. *Covert Racism: Theories, Institutions, and Experiences.* Leiden, the Netherlands: Koninklijke Brill NV.

Cox, Oliver C. 2000. "Race Relations: Its Meaning, Beginning, and Progress." In *Theories of Race and Racism: A Reader*, edited by Les Back, and John Solomos, 71–78. New York, NY: Routledge.

Crenshaw, Kimberle, Neil Gotanda, Gary Peller, and Kendall Thomas, Kendall, eds. 1995. *Critical Race Theory: The Key Writings that Formed the Movement.* New York, NY: The New Press.

Crouch, Robert. 1979. *Human Behavior: An Economic Approach.* North Scituate, MA: Duxbury Press.

Delgado, Richard. 2012. *Critical Race Theory: An Introduction.* New York, NY: New York University Press.

Duckitt, John H. 1992. *The Social Psychology of Prejudice.* New York, NY: Praeger.

Dugger, William M. 1996. "Four Models of Inequality." In *Inequality: Radical Institutionalist Views on Race, Gender, Class, and Nation*, edited by William M. Dugger, 21–38. Westport, CT: Greenwood Press.

Edwards, Richard, Michael Reich, and David Gordon, eds. 1975. *Labor Market Segmentation.* Lexington, MA: D.C. Heath and Company.

Edwards, Richard, Michael Reich, and Thomas Weisskopf, eds. 1978. *The Capitalist System.* Englewood Cliffs, NJ: Prentice-Hall.

Ehrlich, Howard J. 1973. *Social Psychology of Prejudice: A Systematic Theoretical Review and Propositional Inventory of the American Social Psychological Study of Prejudice.* New York, NY: Wiley.

England, Paula. 1992. *Comparable Worth: Theories and Evidence.* New York, NY: Aldine de Gruyter.

Essed, Philomena, and David Theo Goldberg, eds. 2002. *Race Critical Theories: Text and Context.* Malden, MA: Blackwell Publishing, Ltd.

Fanon, Frantz. 2008. *Black Skin, White Masks.* New York, NY: Grove Press.

Feagin, Joe R. 2006. *Systemic Racism: A Theory of Oppression.* New York, NY: Routledge.

Feiner, Susan F., and Barbara A. Morgan. 1987. "Women and Minorities in Introductory Economics Textbooks: 1974 to 1979." *Journal of Economic Education* 18(4): 376–392.

Feiner, Susan F., and Bruce B. Roberts. "Hidden by the Invisible Hand: Neoclassical Economic Theory and the Textbook Treatment of Race and Gender." *Gender and Society* 4(2): 159–181.

Fershtman, Chaim, and Uri Gneezy. 2001. "Discrimination in a Segmented Society: An Experimental Approach." *Quarterly Journal of Economics* 106(1): 351–377.

Figart, Deborah M. 2005. "Gender as More Than a Dummy Variable: Feminist Approaches to Discrimination." *Review of Social Economy* 63(3): 509–536.

Foster, John Bellamy, and Robert W. McChesney. 2004. *Pox Americana: Exposing the American Empire.* New York, NY: Monthly Review Press.

Frankfurt Institute for Social Research. 1972. "Prejudice." In *Aspects of Sociology*, edited by Frankfurt Institute for Social Research, 169–181. Boston, MA: Beacon Press.

Friedman, Milton. 2002. *Capitalism and Freedom.* Chicago, IL: University of Chicago Press.

Fuchs, Victor R. 1986. "His and Hers: Gender Differences in Work and Income, 1959–1979." *Journal of Labor Economics* 4(3): 245–272.

Gordon, David M. 1972. *Theories of Poverty and Unemployment: Orthodox, Radical, and Dual Labor Market Perspectives.* Lexington, MA: Lexington Books.

Gorz, Andre, ed. 1978, *The Division of Labor: The Labor Process and Class Struggle in Modern Capitalism.* London, England: Harvestor Press.

Greenwood, Daphe. 1984. "The Institutional Inadequacy of the Market in Determining Comparable Worth: Implications for Value Theory." *Journal of Economic Issues* 18(2): 457–464.

Gronau, Reuben. 1988. "Sex-Related Wage Differentials and Women's Interrupted Labor Careers – The Chicken or the Egg." *Journal of Labor Economics* 6(3): 277–301.

Gunderson, Morley. 1989. "Male-Female Wage Differentials and Policy Responses." *Journal of Economics Literature* 27(1): 46–72.

Heckman, James J. 1998. "Detecting Discrimination." *Journal of Economic Perspectives* 12(2): 101–116.

Held, David. 1980. *Introduction to Critical Theory.* Berkeley, CA: University of California Press.

Hellman, Deborah. 2008. *When Is Discrimination Wrong?* Cambridge, MA: Harvard University Press.

Hoffman, Emily P., ed. 1991. *Essays on the Economics of Discrimination.* Kalamazoo, MI: W.E. Upjohn Institute for Employment Research.

Humphries, Jane. 1976. "Women: Scapegoats and Safety Valves in the Great Depression." *Review of Radical Economics* 8: 98–121.

Humphries, Jane. 1995. "Introduction." In *Gender and Economics*, edited by Jane Humphries, xiii–xxxix. Aldershot, England: Edward Elgar.

Johnson, Allan G. 2006. *Privilege, Power, and Difference.* New York, NY: McGraw-Hill.

Kahne, Hilda, and Andrew I. Kohen. 1975. "Economic Perspectives on the Roles of Women in the American Economy." *Journal of Economic Literature* 13(4): 1249–1292.

Kennedy, Randall. 2013. *For Discrimination: Race, Affirmative Action, and the Law.* New York, NY: Pantheon Books.

Ladson-Billings, Gloria. 2009. "Just What Is Critical Race Theory and What's It Doing in a Nice Field Like Education?" In *Foundations of Critical Race Theory in Education*, edited by Edward Taylor, David Gillborn, and Gloria Ladson-Billings, 17–36. New York, NY: Routledge.

Lang, Kevin. 2007. *Poverty and Discrimination.* Princeton, NJ: Princeton University Press.

Levy, Sheri R., and Julie Milligan Hughes. 2009. "Development of Racial and Ethnic Prejudice among Children." In *Handbook of Prejudice, Stereotyping, and Discrimination*, edited by Todd D. Nelson, 23–42. New York, NY: Psychology Press.

List, John A. 2004. "The Nature and Extent of Discrimination in the Marketplace: Evidence from the Field." *Quarterly Journal of Economics* 119(1): 49-89.

Longhi, Vittorio. 2013. *The Immigrant War: A Global Movement Against Discrimination and Exploitation.* Bristol, UK: Polity Press.

Loury, Glenn C. 1977. "A Dynamic Theory of Racial Income Differences" In *Women, Minorities and Employment Discrimination*, edited by P.A. Wallace, and A.M. Lamond. Lexington, MA: D.C. Heath and Co.

Loury, Glenn C. 1981. "Intergenerational Transfers and the Distribution of Earnings." *Econometrica* 49(4): 843–867.

Lundberg, Shelly, and Richard Startz. 1998. "On the Persistence of Racial Inequality." *Journal of Labor Economics* 16(2): 292–324.

Lynn, Marvin, and Adrienne D. Dixson, eds. 2013. *Handbook of Critical Race Theory in Education.* New York, NY: Routledge.

Marglin, Stephen A. 1978. "What Do Bosses Do?: The Origins and Functions of Hierarchy in Capitalist Production." In *The Division of Labor: The Labor Process and Class Struggle in Modern Capitalism*, edited by Andre Gorz, 13–54. London, England: Harvestor Press.

Marshall, F. Ray. 1974. "The Economics of Racial Discrimination: A Survey." *Journal of Economic Literature* 12: 849–871.

Medina, Carlos. 2010. *Essays in Economic Discrimination in the Labor Markets: Theory and Evidence.* New York, NY: Routledge.

Miles, Robert. 2000. "Apropos the Idea of 'Race' ... Again." In *Theories of Race and Racism: A Reader*, edited by Les Back, and John Solomos, 125–143. New York, NY: Routledge.

Mills, Charles W. 1997. *The Racial Contract.* Ithaca, NY: Cornell University Press.

Montagu, Ashley. 1957. *Anthropology and Human Nature.* Boston, MA: Porter Sargent Publishers.

Myrdal, Gunnar. 1944. *An American Dilemma.* New York, NY: Harpers.

Nederveen Pieterse, Jan P. 1989. *Empire and Emancipation: Power and Liberation on a World Scale.* New York, NY: Praeger.

Nelson, Todd D., ed. 2009. *Handbook of Prejudice, Stereotyping, and Discrimination.* New York, NY: Psychology Press.

Ore, Tracy E. 2010. *The Social Construction of Difference and Inequality: Race, Class, Gender, and Sexuality.* New York, NY: McGraw-Hill.

Parker, Laurence, and Marvin Lynn. 2009. "What's Race Got to Do with It?: Critical Race Theory's Conflict with and Connections to Qualitative Research Methodology and Epistemology." In *Foundations of Critical Race Theory in Education*, edited by Edward Taylor, David Gillborn, and Gloria Ladson-Billings, 148–160. New York, NY: Routledge.

Phelps, Edmund S. 1972. "The Statistical Theory of Racism and Sexism." *American Economic Review* 62(4): 659–661.

Piore, Michael J. 1970. "Jobs and Training." In *The State and the Poor*, edited by S.H. Beer, 198–219. Cambridge, MA: Winthrop Press.

Polachek, Solomon W. 1995. "Human Capital and the Gender Earnings Gap: A Response to Feminist Perspectives on Economics." In *Out of the Margin: Feminist Perspectives on Economics*, edited by Edith Kuiper, Jolande Sap, Susan Feiner, and Notburga Ott, 61–79. London, England: Rouledge.

Reagan, Barbara B. 1975. "Two Supply Curves for Economists? Implications of Mobility and Career Attachment for Women." *American Economics Review* 65(2): 100–107.

Reich, Michael. 1978. "Who Benefits from Racism?: The Distribution among Whites of Gains and Losses from Racial Inequality." *Journal of Human Resources*, 13(4): 524–544.

Reich, Michael. 1981. *Racial Inequality: A Political-Economic Analysis.* Princeton, NJ: Princeton University Press.

Reich, Michael, David M. Gordon, and Richard C. Edwards. 1973. "A Theory of Labor Market Segmentation." *American Economic Review* 63(2): 359–365.

Riach, Peter A., and Judy Rich. 2002. "Field Experiments of Discrimination in the Market Place." *Economic Journal* 112(483): 480–518.

Rodgers III, William M., ed. 2006. *Handbook on the Economics of Discrimination.* Cheltenham, England: Edward Elgar.

Rose, Arnold M. 1951. *The Roots of Prejudice.* Paris, France: UNESCO.

Rutherglen, George A., and John J. Donohue, III. 2009. *Employment Discrimination: Law and Theory.* New York, NY: West Group.

Saenger, Gerhart. 1953. *The Social Psychology of Prejudice: Achieving Intercultural Understanding and Cooperation in a Democracy.* New York, NY: Harper and Brothers Publishers.

Saunders, Lisa, and William Darity, Jr. 2003. "Feminist Theory and Racial Economic Inequality." In *Feminist Economics Today: Beyond Economic Man*, edited by Marianne A. Ferber, and Julie Nelson, 101–114. Chicago, IL: University of Chicago Press.

Schiller, Bradley R. 2012. *Economics of Poverty and Discrimination.* Englewood Cliffs, NJ: Prentice-Hall, Inc.

Sherman, Howard J. 1996. "A Holistic-Evolutionary View of Racism, Sexism, and Class Inequality." In *Inequality: Radical Institutionalist Views on Race, Gender, Class, and Nation*, edited by William M. Dugger, 39–52. Westport, CT: Greenwood Press.

Sidanius, Jim, and Felicia Pratto. 2001. *Social Dominance: An Intergroup Theory of Social Hierarchy and Oppression.* Cambridge, England: Cambridge University Press.

Smith, Joan, Jane Collins, Terence K. Hopkins, and Akbar Muhammad, eds. 1988. *Racism, Sexism, and the World-System.* Westport, CT: Greenwood Press.

Sokoloff, Natalie J. 1988. "Contributions of Marxism and Feminism to the Sociology of Women and Work." In *Women Working: Theories and Facts in Perspective*, edited by Ann Helton Stomberg, and Shirley Harkess, 116–131. Mountain View, CA: Mayfield Publishing Company.

Stangor, Charles. 2009. "The Study of Stereotyping, Prejudice, and Discrimination within Social Psychology: A Quick History of Theory and Practice." In *Handbook of Prejudice, Stereotyping, and Discrimination*, edited by Toss D. Nelson, 1–22. New York, NY: Psychology Press.

Stefancic, Jean, and Richard Delgado, eds. 2013. *Critical Race Theory: The Cutting Edge.* Philadelphia, PA: Temple University Press.

Stevenson, Mary Huff. 1988. "Some Economic Approaches to the Persistence of Wage Differences between Men and Women." In *Women Working: Theories and Facts in Perspective*, edited by Ann Helton Stomberg, and Shirley Harkess, 87–100. Mountain View, CA: Mayfield Publishing Company.

Taylor, Edward. 2009. "The Foundations of Critical Race Theory in Education: An Introduction." In *Foundations of Critical Race Theory in Education*, edited by Edward Taylor, David Gillborn, and Gloria Ladson-Billings, 1–13. New York, NY: Routledge.

Taylor, Edward, David Gillborn, and Gloria Ladson-Billings, eds. 2009. *Foundations of Critical Race Theory in Education*. New York, NY: Routledge.

Thurow, Lester C. 1969. *Poverty and Discrimination*. Washington, DC: Brookings Institution.

Thurow, Lester C. 1975. *Generating Inequality*. New York, NY: Basic Books.

Valdes, Francisco, Jerome McCristal Culp, and Angela P. Harris, eds. 2002. *Crossroads, Directions, and a New Critical Race Theory*. Philadelphia, PA: Temple University Press.

Wallerstein, Immanuel. 2000. "The Ideological Tensions of Capitalism: Universalism versus Racism and Sexism." In *The Essential Wallerstein*, edited by Immanuel Wallerstein, 344–353. New York, NY: New Press.

Warnke, Georgia. 2007. *After Identity: Rethinking Race, Sex, and Gender*. Cambridge, England: Cambridge University Press.

Williams, Walter E. 2011. *Race and Economics: How Much Can Be Blamed on Discrimination?* Stanford, CA: Hoover Institution.

Wolfson, Beth Anne, Carla M. Palumbo, J. Ralph Lindgren, and Nadine Taub. 2011. *The Law of Sex Discrimination*, Boston, MA: Wadsworth.

Wooley, Frances R. 1993. "The Feminist Challenge to Neoclassical Economics." *Cambridge Journal of Economics* 17: 485–500.

Wright, Erick Olin. 1978. "Race, Class and Income Inequality." *American Journal of Sociology* 83: 1368–1397.

Wright, Erik Olin, David Hachen Costello, and Joey Sprague. 1982. "The American Class Structure." *American Sociological Review* 47: 709–726.

Young, Iris Marion. 1990. *Justice and the Politics of Difference*. Princeton, NJ: Princeton University Press.

Zamudio, Margaret M., Christopher Russell, Francisco A. Rios, and Jacquelyn L. Bridgeman. 2011. *Critical Race Theory Matters: Education and Ideology*. New York, NY: Routledge.

Zarate, Michael A. 2009. "Racism in the 21st Century." In *Handbook of Prejudice, Stereotyping, and Discrimination*, edited by Todd D. Nelson, 387–406. New York, NY: Psychology Press.

Chapter 7

Feminist Economics

Four Paradigmatic Views

Any explanation of feminist economics is based on a worldview. The premise of this book is that any worldview can be associated with one of the four broad paradigms: functionalist, interpretive, radical humanist, and radical structuralist. This chapter takes the case of feminist economics and discusses it from the four different viewpoints. It emphasizes that the four views expressed are equally scientific and informative; they look at the phenomenon from their certain paradigmatic viewpoint; and together they provide a more balanced understanding of the phenomenon under consideration. In this chapter, the first four sections present the four perspectives, and the fifth section concludes the chapter.

FUNCTIONALIST VIEW

The functionalist feminist economics analysis of the relationship between women and knowledge is characterized by the aim of incorporating women into the existing neoclassical economics, both as research practitioners and as objects of study. It takes the incumbent neoclassical framework largely as given, and expands the domain of inquiry to include women in order to make neoclassical economics a more complete representation of the real world. Its intent is to enlarge the content rather than challenge the neoclassical paradigm. For this reason it has been referred to as the "add women and stir" strategy.[1]

The discussion of the work of functionalist feminist economists can be divided into the following three areas. The first area consists of the writings of feminist economists who document and explain the male domination of the profession of academic economics. The second area consists of the writings

177

of feminist economists who have helped to develop the neoclassical theory that has positioned women as economic actors in the same way as men. The third area consists of the writings of feminist economists who belong to the category of "feminist empiricism." These feminists criticize, on both theoretical and empirical grounds, the neoclassical modeling of women, that is, the "oversights" of male economists in their analyses of women's work. These criticisms lead to the development of new work within the neoclassical framework, rather than the rejection of that framework.

The absence of women from the economics discipline: Feminists directed one of their earliest critiques toward the Western knowledge production because women were excluded from the social environments and institutions of knowledge production. The research underlying this critique is referred to as "equity studies," and draws attention to discriminatory practices that lead to a very low number of women to attempt to enter a particular profession, but it does not necessarily highlight any biases within the knowledge itself. An equity study documents the quantity and forms of such discrimination against women. Feminist economists, in turn, have researched and documented the absence or under-representation of women in economic faculty positions, in economic journal publications, in histories of economic thought, and in economics textbook examples. They explain such low representations either as the result of women choosing not to join a profession that is tacitly hostile to their attributes and skills; or as the result of women being subjected to discriminatory practices inherent in the disciplinary employment selection procedures, the journal refereeing process, and the allocation of research funds. They note that, in the context of equal opportunity legislation, such discriminatory practices would have to be abandoned. Their policy recommendation, with respect to the under-representation of women in the profession, therefore, is to eliminate sexist practices and to encourage more women to enter the discipline.

An assumption, whether implicit or explicit, that underlies the explanation of the low representation of women in a discipline is that the male domination of a discipline incorporates bias in the content of that discipline's knowledge. This argument is based on the idea that women, but not men, look at issues and problems relevant to women. The under-representation of women skews choices of problems, the design of experiments, and the interpretation of data. Thus, the male domination of the discipline biases the context of discovery, and furthermore, it affects the context of justification, because the lack of diversity in a scientific community generates a sectarian interest and a limitation of vision. In other words, due to the under-representation of women, they lack numbers and influence, and they cannot properly challenge the prevailing arguments; and as a result better explanations are not advanced, and androcentric and ethnocentric theories are not eradicated. The male domination of knowledge production means that the discipline's notions of good and true as well as interesting are those which are chosen by men. Therefore, there are at least two reasons for examining the extent of the male domination in economics: (1) to satisfy equity considerations; and (2) to criticize the content of the discipline.

Feminist economists have documented the following observations. (1) The absence or under-representation of women within the ranks of economists. (2) Women are concentrated in the lower level academic positions. (3) Male authors cite other male authors in their journal articles. (4) Women disproportionately enter female-intensive specializations such as labor and population economics. (5) The intellectual contributions of women and feminists to economics have been invisible. (6) Discrimination has led to the exclusion of women from the economics profession. (7) Economists have failed to include women's roles in the economy in their courses. (8) Economics "classroom climate" is unfriendly to women. (9) The method by which economics is taught is discriminatory against women.

It must be noted that most contemporary feminist economists in their explanation of the androcentrism of neoclassical economics go beyond the issue of the under-representation of women economists, which is the least confronting of the tasks demanded by feminist economists critical of the discipline of economics. A more challenging critique, which is discussed next, is the absence or inadequate incorporation of women as objects of research in economics.

The inclusion of women as objects of knowledge: Feminist economists have documented the way in which women have been excluded as objects of investigation in neoclassical economics; and they have endeavored to correct this omission by incorporating women as objects of study in the neoclassical framework. Those scholars who have sought to incorporate women in neoclassical economics apply the principles of "feminist empiricism" and they are referred to as "feminist empiricists," who believe that androcentrism can be eliminated through the more rigorous and correct deployment of the scientific method in order to make neoclassical theories more representative of the real world. Their most important research areas are: the definition of economics as a discipline, the household human capital accumulation, discrimination, and the national accounting framework.

The formal definition of the domain of economics excluded women for a large part of the history of the discipline. This omission occurred in the nineteenth century with the definition of political economy as the study of any activity relating to the production or distribution of wealth, where wealth excluded the realm in which the majority of women's activities took place, such as the home, housework, reproduction, and childrearing. This exclusion of the private sphere from political economy was formally addressed in 1935, when political economy was redefined as the science which studies human behavior as a relationship between ends and scarce means which have alternative uses. This no longer excludes women or their activities from economic research. Indeed, post-war neoclassical economists, particularly University of Chicago economists, have developed theories that take both sexes into consideration.

The female labor supply decision was formally incorporated into the neoclassical framework as the result of a "puzzling contradiction" which emerged in the 1950s. On the one hand, cross-sectional data showed an inverse relationship between the participation rate of married women and the wage earnings of married men. On the other hand, time-series data showed a positive relationship between the participation rate of married women and family real income. This puzzle was resolved by arguing that married women choose between hours of paid work, leisure, and work in the home. An increase in the wages which married women could earn entices them to substitute market goods and services for home goods and services as well as leisure. This is because such an increase raises the opportunity cost of both leisure and home-produced goods and services. Empirically, the substitution effect outweighed the income effect of the wage increase. The emergence of this puzzle and its resolution encouraged neoclassical economists to study the labor supply decisions of females (particularly wives), as well as the education and training decisions of women, with due consideration of "family" variables such as marriage, husband's earnings, and children.

The private sphere decisions (including the labor supply decision) were formally incorporated into the neoclassical framework through the development of "new home economics." This research program is associated with Gary Becker, who formalized the role of women in the home by integrating labor-market economics and home economics into a unified theory of economic decision making. That is, in a multi-person household, the allocation of the time of any member is greatly influenced by the opportunities open to other members. If a member becomes more efficient at market activities, other members reallocate their activities in order to allow that person to spend more time at market activities. As a result of this research program, the respectability of the household as an object of economic analysis was significantly raised.

The new home economics developed at the time when the theory of the allocation of time was combined with human capital theory. In the new home economics, non-market decisions are formalized as utility-maximizing decisions. For instance, the decision to marry is theorized as the utility-maximizing choice of an individual; and the decision to have children is theorized as the utility-maximizing choices of a family. This second category has implications for the sexual division of labor. That is, the family seeks to maximize the utility of its altruistic head by producing market and home-produced goods and services. Because women are usually more efficient in doing housework, they specialize in housework, and similarly, men specialize in market work.

The analysis of the lower earnings of women relative to men was formally incorporated into the neoclassical framework at the time when the new home economics was being combined with the human capital theory. That is, female workers devote less time to investing in human capital, such as education and on-the-job training—because they take into account the period of time over which the benefits of such investments will be reaped, that is, their discontinuous labor-market participation, due in large part to their chosen role in the family—and hence earn lower wages. In this way, the individual optimization model offers an explanation of occupational segregation by sex. However, empirical work consistently showed that this model could not fully explain the difference between male and female earnings. In addition, this model left little role for discrimination, which appeared to be a salient reality of the operation of labor markets in the determination of women's wages.

The neoclassical theory of discrimination begun during the 1960s, but its focus was on racial discrimination. Its basic idea was that either employers, employees, or customers have a preference for associating with whites (men) rather than non-whites (women), that is, have a "taste" for discrimination, and require compensation. Discriminating employers pay lower wages to non-whites (women) than whites (men). Discriminatory workers require a wage premium for working with non-whites (women). Discriminatory customers require lower prices for coming into contact with non-white (women) workers, whom should therefore be paid lower wages. However, such wage and price differentials cannot persist in a competitive market. This is because discriminating employers will be driven out of the market, as nondiscriminating employers employ the non-white (women) workers at the lower wage. Similarly, wage premiums paid to discriminatory workers will be eliminated, as firms segment their workforces geographically instead of paying a wage premium. Finally, customer preferences will also lead to a segmented workforce, with both kinds of workers earning the same wage. Nevertheless, empirical evidence confirmed that discriminatory behavior, and its consequent wage differential, was not eliminated by market forces even in the long run.

In response to this empirical finding, neoclassical economists have provided the following variety of arguments. (1) Employers who begin with a white (male) workforce, who prefers not to mix with blacks (women), will not find it profitable to replace white (male) workers with non-white (women) workers because of the transaction costs associated with such change. (2) The theory of statistical discrimination implies that employers who believe that women are, on average, less productive than men (or have higher average turnover rates), and that it is costly to acquire information about the relative productivities of men and women, would rationally discriminate against women. (3) Variables that can explain the wage differential have been missing or have been mismeasured, even in the absence of discrimination. (4) Women's childcare and housework are so effort intensive that married women spend less effort on each hour of market work than married men, and as a result married women have lower hourly earnings than married men with the same market human capital.

National accounts do not include housework, even though housework has been viewed as an activity with economic relevance since the 1960s. In fact, one of the most frequently cited reasons for the exclusion of women as objects of economic research is the omission of unpaid work in the home from the national accounts, which are conventionally used as a measure of the value of the productive work of an economy. Feminist economists have documented the historical processes which led to the exclusion of housework from the national accounts in Australia and the United States. Feminist economists have also discussed the economic impact of such omission, as follows. (1) The value of national output is significantly underestimated when the value of goods and services produced in the household is excluded. (2) Accurate comparisons cannot be made between economies with different relative size of household and market sectors. (3) Measures of income distribution are distorted because the value of household production is different across households. (4) The tax system is distorted because taxes are levied on market income alone. (5) Homemakers are disadvantaged in divorce cases due to the failure in valuing their work. (6) Reliable estimates of home production are needed in cases of injury and life insurance. (7) Rational decision-making about the allocation of resources cannot be made, since the full costs and benefits of all production activities are unknown.

Feminist economists have not been completely satisfied with the way neoclassical economics has taken account of women as economic actors because it is founded on a set of faulty assumptions and misunderstood empirical relationships. The arguments of these feminist economists are taken up next.

Revisions to the modeling of women within neoclassical economics: Feminist economists have taken issue with the new home economics explanation of the sexual division of labor, which is based on the comparative advantage of biologically different sexes. Their three arguments are as follows. (1) There is a self-perpetuating circle in the explanation provided by the new home economics. More specifically, the sexual division of labor is taken as an exogenous variable in order to explain the wage differential between men and women, but the wage differential between men and women is taken as an exogenous variable in order to explain the sexual division of labor. (2) If men have a comparative advantage in some household tasks, it is inefficient for the woman to perform all household tasks. If home-work, home-produced goods, market work, and income yield diminishing marginal utility, both parties can increase their utility by undertaking both activities rather than one. (3) The sexual division of labor in the new home economics is based on the natural biological difference of sex, and thus, ignores the socialization of women into a particular role within the economy, and overlooks the benefits that accrue to men from the sexual division of labor.

There have been two theoretical developments within the neoclassical paradigm for the examination of conflict and distributional issues within the household, as follows. (1) The application of non-cooperative game theory to the family, models the household as two interdependent individuals maximizing their joint gain from the marriage, where the non-marital economic position acts as the threat point. Thus, household decisions become a function of relative economic bargaining power. Specialization of woman in house work is a less likely outcome in such models because it reduces woman's threat point due to her lack of labor market skills. (2) The transactions cost approach explains the economic activities of the family not in terms of production technology, but in terms of a governance structure, or long-term contractual relation, within which bargaining takes place. The family chooses only those activities which can be efficiently performed within the family governance structure.

Feminist economists have not found satisfactory neoclassical economists' explanation of women's voluntary under-investment in human capital which results in women's lower wages. They argue that a large part of wage differential can be explained by societal discrimination. For instance, the "psychic cost" for women in entering traditionally male fields of specialization. In addition, women are systematically excluded from specific occupations by men that result in an expanded supply of labor and lower wages in those occupations. Moreover, both employers and women employees have learned through the social system as to which occupations are appropriate for women. In short, a small amount of direct discrimination can result in a very large cumulative effect, and it is essential to consider both direct and indirect discrimination in explanations of earnings differentials.

INTERPRETIVE VIEW

Many feminist scholars in various disciplines have moved beyond a critique of their disciplines in terms of their content, that is, the "add women and stir" strategy, to a critique of their disciplinary frameworks from a specifically feminist perspective. They have examined the relationship between women and knowledge and have criticized the neoclassical economics by identifying androcentric bias within its core assumptions and its methodological procedures. These feminist economists believe that the problem is not what is said or what is not said about women, but rather, the problem is what can and cannot be said about women within the bounds of a particular philosophical school of thought. In other words, they believe that the fundamental feminist problem in economics is not that the experience of women is omitted from the disciplinary knowledge, but that the experience of women is distorted by that knowledge. Therefore, their main goal is not to merely expand the content of the disciplinary knowledge to include women, but to radically alter, or even displace, the disciplinary knowledge to eliminate its masculinist bias. They believe that the discipline's basic category, that is, the individual, together with its epistemology and methodology cannot capture the realities of women's lives. Whereas, an approach based on a feminist perspective can do much better in this respect, that is, can attain greater truth or realism.[2]

The feminist economists who pursue the above-discussed general orientation can be divided into the following three groups. (1) The first group of feminist economists argue that an expansion of the content of neoclassical economics needs to be done in conjunction with an examination of its categories of analysis——in particular, the category of rational economic man——which are based upon the assumption of the equivalence of man and humanity. These feminist economists advocate alternative theoretical frameworks, such as institutionalist economics. (2) The second group of feminist economists challenge the "add women and stir" strategy based on feminist research on scientific method and epistemology, in general, and feminist philosophy of science (i.e., feminist standpoint theory), in particular. (3) The third group of feminist economists show that, in neoclassical economics, masculinity operates as an implicit rhetorical tool, which supports and perpetuates the assumptions and methodology of neoclassical economics.

The feminist critique of core assumptions of neoclassical economics: This group of feminist economists argue that the core neoclassical assumptions are androcentric and result in the distorted representations of the realities of women's and men's lives. They contend that such assumptions have been accepted by economists because they justify the existing social construction of patriarchal gender relations. More specifically, they argue that the neoclassical assumptions, on the one hand, devalue both the contributions typically made by women, and the traits traditionally deemed appropriate for women. But, the neoclassical assumptions, on the other hand, valorize both the contributions usually made by men, and the traits normally associated with men. This is a distorted representation of reality because, on the one hand, it ignores the important role played by women in economic activity (especially in the private sphere); but on the other hand, hides the many advantages and sites of dominance bestowed on men. This group of feminist economists, therefore, endeavor to overcome the shortcomings of neoclassical assumptions by replacing neoclassical economics with an alternative framework, such as feminist institutionalism. It should be noted that the aim of this group of feminist economists is to counter the processes through which the vocations traditionally assigned to women have come to be seen as natural women's work. This group intends to counter such processes by revaluing women's socially assigned work in order to encourage both men and women to undertake such roles in equal proportions.

This group of feminist economists directs the majority of its criticisms toward those neoclassical assumptions that are related to the individual. In neoclassical economics, the basic unit of analysis is the individual, whom is known as "rational economic man" or "homo economicus," who maximizes his objective function subject to a set of constraints. This group of feminists deem the assumptions underpinning the neoclassical economic agent as androcentric because such an agent is a selfish, and radically separate individual, as well as divested of those traits and uninvolved in those activities which are traditionally associated with women. Consequently, such traits and activities are ignored and devalued within the neoclassical framework. As a result, neoclassical economics misrepresents reality.

This group of feminist economists has criticized the rational economic man along the following points.

1. The rational economic man is unable to make interpersonal utility comparisons. This came about as a result of the shift from a cardinal to an ordinal conception of utility, that is, the shift from a common measure of people's utilities to an individual's ranking of utility. This has had negative implications for women, because it does not allow interpersonal comparisons of wealth and income, that is, wealth and income distribution, and removes a theoretical basis for arguing that existing arrangements benefit the rich more than the poor, as well as, men more than women.

2. The rational economic man has exogenous and stable preferences. Neoclassical economics leaves the question of the formation of individual's preferences to sociobiologists and psychologists. Feminist economists argue that individual's preferences are endogenous and change over time. For instance, individual's preferences change as a result of their long-term involvement in the operation of labor, marriage, and other markets, through which gender inequality is perpetuated. It is very likely that women will develop preferences for occupations in which women have already dominated in response to labor-market discrimination. This means that markets have created gender-related preferences, which will perpetuate women's lower earnings. Therefore, countering indirect discrimination requires a change in preferences, which in turn requires a challenge to one of the core

assumptions of the neoclassical framework rather than a mere extension of that framework.

3. The rational economic man's utility function is independent of others' utility functions in the public sphere. Feminist economists argue that the assumption of selfishness in markets is not only a "male" model of self but also that it fit women less. Feminist economists argue further that the assumption of independent utility functions ignores men's, as well as women's, altruism. Male's altruism may work to the disadvantage of women. For instance, when male employees collude in order to protect their jobs from women, they are exhibiting within-sex altruism.

4. The rational economic man's utility function is interdependent in the non-market sphere. The neoclassical economics assumes that utility functions are interdependent in the home because the benevolent dictator, who works in the market, ensures that everyone acts in the best interest of the family. More specifically, the family maximizes the altruist's utility function subject to the family's budget constraint. Each family member maximizes the altruist's utility function in order to maximize their own utility, and, in this way, also behaves as an altruist toward the rest of the family. According to the neoclassical model, because of the male's comparative advantage in working in the market, the benefactor is a male. Feminist economists argue that although the new home economics relates the family to economics, nevertheless, it maintains the associations between women and the family, and men and the economy, which is to the detriment of women who are considered first as mothers and second as workers. In this way, neoclassical economists avoid considering the way in which the lives of women and men are culturally ordered.

Feminism and the scientific method: There are feminist economists who have challenged the methodology and epistemology which the neoclassical economists have used to derive their central theoretical relationships. A feminist philosophy of science known as feminist standpoint theory, is used as a foundation for such challenges. Feminist economists, on the basis of feminist standpoint theory, question the empiricist or positivist philosophies, which underlie neoclassical economists. They argue that the claim of neoclassical economists in establishing a value-neutral, objective knowledge is unwarranted because knowledge production is always influenced by social background, in general, and gender, in particular. They further explain that masculine and feminine researchers view and appraise "reality" from different perspectives or standpoints; and that, because the masculine perspective has dominated scientific activity for an extended period of time, neoclassical economics research reflects this masculine perspective. It is, therefore, worthwhile to delineate feminist standpoint theory as it applies to scientific research, in general, and as it applies to economic research, in particular.

Feminist standpoint theory plays a dominant role in the field of feminist philosophy of science. According to the standpoint theory, the scientific process is a social activity and, therefore, cannot provide a single, value-neutral, empirical truth. In other words, knowledge is socially situated, and, therefore, there is no Archimedean point, or "view from nowhere." This is an essential initial step in the standpoint program, because standpoint theorists show that the traditional scientific claims of objectivity and neutrality are erroneous. On this basis, standpoint theorists claim that science is gendered. Standpoint theory's emphasis on the idea that the course of scientific thought is not exclusively determined by its own logical and empirical necessities, paved the way for the idea that gender has an important place in the system of knowledge. Feminist standpoint theorists explain that social factors affect the scientific process in the context of both discovery and justification. More specifically, bias affects the process of discovery in various ways: (1) in the selection of research agendas and problems to be studied; (2) in the choice of theories to be considered as explanations; (3) in the choice of facts considered relevant; and (4) in the language used to describe and solve the problems. Furthermore, bias affects the justificatory process through the preconceptions formed in social contexts that shape and order the "facts" which are used to test hypotheses. Feminist standpoint theorists place emphasis on both steps of the scientific process especially the discovery step, because the discovery step has been traditionally deemed not to fall within the domain of the philosophy of science; and feminists' inclusion of the discovery step in the analysis allows for the explanation of bias which is introduced at this step and which cannot be eliminated at the justification step, which is itself biased. This inclusion is important because a philosophy of science that focuses solely on the logic of justification neglects the biases introduced during the selection processes in the context of the discovery step that limit what the research community can learn about.

Feminist standpoint theorists further argue that the biases brought about by these social influences are intrinsic to the scientific process and cannot be eliminated. Their argument is in sharp contrast to the argument of the feminist empiricists who state that masculine bias is an attribute of "bad science;" and can be eliminated by a more appropriate practice of the scientific methods, and a removal of the social influences that shape the identity of the researcher. Feminist standpoint theorists note that: (1) the scientific method does not provide any rules, procedures, or techniques for identifying, let alone eliminating, social influences that variously affect all, or almost all, of the researchers; and (2) the scientific method does not encourage diversity in the social beliefs of researchers in order to increase the effectiveness of the application of the scientific method. Feminist standpoint theorists, in contrast to feminist empiricists, seek to benefit from the identity of the scientist in the production of a more "objective knowledge," where "objectivity" does not refer to the Archimedean standpoint, or "view from nowhere," of the traditional scientific method. Feminist standpoint theorists consider the identity of the knower as important because individuals of different gender, race, and class occupy different positions within society, and their different positions shape their different visions of reality, from which, ultimately, a more objective knowledge can be obtained. Furthermore, individuals, whether men or women, are historically embodied; they are concrete persons, whose perspectives reflect who they are; therefore, in a society, women see and know differently from men. Moreover, the traditional practice of the scientific method has been dominated by a masculine standpoint, to the extent that there is a direct association between the scientific method and norms of masculinity, and non-science and norms of femininity. Consequently, not only there is a history of the lack of participation of women in the process of knowledge production—that is, women's limited access to universities and the practice of science—but also, there is a history of the lack of femininity from such processes. This exclusion of the values which are culturally associated with the female domain, has led to the "masculinization" of science—that is, to a congruence between scientific values and the ideals of masculinity prevailing in Western culture.

Feminist standpoint theorists want to reconceptualize objectivity and reconceive science such that they would no longer be distorted by masculine bias. They advocate a scientific practice in which the researcher transcends the dichotomies—such as the subject/object distinction, which have characterized the traditional scientific method—and unites the cognitive and affective domains. Feminist standpoint theorists note that whereas in masculine science the scientist, that is, the subject, seeks to stay totally separate from the object and to dominate that object, in the feminine approach to science the subject interacts or communicates with the object, and becomes a part of the system in which the object is located, and converses with nature. It is this "dynamic objectivity" that is in the pursuit of knowledge and makes use of subjective experience in order to make science more objective.

Feminist standpoint theorists intend to reformulate objectivity from "weak objectivity" to "strong objectivity." Weak objectivity refers to the scientific method's ill-fated attempt to produce value-neutral knowledge which is independent of the context of discovery. Strong objectivity, on the other hand, increases objectivity by identifying the cultural values and interests that differ among researchers and research communities. It actively searches for socially marginalized vantage points, not to discover uncontestable facts, but to enhance objectivity. Indeed, the consideration of various cultural values spurs scientific progress because it increases the likelihood that previously hidden values will be uncovered. The feminist standpoint theorists play an important role in this process, as the experience arising from the activities assigned to women are seen through feminist theory, provide an impetus to potentially more complete and less distorted knowledge claims than do only men's experiences. In this way, the standards of objectivity are enhanced by the feminist standpoint.

Feminism and rhetoric: This group of feminist economists, based on the "rhetoric of economics" argue that the gendered categories, assumptions, and relationships within neoclassical economics are persuasive to, and accepted by, male economists because they support their interests as men and husbands. They argue that the official, modernist methodologies which are claimed to establish economics as a science are very different from the actual, unofficial, daily methodological procedures which economists follow. The actual procedures which are employed by economists consists, among other things, of a set of rhetorical devices that persuade others to accept or reject particular economic theories. Such devices include: reference to historical precedent, illustration of mathematical expertise, argument by example, symmetry and philosophical consistency, and the use of metaphor, which is the most important device because every component in economic reasoning, including the reasoning of the official rhetoric, is metaphor. Feminist economists argue that the recognition and analysis of the unofficial rhetoric which is actually employed by economists would improve both the quality of the writing and teaching of economics; make economists more modest and tolerant; raise the status of economics among other disciplines and, therefore, enhance the degree of interaction between economics and such other disciplines; make economics more "scientific," or "better," by allowing a wider variety of evidence to be included in research; and encourage much more productive "conversations" among economists.

Feminist economists, more specifically, argue that economists persuade each other by developing a gender analysis of the official and unofficial methodologies of economics. They contend that scientists, in general, and neoclassical economists, in particular, argue by using not only fact and logic but also metaphor and story. This rhetorical "group of four," or tetrad, has been divided, by the philosophers of the modernist age, into two distinct sets: the methodological dyad of fact and logic, and the creative dyad of metaphor and story. Feminist economists continue with their argument using diagrams to represent the rigorous, axiomatic approach of the methodological dyad as a masculine square; and to represent the metaphoric, story approach of the creative dyad as a feminine circle. Feminist economists, then, criticize the scientific method and the neoclassical economics for confining the methodologies of the square and the circle to two separate spheres; and further argue that both the square and the circle are necessary for any adequate undertaking of scientific activity, that both shapes are integral to methodology as well as creativity, and that the active role of the circle in the "sciences" has been neglected. Metaphor may or may not be an alternative to fact, but the construction of facts requires metaphors. For instance, the metaphor of light as quanta, as opposed to waves, is essential for certain measurements in physics. From a feminist perspective, the square masculine approach has been valorized and promoted within economics, while the round feminine approach has been denigrated and "officially" excluded.

RADICAL HUMANIST VIEW

Socialist feminists are not only committed to understanding and changing the system of capitalism, they are also committed to understanding the system of power deriving from capitalist patriarchy. The phrase "capitalist patriarchy" is used to emphasize the mutually-reinforcing dialectical relationship between capitalist class structure and hierarchical sexual structure. Socialist feminists regard the understanding of the interdependence of capitalism and patriarchy to be of essential importance. Although patriarchy, that is, male supremacy, existed before capitalism, and will exist for some time in post-capitalist societies, it is necessary to understand their present relationship in order to be able to demolish the structure of oppression. In this way, socialist feminism holds a wider view than either radical feminist theory or orthodox Marxist analysis.[3]

Radical feminists and Marxist women deal with "power" in a dichotomous way. For the former, power is derived from one's sex; and for the latter, power is derived from one's economic class position. The critique of power rooted in sex, that is, the male/female distinction, focuses on patriarchy. The critique of power rooted in economic class position, that is, the bourgeoisie/proletariat distinction, focuses on capitalism. Radical feminists see the social relations of reproduction; and Marxist women see the social relations of production. Correspondingly, they see as oppressive either: domestic or wage labor; the private or public realms; the family or the economy; ideology or material conditions; the sexual division of labor or capitalist class relations. Socialist feminists believe that most women are implicated on both sides of these dichotomies, which is in contrast to the belief of radical feminists and Marxist women who treat "woman" as though she is implicated only on one side of such dichotomies. These dichotomous conceptual views of woman prevent a more comprehensive understanding of the complexity of her oppression. Such dichotomies obscure reality. Socialist feminists replace such dichotomous views with a dialectical one.

Socialist feminists synthesize radical feminism and Marxist analysis in the formulation of their cohesive political theory. They do not simply add together these two theories of power, but they view these two theories as interrelated through the sexual division of labor. They see capitalist patri-archy as the source of the problem and, therefore, they suggest socialist feminism as the solution to the problem. They use Marxist class analysis as the thesis, radical feminist patriarchal analysis as the antithesis, and their synthesis of the two would generate socialist feminism.

Thesis: Socialist feminists use Marxist class analysis as the thesis. They see a twofold importance in the Marxist analysis of the oppression of women. First, it provides a class analysis of power. Second, it provides a historical and dialectical method of analysis. Although the dialectical method is primarily used by Marxists to analyze class and class conflict, it can also be used to ana-lyze the patriarchal relations and, therefore, women's revolutionary potential. The dialectical and historical method can be used as a tool for understanding all power relations; and its use cannot be limited only to the understanding of class relations. Socialist feminists not only use Marxist analysis of class conflict, but they also use Marxist historical and dialectical method in their analysis of patriarchal relations. That is, they use the dialectical and historical method to expand the orthodox Marxism understanding of material relations in capitalism to material relations in capitalist patriarchy.

According to the orthodox Marxism, the class structure is economic at its base, and reflects in the social, political, and cultural forms of society. Society is divided into two classes: the bourgeoisie and the proletariat. The division of society into two classes and the consequent conflict between the two classes is based on the relation of each class to the modes of production. Such rela-tion results in proletariat's oppression and exploitation, that is, bourgeoisie extracts surplus value from proletariat's productive labor. Such oppression manifests itself as revolutionary class consciousness in society. This Marxist revolutionary ontology can be used as a crucial element in the development of a socialist feminist theory which not only incorporates a theory of class consciousness but also moves beyond it. For this purpose, it is necessary to note that under patriarchy, women are oppressed. Socialist feminists extend to women the revolutionary ontology of Marxism and point to the revolution-ary potential of not only men but also women.

In the discussion of the family in capitalist society, Marxists view family as an element of the superstructure that totally reflects the class society, and that relations of reproduction become subsumed under the relations of production. On the other hand, socialist feminists point out that not only family reflects society but also family structures society through its patriarchal structure, patriarchal ideology, and the need for reproduction. This reciprocal relation-ship—between society and family, production and reproduction—forms the life of women. Any adequate analysis of women's oppression must consider not only women's economic conditions but also women's sexual conditions.

The Marxists' historical materialist method must be extended to incorporate women's relations not only to society but also to the sexual division of labor; and consider women not only as producers but also as reproducers. In addition, there is a need to develop the ideological formulation of this relationship.

Antithesis: Socialist feminists use radical feminist patriarchal analysis as the antithesis. Radical feminists have a revolutionary aim at the destruction of patriarchy. They aim at a fundamental reorganization of: the biological family, the hierarchical sexual division of society, and sex roles. They believe that the sexual division of labor and society underlies the hierarchical division in society between masculine and feminine roles. They view it as the basic mechanism of control in patriarchal culture. Accordingly, it determines: roles, purposes, activity, and one's labor. It means that the biological distinction, male/female, specifies social functions and individual power.

Radical feminists have not only found the analysis of liberal feminists incomplete, but they have also found the politics and theories of Marxists insufficient. They believe that Marxists fail to understand that the structure of the economic class system has its origins in the sexual class system. They regard sexual, not economic, power to be central to any adequate revolutionary analysis. They are neither satisfied with the Marxist definition of power, nor with the equation between women's oppression and exploitation. They do not think that economic class is at the center of social life. They perceive history as patriarchal; and, correspondingly, they view historical struggles as struggles between the sexes. They draw battle lines between men and women, rather than between bourgeoisie and proletariat; and they emphasize that the determining relations are those of reproduction, not production.

Radical feminists define patriarchy as a sexual system of power in which the male possesses superior power and economic privilege. Patriarchy is the hierarchical ordering of society that privileges male. In the past, the legal-institutional base of patriarchy was more explicit; notwithstanding, still the basic relations of power remain intact. The patriarchal system is preserved through marriage and family, as well as the sexual division of labor and society. Patriarchy has its roots in biology, rather than in economics or history. More specifically, patriarchy has its roots in women's reproductive selves, and has its manifestation in the form of male force and control. The patriarchal organization of society, rather than the economic class structure of society, defines woman's position in the power hierarchy.

Radical feminists, through their analyses, bridge the dichotomy between the personal and the public. In their analyses, sex as a personal matter becomes a political matter. The sexual politics of society results in women sharing a common position of oppression. The structuring of society based on sexual division limits women's activities, work, desires, and aspirations. In such society, sex becomes a status category that has strong political implications.

Radical feminists' presentation of the idea of a sex class is in contrast to the Marxist meaning of economic class, which is defined in relation to the means of production. Women form a sex class; and man form the opposing sex class. This social division is used to articulate the dynamic of sexual power. Radical feminists reject the Marxists' economic theory of power; however, they artificially separate the sexual and the economic spheres, and substitute patriarchy for capitalism as the oppressive system. They fail to move further by synthesis because they consider sexuality as the key oppressive factor rather than to view oppression as a more complex phenomenon. Their dichotomous formulation of woman's situation limits their analysis, such that they cannot comprehensively deal with the complex mix of woman's existence. Thus, similar to Marxist analysis which is not extended to include women's oppression, radical feminists cannot fully understand the reality and the historical specificity of the economic existence.

Radical feminists regard patriarchy as a generalized ahistorical power structure. They fail to realize, for example, that although sex roles existed in feudal society they were different from those practiced in advanced capitalist society because their economic and sexual material life were different. As for another example, although nuclear family is experienced in both pre-capitalist and capitalist societies, it is actually experienced in different forms in different societies. It might be true that all history has been patriarchal, but it does not mean that the differences between historical periods are not important. Therefore, patriarchy should be understood not only as a biological system but also as a political system with a specific history. Instead of presenting a historical formulation of women's oppression, radical feminists present a biological determinism. Overall, neither Marxists nor radical feminists comprehensively deal with the interrelationships between ideas and real conditions. Since they segmented reality, their ideological representations of that reality became severed from that reality as well.

Synthesis: Existing power relationships are explained in Marxism in terms of economic class relations; and in radical feminism in terms of biological sex class relations. On the other hand, socialist feminism explains power in terms of not only its class origins but also its patriarchal roots. In such an analysis, current capitalism and patriarchy are mutually dependent. Of course, a more comprehensive explanation would also include the racial dimension of power and oppression.

Socialist feminists do not see oppression and exploitation as equivalent concepts. Exploitation is experienced by men and women in capitalist economic class relations; whereas oppression is experienced by women and minorities in patriarchal, racist, and capitalist relations. Exploitation is experienced by men and women by working in the labor force; whereas oppression is experienced by women not only by being exploited as a wage-laborer but also by being subjected to the patriarchal sexual hierarchy—as mother, domestic laborer, and consumer. Racial oppression is experienced by women through the racist division of society. Oppression includes exploitation, and reflects a more complex reality. Power—and its converse, that is, oppression—derives from sex, race, and class. Power is formed through both the material and ideological aspects of patriarchy, racism, and capitalism. Oppression reflects the hierarchical relations that are formed through the sexual and racial division of labor and society. In dealing with oppression, it is necessary to consider both the material existence (economic and sexual) and ideology. This is because the sexual division of labor and society, which underlies patriarchy, has two inter-related aspects: material (sex roles) and ideological (stereotypes, myths, and ideas which define these roles).

Socialist feminists primarily focus on the understanding of the mutual dependence of capitalism and patriarchy in the existing capitalist patriarchy. Historically, capitalist patriarchy began its development in the mid-eighteenth century in England and the mid-nineteenth century in America. During these periods, there was relationship developing between patriarchy and the new industrial capitalism. Capitalist patriarchy is a terminology chosen to overcome the dichotomies of: sex and class, private and public spheres, domestic and wage labor, family and economy, personal and political, and ideology and material conditions. For instance, the overthrow of the capitalist economy does not in themselves mean either the destruction of patriarchal institutions or the transformation of patriarchal ideology.

Socialist feminists agree with radical feminists that patriarchy precedes capitalism; however, they disagree with Marxists who believe that patriarchy arose with capitalism. Currently, patriarchy—that is, the power of the male obtained through sexual roles in capitalism—is institutionalized in the nuclear family. More specifically, patriarchy reflects the sexual ordering of society, and the sexual ordering is derived from the ideological and political interpretations of biological difference. That is, men have interpreted and politically used the fact that women are the reproducers of humanity. This fact in combination with men's political control of it has turned the relations of reproduction into a particular formulation of woman's oppression. Over time, a patriarchal culture is carried over from one historical period to another and has maintained the sexual hierarchy of society. Material conditions generate necessary ideologies, and ideologies, in turn, impact reality and alter reality. There is a reciprocal relationship: women are products of their social history; and, at the same time, women can shape their own society and their own lives as well.

The sexual division of labor and society forms the context within which patriarchy and capitalism operate. It is at the base of patriarchy and capitalism. It defines, according to biological sex, people's activities, purposes, goals, desires, and dreams. It provides men and women with their respective hierarchical sex roles, and structures their related duties within the domain of family and the economy.

The mutual dependence of patriarchy and capitalism not only implies the malleability of patriarchy to the needs of capital but also implies the malleability of capital to the needs of patriarchy. Capitalism needs patriarchy in order to operate efficiently. This is because male supremacy, as a system of sexual hierarchy, provides the necessary order and control to capitalism (and the systems before it). Capitalism, in turn, protects the patriarchal system because it is necessary for the smooth functioning of the society and the economic system. More specifically, the system of male supremacy underlies the prevailing system of cultural, social, economic, and political control. Since profit-making and societal control are inextricably connected (but cannot be reduced to each other), patriarchy and capitalism form an integrated process, such that specific components of each system are necessitated by the other.

Although this sexual division of labor and society precedes capitalism, it has been specifically defined in terms of the nuclear family, and it has been increasingly institutionalized in order to meet the needs of advanced capitalism. It is now much more sophisticated than what it was in pre-capitalist societies. In a pre-capitalist society, men, women, and children worked together in the home, in the farm, or on the land in order to produce the goods necessary for their survival. Although women were procreators and child-rearers, the organization of work limited the impact of different sexual roles. With the advent of industrial capitalism, men had to leave home and join the wage-labor economy. Women had to stay home and were viewed as nonproductive, although many worked in the factories. They were seen solely in terms of their sex roles. Although, before industrial capitalism, women were mothers, this role was not regarded as an exclusive role. However, in industrial capitalism, women became housewives. The housewife and the proletariat emerged as two characteristic laborers of developed capitalist society. The work that women continued to perform in the home was no longer regarded as work. Productive labor was only considered as wage labor, and it is the labor who produces surplus value.

As it is noted, the conditions of production in society define and shape production, reproduction, and consumption in the family. Conversely, the family mode of production, reproduction, and consumption affects commodity production in society. Their interrelationships define the political economy. In a capitalist patriarchal economy, profit is the basic priority of the ruling class, which requires a system of political order and control. The sexual division of labor and society serves this specific purpose. It stabilizes the society through the family. Furthermore, it organizes a realm of work, for which there is no pay (domestic labor of housewives), limited pay (paid house-workers), or unequal pay (in the paid labor force). This last category shows how women are treated under the sexual division of labor in a class-divided society.

The ruling class protects and preserves the institution of family because family is based on a division of labor that not only secures the ruling class the greatest profit but also hierarchically orders the society culturally and politically. To counter this setting, it is necessary to challenge the sexual division of labor, particularly because of its connection to the capitalist order. It challenges one of the basic forms of work organization—with especial effect on the home, and wide ramifications for the entire society. This challenge endangers the free labor pool, and the cheap labor pool, as well as the sexual hierarchy, which is the fundamental social and political organization of the society.

RADICAL STRUCTURALIST VIEW

Marx, Engels, and their immediate followers contributed more to the understanding of the oppression of women than most participants in the modern women's movement recognize. This is important at a time when the relation between women's struggles and social transformation, which is both practical and theoretical, once again appears as a pressing matter on the revolutionary agenda. A theoretical problem of fundamental significance is the reproduction of labor power in the context of overall social reproduction. Indeed, Marx in his analysis of "social reproduction" has provided the rudiments of a usable approach to this problem. In the following discussion, a theoretical framework is discussed that situates the phenomenon of women's oppression in terms of social reproduction.[4]

Women's oppression is a highly individual and subjective experience, and it has been expressed in elaborate descriptive terms that emphasize issues such as sexuality, interpersonal relations, and ideology. Consequently, the women's liberation movement has placed great emphasis on the experiential aspects of oppression in marriage and in sexual relationships, as well as in the ideology of femininity and male dominance. Furthermore, the women's liberation movement has established "sexual politics" as a central area of struggle; and in doing so it has succeeded in bringing to the fore the privatized relationships. Indeed, the politicization of personal life is a major achievement of feminist activity. However, such analyses are not enough, because they ignore the ways in which private oppression is related to broader questions of relations of production and the class structure. In the following discussion, the emphasis will be placed on this latter question, that is, on the economic, or material, aspect of women's situation. It starts with a theoretical perspective on social reproduction, but the ultimate goal is to deal with the twin problems of women's oppression and the conditions for women's liberation.

To analyze women's oppression in the context of social reproduction and the reproduction of labor power, several concepts need to be explained. The first concept is "labor power," which is something latent in all persons, or more specifically, labor-power or capacity for labor is the aggregate of those mental and physical capabilities existing in a human being, which he exercises whenever he produces a use-value of some kind. A "use-value," which is "a useful thing," or more specifically, a use value is something that has properties which satisfy some of the human wants. Use-values, and the useful labor that go into their production, exist in every society, but their specific social form varies. The labor that creates the use-value is useful labor, it is a necessary condition for the existence of the human race, and it exists independently of the form of society. Consequently, labor power, which is the capacity for useful labor, is also independent of the social phase of human existence, that is, it is common to every form of human society.

Labor power is a dormant capacity which human beings have. The potentiality of labor power becomes realized when labor power is put to use, that is, consumed, in a labor process. When the bearer of labor power enters the labor process, the bearer of labor power contributes labor, that is, labor-power in use is labor itself. Labor power needs to be distinguished from the bodily and social existence of its bearer.

Labor processes do not exist by themselves. They are components of specific modes of production. Furthermore, any production involves reproduction. A society that decides to cease production, it needs to cease consumption. With this holistic view, where its components are connected, and noting the incessant renewal, every social process of production is, at the same time, a process of social reproduction. Social reproduction, in turn, entails the reproduction of the conditions of production. For instance, in feudal society, the serf produced enough to not only reproduce his conditions of labor but also his subsistence. This relationship holds true under all modes of production. This is because such relationship is not the result of their specific form, but it is a general requirement of all continuous and reproductive labor. It is a requirement of any continuing production, which is always simultaneously reproduction, that is, reproduction of its own operating conditions. Social reproduction requires, among other things, that a supply of labor power always be available to enter into the labor process.

The bearers of labor power, however, do not work indefinitely. Those who work are subject to wear and tear. Some of them are too young to participate in the labor process, and some others too old to participate in the labor process. Eventually, every person dies. Therefore, a requirement of social reproduction is not only some process that meets the ongoing personal needs of the bearers of labor power as human beings but also some process that replaces workers who have died or withdrawn from the active workforce. These processes of maintenance and replacement are often imprecisely, if usefully, conflated and called the "reproduction of labor power."

Although from a linguistic point of view, the terms production and reproduction are similar; from a theoretical point of view, the processes that make up society's production, and those that form the reproduction of labor power are not comparable. Reproduction of labor power is a condition of production, because it replaces the labor power which is necessary for production. However, reproduction of labor power is not a form of production. This is because, it does not necessarily involve specific raw materials and means of production which are combined in a labor process whose product is labor power. Of course, under special circumstances, the reproduction of labor power becomes a production process which takes place in family households, but such activities represent only one possible mode of renewing the bearers of labor power. Indeed, the workers can be maintained and the workforce can be replenished through: labor camps, dormitory facilities, immigration, enslavement, as well as generational replacement of existing workers.

So far, in the discussion, it has not been necessary to specify the gender of direct producers. However, it becomes necessary when the discussion includes the phenomenon of generational replacement of bearers of labor power, that is, replacement of existing workers by new workers from the next generation. This is because for generational replacement it becomes necessary for biological reproduction to take place, in which women and men are different. Therefore, the biological distinction between women and men with respect to childbearing appears at the level of total social reproduction.

In a class-divided society, the reproduction of labor power plays a special role. Class relations are founded on the appropriation of surplus labor, that is, exploitation. In a class society, the ruling class appropriates surplus labor which is performed by an exploited class of direct producers. More specifically, labor power refers to the capacity of direct producers to perform the surplus labor which the ruling class appropriates. The bearers of labor power constitute the exploited class. For a class society, the reproduction of labor power means, strictly speaking, the maintenance and renewal of the class of bearers of labor power, whom are subject to exploitation. In contrast, the maintenance and replacement of the individuals who make up the ruling class cannot be considered part of the reproduction of labor power in society. This is because, by definition, in a class society, labor power is borne only by members of the class of direct producers.

Marx contrasts the "necessary labor" with the "surplus labor" which are performed by direct producers in a class society. Marx defines both kinds of labor in terms of the time expended by a single producer during one working day. Necessary labor is that portion of the day's work that enables the producer to achieve his own reproduction. The remainder of the day's work is surplus labor, which is appropriated by the exploiting class. In reality, a portion of the direct producer's necessary labor may be allocated to the reproduction of the other members of the exploited class, for example, children, the elderly, or a wife of a direct producer may not enter into surplus production as direct producers, and therefore, a certain amount of labor time must be allocated to their maintenance. Necessary labor also includes a certain amount of supplementary labor which must be performed in order that the necessaries can be consumed in appropriate form; for example, firewood must be chopped, meals must be cooked, garden plots must be tended, clothes must be repaired, and so on. Necessary labor also includes an important series of labor processes associated with the generational replacement of labor power, that is, the bearing and raising of the children of the subordinate class.

This last component of necessary labor, that is, the generational replacement of labor power, requires a sex division of labor. That is, women carry and deliver children. In the context of the generational replacement of labor power, women belonging to the subordinate class play this special role. Even if women are direct producers, it is their differential role in the reproduction of labor power that underlies their oppression in class society.

This argument is based on the relationship between childbearing and the appropriation of surplus labor in class society. Childbearing by a woman in the subordinate class can reduce her contribution as a direct producer and as a participant in necessary labor. This is because pregnancy and lactation are associated with, at least, several months of lower capacity to work. Even when a woman is participating in surplus production, childbearing interferes with the appropriation of surplus labor by the ruling class. In addition, pregnancy and lactation lessen a woman's capacity in that portion of labor which is ordinarily required for the maintenance of labor power. From the short-term point of view of the ruling class, childbearing involves a costly decline in the mother's capacity to work, if she is maintained during the period of diminished contribution. This is because, some of the necessary labor that provides for her during that time could have formed part of the surplus labor which would have been appropriated by the ruling class. In other words, necessary labor has to increase in order to cover her maintenance during the childbearing period, which implies a corresponding decrease in surplus labor. At the same time, from the long-term point of view of the ruling class, childbearing is beneficial to the ruling class, because it is necessary to replenish the labor force through generational replacement. Overall, from the point of view of the dominant class, there is therefore, a contradiction between its short-term need to appropriate surplus labor, and its long-term requirement for the existence of a class to perform it. To resolve the contradiction, the ruling class attempts to minimize necessary labor over the long term while ensuring the reproduction of labor power. The extent to which the ruling class succeeds in implementing such strategies is, of course, dependent on the extent of the class struggle.

The resolution of this contradiction involves taking advantage of relationships between women and men which are based on sexuality and kinship. Men of the subordinate class, historically have had the responsibility, with respect to the generational replacement of labor, for making sure that the woman is provided for during the period of diminished activity associated with childbearing. The differential roles for women and men in the reproduction of labor power are of finite duration, that is, only during the woman's childbearing months. This division of labor reflects a wider historical division of labor, according to which women have had greater responsibility for the ongoing tasks associated with necessary labor, and especially for work related to children; and men, correspondingly, have had greater responsibility for the provision of material means of subsistence, a responsibility which is accompanied by their disproportionately greater involvement in the performance of surplus labor.

The exact arrangement through which men obtain more means of subsistence than they need for their own individual consumption varies from society to society. The arrangement, however, is ordinarily legitimated by men's domination of women, and reinforced by structures of female oppression. The ruling class, in its attempt to ensure the reproduction of labor power, and to minimize the amount of necessary labor, encourages male supremacy in the exploited class.

It is important to note that men's provision of means of subsistence to women during the childbearing period, and not the sex division of labor in itself, forms the material basis for women's subordination in class society. The sex division of labor, in the reproduction of labor power, during pregnancy and lactation, and often long thereafter, does not in itself constitute a source of oppression. This is because divisions of labor prevail in all societies. For instance, even in the most egalitarian hunting and gathering society, a variety of daily tasks is accomplished through divisions of labor. At the same time, differences among people, arising from biological and social development, prevail in all societies. That is, individuals may be: mentally retarded or physically handicapped; heterosexual or homosexual; single or married; and men or women, with the capacity to bear children. The social significance of divisions of labor, and of individual differences, is determined in the context of the actual society in which they are embedded. In class societies, women's childbearing capacity creates contradictions for the dominant class's need to appropriate surplus labor. The oppression of women in the exploited class emanates from the process of the class struggle with respect to the resolution of these contradictions.

In the ruling class, women may be subordinated to their men. The existence of such subordination ultimately rests on women's special role with respect to the generational replacement of individual members of the ruling class. What is of prime importance to the ruling class is property. If property comes to be held by men, and it is to be inherited by children, female oppression paves the way to the paternity of those children.

The working-class family can now be situated in the context of capitalist social reproduction. The working-class family is a kin-based unit for the reproduction of labor power. Similarly to most other units for domestic labor in capitalist society, it is isolated from the social sphere of wage labor. The working-class family commonly appears as a household, or a series of households, linked by networks of mutual obligation. In most capitalist societies, the major responsibility for working-class family households is the maintenance and renewal of the bearers of labor power.

In the working-class family household, the performance of the domestic component of necessary labor forms its material pivot. Historically, this task has been primarily performed by women, in a context which has usually been characterized by male supremacy, and therefore, the working-class family has acted as a repository of women's oppression. Women, in the private household, act as domestic laborers, and devote much of their time to performing unpaid services for wage-earning men. This situation can give rise to antagonistic relationships between the sexes. In addition, women's political and social inequality in comparison with men, and their struggle to acquire equal rights with men, constitute another source of conflict between the sexes. This chronic tension and women's oppression may appear to be rooted in the sex division of labor within the family. However, women's responsibility for the domestic labor necessary for capitalist social reproduction—but, not the sex division of labor within the family per se—is the underlying cause of not only the perpetuation of women's oppression but also their inequality in capitalist society.

Commonly, the experience of the working-class family reflects the contradictory role that exists in capitalist social reproduction of domestic labor and the reproduction of labor power. On the one hand, family life, which is characterized by male supremacy and women's oppression, produces tensions and conflict that further fragment an already divided working class. On the other hand, families are important supportive units in working-class communities that offer meaning and warmth to their members, and provide a base for opposition to the capitalist class who attempts to enforce or extend its economic, political, or ideological domination. In other words, the family is neither a united front of defense and solidarity for the working class, nor a site full of internal struggle and male domination that it must be abolished. Instead, working-class families are carriers of elements of both support and conflict, and are bound together in a dynamic system, which is not fixed. Indeed, many case studies in the nineteenth- and twentieth-century social history demonstrate the vital and contradictory role of the working-class family: a haven for its members against the onslaughts of capitalist accumulation, and at the same time a condensed site of patriarchal relations.

Since the late twentieth century, the success of working-class and popular struggles has become increasingly dependent on the inclusion of women as well as men in their mobilization. Male chauvinism and women's oppression in working-class families are severe obstacles in achieving socialist goals. A socialist movement should avoid uncritical support of existing forms of working-class family life, and should also avoid perfunctorily addressing the problem of female subordination; otherwise, the socialist movement alienates more than half its activists and allies. Conversely, popular social movements that vigorously confront male chauvinism, and oppose women's oppression would be laying the groundwork for a future society in which the real social equality of women and men can be built.

CONCLUSION

This chapter briefly discussed four views expressed with respect to feminist economics. The functionalist feminist economics incorporates women into the existing neoclassical economics, both as research practitioners and as objects of study. The interpretive feminist economics believes that the main goal is not to merely expand the content of the disciplinary knowledge to include women, but to radically alter, or even displace, the disciplinary knowledge to eliminate its masculinist bias. The radical humanist feminist economics is not only committed to understanding and changing the system of capitalism, it is also committed to understanding the system of power deriving from capitalist patriarchy. The radical structuralist feminist economics believes that the emphasis should be placed on the economic, or material, aspect of women's situation, but the ultimate goal should be to deal with the twin problems of women's oppression and the conditions for women's liberation.

Each paradigm is logically coherent—in terms of its underlying assumptions—and conceptualizes and studies the phenomenon in a certain way, and generates distinctive kinds of insight and understanding. Therefore, different paradigms in combination provide a broader understanding of the phenomenon under consideration. An understanding of different paradigms leads to a better understanding of the multifaceted nature of the phenomenon.

NOTES

1. For this literature, see Abdela (1995), Arrow (1972), Bahr (1980), Becker (1965, 1973, 1974, 1981, 1981, 1985), Blau (1987), Blecker and Seguino (2007), Cigno (1991), Darity (2007), Eisner (1988), Friedman (1953), Fuchs (1988, 1989), Goldschmidt-Clermont (1990), Gronau (1977), Hewitson (1999), Hirschfeld, Moore, and Brown (1995), Lundberg and Pollack (1996), McCrate (1988), Nussbaum and Glover (2001), Paludi and Strayer (1985), Pollak (1985), Robbins (1937), Sandler (1994), Schultz (1974), Seiz (1992), Thornton (1994), and Wolf (2013). This section is based on Hewitson (1999).

2. For this literature, see Beneria (2007), Bettio and Verashchagina (2008), Blau, Ferber, and Winkler (1986), Bordo (1986, 1987), Dolfsma and Hoppe (2003), England (1989, 1992, 1993), England and Farkas (1986), Fee (1983, 1986), Ferber and Nelson (1993a, b, 2003), Feyerabend (1976), Folbre, and Bittman (2004), Gergen (1985), Grapard (1996), Harding (1986, 1995), Hewitson (1999), Horwitz (1995), Humphries (1995), Hyman (1994a, b), Jennings (1993), Jennings and Waller (1990), Karamessini and Rubery (2014), Keller (1985), Kessler-Harris (2001), Kuhn (1962), Kuiper, Sap, Feiner, Ott, and Tzannatos (1995), Longino (1990), McCloskey (1983, 1994, 1998), Merchant (1980), Nelson (1992, 1993a, b, 1995, 1996, 2001, 2010), Nicholson (1986), Pujol (1995), Rosaldo (1980), Seiz (1995), Stewart (1992), Strassmann (1994), Tilly and Scott (1978), Veblen (1904), Waller and Jennings (1990), and Wooley (1993). This section is based on Hewitson (1999).

3. For this literature, see Alcoff (1988), Amariglio (1988), Amariglio, Callari, Resnick, Ruccio, and Wolff (1996), Barker (2004), Barker and Feiner (2004), Beasley (1994), Bebel (1904), Beneria (2003), Benhabib and Cornell (1987), Blum (1991), Bowden and Mummery (2009), Brown (1994), Butler and Weed (2011), De Beauvoir (1952), Diamond and Quinby (1988), Ehrenreich (1984), Eisenstein (1979), Eisenstein (1993), Elliot (1991), England (1992), Ferguson (1989), Ferguson and Folbre (1981), Folbre (1993, 2009), Gatens (1991), Gibson-Graham (2006), Gilman (1998), Gottlieb (1989), Greer (1970), Gunewardena and Kingsolver (2007), Harding (1991), Hartsock (1979), Hartsock (1985), Hewitson (1999), Hewitt (2010), Jacoby (1976), Johnson (2007), MacKinnon (1982), Marcuse (1974), Martin (2003), Matthaei (1992), McRobbie (2009), Mohanty (2003), Morgan (1976), Morgan (1977), Narayan (1997), Nicholson (1990), Oliver and Walsh (2004), Peterson (1997), Poovey (1988), Quick (1977), Redstockings (1975), Rosetti (1992), Sargent (1981), Schonpflug (2008), Scott (1988), Taylor (1983), Walker (1995), Waring (1988), and Wing and Davis (2000). This section is based on Eisenstein (1979b).

4. For this literature, see Atkinson (1974), Bebel (1904), Delmar (1976), Delphy (1977, 1984), Donovan (2006), Draper (1970), Engels (1948), Ferguson and Folbre (1981), Firestone (1970), Griffin (1978), Hartmann (1981), Kuhn and Wolpe (1978), Marx, Engels, Lenin, and Stalin (1951), Phillips (1987), Sacks (1974), Sargent (1981), Slaughter and Kern (1981), Storkey (1985), Wallerstein (2000), and Zetkin (1934). This section is based on Vogel (1983, 2014).

REFERENCES

Abdela, Randy. 1995. "The Impact of Feminism in Economics—Beyond the Pale? A Discussion and Survey Results." *Journal of Economic Education* 26(3): 253–273.

Alcoff, Linda Martin. 1988. "Cultural Feminism versus Post-Structuralism: The Identity Crisis in Feminist Theory." *Signs* 13: 405–436.

Amariglio, Jack L. 1988. "The Body, Economic Discourse, and Power: An Economist's Introduction to Foucault." *History of Political Economy* 20(4): 583–613.

Amariglio, Jack, Antonio Callari, Stephen Resnick, David Ruccio, and Richard D. Wolff. 1996. "Nondeterminist Marxism: The Birth of a Postmodern Tradition in Economics." In *Beyond Neoclassical Economics: Heterodox Approaches to Economic Theory*, edited by Fred E. Foldvary, 134–147. Cheltenham, England: Edward Elgar.

Arrow, Kenneth J. 1972. "Models of Job Discrimination." In *Race Discrimination in Economic Life*, edited by A.H. Pascal, 83–102. Lexington, MA: D.C. Heath.

Atkinson, Ti-Grace. 1974. *Amazon Odyssey.* New York, NY: Links Books.

Bahr, Stephen J., ed. 1980, *Economics and the Family.* Lexington, MA: Lexington Books.

Barker, Drucilla K. 2004. "From Feminist Empiricism to Feminist Poststructuralism: Philosophical Questions in Feminist Economics." In *The Elgar Companion to Economics and Philosophy*, edited by John B. Davis, Alain Marciano, and Jochen Runde, 213–230. Cheltenham, England: Edward Elgar.

Barker, Drucilla K., and Susan F. Feiner. 2004. *Liberating Economics: Feminist Perspectives on Families, Work, and Globalization.* London, England: Routledge.

Beasley, Chris. 1994. *Sexual Economyths: Conceiving a Feminist Economics.* New York, NY: St. Martin's Press.

Bebel, August. 1904. *Woman under Socialism.* New York, NY: Source Book Press.

Becker, Gary Stanley. 1965. "A Theory of the Allocation of Time." *Economic Journal* 75: 493–517.

Becker, Gary Stanley. 1973. "A Theory of Marriage: Part I." *Journal of Political Economy* 81(4): 13–846.

Becker, Gary Stanley. 1974. "A Theory of Marriage: Part II." *Journal of Political Economy*, 82(2): 1063–1093.

Becker, Gary Stanley. 1981a. *A Treatise on the Family.* Cambridge, MA: Harvard University Press.

Becker, Gary Stanley. 1981b. "Altruism in the Family and Selfishness in the Market Place." *Economica* 48(189): 1–15.

Becker, Gary Stanley. 1985. "Human Capital, Effort, and the Sexual Division of Labor." *Journal of Labor Economics* 3(S): 33–58.

Beneria, Lourdes. 2003. *Gender, Development, and Globalization: Economics as if All People Mattered.* New York, NY: Routledge.

Beneria, Lourdes. 2007. "Gender and the Social Construction of Markets." In *The Feminist Economics of Trade*, edited by Irene Van Staveren, Diane Elson, Caren Grown, and Nilufer Cagatay, 13–32. New York, NY: Routledge.

Benhabib, Seyla and Drucilla Cornell, eds. 1987. *Feminism as Critique: On the Politics of Gender.* Minneapolis, MN: University of Minnesota Press.

Bettio, Francesca and Aline Verashchagina, eds. 2008. *Frontiers in the Economics of Gender.* New York, NY: Routledge.

Blau, Francine D. 1987. "Gender." In *The New Palgrave: A Dictionary of Economics*, Vol. 2, edited by John Eatwell, Murray Milgate, and Peter Newman, Peter, 492–498. New York, NY: Stockton.

Blau, Francine D., Marianne A. Ferber, and Anne E. Winkler. 1986. *The Economics of Women, Men, and Work.* Englewood Cliffs, NJ: Prentice Hall.

Blecker, Robert A. and Stephanie Seguino. 2007. "Macroeconomic Effects of Reducing Gender Wage Inequality in an Export-Oriented, Semi-Industrialized Economy." In *The Feminist Economics of Trade*, edited by Irene Van Staveren, Diane Elson, Caren Grown, and Nilupher Cagatay, 91–114. New York, NY: Routledge.

Blum, Linda M. 1991. *Between Feminism and Labor: The Significance of the Comparative Worth Movement.* Berkley, CA: University of California press.

Bordo, Susan. 1986. "The Cartesian Masculinization of Thought." *Signs* 11: 439–456.

Bordo, Susan. 1987. *The Flight to Objectivity: Essays on Cartesianism and Culture.* Albany, NY: State University of New York Press.

Bowden, Peta and Jane Mummery. 2009. *Understanding Feminism.* Durham, England: Acumen.

Brown, Doug. 1994. "Radical Institutionalism and Postmodern Feminist Theory." In *The Economic Status of Women under Capitalism: Institutional Economics and Feminist Theory*, edited by Janice Peterson, and Doug Brown, 35–52. Aldershot, England: Edward Elgar.

Butler, Judith, and Elizabeth Weed, Elizabeth, eds. 2011. *Question of Gender: Joan W. Scott's Critical Feminism.* Bloomington, IN: Indiana University Press.

Cigno, Alessandro. 1991. *Economics of the Family.* Oxford, England: Claredon Press.

Darity, Jr., William A. 2007. "The Formal Structure of a Gender-Segregated Low-Income Economy." In *The Feminist Economics of Trade*, edited by Irene Van Staveren, Diane Elson, Caren Grown, and Nilupher Cagatay, 78–90. New York, NY: Routledge.

De Beauvoir, Simone. 1952. *The Second Sex.* New York, NY: Bantam.

Delmar, Rosalind. 1976. "Looking Again at Engels' Origin of Family, Private Property and the State." In *The Rights and Wrongs of Women*, edited by Juliet Mitchell, and Ann Oakley, 271–287. Hamondsworth, Middlesex, England: Penguin Books.

Delphy, Christine. 1977. *The Main Enemy: A Materialist Analysis of Women's Oppression.* London, England: Women's Research and Resources Center Publications.

Delphy, Christine. 1984. *Close to Home: A Materialist Analysis of Women's Oppression.* Amherst, MA: University of Massachusetts Press.

Diamond, Irene, and Lee Quinby, eds. 1988. *Feminism and Foucault: Reflections on Resistance.* Boston, MA: Northeastern University Press.

Dolfsma, Wilfred, and Hella Hoppe. 2003. "On Feminist Economics." *Feminist Review* 75: 118–128.

Donovan, Josephine. 2006. *Feminist Theory: The Intellectual Traditions of American Feminism.* New York, NY: Continuum International Publishing Group Inc.

Draper, Hal. 1970. "Marx and Engels on Woman's Liberation." *International Socialism* 57(July/August): 20–29.

Ehrenreich, Barbara. 1984. "Life without Father: Reconsidering Socialist-Feminist Theory." *Socialist Review* 68(3): 48–57.

Eisenstein, Zillah R., ed. 1979a. *Capitalist Patriarchy and the Case for Socialist Feminism.* New York, NY: Monthly Review Press.

Eisenstein, Zillah R. 1979b. "Developing a Theory of Capitalist Patriarchy and Socialist Feminism." In *Capitalist Patriarchy and the Case for Socialist Feminism*, edited by Zillah R. Eisenstein, 5–40. New York, NY: Monthly Review Press.

Eisenstein, Zillah R. 1993. *The Radical Future of Liberal Feminism.* Boston, MA: Northeastern University Press.

Elliot, Patricia. 1991. *From Mastery to Analysis: Theories of Gender in Psychoanalytic Feminism.* Ithaca, NY: Cornell University Press.

Engels, Friedrich. 1948. *The Origin of the Family, Private Property and the State.* Moscow, USSR: Progress Publishers.

England, Paula. 1989. "A Feminist Critique of Rational-Choice Theories: Implications for Sociology." *American Sociologist* 20: 14–28.

England, Paula. 1992. *Comparative Worth: Theory and Evidence.* New York, NY: Aldine de Gruyter.

England, Paula. 1993. "The Separate Self: Androcentric Bias in Neoclassical Assumptions." In *Beyond Economic Man: Feminist Theory and Economics*, edited by Marianne Ferber, and Julie A. Nelson, 37–53. Chicago, IL: University of Chicago Press.

England, Paula, and George Farkas. 1986. *Households, Employment, and Gender: A Social, Economic, and Demographic View.* New York, NY: Aldine de Gruyter.

Eisner, Robert. 1988. "Extended Accounts for National Income and Product." *Journal of Economic Literature* 26: 1161–1185.

Fee, Elizabeth. 1983. "Women's Nature and Scientific Objectivity." In *Women's Nature: Rationalization of Inequality*, edited by Marian Lowe, and Ruth Hubbard, 9–28. New York, NY: Pergamon Press.

Fee, Elizabeth. 1986. "Critiques of Modern Science: The Relationship of Feminism to Other Radical Epistemologies." In *Feminist Approaches to Science*, edited by Ruth Bleier, 42–56. New York, NY: Pergamon Press.

Ferber, Marianne A., and Julie A. Nelson, eds. 1993a. *Beyond Economic Man: Feminist Theory and Economics.* Chicago, IL: University of Chicago Press.

Ferber, Marianne A., and Julie A. Nelson. 1993b. "The Social Construction of Economics and the Social Construction of Gender." In *Beyond Economic Man: Feminist Theory and Economics*, edited by Marianne Ferber, and Julie A. Nelson, 1–22. Chicago, IL: University of Chicago Press.

Ferber, Marianne A., and Julie A. Nelson, eds. 2003. *Feminist Economics Today: Beyond Economic Man.* Chicago, IL: University of Chicago Press.

Ferguson, Ann. 1989. "Sex and Work: Women as a New Revolutionary Class in the United States." In *An Anthology of Western Marxism: From Lukacs and Gramsci to Socialist-Feminism*, edited by Roger S. Gottlieb, 348–380. Oxford, England: Oxford University Press.

Ferguson, Ann, and Nancy Folbre. 1981. "The Unhappy Marriage of Patriarchy and Capitalism." In *Women and Revolution: A Discussion of the Unhappy Marriage of Marxism and Feminism*, edited by Lydia Sargent, 313–337. Boston, MA: South End Press.

Feyerabend, Paul. 1976. *Against Method.* New York, NY: Humanities Press.

Firestone, Shulamith. 1970. *The Dialectic of Sex: The Case for Feminist Revolution.* New York, NY: Bantam Books.

Folbre, Nancy. 1993. "Socialism, Feminism and Scientific." In *Beyond Economic Man: Feminist Theory and Economics*, edited by Marianne Ferber, and Julie A. Nelson, 94–110. Chicago, IL: University of Chicago Press.

Folbre, Nancy. 2009. *Greed, Lust and Gender: A History of Economic Ideas.* Oxford, England: Oxford University Press.

Folbre, Nancy, and Michael Bittman, eds. 2004. *Family Time: The Social Organization of Care.* New York, NY: Routledge.

Friedman, Milton. 1953. *Essays in Positive Economics.* Chicago, IL: University of Chicago Press.

Fuchs, Victor R. 1988. *Women's Quest for Economic Equality.* Cambridge, MA: Harvard University Press.

Fuchs, Victor R. 1989. "Women's Quest for Economic Equality." *Journal of Economic Perspectives* 3(1): 25–41.

Gatens, Moira. 1991. *Feminism and Philosophy: Perspectives on Difference and Equality.* Bloomington, IN: Indiana University Press.

Gergen, Kenneth J. 1985. "The Social Constructionist Movement in Modern Psychology." *American Psychologist* 40: 266–275.

Gibson-Graham, J.K. 2006. *The End of Capitalism (As We Know It): A Feminist Critique of Political Economy.* Minneapolis, MN: University of Minnesota Press.

Gilman, Charlotte Perkins. 1998. *Women and Economics: A Study of the Economic Relation between Men and Women as a Factor in Social Evolution.* Berkeley, CA: University of California Press.

Goldschmidt-Clermont, Luisella. 1990. "Economic Measurement of Non-Market Household Activities: Is It Useful and Feasible?" *International Labor Review* 129(3): 279–299.

Gottlieb, Roger S., ed. 1989. *An Anthology of Western Marxism: From Lukacs and Gramsci to Socialist-Feminism.* Oxford, England: Oxford University Press.

Grapard, Ulla. 1996. "Feminist Economics: Let Me Count the Ways." In *Beyond Neoclassical Economics: Heterodox Approaches to Economic Theory*, edited by Fred E. Foldvary, 100–114. Cheltenham, England: Edward Elgar.

Greer, Germaine. 1970. *The Female Eunuch.* New York, NY: McGraw-Hill Book Company.

Griffin, Susan. 1978. *Woman and Nature: The Roaring inside Her.* New York, NY: Harper and Row, Publishers.

Gronau, Reuben. 1977. "Leisure, Home Production and Work: The Theory of the Allocation of Time Revisited." *Journal of Political Economy* 85: 1099–1123.

Gunewardena, Nandini, and Ann Kingsolver. 2007. *The Gender of Globalization: Women Navigating Cultural and Economic Marginalities.* Santa Fe, New Mexico: School for Advanced Research Press.

Harding, Sandra. 1986. *The Science Question in Feminism.* Ithaca, NY: Cornell University Press.

Harding, Sandra. 1991. *Whose Science? Whose Knowledge? Thinking from Women's Lives.* Ithaca, NY: Cornell University Press.

Harding, Sandra. 1995. "Can Feminist Thought Make Economics More Objective?" *Feminist Economics* 1(1): 7–32.

Hartmann, Heidi. 1981. "The Unhappy Marriage of Marxism and Feminism: Toward a More Progressive Union." In *Women and Revolution: A Discussion of the Unhappy Marriage of Marxism and Feminism*, edited by Lydia Sargent, 1–41. Boston, MA: South End Press.

Hartsock, Nancy C. 1979. "Feminist Theory and the Development of Revolutionary Strategy." In *Capitalist Patriarchy and the Case for Socialist Feminism*, edited by Zillah R. Eisenstein, 56–82. New York, NY: Monthly Review Press.

Hartsock, Nancy C., 1985, *Money, Sex, and Power: Toward a Feminist Historical Materialism*, Boston, MA: Northeastern University Press.

Hewitson, Gillian J. 1999. *Feminist Economics: Interrogating the Masculinity of Rational Economic Man.* Cheltenham, England: Edward Elgar.

Hewitt, Nancy A., ed. 2010. *No Permanent Waves: Recasting Histories of U.S. Feminism.* New Brunswick, NJ: Rutgers University Press.

Hirschfeld, Mary, Robert L. Moore, and Eleanor Brown. 1995. "Exploring the Gender Gap on the GRE Subject Test in Economics." *Journal of Economic Education* 26(1): 3–15.

Horwitz, Steven. 1995. "Feminist Economics: An Austrian Perspective." *Journal of Economic Methodology* 2(2): 259–279.

Humphries, Jane. 1995. "Introduction." In *Gender and Economics*, edited by Jane Humphries, xiii–xxxix. Aldershot, England: Edward Elgar.

Hyman, Prue J. 1994a. "Feminist Critiques of Orthodox Economics: A Survey." *New Zealand Economic Papers* 28(1): 53–80.

Hyman, Prue J. 1994b. *Women and Economics: A New Zealand Perspective.* Wellington, New Zealand: Bridget Williams Books.

Jacoby, Robin Miller. 1976. "Feminism and Class Consciousness in the British and American Women's Trade Union Leagues, 1890–1925." In *Liberating Women's History: Theoretical and Critical Essays*, edited by Berenice A. Carroll, 137–160. Urbana, IL: University of Illinois Press.

Johnson, Merri Lisa, ed. 2007. *Third Wave Feminism and Television: Jane Puts It in a Box.* New York, NY: Palgrave Macmillan.

Jennings, Ann L. 1993. "Public or Private? Institutional Economics and Feminism." In *Beyond Economic Man: Feminist Theory and Economics*, edited by Marianne Ferber, and Julie A. Nelson, 111–129. Chicago, IL: University of Chicago Press.

Jennings, Ann, and William Waller. 1990. "Constructions of Social Hierarchy." *Journal of Economic Issues* 24: 623–632.

Karamessini, Maria, and Jill Rubery, eds. 2014. *Women and Austerity: The Economic Crisis and the Future for Gender Equality.* New York, NY: Routledge.

Keller, Evelyn Fox. 1985. *Reflections on Gender and Science.* New Havens, CT: Yale University Press.

Kessler-Harris, Alice. 2001. *In Pursuit of Equity: Women, Men, and the Quest for Economic Citizenship in 20th-Century America.* Oxford, England: Oxford University Press.

Kuhn, Annette, and Ann Marie Wolpe, eds. 1978. *Feminism and Materialism: Women and Modes of Production.* London, England: Routledge and Kegan Paul.

Kuhn, Thomas. 1962. *The Structure of Scientific Revolutions.* Chicago, IL: University of Chicago Press.

Kuiper, Edith, Jolande Sap, Susan Feiner, Notburga Ott, and Aafiris Tzannatos, eds. 1995. *Out of the Margin: Feminist Perspectives on Economics.* London, England: Routledge.

Longino, Helen E. 1990. *Science as Social Knowledge: Values and Objectivity in Scientific Inquiry.* Princeton, NJ: Princeton University Press.

Lundberg, Shelly, and Robert A. Pollack. 1996. "Bargaining and Distribution in Marriage." *Journal of Economic Perspectives* 10(4): 139–158.

MacKinnon, Catherine A. 1982. "Feminism, Marxism, Method, and the State: An Agenda for Theory." *Signs* 7(3): 515–544.

Marcuse, Herbert. 1974. "Marxism and Feminism." *Women's Studies* 2(3): 279–288.

Martin, Joanne. 2003. "Feminist Theory and Critical Theory: Unexplained Synergies." In *Studying Management Critically*, edited by M. Alvesson, and H. Willmott, 66–91. London, England: Sage Publications.

Marx, Karl, Friedrich Engels, V.I. Lenin, and Joseph Stalin. 1951. *The Woman Question: Selections from the Writings of Karl Marx, Friedrich Engels, V.I. Lenin, and Joseph Stalin.* New York, NY: International Publishers.

Matthaei, Julie. 1992. "Marxist Feminist Contributions to Radical Economics." In *Radical Economics*, edited by Bruce Roberts and Susan Feiner, 117–144. Boston, MA: Kluwer Academic Publishers.

McCloskey, Donald/Deirdre N. 1983. "The Rhetoric of Economics." *Journal of Economic Literature* 21(2): 481–517.

McCloskey, Donald/Deirdre N. 1994. *Knowledge and Persuasion in Economics.* Cambridge, England: Cambridge University Press.

McCloskey, Donald/Deirdre N. (1998/1985), *The Rhetoric of Economics,* 2nd edition. Madison, WI: University of Wisconsin Press.

McCrate, Elaine. 1988. "Gender Difference: The Role of Endogenous Preferences and Collective Action." *American Economic Review* 78(2): 235–239.

McRobbie, Angela. 2009. *The Aftermath of Feminism: Gender, Culture and Social Change.* Thousand Oakes, CA: Sage Publications.

Merchant, Carolyn. 1980. *The Death of Nature: Women, Ecology and the Scientific Revolution.* San Francisco, CA: Harper and Row.

Mohanty, Chandra Talpade. 2003. *Feminism without Borders: Decolonizing Theory, Practicing Solidarity*. Durham, NC: Duke University Press.

Morgan, Robin. 1976. *Papers on Patriarchy, Patriarchy Conference, London, 1976*. Brighton, England: Women's Publishing Collective.

Morgan, Robin. 1977. *Going Too Far: The Personal Chronicle of a Feminist*. New York, NY: Random House.

Narayan, Uma. 1997. *Dislocating Cultures: Identities, Traditions, and Third-World Feminism*. New York, NY: Routledge.

Nelson, Julie A. 1992. "Gender, Metaphor, and the Definition of Economics." *Economics and Philosophy* 8(1): 103–125.

Nelson, Julie A. 1993a. "Gender and Economic Ideology." *Review of Social Economy* 51(3): 287–301.

Nelson, Julie A. 1993b. "The Study of Choice or the Study of Provisioning? Gender and the Definition of Economics." In *Beyond Economic Man: Feminist Theory and Economics*, edited by Marianne Ferber, and Julie A. Nelson, 23–36. Chicago, IL: University of Chicago Press.

Nelson, Julie A. 1995. "Feminism and Economics." *Journal of Economic Perspectives* 9(2): 131–148.

Nelson, Julie A. 1996. *Feminism, Objectivity and Economics*. New York, NY: Routledge.

Nelson, Julie A. 2001. "Feminist Economics: Objective, Activist, and Postmodern?" In *Postmodernism, Economics, and Knowledge*, edited by Stephen Cullenberg, Jack Amariglio, and David F. Ruccio, 286–304. London, England: Routledge.

Nelson, Julie A. 2010 "Sociology, Economics, and Gender: Can Knowledge of the Past Contribute to a Better Future?" *American Journal of Economics and Sociology* 69(4): 1127–1154.

Nicholson, Linda J. 1986. *Gender and History*. New York, NY: Columbia University Press.

Nicholson, Linda J., ed. 1990. *Feminism/Postmodernism*. New York, NY: Routledge.

Nussbaum, Martha C., and Jonathan Glover, eds. 2001. *Women, Culture, and Development: A Study of Human Capabilities*. Oxford, England: Oxford University Press.

Oliver, Kelly, and Lisa Walsh, eds. 2004. *Contemporary French Feminism*. Oxford, England: Oxford University Press.

Paludi, Michelle A., and Lisa A. Strayer. 1985. "What's in an Author's Name? Differential Evaluations of Performance as a Function of Author's Name." *Sex Roles* 12(3/4): 353–361.

Peterson, V. Spike. 1997. "Seeking World Order beyond the Gendered Order of Global Hierarchies." In *The New Realism: Perspectives on Multilateralism and World Order*, edited by Robert W. Cox, 38–56. New York, NY: St. Martin's Press.

Phillips, Anne, ed. 1987. *Feminism and Equality*. New York, NY: New York University Press.

Pollak, Robert A. 1985. "A Transaction Cost Approach to Families and Households." *Journal of Economic Literature* 23(2): 581–608.

Poovey, Mary. 1988. "Feminism and Deconstruction." *Feminist Studies* 14: 51–65.

Pujol, Michele A. 1995. "Into the Margin." In *Out of the Margin: Feminist Perspectives on Economics*, edited by Edith Kuiper, and Jolande Sap, 17–34. London, England: Routledge.

Quick, Paddy. 1977. "The Class Nature of Women's Oppression." *Review of Radical Political Economics* 9(3): 42–53.

Redstockings. 1975. *Feminist Revolution.* New Paltz, NY: Random House.

Robbins, Lionell. 1937. *An Essay on the Nature and Significance of Economic Science.* London, England: Macmillan.

Rosaldo, Michelle. 1980. "The Use and Abuse of Anthropology." *Signs* 5: 391–417.

Rosetti, Jane. 1992. "Deconstruction, Rhetoric, and Economics." In *Post-Popperian Methodology of Economics: Recovering Practice*, edited by Neil de Marchi. Boston, MA: Kluwer Academic Publishers.

Sacks, Karen. 1974. "Engels Revisited: Women, the Organization of Production and Private Property." In *Women, Culture, and Society*, edited by Michelle Zimbalist Rosaldo, and Louise Lamphere, 207–222. Stanford, CA: Stanford University Press.

Sandler, Bernice R. 1994. "The Classroom Climate for Women." In *Race and Gender in the American Economy: Views from Across the Spectrum*, edited by Susan F. Feiner, 166–168. New York, NY: Prentice-Hall.

Sargent, Lydia, ed. 1981. *Women and Revolution: A Discussion of the Unhappy Marriage of Marxism and Feminism.* Boston, MA: South End Press.

Schonpflug, Karin. 2008. *Feminism, Economics and Utopia: Time Traveling through Paradigms.* New York, NY: Routledge.

Schultz, Theodore W., ed. 1974. *Economics of the Family: Marriage, Children and Human Capital.* Chicago, IL: University of Chicago Press.

Scott, Joan W. 1988. "Deconstructing Equality-versus-Difference: Or, the Use of Poststructuralist Theory for Feminism." *Feminist Studies* 14: 33–50.

Seiz, Janet A. 1992. "Gender and Economic Research." In *Post-Popperian Methodology of Economics: Recovering Practice*, edited by Neil De Marchi, 273–319. Boston, MA: Kluwer Academic Publishers.

Seiz, Janet A. 1995. "Bargaining Models, Feminism, and Institutionalism." *Journal of Economic Issues* 29(2): 609–618.

Slaughter, Jane, and Robert Kern, eds. 1981. *European Women on the Left: Socialism, Feminism, and the Problems Faced by Political Women, 1880 to the Present.* Westport, CT: Greenwood Press.

Stewart, Hamish. 1992. "Rationality and the Market for Human Blood." *Journal of Economic Behavior and Organization* 19: 125–143.

Storkey, Elaine. 1985. *What's Right with Feminism.* Grand Rapids, MI: William B. Eerdmans Publishing Company.

Strassmann, Diana L. 1994. "Feminist Thought and Economics; or, What Do the Visigoths Know?" *American Economic Review, Papers and Proceedings* 84(2): 153–158.

Taylor, Barbara. 1983. *Eve and the New Jerusalem: Socialism and Feminism in the Nineteen Century.* New York, NY: Pantheon Books.

Thornton, Merle. 1994. *Gender in the Economics Curriculum.* Melbourne, Australia: University of Melbourne.

Tilly, Louise A., and Joan W. Scott. 1978. *Women, Work and Family.* London, England: Holt, Rinehart and Winston.

Veblen, Thorstein. 1904. *The Theory of Leisure Class.* New York, NY: Mentor.

Vogel, Lise. 1983/2014. Marxism and the Oppression of Women: Toward a Unitary Theory. New Brunswick, NJ: Rutgers University Press.

Walker, Rebecca, ed. 1995. *To Be Real: Telling the Truth and Changing the Face of Feminism.* New York, NY: Anchor Books.

Waller, William, and Ann Jennings. 1990. "On the Possibility of a Feminist Economics: The Convergence of Institutional and Feminist Methodology." *Journal of Economic Issues* 24(2): 613–622.

Wallerstein, Immanuel. 2000. "The Ideological Tensions of Capitalism: Universalism versus Racism and Sexism." In *The Essential Wallerstein*, edited by Wallerstein, Immanuel, 344–353. New York, NY: New Press.

Waring, Marilyn. 1988. *If Women Counted: A New Feminist Economics.* San Francisco, CA: Harper San Francisco.

Wing, Adrien Katherine, and Angela Y. Davis. 2000. *Global Critical Race Feminism: An International Reader.* New York, NY: New York University Press.

Wolf, Alison. 2013. *The XX Factor: How the Rise of Working Women Has Created a Far Less Equal World.* New York, NY: Random House.

Wooley, Frances R. 1993. "The Feminist Challenge to Neoclassical Economics." *Cambridge Journal of Economics* 17: 485–500.

Zetkin, Clara. 1934. *Lenin on the Woman Question.* New York, NY: International Publishers Co., Inc.

Chapter 8

Feminist Research

A Paradigmatic View

The purpose of this chapter is to show that, according to Sandra Harding (1995), feminists have a subjective, rather than, an objective, view of reality, and therefore, prefer research methods that correspond to the interpretive paradigm, rather than the functionalist paradigm. The paper, therefore, first briefly discusses the work of the prominent feminist philosopher of science Sandra Harding (1995) to show that indeed her view of reality emphasizes the subjective, rather than the objective, nature of it; and then the paper compares and contrasts the research methodologies of feminists with those of the conventional economics, which emphasizes the objective nature of the world.

Feminists' Philosophy of Science: Values and interests act as the driving force and provide the context for advancing the growth of knowledge. But often, it has been only the contextual elements that have been considered problematic. According to the conventional philosophies of science, the methods of the sciences should eliminate these contextual, normative elements from research, leaving only "information" that is neutral ("positive") to those normative social, psychological, political, and economic commitments that make societies culturally distinctive. In contrast, feminists and other critics of the conventional philosophies of science have pointed out that, in fact, contextual values, such as androcentrism, function as constitutive elements in social sciences and biology, and construct scientific projects that express and serve the dominant institutions, and from the process of its design and direction women have systematically been excluded. Similarly, there have been longstanding arguments made regarding bourgeois, racist, and Eurocentric values and interests. Moreover, feminists have also shown that at least some of the constitutive values and interests—such as simplicity, comprehensiveness, and preserving the data—have political effects in the same way that contextual values do, and have concluded that they are neither "only internal"

213

nor apolitical. Finally, it has become clear that, in the natural sciences, some contextual values and interests improve the quality of research, rather than deteriorate it. Thus, neutrality, that is, the exclusion of all social values and interests, is neither possible nor desirable.[1]

Since the exclusion of all social values and interests is neither possible nor desirable for the natural sciences, there is no grounds on which it can be claimed that it is possible and desirable for the social sciences. It is very ironic if the conventional "positivist" philosophy which is increasingly regarded as misleading for the natural sciences is to remain dominant in the social sciences. These findings are very beneficial to the research performed in the social sciences. First, economics research cannot achieve value- and interest-neutrality because it is saturated with both constitutive and contextual values and interests. Second, contextual values and interests—those that "intrude" from the social communities within which economics research occurs—often act as constitutive elements as well. Finally, constitutive ones—which are supposedly "only internal" to economics research and, therefore, they are regarded as neutral to external values and interests—in fact are not neutral because they "take sides" with "external" positions with respect to values and interests.

Feminist economists have identified various androcentric values and interests that have formed the fundamental concepts and analytic methods of economics. They warn that an exclusive focus on those values and interests which are important to the dominant institutions provide only a partial and distorted account of how economic relations actually work. Feminist economists argue that for economic theory to become more comprehensive and accurate, research must value—that is, be interested in—nature, childhood, bodily needs, human connectedness, women's work in the household, the gender-differing values and interests within every household, and gendered power relations. They emphasize that the neutrality, which is the ideal of "positive" economics, has been shown to limit the empirical and theoretical adequacy of economic theories.

Science is not a mirror of nature, but it is practice and culture. Some philosophers of science have shown how the cognitive, technical cores of the natural sciences have always been consistent with diverse social formations and belief systems of their eras. Such cognitive, technical cores have been part of their era's social history as well as part of their intellectual traditions. These cognitive, technical cores of the sciences have been partially created by and have partially created cultural assumptions. Sometimes, these assumptions have belonged to the marginalized or not yet dominant groups. For instance, the materialist assumptions of early modern scientists whose methods and results of research challenged the spiritual assumptions of the Church. At other times, the assumptions have belonged to the dominant groups. For instance, the racist, sexist, and class-bound biological determinist assumptions that shaped nineteenth century craniology and other studies of "intelligence."

Furthermore, some philosophers of science have noted that observations are theory laden, and that theories are value, interest, and culture laden. Facts are facts and remain as facts as long as one does not question the theories and their underlying assumptions that conceptualize them as the only reasonable ones. The following few examples provide some clarification on this point. Do we observe the sun rising or do we ourselves "fall towards" it? Was it a riot or a strike at the factory gates? Do women do a double-day of work because of their "natures" or because of the exploitative social relations? Are the fewer numbers of women seeking careers in mathematics due to women's biologically inferior intellects or due to systematic discrimination? The answer to each question depends on one's theory, and all theories are shaped by and play a role in shaping cultural assumptions and practices. When our hypotheses appear rejected by "the data," we should reasonably ask whether it is due to our explicit hypotheses or our implicit underlying beliefs with which they are enmeshed—that is, assumptions about the way we have posed the problem, the adequacy of our central concepts, the suitability of our testing instruments, the level of evidence required, the way we interpret the data, and so on. We always get involved in controversy whenever we attempt to distinguish "the facts" from the values and interests that select them as evidentially supported, meaningful, and relevant. The total set of beliefs (common sense and scientific) of a person forms an interlocked network such that none of its logical, empirical, or normative constituents are in principle immune from revision. People, reasonably and unreasonably, "revise" or ignore observations because of their theoretical commitments, as often as, they revise or abandon their theories because of observations. And even definitions, as well as logical and mathematical principles, have been modified in the processes of achieving empirically and theoretically more useful knowledge claims. Theories are underdetermined not by any unbiased evidence that has been collected, but by any possible evidence for them. These findings illustrate that there is enough slack in scientific belief sorting to permit social values and interests to permeate such processes and their results.

This slack is not an unmitigated defect but, instead, it is a crucial resource for the growth of scientific knowledge. The looseness with which our theories fit the world allows more than one theory to reasonably fit any set of observations, and more than one interpretation to reasonably fit any theory. For instance, both Ptolemaic and Galilean/Copernican astronomical theories are supported by "the same data." Everyday most research projects have the task of deciding how best to apply their theory to new situations, that is, what phenomena and processes are to be interpreted as relevant to their theory.

The slack gives us the opportunity to "see" nature in variously new and more illuminating ways. This is because we can always see more than what can be captured by any simple representational model, no matter how fully it is elaborated. Theories act like maps. Each theory can represent only a part of reality, and other theories can illuminate other characteristics of that reality. Feminist economic theory not only reasonably fits well the "same data" which are used to support the conventional, pre-feminist accounts but also illuminates aspects of economic relations which were not visible based on the assumptions of pre-feminist theories. After all, feminist theory is neither the first economic theory nor the last economic theory to provide illuminating alternative interpretations of economic data. These are in contrast to the central conventional assumptions regarding the possibility of scientific images of nature that merely reflect regularities and underlying causal determinants that are "out there" in nature.

Paradigms and Research Methodologies: In order to understand the role of paradigms in research methodology, it is necessary to understand the relationship between specific modes of research and the worldviews that they reflect. A research methodology, whether scientific or clinical (of course, this is an oversimplified dichotomization), cannot be considered in the abstract. The choice and adequacy of a method embodies assumptions regarding; the nature of the phenomenon to be investigated, the nature of knowledge, and the methods through which that knowledge can be obtained. Therefore, it is necessary to examine methodology within this wider and deeper context, in order to develop a framework within which the extent of appropriate use of different methodologies might be inferred.[2]

The methodology traditionally favored in the study of social sciences and economics is called scientific. It is based on its functionalist paradigmatic assumptions, and, therefore, committed to the method of observation.

The scientific methodology, which corresponds to the functionalist paradigm and the conventional economics' philosophy of science, consists of the following five principal stages:

1. Observation,
2. Theory building,
3. Hypothesis: systematic doubt,
4. Experimental framework/design, and
5. Test: rejection, reformulation, or confirmation of the theory.

The scientific methodology begins with the observation of the phenomenon. It is based on the idea that the researcher observes what is "out there." Reality is the source of ideas, which is the basis for the development of theory. This is the process which is called theory building. The scientist makes sense of what is observed "out there" in the "real world."

The theory often starts as a very broad idea, which is rather imprecise. In the next stage, the scientist comes up with a hypothesis, or a set of hypotheses, which translates the theory into a testable form.

A hypothesis should have the crucial property of being refutable, that is, the possibility that it is untrue. In other words, the development of a hypothesis is based on "systematic doubt," which is crucial for the scientific process. Without bringing doubt on research, it is not scientific. The scientist should try to refute, or disprove, his or her favored theory, perhaps not to reject it altogether, but to proceed in terms of a methodological process of rejection, reformulation, or confirmation of the theory.

The test of a hypothesis is based on the specification of the hypothesis in a testable form, so that it can be refuted. The testing, based on systematic doubt, leads to the rejection or confirmation of the hypothesis. But, to be scientific, confirmation should not be sought, but should come through the process of attempting to reject. This process is an open one: when the hypothesis is not confirmed, it is reformulated, which, in turn, may lead to the reformulation of the theory. In other words, the results of the experiments may lead to the recommencement of the process.

The scientific methodology is an iterative process. It begins with stage 1, goes through the various steps to stage 5, and then goes back to stages 2 or 1. This is to obtain an improved understanding of the subject of study.

The above-mentioned model represents the scientific methodology. Its aim is to generate ever better descriptions and explanations of reality.

The clinical methodology, which corresponds to the interpretive paradigm and the feminists' philosophy of science, consists of the following five stages:

1. Get inside: get deeply involved in the situation,
2. Adopt the role of a learner,
3. Map the system of symbols and their meanings,
4. Identify key themes and explanations, and
5. Test against opinion in the situation: reject, reformulate, or confirm themes and explanations.

The clinical methodology starts with the idea that, instead of observing reality from the outside, one should attempt to understand it from within. Whereas the scientist applying the scientific methodology observes the phenomenon from a distance, the clinical scientist makes direct and unstructured contact with it, with no preconception in terms of what is to be discovered. The clinical scientist becomes a participant in the situation to be investigated. In fact, one of the techniques in clinical research is called "participant observation," which is very flexible. The main goal is to understand how people construct their world.

The clinical scientist gets inside the situation to understand how it is put together from within. This is done without taking on the role of an expert, with a theory about how that phenomenon works, as is done in the scientific methodology. Rather, the clinical scientist takes on the role of a learner, who attempts to understand the situation being researched.

The next stage of research is mapping the rich fabric of the phenomenon: the symbols, the meanings, the rituals, the routines, the folklore, and the history, which the researcher documents. Actually, this process starts at the beginning of research, and continues throughout. Clinical methodology relies heavily on keeping rigorous documentation of the scientist's observations and actions within the phenomenon. The scientist keeps journals of his or her visits about; observation of events and situations; who interacts and talks with whom, conversations, and interviews. Such journals sensitively document from within, what people are seeing, and saying from their standpoint. Once the clinical scientist is well advanced with this mapping stage, he or she will have built a large file of documents containing explanations and descriptions of the pattern of symbols and meanings that seem relevant to the phenomenon.

The next stage of the research process is identifying the key themes and interpretations of the situation. This is similar to the theory building, stage 2, of the scientific methodology. In clinical methodology, it is delayed until stage 4. This is because it believes that the theory should not be brought in from the outside, but should make sense from the inside. The clinical scientist attempts to explain how reality is constructed. Therefore, the methodology used should be compatible with the internal mechanisms of this reality construction process.

The next stage of research is to test the validity of the theory, by bringing systematic doubt into the explanations and themes. In other words, the clinical scientist tests whether the explanations produced from the situation make sense to the people in it. This is diametrically different from the scientific methodology, since the scientist applying the scientific methodology leaves the situation with the data. Often, the statistics collected are tested through mathematical statistical techniques to bring systematic doubt.

Clinical research is not the replication of what is obvious. It might be a new, novel insight, but one which makes sense to the members in the situation. The clinical research must employ a process of systematic doubt if it is to constitute a scientific one. An unfavorable test result leads to the reformulation of the initial insight, explanation, and theory. There is a feedback loop which goes from stage 5 to stage 4; in an iterative manner. The final outcome is an explanation which is consistent with the process of reality construction within the situation. This case study is the knowledge product of clinical research.

Scientific and clinical methodologies are totally different, because they view knowledge in totally different ways. A case study may produce an insight which can be generalized to other situations. The scientific methodology is concerned with generalizability of facts, laws, and relationships. The clinical scientist looks for the generalizability of insights.

NOTES

1. For this literature, see Belenky, Clinchy, Goldberger, and Tarule (1986), Bordo (1986, 1987), Bowles and Klein (1983), Caldwell (1994), Chodorow (1978, 1994), Farganis (1989), Fee (1986), Flax (1983), Gorsz and De Lepervanche (1988), Harding (1986, 1989, 1993, 1995, 2004), Hartsock (1987), Keller (1983a, b, 1985, 1986, 1989a, b), Klamer (1991, 1995), Klein (1983), Longino (1988, 1989, 1993a, b), Longino and Doell (1987), McCloskey (1985), Merchant (1980), Miles (1983), Nelson (1995), Reinharz (1983), Rose (1986, 1987), Schiebinger (1987), Seiz (1992, 1995), Sheman (1983), Smith (1974, 1987), Stanley and Wise (1983), Taylor, Gillborn, and Ladson-Billings (2009), Westkott (1983), Whatley (1986), and Young (1990). This section is based on Harding (1995).

2. For this literature, see Ardalan (2008), Berg and Smith (1985), Bettner, Robinson, and McGoun (1994), Frankfurter, Carleton, Gordon, Horrigan, McGoun, Philippatos, and Robinson (1994), Friedman (1953), Merton (1995), McGoun (1992), Morgan (1983, 1985), Taylor and Bogdan (1984), Weston (1966). This section is taken from Ardalan (2008), which is based on Morgan (1983, 1985).

REFERENCES

Ardalan, Kavous. 2008. *On the Role of Paradigms in Finance.* Aldershot, Hampshire, England: Ashgate Publishing Limited.

Belenky, Mary Field, Blythe McVicker Clinchy, Nancy Rule Goldberger, and Jill Mattuck Tarule. 1986. *Women's Ways of Knowing: The Development of Self, Voice, and Mind.* New York, NY: Basic Books.

Berg, D.N., and K.K. Smith. 1985. *Exploring Clinical Methods for Social Research.* Beverly Hills, CA: Sage Publications, Inc.

Bettner, Mark S., Chris Robinson, and Elton McGoun. 1994. "The Case for Qualitative Research in Finance." *International Review of Financial Analysis* 3(1): 1–18.

Bordo, Susan. 1986. "The Cartesian Masculinization of Thought." *Signs: Journal of Women in Culture and Society* 11(3): 439–456.

Bordo, Susan. 1987. *The Flight to Objectivity: Essays on Cartesianism and Culture.* Albany, NY: State University of New York Press.

Bowles, Gloria, and Renate Duelli Klein, eds. 1983. *Theories of Women's Studies.* London, England: Routledge and Kegan Paul.

Caldwell, Bruce J. 1994. *Beyond Positivism: Economic Methodology in the Twentieth Century.* London, England: Routledge.

Chodorow, Nancy. 1978. *The Reproduction of Mothering: Psychoanalysis and the Sociology of Gender.* Berkeley, CA: University of California Press.

Chodorow, Nancy. 1994. "Gender, Relation and Difference in Psychoanalytic Perspective." In *The Polity Reader in Gender Studies,* edited by David Held, Dan Hillman, Don Hubert, Debbie Seymour, Michelle Stannorth, and John Thompson, 41–49. Cambridge England: Polity Press.

Farganis, Sondra. 1989. "Feminism and the Reconstruction of Social Science." In *Gender/Body/Knowledge: Feminist Reconstructions of Being and Knowing,* edited by Alison M. Jaggar, and Susan R. Bordo, 207–223. New Brunswick, NJ: Rutgers University Press.

Fee, Elizabeth. 1986. "Critiques of Modern Science: The Relationship of Feminism to Other Radical Epistemologies." In *Feminist Approaches to Science,* edited by Ruth Bleier, 42–56. New York, NY: Pergamon Press.

Flax, Jane. 1983. "Political Philosophy and the Patriarchal Unconscious: A Psychoanalytic Perspective on Epistemology and Metaphysics." In *Discovering Reality: Feminist Perspectives on Epistemology, Metaphysics, Methodology and Philosophy of Science,* edited by Sandra Harding, and Merrill B. Hintikka, 245–282. Dordrecht, the Netherlands: Reidel Publishing Company.

Frankfurter, George M., Willard Carleton, Myron Gordon, James Horrigan, Elton McGoun, George Philippatos, and Chris Robinson. 1994. "The Methodology of Finance: A Round Table Discussion." *International Review of Financial Analysis* 3(3): 173–207.

Friedman, Milton. 1953. *Essays in Positive Economics.* Chicago, IL: University of Chicago Press.

Gorsz, E.A., and Marie De Lepervanche. 1988. "Feminism and Science." In *Crossing Boundaries: Feminisms and the Critique of Knowledges,* edited by Barbara Caine, E.A. Gorsz, and Marie De Lepervanche, 5–27. Sydney, Australia: Allen and Unwin.

Harding, Sandra. 1986. *The Science Question in Feminism.* Ithaca, NY: Cornell University Press.

Harding, Sandra. 1989. "Feminist Justificatory Strategies." In *Women, Knowledge, and Reality: Explorations in Feminist Philosophy,* edited by Ann Garry, and Marilyn Pearsall, 189–201. Boston, MA: Unwin Hyman.

Harding, Sandra. 1993. "Rethinking Standpoint Epistemology: What Is 'Strong Objectivity'?" In *Feminist Epistemologies,* edited by Linda Alcoff, and Elizabeth Potter, 49–82. New York, NY: Routledge.

Harding, Sandra. 1995. "Can Feminist Thought Make Economics More Objective?" *Feminist Economics* 1(1): 7–32.

Harding, Sandra, ed. 2004. *The Feminist Standpoint Theory Reader: Intellectual and Political Controversies.* New York, NY: Routledge.

Hartsock, Nancy C.M. 1987. "The Feminist Standpoint: Developing the Ground for a Specifically Feminist Historical Materialism." In *Feminism and Methodology,* edited by Sandra Harding, 157–180. Bloomington, IN: Indiana University Press.

Keller, Evelyn Fox. 1983a. "Gender and Science." In *Discovering Reality: Feminist Perspectives on Epistemology, Metaphysics, Methodology and Philosophy of Science*, edited by Sandra Harding, and Merrill B. Hintikka, 187–205. Dordrecht, The Netherlands: D. Reidel Publishing Company.

Keller, Evelyn Fox. 1983b. *A Feeling for the Organism: The Life and Work of Barbara McClintock*. New York, NY: W.H. Freeman and Company.

Keller, Evelyn Fox. 1985. *Reflections on Gender and Science*. New Havens, CT: Yale University Press.

Keller, Evelyn Fox. 1986. "How Gender Matters: Or, Why It's So Hard for Us to Count Past Two." In *Perspectives on Gender and Science*, edited by Jan Harding, 168–183. London, England: Falmer Press.

Keller, Evelyn Fox. 1989a. "Feminism and Science." In *Women, Knowledge, and Reality: Explorations in Feminist Philosophy*, edited by Ann Garry, and Marilyn Pearsall, 175–188. Boston, MA: Unwin Hyman.

Keller, Evelyn Fox. 1989b. "Women Scientists and Feminist Critics of Science." In *Learning about Women: Gender, Politics, and Power*, edited by Jill K. Conway, Susan C. Bourque, and Joan W. Scott, 77–91. Ann Arbor, MI: University of Michigan Press.

Klamer, Arjo. 1991. "On Interpretive and Feminist Economics." In *Economics, Culture and Education: Essays in Honor of Mark Blaug*, edited by G.K. Shaw, 133–141. Aldershot, England: Edward Elgar.

Klamer, Arjo. 1995. "Feminist Interpretive Economics: Comments on Chapters by Strassmann and Polanyi, and Feiner." In *Out of the Margin: Feminist Perspectives on Economics*, edited by Judith Kupier, and Jolande Sap, 167–171. London, England: Rouledge.

Klein, Renate Duelli. 1983. "How to Do What We Want to Do: Thoughts about Feminist Methodology." In *Theories of Women's Studies*, edited by Gloria Bowles, and Renate Duelli Klein, 88–104. London, England: Routledge and Kegan Paul.

Longino, Helen E. 1988. "Science, Objectivity, and Feminist Values." *Feminist Studies* 14(3): 561–574.

Longino, Helen E. 1989. "Can There Be a Feminist Science?" In *Women, Knowledge, and Reality: Explorations in Feminist Philosophy*, edited by Ann Garry, and Marilyn Pearsall, 203–216. Boston, MA: Unwin Hyman.

Longino, Helen E. 1993a. "Feminist Standpoint Theory and the Problems of Knowledge." *Signs* 19(11): 201–212.

Longino, Helen E. 1993b. "Subjects, Power, and Knowledge: Description and Prescription in Feminist Philosophy of Science." In *Feminist Epistemologies*, edited by Linda Alcoff, and Elizabeth Potter, 101–120. New York, NY: Routledge.

Longino, Helen E., and Ruth Doell. 1987. "Body, Bias, and Behavior: A Comparative Analysis of Reasoning in Two Areas of Biological Science." In *Sex and Scientific Inquiry*, edited by Sandra Harding, and Jean F. O'Barr, 165–186. Chicago, IL: University of Chicago Press.

McCloskey, Donald/Deirdre N. 1985. *The Rhetoric of Economics*. Madison, WI: University of Wisconsin Press.

McGoun, Elton G. 1992. "On Knowledge of Finance." *International Review of Financial Analysis* 1(3): 161–177.

Merchant, Carolyn. 1980. *The Death of Nature: Women, Ecology and the Scientific Revolution.* San Francisco, CA: Harper and Row.

Merton, Robert C. 1995. "Influence of Mathematical Models in Finance on Practice: Past, Present, and Future." *Financial Practice and Education* 5(1): 7–15.

Miles, Maria. 1983. "Towards a Methodology for Feminist Research." In *Theories of Women's Studies*, edited by Gloria Bowles, and Renate Duelli Klein, 117–139. London, England: Routledge and Kegan Paul.

Morgan, Gareth. 1983. *Beyond Method: Strategies for Social Research.* Beverley Hills, CA: Sage Publications.

Morgan, Gareth. 1985. "Qualitative and Action Based Research." In *Actes du Colloque, Perspective de Recherche Pour lo Praticien*, edited by Y. Allaire, M. Landry, H. Mintzberg, and G. Morgan, 81–187. University of Quebec at Abitibi-Temiscaminque.

Nelson, Julie A. 1995. "Feminism and Economics." *Journal of Economic Perspectives* 9(2): 131–148.

Reinharz, Shulamit. 1983. "Experiential Analysis: A Contribution to Feminist Research." In *Theories of Women's Studies*, edited by Gloria Bowles, and Renate Duelli Klein, 162–191. London, England: Routledge and Kegan Paul.

Rose, Hilary. 1986. "Beyond Masculine Realities: A Feminist Epistemology for the Sciences." In *Feminist Approaches to Science*, edited by Ruth Bleier, 57–76. New York, NY: Pergamon Press.

Rose, Hilary. 1987. "Hand, Brain, and Heart: A Feminist Epistemology for the Natural Sciences." In *Sex and Scientific Inquiry*, edited by Sandra Harding, and Jean F. O'Barr, 265–282. Chicago, IL: University of Chicago Press.

Schiebinger, Londa. 1987. "The History and Philosophy of Women in Science: A Review Essay." In *Sex and Scientific Inquiry*, edited by Sandra Harding, and Jean F. O'Barr, 7–34. Chicago, IL: University of Chicago Press.

Seiz, Janet A. 1992. "Gender and Economic Research." In *Post-Popperian Methodology of Economics: Recovering Practice*, edited by Neil De Marchi, 273–319. Boston, MA: Kluwer Academic Publishers.

Seiz, Janet A. 1995. "Epistemology and the Tasks of Feminist Economics." *Feminist Economics* 1(3): 110–118.

Sheman, Naomi. 1983. "Individualism and the Objects of Psychology." In *Discovering Reality: Feminist Perspectives on Epistemology, Metaphysics, Methodology and Philosophy of Science*, edited by Sandra Harding, and Merrill B. Hintikka, 225–244. Dordrecht, the Netherlands: Reidel Publishing Company.

Smith, Dorothy E. 1974. "Women's Perspective as a Radical Critique of Sociology." *Sociological Inquiry* 44(1): 7–13.

Smith, Dorothy E. 1987. *The Everyday World as Problematic: A Feminist Sociology.* Boston, MA: Northeastern University Press.

Stanley, Liz, and Sue Wise. 1983. "'Back into the Personal' or: Our Attempt to Construct 'Feminist Research'." In *Theories of Women's Studies*, edited by Gloria Bowles, and Renate Duelli Klein, 192–209. London, England: Routledge and Kegan Paul.

Taylor, Edward, David Gillborn, and Gloria Ladson-Billings, Gloria, eds. 2009. *Foundations of Critical Race Theory in Education.* New York, NY: Routledge.

Taylor, S.J., and R. Bogdan. 1984. *Introduction to Qualitative Research Methods: The Search for Meanings*, 2nd edition. New York, NY: John Wiley and Sons.

Westkott, Marcia. 1983. "Women's Studies as a Strategy for Change: Between Criticism and Vision." In *Theories of Women's Studies*, edited by Gloria Bowles, and Renate Duelli Klein, 210–218. London, England: Routledge and Kegan Paul.

Weston, Fred J. 1966. *The Scope and Methodology of Finance.* Englewood Cliffs, NJ: Prentice-Hall, Inc.

Whatley, Mariamne H. 1986. "Taking Feminist Science to the Classroom: Where Do We Go from Here?" In *Feminist Approaches to Science*, edited by Ruth Bleier, 181–190. New York, NY: Pergamon Press.

Young, Iris Marion. 1990. *Throwing Like a Girl and Other Essays in Feminist Philosophy and Social Theory.* Bloomington, IN: Indiana University Press.

Chapter 9

Feminist Education

A Paradigmatic View

This chapter intends to show that, according to Belenky, Clinchy, Goldberger, and Tarule (1986), currently women's way of learning and knowing corresponds to the interpretive paradigm. For this purpose, first "Women's Way of Knowing" is briefly discussed, and then, in a more fundamental way, it is shown that women's way of learning and knowing is consistent with the interpretive paradigm's case method of teaching and learning, which is in contrast to the functionalist paradigm's lecture method of teaching. Again, this chapter does not get involved in the explanation of the reason why currently women's way of learning is the way that it is. This has been discussed in previous chapters.

Women's Way of Knowing: Based on intensive interviews with women in the United States, we describe the ways of knowing that women have cultivated and learned to value, ways that are powerful but have been neglected by dominant male institutions. Although the number of women students in higher education and professional schools has increased, faculties, who are mostly male, disagree with having a special focus on women students, and disagree with the idea that women's educational needs are different from men's educational needs. Even when the focus of the content of a course is on issues of concern to women, strategies of teaching and methods of evaluation are rarely checked by faculty for compatibility with women's preferred styles of learning. Faculty often assume that pedagogical techniques which are appropriate for men are suitable for women as well.[1]

Feminists believe that the current articulated and accepted conceptions of knowledge and truth have historically been shaped by the male-dominated majority culture. Our educational institutions were originally founded by men in order to educate men. Even female educational institutions have been modeled similar to male educational institutions in order to give women an education which is equivalent to that of men. Almost no attention has been paid to modes of learning, knowing, and valuing that may be specific to, or common in, women. Perhaps the stereotype of women's thinking as emotional, intuitive, and personalized has contributed to the denigration of women's minds and contributions, particularly in Western cultures, in which rationalism and objectivity are valued. Generally, it is assumed that intuitive knowledge is more primitive, and therefore, less valuable than "objective" modes of knowing. Traditional educational curricula and pedagogical standards have been subjected to such way of thinking. Feminists have shown that there is a masculine bias at the core of almost all academic disciplines, methodologies, and theories. Feminist teachers and scholars have questioned the structure, the curriculum, and the pedagogical practices of institutions of higher education, and have made proposals for change.

The traditional lecture method of education is similar to "banking," in which the teacher attempts to "fill" the students by making deposits of information, which the teacher regards as true knowledge. The student's role is to "store the deposits." The teacher does not take almost any risks. He privately composes his thoughts. The students are permitted to see the product of the teacher's thinking, but not the process of gestation. The lecture appears like magic. The teacher invites students to find fallacies in his arguments, but he has taken every precaution to make it airtight. He does not allow for his arguments to become more permeable, because he believes he needs to uphold the standards of his discipline and the vigor of his interpretation. The students have learned to admire it too. They see it as an act of vandalism to "rip into" an argument which they regard as the private property of the teacher.

In contrast, a woman should know that her own ideas can be very good and completely reliable, and that a theory is only something that someone thought up. In other words, a theory is not a mysterious thing which only Einstein could figure out. Teachers are in the position of power, and when they speak in their own voices they risk converting their students' voices into echoes of their own, and when they speak in utterly objective and disembodied voice they not only obscure the influence of the personal or subjective but also give the impression of divine origin. As long as teachers hide the imperfect processes of their thinking, and allow students to see only the finished product, students continue to believe that only Einstein, or a professor, can think up a theory. This problem is especially acute in science, where students are led to believe that the professors do not indulge in conjecture, but tell the truth. In addition, science students come to believe that science is not a creation of the human mind, and that professors talk about facts not models.

Teachers appear to students first in the guise of gods and they are later revealed to be humans. Such revelation should occur sooner by the help of those teachers who have the courage, and the institutional support, and can think out loud with their students. Indeed, the deflation of authority is a powerful learning experience.

Women do not want a system in which knowledge flows in only one direction, that is, from teacher to student. They praise teachers who can help them articulate and expand their latent knowledge, that is, midwife-teachers, who are the opposites of banker-teachers. In contrast to the banker-teacher who attempts to deposit knowledge in the learner's head, the midwife-teacher helps to draw it out. The midwife-teacher assists the students in giving birth to their own ideas, in making their own tacit knowledge explicit, and in elaborating it. The midwife-teacher supports students' thinking, and he or she neither does the students' thinking for them nor does expect the students to think as he or she does. A midwife-teacher is a partner-teacher and assists in the emergence of consciousness. He or she encourages students to speak in their own active voice.

Women need a teacher who supports the evolution of the students' thinking. A midwife-teacher does not focus on his or her own knowledge (as the lecturer does) but on the students' knowledge. A midwife-teacher contributes when needed, but the priority is always given to the students' ideas. It works back and forth between the students and the teacher, like a two-way street. It is a process which involves confirmation-evocation-confirmation. A midwife-teacher helps students to deliver their ideas to the world and get involved with other voices in the culture, whether past or present.

A midwife-teacher encourages students to use their knowledge in everyday life. Women often need practical information, which cover a wide range from obviously immediate to seemingly remote matters.

Women need a teacher who does not believe that the object of knowledge is the private property of the teacher, but that it is a medium that evokes the critical reflection of both teacher and students. Instead of the teacher privately thinks about the object and publically talks about it so that the students can store it, both teacher and students think together and engage in a public dialogue in order to exchange their thoughts. In the process of thinking and talking, their roles merge. That is, the teacher-of-the-students and the students-of-the-teacher become replaced by teacher-student and students-teachers. This connected class has a growth culture, which is different from a "movie" class, in which students are spectators. The connected teacher creates groups in which group members can nurture each other's thoughts to maturity. In a connected class, everyone knows that evolving thoughts are tentative, and therefore, no one apologizes for uncertainty. Students in the connected class recognize that truth is subjective, that each student has a unique perspective, and that the class provides the opportunity for personal perspectives to become publically available to the members of the class, so that through stretching and sharing students revise their ideas as they become exposed to their classmates' ideas. Women welcome the diversity of opinion in class discussion. In a connected education, each student is treated as an independent subject, not as a subordinate object.

Lecture versus Case Method, Roles of Teachers and Students: Any adequate comparison between the lecture and the case methods of instruction necessarily requires a comparison of their underlying philosophies and methodologies. This is based on the premise that foundational philosophies or worldviews underlie educational philosophies, and each educational philosophy favors a certain instructional methodology, which in turn implies a certain way or method of instruction. This section, therefore, by reference to the four basic worldviews or paradigms (functionalist, interpretive, radical humanist, and radical structuralist) discusses the major educational philosophies and their correspondence with these paradigms. It notes that each educational philosophy favors a certain instructional methodology, which in turn determines the way that the instruction is performed. More specifically, this paper shows how each foundational philosophy implies specific roles for teachers and students.[2]

This section is organized as follows. Subsection A discusses the major educational philosophies and their correspondence with the four paradigms. Subsection B notes that each educational philosophy favors a certain educational methodology, which in turn determines the way or the method that the instruction is performed. More specifically, this subsection shows how each foundational philosophy implies specific roles for teachers and students.

Educational Philosophies: Educational philosophy can usefully be conceived in terms of four key worldviews or paradigms: functionalist, interpretive, radical humanist, and radical structuralist. The four paradigms are founded upon mutually exclusive views of the social world. Each generates educational philosophies, instructional methodologies, ways or methods of instructions, theories, concepts, and analytical tools which are different from those of other paradigms. This subsection discusses the major educational philosophies (i.e., realism and pragmatism) that correspond to the functionalist and the interpretive paradigms.

Realism and Education: Realists strongly promote the study of science and the scientific method. They believe that knowledge of the world is needed for humankind's proper use of it for his or her survival. The idea of survival has important implications for education. It places self-preservation as the primary aim of education.

Realists maintain that knowing the world requires an understanding of facts and classifying the knowledge obtained about them. Schools should teach essential facts about the universe and the method of arriving at facts. Realists place enormous emphasis upon critical reason based on observation and experimentation.

Realists emphasize the practical side of education. Their concept of "practical" includes education for moral and character development, where moral education is founded on knowledge itself. Realists' essentials and the practicalities of education lead themselves further. They proceed from matter to idea, from imperfection to perfection, and all to the good life.

Realists promote the education which is primarily technical and leads to specialization. The idea of specialization is the natural outcome of the efforts to refine and establish definitive scientific knowledge. The expansion of our knowledge can be accomplished by many people, each one working on a small component of knowledge.

Realists support the lecture methodology and other formalized methodologies of teaching. They maintain that such objectives as self-realization can best occur when the learner is knowledgeable about the external world. Consequently, the learner must be exposed to the facts, and the lecture method can be an efficient, organized, and orderly way to accomplish this. Realists insist that any method used should be characterized by the integrity which comes from systematic, organized, and dependable knowledge.

Realists consider the role of the teacher in the educational process to be of primary importance. The teacher presents material in a way which is systematic and organized. He or she promotes the idea that there are clearly defined criteria making judgment about art, economics, politics, and education. For example, in education there are certain objective criteria to judge whether particular educational activities are worthwhile, such as type of material presented, how it is organized, whether or not it suits the psychological make-up of the learner, whether the delivery system is suitable, and whether it achieves the desired results.

Realists expect that institutions of higher education turn out teaching specialists who are knowledgeable, and who can serve as role models for their students. Realists place a lower priority on the personality and character of the teacher than they do on the effectiveness of the teacher to impart knowledge about the world that the learner can use.

Realism results in practices with five formal steps of learning: preparation, presentation, association, systematization-generalization, and application. This is due to the realists' desire for precision and order. These desires are found in such school practices as ringing bells, set time periods for study, departmentalization, daily lesson plans, course scheduling, increasing specialization in curriculum, prepackaged curriculum materials, and line-staff forms of administrative organization.

Pragmatism and Education: Pragmatism seeks out the processes which work best to achieve desirable ends. Pragmatism examines traditional ways of thinking and doing to reconstruct approaches to life more in line with contemporary conditions.

Pragmatists stress that educational aims grow out of existing conditions. They are tentative and flexible, at least in the beginning. People—parents, students, and citizens—are the ones who have educational aims, and not the process of education.

Pragmatists point out that the philosophy of education is the formation of proper mental and moral attitudes to be used in tackling contemporary problems. When social life changes, the educational program must be reconstructed to meet the change.

For pragmatists, the process of education is fulfilled only when the student really understands why he or she does things. School fosters habits of thought, invention, and initiative which assist the individual in growing in the desired direction. School is a place where the other environments which the student encounters—the family environment, the religious environment, the work environment, and others—are combined into a meaningful whole.

Pragmatists do not view education as preparation for life, but as life itself. The lives of learners are important to them. Thus, educators should be aware of the background, interests, and motivations of the learners. Pragmatists believe that educators should also look at learners in terms of their cognitive, physical, emotional, and all their other factors. Pragmatists maintain that individuals should be educated as social beings, capable of participating in and directing their social affairs.

Pragmatists champion a diversified and integrated curriculum. It is composed of both process and content, but it is not fixed or an end in itself. Pragmatists recommend developing a "core" approach to curriculum. Learners can select an area of concentration or "core" for a period of study such that all other subject areas revolve around it. Learners are capable of knowing the general operating principles of nature and social conditions, which serve as general guides for participation.

Pragmatists believe that life is ever-changing and there is a constant need for improvement. Therefore, pragmatic education is based on experimental method which realizes that there are no fixed or absolute conclusions. The students learn the process of discovery and self-sufficiency as much as the facts which are uncovered. One of the approaches suggested by pragmatic educators is the project approach to learning. Students cooperate in pursuing the goals of the project. Projects are decided by group discussion with the teacher as moderator. Pragmatists favor the use of case methodology in class.

Pragmatists adhere to action-oriented education. They suggest an activity-oriented core approach. School can arrange for students to reconstruct past events and life situations in order to better appreciate the difficulties involved in a given actual situation. Learners become involved with the fundamentals of knowledge in a practical and applied way so that the usefulness of knowledge becomes more apparent to them. This approach demonstrates the relationship of various disciplines, shows the wholeness of knowledge, and helps learners to utilize such a knowledge in novel and creative ways when tackling problems.

Roles of Teachers and Students: This subsection discusses the implications of the previous subsection with respect to the lecture-versus-case methods of instruction. For this purpose, this section brings major aspects of the previous subsection to the forefront, elaborates on its implications for the way or the method instructions are performed.

The previous subsection, in essence, has shown that foundational philosophies or worldviews underlie educational philosophies, and each educational philosophy favors a certain instructional methodology. In other words, as one moves from the objective to the subjective end of the spectrum in figure 1.1, the in-class instructional methodology favored changes from totally having a lecture orientation to completely having a discussion orientation, for example, a case orientation. This subsection shows how these in turn determine the way instructions are performed.

In fact, for the realist, whose position on the objective-subjective continuum in figure 1.1 is to the far right, the teacher is a guide. The real world exists, and the teacher is responsible for introducing the student to it. To do this, the teacher uses lectures, demonstrations, and sensory experiences. The teacher does not do it in a random or haphazard way; he or she must not only introduce the students to nature but also show them its regularities.

At the other extreme on the objective-subjective continuum in figure 1.1, for the pragmatist, truth is relative, reality is probabilistic, and structural relationships are contingent. Therefore, teaching and learning are most effectively accomplished through discussion rather than exploration. Since phenomena are intrinsically complex, simple theoretical relationships cannot explain them and little of value can be communicated directly from the teacher to the student. Under these circumstances, the learning process must emphasize the development of understanding, judgment, and even intuition.

In short, as one moves from the objective to the subjective end of the continuum in figure 1.1 the nature of reality viewed changes and along with it changes the foundational philosophy, its corresponding educational philosophy, and its instructional methodology. That is, a move from lecture methodology to discussion methodology, for example, case methodology.

In the lecture method teaching is telling, knowledge is facts, and learning is recall. Teachers deliver content, in the form of factual information, and students receive it. Learning is satisfactorily completed when the student transfers the material back to the teacher at the specified time.

The lecture method is efficient with respect to the use of time, energy, and the patience of instructor and student. A student trained under the lecture method possesses a certainty, a precision, and a firming of grasp which is remarkable for the relatively short time he or she spends on acquiring his or her knowledge.

The lecture method is of great power when the transfer of knowledge is the primary academic objective. But when the objective is critical thinking (in the liberal arts setting, for example) or problem-solving (in the professional school milieu), and the development of qualities such as sensitivity, cooperation, and zest for discovery, then discussion pedagogy offers substantial advantages. To achieve these goals, both teachers and students must modify their traditional roles and responsibilities.

The case method has an entirely different purpose and provides an entirely different result. Businesspeople must be able to solve problems arising in new situations in the real life. Accordingly, education would consist of acquiring skills to act in a changing environment. It is not that how a student may be trained to know, but how a student is to be trained to act. The case method is most effective wherever decisions are to be made and problems are to be solved. There is no one best way of teaching with cases.

The case method is a learning process which consists of the interaction of the case situation, individual student, overall class section, and the teacher. It blends cognitive and affective learning modes.

There are other methods of teaching such as lectures, movies, field trips, readings. Any way students can learn is a good way. There are situations where the case method is not a good match. But, in business environment it is one of the best fit.

Next, this subsection shows that the sequence of foundational philosophy, educational philosophy, and educational methodology affects the way that an instructional method is used in practice. In order to show this, the section focuses on certain aspects of the lecture and case methods of instruction and compares them. Since most readers are familiar with the lecture method, the discussions in this subsection elaborate on the case method.

Passive Students v. Active Students: In the lecture method, teaching is telling, knowledge is facts, and learning is recall. Teachers deliver content, in the form of factual information. Students receive it. Learning is satisfactorily completed when the student transfers the disciplinary knowledge back to the teacher at the required moment. The lecture method constructs formal learning such that it discourages social interaction. It emphasizes individual cognition over social interaction, abstract manipulation of symbols over concrete application in practical settings, and generalized learning over specific social context application learning. Consequently, learning progressively diminishes student's competencies for the real social life.

In the case method, human learning, that is, the acquisition and application of knowledge, is regarded as fundamentally a social act. The social dimension of learning is critical to the practical application of knowledge. For instance, children acquire language through social interactions with adults and other children. Carpenters, bookmakers, chefs, surgeons, experimental scientists, and practitioners of other occupations which require strategies for decision making, acquire most of their practical knowledge from observing and interacting with other skilled practitioners.

In the case method, teaching is considered a transformation vocation. The teacher should not only transmit information but also transform students from passive recipients of teacher's knowledge into active constructors of their own and others' knowledge. Of course, the teacher cannot transform students without their own active participation. Teachers should create the pedagogical, social, and ethical conditions in which students take charge of their own learning, individually and collectively.

In the case method, discussion is a systematic way of constructing a context for learning from the knowledge and experience of students, in addition to the disciplinary knowledge. Collectively, students should take responsibility for determining the direction of the discussion. Teachers should enable that responsibility. Teachers believe that learning occurs when students actively form the relationship of new knowledge to its intellectual and social context.

In the case method, students are responsible for performing a thorough analysis of the case in hand. They are expected to be prepared for presenting or communicating their analysis to their classmates in a similar fashion to what they would if they were in a managerial position in the real world. They are expected to define and change their analysis under the critical examination of their classmates and teacher. Their role varies according to whether they are offering their analysis or criticizing a classmate's. But they are always expected to remain actively involved, especially when there is disagreement on the definition of the problem or its solution.

In the case method, students are required to participate in class discussion, are expected to define problems and develop their solutions, and are expected to develop their problem-solving skills. If students rely on their classmates and the teacher to do the case analysis and problem-solving exercise, they miss one of the fundamental intended benefits of the case method. Moreover, they do not develop communication and interpersonal skills which are required in a real-life managerial position.

The transition from the lecture method to the case method involves a basic change in culture. It involves a move from the individual, competitive model of the lecture method to teamwork with cooperation. Furthermore, it involves a move from a conception of curriculum as discrete pieces of factual information of the lecture method to synthetic, analytic structures for ideas.

Teacher Responsible v. Student Responsible: In the case method, it is not the teacher, but the student who is responsible for the exploration and argumentation of both the analysis and the plan of action. The focus is on students' learning through their joint, cooperative effort, rather than on the teacher's views conveyed to the students (this is what is done in the lecture method). The teacher has important roles to play, but it does not include telling the students the facts (this is what is done in the lecture method). Teachers ask questions to guide students' discussion into unconsidered but important areas. Teachers manage the progress of discussion according to the time available. When other students do not challenge superficial thinking of a student, teachers lead the student along the path of his or her thinking until he or she sees the consequences of his or her thinking.

In the case method, each student is expected to contribute to the learning of the class: (a) by actively participating; (b) by taking risks; (c) by teaching others; and (d) by learning from the teacher and classmates.

In the case method, each student is expected to take a series of steps in the following order:

1. Before Class: Each student receives the case and the reading assignments, reads and prepares individually, participates in a small group discussion of the case.
2. During Class: Each student asks questions on reading assignments, participates in class discussion of the case by sharing his or her insight and listening carefully to the insight of others.
3. After Class: Each student reviews his or her preparation along with the class discussion and notes the concepts learned.

In the case method, each student is expected to perform the following activities:

1. To prepare, through reading of materials and analysis of the case under consideration.
2. To offer viewpoints where these differ from the class in order to:
   a. Improve his or her thinking and skills at analysis.
   b. Improve the class discussion of the case.
3. To develop both his or her theoretical and conceptual model(s) of the topic and the field under study, and his or her skill of problem-solving.
4. To try to make inferences or generalizations on the basis of each case discussed.

In the case method, small group discussions are considered very beneficial. Each student brings some insight into the group discussion, which consequently covers a variety of points faster than the individual, surpasses each separate individual preparation, and reduces the total preparation time. They also learn that it is a good managerial skill to recognize good ideas when presented.

Small group discussions give the student the opportunity to learn to work with others. Students learn to use resource persons more effectively and to appreciate the ideas of others. Small-group skills are particularly useful in practice because much of a manager's time is spent on task forces and committees.

In the case method, teachers may ask students to form their own groups for an initial probationary period, during which they work on a case to decide whether they want to change membership, with no questions asked.

In the case method, in small group discussions, each student is expected to check his or her insights, assumptions, and preparation against those of others; to clarify understanding; to listen attentively and critically to others; and to argue for his or her positions developed during the individual preparation stage.

In the case method, in group and class discussions, students are expected to participate based on the willingness to give and take. Class discussion involves a lot of new ideas which would take a much longer time for a student to uncover alone. The synergy generated by class discussion shows how far the class can go beyond the analysis reached by each student in isolation. It is almost impossible for any student preparation or small group discussion to reach the level of understanding which is achievable by class discussion.

In the case method, the purpose of the class discussion is not just to arrive at a thorough understanding of the case and an optimal resolution of the problem, which is expected in the lecture method. The class discussion also expects students to practice in the large group to share their individual preparations and small group discussions with the rest of the class and to be evaluated by them and the instructor.

In the case method, teachers do not expect that only right answers be part of class discussions. From a pedagogical perspective, wrong answers can provide valuable insights. Mistakes are expected to occur and have to occur for true learning to occur.

In the case method, discussion is based on the idea of the reciprocity between students and teachers. That is, the roles of teacher and student are reversible. Students teach each other, and they teach the teacher. Teachers learn through class discussion, not only by being exposed to students' understandings of the subject but also by accumulating knowledge about teaching.

The case method presents many ideas regarding participatory, student-oriented, active-learning arrangements. The case method involves student participation in discussing the analysis and solution of relevant and practical problems. The case method deals with the testing of theory in practice. The move from the lecture method to the case method involves the move from the position of students as simple recipients of knowledge to participatory education.

Student as an Outsider v. Student as an Insider: In the lecture method, the purpose is to find the most efficient solution to the company's problems. In the case method, it is important that every student tries to solve the problem because it is only through participation that students can become part of that process.

In the lecture method, students do not role-play and they do not know who they are in relation to the problem. They spend a lot of time and energy with numbers and expect those numbers to lead them to the answer because they believe the answer is in the numbers. If they do not find the answer, it is because they do not know how to deal with numbers.

In the case method, the case is translated into an experience. Students take the role of the manager in the case. To show the importance of qualitative aspects of the situation, case teachers discuss a case without reference to numbers. They ask the students to regard the case as an experience, get inside it, start somewhere, and find his or her solution to the problem.

In the case method, the group discussion process provides students with valuable practical learning opportunities. In practice, business problems are decided on after they are discussed among smaller or larger groups. Each case class is a practical experience both in group's behavior and group discussions in arriving at business decisions. Each case class provides a learning experience in how to listen to the views of others, how to express one's view, and how to persuade others to one's point of view. It gives opportunities to express one's view and gain confidence in one's own judgment, and at times become humiliated. It also provides students with the opportunity to learn how far one can proceed by rigorous logical analysis of some aspects of the problem (which is what the lecture method teaches) and to what extent judgment has to be used in order to weigh many factors which have no common denominator.

In the case method, the basic idea is that students think and learn most when they wrestle with the conditions of the problem, and seek and find their own solution. If they cannot find their own solution (with the help of the teacher and other students) they do not learn, not even if they can accurately recite some correct answer.

In the case method, education is regarded as consisting of the cumulative and unending acquisition, combination, and reordering of individual experiences; that is, learning experiences should not be described in isolation. Educational growth is considered to consist of combining past experiences with present experiences in order to understand future experiences. That is, students must continually and cohesively reorganize and reformulate past experiences with new experiences.

In the case method, students routinely apply the classical problem-solving model of case analysis: problem, causes, analysis, alternatives, evaluation, decision, and implementation. There are two major benefits for students when they go through these steps routinely. First, they assume the active participation role in the case. Second, they develop the managerial, decision-making skills.

In the case method, the student takes the place of the decision-maker in the case, without assuming the personality and gender of the individual in the case. Thus, the student brings his or her personal skills, background, and biases to the situation at hand. In the individual preparation stage, the student faces the problem, takes advantage of opportunities, and makes a decision. The student's acceptance of this role and the assumption of responsibilities are major challenges in the use of cases. It is very comfortable to be an observer of and commentator about the situation, which is the role of students in the lecture method. The student benefits more if the acceptance of the ownership of the situation and the assumption of the role take place earlier.

In the case method, a standard case assignment question is as follows: "If you were in John Doe's position in this organization, what would be your analysis of the situation described, and what action would you take and why?" If no assignment questions are provided with the case, the student is expected to ask him- or her-self that question.

In their case analysis, students take the role of the focal person in the case. They do not change their age, gender, personality, or experience, but imagine themselves in the shoes of John Doe. The student brings his or her values, age, gender, background, theoretical and practical understanding, training, expertise, and culture into the position. The background of the organization and the problem remain as identified in the case, but the task facing John Doe has now become that of the student.

Fundamental to the case learning process is the student's acceptance of the ownership of the problem. Questions such as "If the student were a consultant to John Doe, what would the student recommend?" and "What is the student's assessment of this organization's situation?" distant the student from the role the student should play. That is, the student is turned into a spectator, commentator, or bystander, rather than a problem-solver or decision-maker.

In the case method, students are enabled to discover and develop their unique framework for approaching, understanding, and dealing with business problems.

Theoretical Exposure v. Theoretical and Practical Exposure: Integration of theory with practice has been one of the enduring questions in business education. In the lecture method, the teacher's goal is to teach the theory. In the case method, the teacher's goal is to integrate theory and practice. The case method is based on the principle of growth through experience, that is, practice makes perfect and permanent.

In the case method, teacher's emphasis is on relating analysis and action. The lecture method's goal has been to know, while the practitioner's necessity has been to act. The case method's goal has been to combine these two activities. This is because the application of knowledge has been the manager's primary task. Knowledge has always been partial to the complexities of administrative problems and has never been capable of providing complete solutions.

In the case method, teachers believe that learning is contextual in at least the following three ways: (1) New knowledge is acquired by extending and revising prior knowledge; (2) New ideas gain meaning when they are presented in a coherent relationship to one another; and (3) Knowledge becomes usable when it entails applications to concrete problem-solving situations.

In the case method, teachers use cases as an effective way of bringing actual experience into the classroom which leads to rich educational discussion. It is learning by doing, learning from others, and teaching others. It is a learning which remains deeply ingrained in students. The routine exercise to identifying, analyzing, and solving problems in different settings converts students to professionals for their field of work. Students experience the world of management, that is, a rehearsal of life.

Typically, a case is a partial, historical, and clinical record for the study of a business situation, which involves an opportunity, a challenge, a decision confronted actually by a practicing administrator or managerial group. Furthermore, a case also provides information about the surrounding facts, opinions, and prejudices upon which executive decisions have to depend. Normally, it is written from the viewpoint of the decision-maker and the student is expected to play the role of the decision-maker. Students analyze, discuss, and decide on these real and company-specific cases with due consideration of the complexity and ambiguity of the practical world.

In the case method, teacher's emphasis is on the primacy of situational analysis. This situational orientation focuses on what can be said to a specific manager, at a specific time, and on a specific issue, which stands in contrast to the generalized prescriptions of the lecture method. From the experience accumulated after many case discussions, the student derives generalization, but they are stated tentatively, tested frequently, and used carefully.

In general, teachers set priorities for their courses. This means that, during the limited class time, topics with higher priority will receive preference over others. In the case method, this starts with a review of course objectives, case objectives, plans for this particular class within the sequence of all classes, and the importance of having this class and this case within this class. In teaching with cases, priority is not only given to making sure that certain concepts are fully understood but also to sorting or specification of information, problem identification and analysis, proper application of relevant theory to practice, alternative generation, decision-making, and implementation planning. Initially, priority is given to familiarizing students with the discussion process and the teacher's expectations regarding proper student preparation and participation in class. Priorities are, therefore, multidimensional, and are both process and content based. In the lecture method, priority is given only to making sure that certain concepts are fully understood.

In the case method, teachers help students to develop a disciplined mental approach to an unstructured problem. Students learn to distinguish and define the problem and select the proper tool. In the lecture method, teachers place too much emphasis on the technical details in class. This allows knowledgeable teachers to gain the respect of students, but, many students do not know how to define the problem in tackling a managerial issue.

In the case method, teachers aim at preparing students for decision making in business. Therefore, they do not expect students to perform detailed numerical calculations which are not necessary. This is in contrast to the lecture method.

In the lecture method, students graduate with the impression that their education has provided them with anybody of specific knowledge, any set of formulae, any answers, or any patterns of behavior that enable students immediately to become successful administrators. In the case method, students are trained to analyze a situation, to formulate a program of action, and to effectively implement that program through the people in their organization. These students are aware that business problems do not lend themselves to one simple, right method of analysis which arrives at the end at the only correct answer. This is in contrast to the lecture method. Business and social communities vitally need qualities of judgment and leadership.

In the case method, teachers place students in cases which involve serious and important experiences for them in their careers, including activities which they must perform well in their careers. In designing their new case course, teachers get excited, concerned, worried, enthusiastic, and very much involved with problems that they see in business, in the economy, and with managers who are struggling and attempting to cope.

As an example, consider the Human Resources course. A teacher, who uses either the case method or the lecture method, knows that the conceptual theoretical knowledge for human resources management is in the library. But only the case teacher asks: What are some companies doing about it? What are some managers of human resources doing about it? What is their role? What is their opportunity?

As another example, consider the Investment Management course. There are at least two ways to organize the course. One way is to decide on the textbooks and the literature, which is what both the lecture method teacher and the case method teacher would do. However, the case teacher is aware that the investment textbooks do not have much to offer about the management of investments. The case teacher, therefore, adds a second way of organizing the course by talking to people in the investment business. In this way, the case teacher gets an accurate picture of what issues leading practitioners wrestle with, specific examples, possible cases, as well as recommendations of who else the case teacher should talk to about the business in general. Then the case teacher decides on the organization of the course.

In the lecture method, the proper relationship of theory and practice is as follows. Rigorous professional practice is essentially technical. Its rigor is defined by the use of describable, testable, replicable techniques derived from scientific research, based on knowledge which is objective, consensual, cumulative, and convergent. Accordingly, rigorous management requires the use of management science.

In the lecture method, practice is technical only when certain things are kept isolated from one another. Deciding and doing must be kept separate from one another. Means and ends must be kept separate from one another. Research and practice must be kept separate from one another. Research can generate new knowledge only in the protected setting of the scholar's study or in the carefully controlled environment of a scientific laboratory.

In the case method, managers convert an uncertain situation into a solvable problem. They construct not only the means to be used but also the ends to be achieved. That is, ends and means are reciprocally determined. In the unstable world of practice, where methods and theories developed and applicable in one context are not suitable in another, practitioners function as researchers and invent the techniques and models which are appropriate for the situation at hand. The world of practice is notoriously unprotected and uncontrollable. The lecture method's view of practice leads to the dilemma of rigor or relevance.

In the lecture method, professional rigor and rigorous practice depend on well-formed problems of instrumental choice which require research-based theory and technique to obtain their solutions. In the case method, real-world problems are not well-formed. They are messy, indeterminate, problematic situations. The term practice takes full account of the competencies practitioners display in situations of uncertainty, complexity, and uniqueness. Case teachers and students should analyze how skilled practitioners build up repertoires of exemplars, images, and strategies of description in terms of which they learn to see novel, one-of-a-kind phenomena.

Competitive Education v. Collaborative Education: In the case method, discussion forms the basis of learning. Cases provide the focus for the exchange of ideas and the joint stakeholders are instructors and students. The class discussion requires individual preparation and small group discussion as prerequisites. Small groups—alternatively referred to as study groups, learning teams, syndicates, or break-out groups—give students the opportunity to discuss their insights about the case.

In the case method, the climate of case discussion is one of collaboration, not competition, which prevails in the lecture method. All class participants share their ideas and insights, which become public knowledge. The students learn to be flexible in the give and take and exchange of ideas.

In the case method, the class discussion reflects the collective efforts of all students, helped by a teacher, which provides the opportunity for further improvement of each student's learning. The group synergy is achieved by the commitment of the whole class to the best utilization of the limited class time and to the collective search for superior insights.

In the case method, at the core of the case discussion process, there is a fundamental insight that teaching and learning are inseparable as both are parts of a single continuum of reciprocal giving and receiving. In class discussion, students share the task of teaching with the teacher and one another, that is, all teach, and all learn.

In the case method, class discussion is based on the idea of learning by teaching, adding to the collective wisdom of the whole class, comparing self-preparation and delivery with a sample of colleagues one may professionally work with in a future career. Students' performance in the case classroom is a reliable indication of their performance in the real organization. Performance means being active in contributing, listening, questioning, and responding.

In the case method, case discussions provide a safe environment for the students' evolving ideas. This is because the case method emphasizes cooperation and values contributions. Not all opinions are equally correct as most of the discussions tend toward a consensus that finds some approaches to be more correct than others. Of course, class discussion reaches its goals only when all contributors' ideas are explored.

In the case method, students learn through case discussion by listening, talking, and reflecting. The effective participation in a case discussion requires listening and thinking at the same time. Meaningful contributions relate to both the case content and the discussion process. The way a student expresses his or her ideas significantly affects its acceptance.

In the case method, active listening requires understanding not only what is being said but also what it being meant. Listening should accompany an open mind. Preconceptions and experiences greatly limit the capacity to hear and understand. It takes a lot of time and effort to really hear and understand someone's spoken words and implied feelings. The goal should be listening for the total meaning, which includes both the verbal and nonverbal components of the message, that is, both the content and the underlying attitudes and values which are conveyed.

In the case method, active listening has an evaluative component. Students compare their peers' views with their own ideas and positions. Students tend to determine whether they agree with their peers' views or not and explain why. These encourage students to further participate in the discussion.

In the case method, class discussion allows students to reflect on their own preparation in comparison with the class position at the end of the class period. Students determine whether they agreed or disagreed with others and why. Students realize whether they did well or poorly in their individual preparation and in their small group discussion and why.

In the case method, in their discussions, students share their analysis, subject their ideas to open debate, take risks, and critique others' positions in a positive manner. Students regard participation not as a problem, but as an opportunity with high pay-off which allows them to develop a set of skills for effectiveness and success in their chosen profession. The process of case discussion is similar to real-life public and private meetings which are conducted after the business issue has been discussed by smaller units such as project teams, taskforce, or committees.

In the case method, small groups provide opportunities to increase student's performance and to improve student's learning. Small group working sessions, when properly undertaken, constitute an enriching component of the case learning experience.

In the case method, ideally, each discussion group should contain a variety of skills, cultures, experiences, and expertise. The variety of perspectives from members with diverse backgrounds enriches the group discussions. A balanced distribution of members with quantitative and qualitative skills improves the overall learning in the group discussions.

In the case method, each small group develops its own rules of conduct, standards of participation, and expectations of members' behavior.

In the case method, each student arrives at his or her own decisions based on both the individual preparation as well as the small group discussion. It is not always necessary for a group discussion to achieve consensus or a group position. That is, students do not need to agree with each other on the solution of the case. In real life, consensus becomes important because then key stakeholders would support the implementation of major decisions. In small group discussion, diversity of opinions and options enriches student learning but with insufficient availability of time group's ability to achieve consensus becomes limited.

In the case method, case discussion allows each student to influence the outcome. Students who plan and regularly hold short small group meetings to exchange views on each case will acquire superior learning, better team management skills, and increased self-confidence.

In the case method, many factors influence the level of student's participation: the teaching style and skills of the teacher; student's own personality, background, experience, and culture; course content; and the cases themselves.

In the case method, students in case classes have the opportunity to stretch, test, push, fend, and grow such that they will be prepared for the challenges ahead in the professional world.

In the case method, the program involves a culture which is fundamentally different from the culture of the lecture method. The case method involves a change in culture away from the individual, competitive model of the lecture method to one in which students succeed through teamwork. Furthermore, the case method involves a change in culture away from a conception of curriculum as discrete bits of factual information of the lecture method to one in which students are introduced to powerful synthetic, analytic structures for ideas.

Knowledge v. Knowledge and Skills: In the lecture method, students study by themselves and take examinations. In the case method, the ability to communicate well, whether with another person or with a group, is considered more important than the ability to write a good examination. This is what the business world prefers as well.

In the case method, the goal is the development of analytical and decision-making skills rather than the acquisition of knowledge of management theories and techniques, which is the goal in the lecture method. Of course, such knowledge is important and its acquisition is more effective through lectures and readings.

In the case method, students develop their critical-thinking skills because they believe that these skills, and not the sole pursuit of management theories, that differentiate between managers in successful and less successful organizations.

In the case method, students develop skills such as oral communication, debating, persuasion, resolving issues, and time management. They gain a sense of confidence in themselves and in relating to their peers. Their exposure to a variety of business situations broadens their views and skills.

In the case method, students develop presentation skills. They learn that in any presentation there are certain common elements. They learn that their presentation is not just for content but also for style of delivery, eye contact, poise, timing, linking between various presenters, and use of visual aids. They become aware of the importance of mannerism and asking for feedback. They improve their presentation skills through rehearsal and gain confidence.

The overriding goal for an educational experience is that students who go through it change in certain desirable ways. There is a broad range of learning goals to choose from. The case method provides the students with the opportunity to develop a wide range of skills as follows:

Acquire knowledge
Develop concepts
Understand techniques
Acquire skill in the use of a technique, concept, or knowledge
Acquire skill in analysis of complex and unstructured problems
Acquire skill in synthesis of plans for action and implementation
Grow in ability to listen
Grow in ability to form trustworthy relationships
Develop certain attitudes, (e.g., Responsibility—for own decision, for
   outcomes; Skepticism; Criticism—of self, of status quo; Confidence—
   "can do")
Develop ability to communicate—briefly, effectively, persuasively
Develop certain qualities of mind, (e.g., Distinguishing between hopes,
   beliefs, inferences, facts; Clarity of objectives and purposes; Analysis;
   Self-starting—initiative; A set of standards—moral, business, institutional)
Develop judgment and wisdom, (e.g., To foresee implications, outcomes;
   To place situations in a long range, broad perspective; To generalize—
   accurately from specifics at the level of detail, to perceive trends and
   develop useful concepts).

The above is in line with Bloom's Taxonomy of learning outcomes:

Evaluation: Form criteria, make judgments, detect fallacies, evaluate,
decide

Synthesis: Produce a new communication not clearly evident before
(requires originality or creativity).

Analysis: Identify components, how they are related and arranged; distinguishing fact from fiction.

Application: Apply understandings to solve new problems in new situations when no directions or methods of solution are specified.

Comprehension: Change the information to a more meaningful parallel form, paraphrase, interpret, infer, imply, extrapolate when told to do so (lowest level of understanding).

Knowledge: State terms, specific facts, definitions, categories, ways of doing things (No evidence of understanding is required. The learner needs only to "boomerang" back information given).

In the case method, students are expected to analyze and evaluate the circumstances of the problems, to make decisions, and construct programs of action for their execution appropriate for the particular situations. The process is inductive rather than deductive. Students are expected to become proficient in analyzing administrative problems, reaching decisions for desirable actions, and formulating programs for effecting the decision. They are expected to realize that the purpose is not the development of generalizations or principles even though such development may provide ideas for consideration in dealing with a specific situation.

The case method is excellent for developing a variety of ideas, a depth of understanding of factors involved in administrative problems, considerable skill in the analysis of these factors, significant skill in thinking of and appraising alternative courses of action, reaching a sensible decision among them, and in planning to make the decision effective.

NOTES

1. For this literature, see Alford (1996), Belenky, Clinchy, Goldberger, and Tarule (1986), Bergmann (1990), Ferber, Birnbaum, and Green (1983), Hirschfeld, Moore, and Brown (1995), Kruger, Arrow, Blanchard, Blinder, Goldin, Leamer, Lucas, Panzar, Penner, Schultz, Stiglitz, Summers, (1991), Lumsden and Scott (1987), Nelson (1995), Niederle and Vesterlund (2010), Niederle and Vesterlund (2011), Olsen and Cox (2001), Quade (1994), Richardson (1996), Rosener (1990), Rutenberg (1983), Shackleford (1992), Westkott (1983), and Whatley (1986). This section is based on Belenky, Clinchy, Goldberger, and Tarule (1986).

2. For this literature, see Ardalan (2003a, b, 2006, 2008, 2013), Barnes, Hansen, and Christensen (1994), Barrow and White (1993), Barrow and Woods (1989), Blake, Smeyers, Standish, and Smith (2000), Brosio (1998), Burrell and Morgan (1979), Byrne (2009), Cahn (1996), Carr (2003), Chambliss (1996), Christensen and Garvin (1991), Cromer (1997), Curren (2003), Dooley and Skinner (1977), Ellis, Cogan, and Howey (1991), Erskine, Leenders, and Mauffette-Leenders (2003), Freedman (1996), Gragg (1954), Gutek (2000a, b, 2003), Hancock (1999), Hare and Portelli (2001), Hickman and Alexander (1998), Kimball and Orrill (1995), Larochelle, Bednarz, and Garrison, (1998), Marples (1999), Mauffette-Leenders, Erskine, and Leenders (2005), McLaren (1998), Morgan (1983), Noddings (1998), Orrill (1999), Ozmon and Craver (2002), Philosophy of Education Society (2003), Popkewitz and Fendler (1999), Power (1995), Reynolds (1978), Rorty (1998), Sadovnik, Semel, and Cookson (2000), Schrag (1995), Talisse and Hester (2002), and Winch and Gingell (1999). This section is based on Ardalan (2006, 2008, 2013).

REFERENCES

Alford, Katrina. 1996. "Gender and Economics." *Academy of the Social Sciences in Australia Newsletter* 15(4): 21–26.

Aralan, Kavous. 2008. "The Philosophical Foundation of the Lecture-versus-Case Controversy: Its Implications for Course Goals, Objectives, and Contents." *International Journal of Social Economics* 35(1/2): 15–34.

Ardalan, Kavous. 2003a. "The Lecture-versus-Case Controversy: Its Philosophical Foundation." *Southwestern Economic Review* 30(1): 99–118.

Ardalan, Kavous. 2003b. "Alternative Approaches Utilized in the Case Method: Their Philosophical Foundations." *Academy of Educational Leadership Journal* 30(3): 103–120.

Ardalan, Kavous. 2006. "The Philosophical Foundation of the Lecture-versus-Case Controversy: Its Implications for Faculty Teaching, Research, and Service." *International Journal of Social Economics* 33(3): 261–281.

Ardalan, Kavous. 2013. "The Philosophical Foundation of the Lecture Method of Instruction and the Case Method of Instruction: Implications for Examinations." *Contemporary Issues in Education Research* 6(1): 1–7.

Barnes, Louis B., Abby J. Hansen, and C. Roland Christensen. 1994. *Teaching and the Case Method: Text, Cases, and Readings.* Cambridge, MA: Harvard Business School Press.

Barrow, Robin, and Patricia White, eds. 1993. *Beyond Liberal Education: Essays in Honor of Paul H. Hirst.* New York, NY: Routledge.

Barrow, Robin, and Ronald Woods. 1989. *An Introduction to Philosophy of Education.* New York, NY: Routledge.

Belenky, Mary Field, Blythe McVicker Clinchy, Nancy Rule Goldberger, and Jill Mattuck Tarule. 1986. *Women's Ways of Knowing: The Development of Self, Voice, and Mind.* New York, NY: Basic Books.

Bergmann, Barbara R. 1990. "Reading Lists on Women's Studies in Economics." *Women's Studies Quarterly* 18(3/4): 75–86.

Blake, Nigel, Paul Smeyers, Paul Standish, and Richard Smith, eds. 2000. *The Blackwell Guide to the Philosophy of Education.* Hoboken, NJ: Blackwell Publishers.

Brosio, Richard A. 1998. "The Continuing Correspondence Between Political Economy and Schooling: Telling the News." *Journal of Thought* 33(3): 85–105.

Burrell, Gibson, and Gareth Morgan. 1979. *Sociological Paradigms and Organizational Analysis.* Hants, England: Gower Publishing Company Limited.

Byrne, D. 2009. "Case-Based Methods: What They Are; Why We Need Them; How to Do Them." In *The Sage Handbook of Case-Based Methods*, edited by D. Byrne, and C. Ragin, 1–10. London, England: Sage Publications.

Cahn, Steven M., ed. 1996. *Classic and Contemporary Readings in the Philosophy of Education.* New York, NY: McGraw-Hill College Division.

Carr, David. 2003. *Making Sense of Education: An Introduction to the Philosophy and Theory of Education.* New York, NY: Routledge.

Chambliss, J.J., ed. 1996. *Philosophy of Education: An Encyclopedia.* New York, NY: Garland Publishers.

Christensen, C. Roland, and David A. Garvin, eds. 1991. *Education for Judgment.* Cambridge, MA: Harvard Business School Press.

Cromer, Alan H. 1997. *Connected Knowledge: Science, Philosophy, and Education.* Oxford, England: Oxford University Press.

Curren, Randall R., ed. 2003. *Companion to the Philosophy of Education.* Hoboken, NJ: Blackwell Publishers.

Dooley, Arch R., and Wickham Skinner. 1977. "Casing Casemethod Methods." *Academy of Management Review* (April): 277–289.

Ellis, Arthur K., John J. Cogan, and Kenneth R. Howey. 1991. *Introduction to the Foundations of Education.* New York, NY: Prentice Hall.

Erskine, James A., Michiel R. Leenders, and Louise A. Mauffette-Leenders. 2003. *Teaching with Cases,* 3rd edition, London, ON: University of Western Ontario, Ivey Business School, Erskine Associate Inc., and Leenders and Associates Inc.

Ferber, Marianne A., Bonnie G. Birnbaum, and Carole A. Green. 1983. "Gender Differences in Economic Knowledge: A Reevaluation of the Evidence." *Journal of Economic Education* 14(2): 24–37.

Freedman, James O. 1996. *Idealism and Liberal Education.* Ann Harbor, MI: University of Michigan Press.

Gragg, Charles I. 1954. "Because Wisdom Can't Be Told." In *The Case Method at the Harvard Business School,* edited by Malcolm P. McNair, 6–12. New York, NY: McGraw-Hill Book Company, Inc.

Gutek, Gerald Lee. 2000a. *Philosophical and Ideological Perspectives on Education,* 3rd edition. Boston, MA: Allyn and Bacon.

Gutek, Gerald Lee. 2000b. *Historical and Philosophical Foundations of Education: Selected Readings.* New York, NY: Prentice Hall, College Division.

Gutek, Gerald Lee. 2003. *Philosophical and Ideological Voices in Education,* 1st edition. Boston, MA: Allyn and Bacon.

Hancock, Ralph C., ed. 1999. *America, the West, and Liberal Education.* New York, NY: Rowman and Littlefield.

Hare, William, and John P. Portelli, eds. 2001. *Philosophy of Education: Introductory Readings,* 3rd edition. Middlesex, NJ: Detseling Enterprises.

Hickman, Larry, and Thomas M. Alexander, eds. 1998. *The Essential Dewey: Pragmatism, Education, Democracy.* Bloomington, IN: Indiana University Press.

Hirschfeld, Mary, Robert L. Moore, and Eleanor Brown. 1995. "Exploring the Gender Gap on the GRE Subject Test in Economics." *Journal of Economic Education* 26(1): 3–15.

Kimball, Bruce A., and Robert Orrill, eds. 1995. *The Condition of American Liberal Education: Pragmatism and a Changing Tradition.* New York, NY: College Entrance Examination Board.

Kruger, Ann O., Kenneth J. Arrow, Olivier Jean Blanchard, Alan S. Blinder, Claudia Goldin, Edward E. Leamer, Robert Lucas, John Panzar, Rudolph G. Penner, T. Paul Schultz, Joseph E. Stiglitz, and Lawrence H. Summers. 1991. "Report of the Commission on Graduate Education in Economics." *Journal of Economic Literature* 29(3): 1035–1053.

Larochelle, Marie, Nadine Bednarz, and Jim Garrison, eds. 1998. *Constructivism and Education.* Cambridge, England: Cambridge University Press.

Lumsden, Keith G., and Alex Scott. 1987. "The Economics Student Reexamined: Male-Female Differences in Comprehension." *Journal of Economic Education* 18(4): 365–375.

Marples, Roger, ed. 1999. *The Aims of Education.* New York, NY: Routledge.

Mauffette-Leenders, Louise A., James A. Erskine, and Michiel R. Leenders. 2005. *Learning with Cases,* 3rd edition. London, ON: University of Western Ontario, Ivey Business School, Ivey Publishing.

McLaren, Peter. 1998. "Revolutionary Pedagogy in Post-Revolutionary Times: Rethinking the Political Economy of Critical Education." *Educational Theory* 48(4): 431–462.

Morgan, Gareth. 1983. *Beyond Method: Strategies for Social Research.* Beverley Hills, CA: Sage Publications.

Nelson, Julie A. 1995. "Feminism and Economics." *Journal of Economic Perspectives* 9(2): 131–148.

Niederle, Muriel, and Lise Vesterlund. 2010. "Explaining the Gender Gap in Math Test Scores: The Role of Competition." *Journal of Economic Perspectives* 24(2): 129–144.

Niederle, Muriel, and Lise Vesterlund. 2011. "Gender and Competition." *Annual Review Economics* 3: 601–630.

Noddings, Nel. 1998. *Philosophy of Education.* Boulder, CO: Westview Press.

Olsen, Robert A., and Constance M. Cox. 2001. "The Influence of Gender on the Perception and Response to Investment Risk: The Case of Professional Investors." *Journal of Psychology and Financial Markets* 2(1): 29–36.

Orrill, Robert, ed. 1999. *Education and Democracy: Re-Imaging Liberal Learning in America.* New York, NY: College Entrance Examination Board.

Ozmon, Howard A., and Samuel M. Craver. 2002. *Philosophical Foundations of Education*, 7th edition. New York, NY: Prentice Hall.

Philosophy of Education Society. 2003. *Philosophy of Education 2002.* New York, NY: Philosophy of Education Society Press.

Popkewitz, Thomas S., and Lynn Fendler, eds. 1999. *Critical Theories in Education: Changing Terrains of Knowledge and Politics.* New York, NY: Routledge.

Power, Edward J. 1995. *Educational Philosophy: A History from the Ancient World to Modern America.* New York, NY: Garland Publishers.

Quade, Ann, ed. 1994. *The Feminist Economics Curriculum Project.* Sacramento, CA: California State University at Sacramento, Committee of the International Association for Feminist Economics.

Reynolds, John I. 1978. "There's Method in Cases." *Academy of Management Review* (January): 129–133.

Richardson, Sue. 1996. "Why Women Make Lousy Economists." *Academy of Social Sciences in Australia Newsletter* 15(4): 19–20.

Rorty, Amelie Oksenberg, ed. 1998. *Philosophers on Education: Historical Perspectives.* New York, NY: Routledge.

Rosener, Judy B. 1990. "Ways Women Lead." *Harvard Business Review* (Nov./Dec.): 3–10.

Rutenberg, Taly. 1983. "Learning Women's Studies." In *Theories of Women's Studies*, edited by Gloria Bowles, and Renate Duelli Klein, 72–78. London, England: Routledge and Kegan Paul.

Sadovnik, Alan R., Susan Semel, and Peter Cookson. 2000. *Exploring Education: An Introduction to the Foundations of Education*, 2nd edition. Boston, MA: Allyn and Bacon.

Schrag, Francis. 1995. *Back to Basics: Fundamental Educational Questions Reexamined.* Hoboken, NJ: Jossey-Bass Education Series.

Shackleford, Jean. 1992. "Feminist Pedagogy: A Means for Bringing Critical Thinking and Creativity to the Economics Classroom." *American Economic Review* 82(2): 570–576.

Talisse, Robert B. and D. Micah Hester. 2002. *On the Philosophy of Education.* Belmont, CA: Wadsworth Publishing.

Westkott, Marcia. 1983. "Women's Studies as a Strategy for Change: Between Criticism and Vision." In *Theories of Women's Studies*, edited by Gloria Bowles, and Renate Duelli Klein, 210–218. London, England: Routledge and Kegan Paul.

Whatley, Mariamne H. 1986. "Taking Feminist Science to the Classroom: Where Do We Go from Here?" In *Feminist Approaches to Science*, edited by Ruth Bleier, 181–190. New York, NY: Pergamon Press.

Winch, Christopher, and John Gingell. 1999. *Key Concepts in the Philosophy of Education.* New York, NY: Routledge.

Chapter 10

Economics versus Sociology

A Paradigmatic View

This chapter briefly reviews the work of the prominent feminist Julie Nelson (2010) in order to show that the idea that underlies such work is that economics, as is currently practiced, is associated with the functionalist paradigm; and sociology, as it is proposed by Julie Nelson, is associated with the interpretive paradigm. The work shows the gendered nature of the division into two disciplines of economics and sociology that took place in the late nineteenth and early twentieth centuries, and appreciates current efforts, such as economic sociology, devoted to bringing the fields more closely together. It performs a historical investigation of the gendered processes underlying the divergence of the two disciplines in terms of definition, method, and degree of engagement with social problems.[1]

Consider the following two declarations which are made by two scholarly associations. The first one, which reflects the "Scope of the Society" adopted by the Econometric Society on the occasion of its founding in 1930 in Cleveland, Ohio, is as follows. The Society will operate as a completely disinterested, scientific organization. Its main objective will be to promote studies that attempt to unify the theoretical-quantitative and the empirical-quantitative approach to economic problems; and that are penetrated by constructive and rigorous thinking similar to that which has dominated in the natural sciences.

The second one, which reflects the editorial announcement of the formation of the American Sociological Association (then called the American Sociological *Society*), reporting on its first conference in 1907 in Providence, Rhode Island, is as follows. The members of our Society do not intend to destroy the vocation of other investigators of society. They intend to represent factors in the problems of human association which have thus far received less than their required attention. They, in organizing a society, are not beginning, but continuing, the appreciation of those neglected factors. The society does not ask for credit. It simply encourages sociological inquiry and competent judgment of results.

The first declaration emphasizes scientific method, quantitative analysis, and "hard" sciences. It uses strong verbs and adjectives, and especially the quasi-sexual (from a sexist and macho-masculine viewpoint) language, that is, penetrate and dominate. Its gender is decidedly masculine.

The second declaration, in contrast, is very considerate and supportive. It is very subservience and passive, and strongly reflects the sexist imagination of feminine sexual and social roles. Its gender is decidedly feminine.

The fields of economics and sociology, in the United States, through various means, chose separate methodological and subject-matter territories at the turn of the twentieth century. It is very important to recognize the heavily gendered nature of the historical, and still-existing, division between the discipline of economics and the discipline sociology. Such recognition enhances any future development of a rapprochement between the two fields. Understanding the way sexist, dualistic, and hierarchical notions of gender have shaped the two disciplines would enable richer, stronger, more resilient, and less biased forms of economic and social knowledge.

The concern is not with respect to the sex of the subjects of study or the sex of the practitioners, but the concern is with respect to "gender," that is, the associations cultures build up on top of the sexual differences. More specifically, the concern is with respect to the "cognitive" functions of gender, that is, how gender shapes the way people think. Indeed, such gender associations become a part of automatic, unconscious mental processes. For instance, in contemporary U.S. culture, dogs are gendered masculine, and cats are gendered feminine. Similarly, abstract shapes are gendered: curvy, enveloping ones are perceived as feminine; and sharp, angular ones are perceived as masculine. The purpose of discussing these associations is not to endorse or reinforce them. Rather, the purpose is to highlight the cognitive role of gendering as an extant psychological phenomenon. This can be done by bringing out into the open the phenomenon which is at the unexamined and unconscious level.

Feminist philosophers of science have noted the way gendered patterns of thought have influenced the development of scientific endeavor, from the time of the Enlightenment onward. Metaphors used to describe the rise of scientific thinking over prescientific thought and nature have often been in the form of contrasts between masculine and feminine, such as: mind v. nature and the body; reason v. emotion and social commitment; subject v. object and objectivity v. subjectivity; and the abstract v. the concrete and the general v. the particular. In each opposition, the former (which is masculine) dominates the latter (which is feminine).

Furthermore, on the one hand, separation, logical consistency, individual accomplishment, and mathematics have been culturally and cognitively associated with rigor, hardness, and masculinity. On the other hand, connection, intuitive understanding, sociality, and qualitative analysis have been associated with weakness, softness, and femininity. Such associations were sometimes made as explicit as stating the goal of scholarly activity as raising a masculine philosophy so that the mind of man can be promoted by the knowledge of solid truths.

Cognitive gender is also crucially hierarchical in the dominant culture. For instance, "reason" refers to a masculine trait with a positive "up" connotation, while "emotion" refers to a feminine trait and carries a negative "down" connotation.

The history of professional societies in the United States shows a recurring concern with defining disciplines that could be thought to be scientific. What are currently known as the separate fields of economics and sociology were formed out of an earlier, more general "social science," which, in the 1860s, included history, "political economy," politics, social work, and other similar fields of study. Over time, the gendered understandings of science shaped the disciplines of economics and sociology.

Perhaps Descartes' division between "res cogitans" and "res extensa" underlies how economics modeled itself based on assumptions of (hyper-) rationality and detachment, and on the belief that the economy should be considered as being a-social. Adam Smith brought in the idea that the economy is an inhuman, purely mechanical system (driven by the "energy" of self-interest). In 1836 John Stuart Mill wrote an essay, in which he carefully distinguished economics from other disciplines, laid out both the central assumptions and the methodology (including the rational-choice-theory definition of economics and the original description of "economic man"), which neoclassical economists adopted.

Neoclassical economists, that is, "marginalists," in the nineteenth century, developed Mill's idea that political economy must become an axiomatic-deductive enterprise in order to be "scientific." The major neoclassical economists were Francis Edgeworth, Stanley Jevons, Leon Walras, and Vilfredo Pareto. These scholars mathematically formalized Mill's idea of economic behavior based on the pursuit of "wealth" using models borrowed from Newtonian physics. These notions led to abstract mathematical modeling of consumers' desire to maximize utility, and firms' desire to maximize profit. By the 1930s the victory of neoclassical approach—whether called "scientism," "objectivism," or "positivism"—among mainstream economists had been almost complete.

Economics, then, rose to the high status. It captured the "masculine" subjects of markets and business. It undertook the study of such subjects with a "masculine" armory of rigorous, precise, mathematical, deductive, abstract tools. It considered individuals to be thoroughly (in masculine way) rational and detached from all social connection, as well as living in a world of cut-throat competition for scarce resources. Its notion of scientific objectivity promoted detachment, that is, detachment from social influences, detachment from the object of study, detachment from other researchers, and detachment from practical and ethical concerns.

As economics captured the high status ground, sociology took the left-overs: marriage, the family, poverty, crime, education, religion, and sex, that is, areas of women's traditional activity and of pressing social problems. Sociology's methods and models are more diverse, and its connection to social change more salient. But, the issue that sociology is not quite a sci-ence has been a strong recurring theme in the discipline. Whereas economists took the up and masculine position, sociologists, as a group, took the down and feminine position, no matter what their particular sex, interests, abilities, or degree of critical leaning was. As long as, on the one hand, economics is associated with the hierarchical and sexist values of masculinity, detachment, science, and high value; and on the other hand, sociology is associated with femininity, sociality, softness, and lesser value, the situation is unlikely to change.

People have sexist and hierarchical habits of thinking that are strong (and are strongly reinforced by social patterns), but they can be changed. The first stage is to decouple gender and sex, so that from the acknowledgment that some characteristic is culturally coded as, say, feminine, one does not errone-ously conclude that it is shared by, or is predominant in, women. Unlinking gender and sex leads to the conclusion that men and women (and transsexual and transgendered persons and persons of ambiguous sexual identity) all have, for instance, both emotional and rational capacities.

The second stage is that in dealing with any prevailing dualism, one should also consider the opposites of the elements of that dualism in order to arrive at a more balanced view of the given dualism. Furthermore, one should con-sider the complementarity nature of the two elements which are involved in the dualism.

For instance, in terms of the comparison of the methodology of econom-ics versus social science, consider the dualism that claims that masculine, precise, quantitative methods are always preferable to feminine, less precise, qualitative analysis. In order to have a more balanced view of this claim, one should consider the opposites of each element of the dualism. One element is quantitative method which is precise, and the other element is qualita-tive method which is imprecise. On the one hand, although the quantitative method is precise and is to be admired, it is unrealistic because it ignores lots of relevant factors. On the other hand, although qualitative method is less precise, it is richer in its analysis. Furthermore, one should take advantage of the complementarity of quantitative and qualitative methods and use them in conjunction with one another.

Good research, as opposed to macho research, should be both as precise and as rich as possible. In many cases, this means combining data crunching with case studies, or survey research with ethnography. At the least, it means appreciating the shortcomings of any study that draws on only one methodology.

NOTE

1. For this literature, see Abbott (2001), Acker (2006), American Economic Association (1895), American Sociological Society (1907), Bem (1981), Bernard (1973), Bordo (1986), Calhoun (2007), Deegan (1988), Ely (1936), England (2003), England and Folbre (2005), Ferber and Nelson (1993), Ferber and Nelson (2003), Furner (1975), Gillin (1927), Harding (1986), Haskell (1977), Keller (1985), Knutson, Mah, Manly, and Grafman (2007), Lakoff and Johnson (1980), Laslett (1990), Longino (1990), Mill (1836), Nelson (1992a, b, 1993, 2001, 2006a, b, 2010), Ogburn (1930), Robbins (1935), Roos (1933), Ross (1991), Silverberg (1998), Small (1916), Smelser and Swedberg (2005), Smith (1994), Spalter-Roth and Scelza (2008), Stacey and Thorne (1985), and Tobin (1985). The rest of this chapter is based on Nelson (2010).

REFERENCES

Abbott, A. 2001. *Chaos of Disciplines*. Chicago, IL: University of Chicago Press.

Acker, J. 2006. "Introduction: 'The Missing Feminist Revolution' Symposium." *Social Problems* 53(4): 444–447.

American Economic Association. 1895. "Constitution." *Publications of the American Economic Association* 10: 10.

American Sociological Society. 1907. "The American Sociological Society." *American Journal of Sociology* 12(5): 579–580.

Bem, S.L. 1981. "Gender Schema Theory: A Cognitive Account of Sex Typing." *Psychological Review* 88(4): 354–364.

Bernard, J. 1973. "My Four Revolutions: An Autobiographical History of the ASA." *American Journal of Sociology* 78(4): 773–791.

Bordo, S. 1986. "The Cartesian Masculinization of Thought." *Signs: Journal of Women in Culture and Society* 11(3): 439–456.

Calhoun, C., ed. 2007. *Sociology in America: A History*. Chicago, IL: University of Chicago Press.

Deegan, M.J. 1988. *Jane Addams and the Men of the Chicago School, 1892–1918*. New Brunswick, NJ: Transaction Publishers.

Ely, R.T. 1936. "The Founding and Early History of the American Economic Association." *American Economic Review* 26(1): 141–150.

England, P. 2003. "Separative and Soluble Selves: Dichotomous Thinking in Economics." In *Feminist Economics Today: Beyond Economic Man*, edited by M.S. Ferber, J.A. Nelson, 33–60. Chicago, IL: University of Chicago Press.

England, P., and N. Folbre. 2005. "Gender and Economic Sociology." In *Handbook of Economic Sociology*, edited by N.J. Smelser, and R. Swedberg, 627–649. Princeton, NJ: Princeton University Press.

Ferber, M.A., and J.A. Nelson. 1993. *Beyond Economic Man: Feminist Theory and Economics.* Chicago, IL: University of Chicago Press.

Ferber, M.A., and J.A. Nelson, eds. 2003. *Feminist Economics Today.* Chicago, IL: University of Chicago Press.

Furner, M.O. 1975. *Advocacy and Objectivity: A Crisis in the Professionalization of American Social Science, 1865–1905.* Lexington, KY: University Press of Kentucky.

Gillin, J.L. 1927. "The Development of Sociology in the United States." *Papers and Proceedings Twenty-First Annual Meeting American Sociological Society* 21: 1–25.

Harding, S. 1986. *The Science Question in Feminism.* Ithaca, NY: Cornell University Press.

Haskell, T.L. 1977. *The Emergence of Professional Social Science: The American Social Science Association and the Nineteenth-Century Crisis of Authority.* Urbana, IL: University of Illinois Press.

Keller, E.F. 1985. *Reflections on Gender and Science.* New Haven, CT: Yale University Press.

Knutson, K.M., L. Mah, C.F. Manly, and J. Grafman. 2007. "Neural Correlates of Automatic Beliefs about Gender and Race." *Human Brain Mapping* 28: 915–930.

Lakoff, G., and M. Johnson. 1980. *Metaphors We Live By.* Chicago, IL: University of Chicago Press.

Laslett, B. 1990. "Unfeeling Knowledge: Emotion and Objectivity in the History of Sociology." *Sociological Forum* 5: 413–433.

Longino, H. 1990. *Science as Social Knowledge: Values and Objectivity in Scientific Inquiry.* Princeton, NJ: Princeton University Press.

Mill, J.S. 1836. "On the Definition of Political Economy; and on the Method of Philosophical Investigation in that Science." *London and Westminster Review* 6(1) 1–29.

Nelson, Julie A. 1992a. "Gender, Metaphor, and the Definition of Economics." *Economics and Philosophy* 8(1): 103–125.

Nelson, Julie A. 1992b. "Thinking about Gender." *Hypatia: A Journal of Feminist Philosophy* 7(3): 138–154.

Nelson, Julie A. 1993. "The Study of Choice or the Study of Provisioning? Gender and the Definition of Economics." In *Beyond Economic Man*, edited by M. Ferber, and J.A. Nelson, 23–36. Chicago, IL: University of Chicago Press.

Nelson, Julie A. 2001. "Feminist Economics: Objective, Activist and Postmodern?" In *Postmodernism, Economics and Knowledge*, edited by S. Cullenberg, J. Amariglio, and D.F. Ruccio, 286–304. London, England: Routledge.

Nelson, Julie A. 2006a. "Can We Talk? Feminist Economists in Dialogue with Social Theorists." *Signs: Journal of Women in Culture and Society* 31(4): 1052–1074.

Nelson, Julie A. 2006b. *Economics for Humans.* Chicago, IL: University of Chicago Press.

Nelson, Julie A. 2010. "Sociology, Economics, and Gender: Can Knowledge of the Past Contribute to a Better Future?" *American Journal of Economics and Sociology* 69(4): 1127–1154.

Ogburn, W.F. 1930. "The Folkways of a Scientific Sociology." *Publications of the American Sociological Society* 24: 1–11.

Robbins, L. 1935. *An Essay on the Nature and Significance of Economic Science.* London, England: Macmillan.

Roos, C.F. 1933. "The Organization of the Econometric Society in Cleveland, Ohio, December 1930." *Econometrica* 1: 71–72.

Ross, D. 1991. *The Origins of American Social Science.* Cambridge, England: Cambridge University Press.

Silverberg, H., ed. 1998. *Gender and American Social Science: The Formative Years.* Princeton, NJ: Princeton University Press.

Small, A.W. 1916. "Fifty Years of Sociology in the United States." *American Journal of Sociology* 21(6): 721–864.

Smelser, N.J., and R. Swedberg. 2005. *The Handbook of Economic Sociology.* Princeton, NJ: Princeton University Press.

Smith, M.C. 1994. *Social Science in the Crucible: The American Debate over Objectivity and Purpose, 1918–1941.* Durham, NC: Duke University Press.

Spalter-Roth, R., and J. Scelza. 2008. "Sociology Faculty Salaries, 2007–2008." In *Research Brief: Department of Research and Development*, edited by American Sociological Association, 1–4. Washington, DC: American Sociological Association.

Stacey, J., and B. Thorne. 1985. "The Missing Feminist Revolution in Sociology." *Social Problems* 32(4): 301–316.

Tobin, J. 1985. "Neoclassical Theory in America: J.B. Clark and Fisher." *American Economic Review* 75: 28–38.

Chapter 11

Men versus Women

A Paradigmatic View

In Western world, there are qualities which are associated with men and there are other qualities which are associated with women. These qualities are commonly used in pairs such as: men v. women or masculine v. feminine. The purpose of this chapter is to briefly review the model proposed by the prominent feminist Julie Nelson (1992a), in order to point out that the qualities that are associated with men associate them with the functionalist paradigm, and the qualities that are associated with women associate them with the interpretive paradigm. In other words, currently, in the Western world, a typical person believes that men believe in and act according to the functionalist paradigm, and that women believe in and act according to the interpretive paradigm. This chapter does not intend to get involved with the discussion of why a typical person in the Western world has developed such beliefs about men versus women. This is because such discussion has been provided in previous chapters. Therefore, this chapter takes the prevailing beliefs in the Western world as given and moves forward.[1]

A simple model can be used to revise the relationships between the constructions of "masculine" and "feminine." This model is helpful in organizing the ideas of hierarchies, polarities, dualisms, "differences," and "complementarities."

In this model, the term "gender" does not refer either to biological sex differences between females and males, or to attributes that might be differentially possessed by actual women and men due to social influences, but refers to the way in which people use the categories "masculine" and "feminine" as cognitive organizers. These patterns of mapping may have little or nothing to do with sex differences. These patterns of mapping concepts onto the two sexes, may be called "gender schema" or "gender-based metaphors." For instance, in contemporary American culture, cats are generally considered as more feminine (regardless of their actual sex), whereas dogs are considered as more masculine. Similarly, the Pythagoreans associated masculinity with odd numbers and femininity with even numbers. In both of these cases, the attribution of gender tells more about how human minds work than about any characteristics inherent in cats and dogs or in numbers.

The model offers a template for organizing thinking about gender. The model is intended to replace the dominant conception of gender, in the English-speaking world, as an oppositional, hierarchical dualism, which is deeply entrenched in the cognitive faculties of people. Feminists who work within the oppositional model tend to swing back and forth between the extremes of trying to erase the dualism (which is called "counting to one"), and emphasizing the dualism, for example, when a feminist revalues "the feminine," (which is called "counting to two"). To avoid this problem, the model takes the relationships contained in the traditionally dominant conception of gender as a bipolar (dualistic), one-dimensional, hierarchical relationship and expands it into a two-dimensional relationship that is simple, but has radically different implications.

In the traditional, dominant conception of gender, masculinity and femininity are construed as opposites, with masculinity claiming the high status. This duality and its metaphorical connection with numerous other hierarchical dualisms—in post-Enlightenment Western, white, thought—are endemic in feminist scholarship, such that one frequently encounters a two-column list as follows:

Masculine-Positive v. Feminine-Negative Dualisms:

Masculine v. Feminine
Masculinity v. Femininity
Man v. Woman
Men v. Women
Self-Interested v. Other-Interested/Concerned about others' welfare
Separation v. Connection
Detached v. Committed
Individual v. Social
Individuality v. Relatedness
Individual accomplishment v. Sociality
Independent/Autonomous v. Dependent
Autonomy v. Situatedness
Rational v. Emotional
Reason v. Emotion/Passion
Free to choose v. Subject to decisions made by others
Free to choose v. Influenced by the social and natural environment

Acts by choice v. Acts by nature

Goes out and acts in the world v. Takes care of connections, feeding, clothing, children, and so on.

Achiever v. Supporter

Breadwinner v. Background

Universal/General v. Particular

Abstract v. Concrete

Abstraction v. Concreteness

Abstract analysis v. Concrete analysis

Science v. Humanities

Scientific v. Humanistic

Hard v. Soft

Hardness v. Softness

Rigorous v. Intuitive

Logic v. Intuition

Logical v. Intuitive

Logical consistency v. Intuitive Understanding

Subject v. Object

Objective v. Subjective

Objectivity v. Subjectivity

Formal v. Informal

Quantitative/Mathematical analysis v. Qualitative analysis

Mathematical v. Verbal

Precise v. Vague

Competition v. Cooperation

Competitive v. Nurturing

Efficiency v. Equity

The metaphorical association of traits, behaviors, activities, and attributes with masculinity or femininity not only includes cultural conceptions of appropriate social roles for women and men but also goes far beyond, as in the cat and dog example which was given earlier.

"Difference" is not a binary, that is, a dualistic, relationship. For instance, "emotional" is not the antonym, that is, the opposite, for "rational." The antonym, or opposite, for "rational" is "irrational," that is, "lack" of rationality. Indeed, "emotional" and "rational" have a "complementarity" relationship, in the sense that there is some value to achieving a balance including both capacities.

The word "difference" includes the concepts of "lack," "complementarity," and "perversion." A concept is a perversion of another if it is the distortion, corruption, or degradation of it. For instance, emotionalism, which is judgments made on purely emotional terms (and hence irrationally), is a perverse use of emotional capacity. Similarly, rationalism, in which all emotion is suppressed, is a perverse use of rationality.

For instance, consider the dualisms that relate to the gendered conception of "reason" in post-Enlightenment Western thought. This simple dualism relates reason to masculine-logical-scientific-hard, and intuition to feminine-intuitive-humanistic-soft. However, broader conceptions of "reasoning" are more complex. That is, reason consists of both "logic," that is, "reasoning why," and "intuition," that is, "seeing that." Therefore, both "logic" and "intuition" are necessary for comprehension, that is, they play a "complementarity" role.

An example of logic without intuition is the student who on an exam writes a rigorous and detailed essay that is not related to the question asked: this is "missing the point." Intuition, or apprehension of the whole, degenerates into vagueness and contradiction if it is not combined with logic.

The central task of the feminist project on gender should be the exploration and valuation of the positive aspects of feminine, that is, feminine-positive, and exposing the negative aspects of masculine, that is, masculine-negative. This project is related to various dimensions of difference—racial, class, cultural—which have been similarly distorted by dualistic thinking.

NOTE

1. For this literature, see Alford (1996), Barker and Feiner (2004), Belenky, Clinchy, Goldberger, and Tarule (1986), Bordo (1986, 1987), Chodorow (1978), Costa (1994), Croson and Gneezy (2009), England (1993), Fee (1986), Ferber, Birnbaum, and Green (1983), Ferber and Nelson (1993), Flax (1983), Friedl (1975), Grapard (2001), Harding (1986), Heath (1989), Jennings (1993), Keller (1985), Kuiper, Sap, Feiner, Ott, and Tzannatos (1995), Lumsden and Scott (1987), Merchant (1980), Nelson (1992a, b, 1993a, b, 1994, 1995a, b, 1996a, b, 2001, 2010), Nelson and Vilela (2012), Niederle and Vesterlund (2010), Niederle and Vesterlund (2011), Olsen and Cox (2001), Otnes and Zayer (2012), Ourahmoune (2012), Richardson (1996), Rose (1986), Rosener (1990, 1995, 1997), Roszkowski and Grable (2005), Sheman (1983), Unger (1989), Weinreich-Haste (1986), Williams (1993), and Zayer and Otnes (2012). The rest of this chapter is based on Nelson (1992a).

REFERENCES

Alford, Katrina. 1996. "Gender and Economics." *Academy of the Social Sciences in Australia Newsletter* 15(4): 21–26.
Barker, Drucilla K., and Susan F. Feiner. 2004. *Liberating Economics: Feminist Perspectives on Families, Work, and Globalization.* London, England: Routledge.

Belenky, Mary Field, Blythe McVicker Clinchy, Nancy Rule Goldberger, and Jill Mattuck Tarule. 1986. *Women's Ways of Knowing: The Development of Self, Voice, and Mind.* New York, NY: Basic Books.

Bordo, Susan. 1986. "The Cartesian Masculinization of Thought." *Signs* 11: 439–456.

Bordo, Susan. 1987. *The Flight to Objectivity: Essays on Cartesianism and Culture.* Albany, NY: State University of New York Press.

Chodorow, Nancy, 1978. *The Reproduction of Mothering: Psychoanalysis and the Sociology of Gender.* Berkeley, CA: University of California Press.

Costa, Janeen Arnold, ed. 1994. *Gender Issues and Consumer Behavior.* Thousand Oaks, CA: Sage Publications.

Croson, Rachel, and Uri Gneezy. 2009. "Gender Differences in Performances." *Journal of Economic Literature* 47(2): 448–474.

England, Paula. 1993. "The Separate Self: Androcentric Bias in Neoclassical Assumptions." In *Beyond Economic Man: Feminist Theory and Economics*, edited by Marianne Ferber, and Julie A. Nelson, 37–53. Chicago, IL: University of Chicago Press.

Fee, Elizabeth. 1986. "Critiques of Modern Science: The Relationship of Feminism to Other Radical Epistemologies." In *Feminist Approaches to Science*, edited by Ruth Bleier, 42–56. New York, NY: Pergamon Press.

Ferber, Marianne A., Bonnie G. Birnbaum, and Carole A. Green. 1983. "Gender Differences in Economic Knowledge: A Reevaluation of the Evidence." *Journal of Economic Education* 14(2): 24–37.

Ferber, Marianne A., and Julie A. Nelson. 1993. "Introduction: The Social Construction of Economics and the Social Construction of Gender." In *Beyond Economic Man: Feminist Theory and Economics*, edited by Marianne Ferber, and Julie A. Nelson, 1–22. Chicago, IL: University of Chicago Press.

Flax, Jane. 1983. "Political Philosophy and the Patriarchal Unconscious: A Psychoanalytic Perspective on Epistemology and Metaphysics." In *Discovering Reality: Feminist Perspectives on Epistemology, Metaphysics, Methodology and Philosophy of Science*, edited by Sandra Harding, and Merrill B. Hintikka, 245–282. Dordrecht, the Netherlands: Reidel Publishing Company.

Friedl, Ernestine. 1975. *Women and Men: An Anthropologist's View.* New York, NY: Holt, Rinehart and Winston.

Grapard, Ulla. 2001. "The Trouble with Women and Economics: A Postmodern Perspective on Charlotte Perkins Gilman." In *Postmodernism, Economics, and Knowledge*, edited by Stephen Cullenberg, Jack Amariglio, and David F. Ruccio, 261–285. London, England: Routledge.

Harding, Sandra. 1986. *The Science Question in Feminism.* Ithaca, NY: Cornell University Press.

Heath, Julia A. 1989. "An Econometric Model of the Role of Gender in Economic Education." *American Economic Review* 79(2): 226–230.

Jennings, Ann L. 1993. "Public or Private? Institutional Economics and Feminism." In *Beyond Economic Man: Feminist Theory and Economics*, edited by Marianne Ferber, and Julie A. Nelson, 111–129. Chicago, IL: University of Chicago Press.

Keller, Evelyn Fox. 1985. *Reflections on Gender and Science*. New Havens, CT: Yale University Press.

Kuiper, Edith, Jolande Sap, Susan Feiner, Notburga Ott, and Aafiris Tzannatos, eds. 1995. *Out of the Margin: Feminist Perspectives on Economics*. London, England: Routledge.

Lumsden, Keith G., and Alex Scott. 1987. "The Economics Student Reexamined: Male-Female Differences in Comprehension." *Journal of Economic Education* 18(4): 365–375.

Merchant, Carolyn. 1980. *The Death of Nature: Women, Ecology and the Scientific Revolution*. San Francisco, CA: Harper and Row.

Nelson, Julie A. 1992a. "Thinking about Gender." *Hypatia* 7(3): 138–154.

Nelson, Julie A. 1992b. "Gender, Metaphor, and the Definition of Economics." *Economics and Philosophy* 8(1): 103–125.

Nelson, Julie A. 1993a. "Gender and Economic Ideology." *Review of Social Economy* 51(3): 287–301.

Nelson, Julie A. 1993b. "The Study of Choice or the Study of Provisioning? Gender and the Definition of Economics." In *Beyond Economic Man: Feminist Theory and Economics*, edited by Marianne Ferber, and Julie A. Nelson, 23–36. Chicago, IL: University of Chicago Press.

Nelson, Julie A. 1994. "More Thinking about Gender: Reply." *Hypatia* 9(1): 199–205.

Nelson, Julie A. 1995a. "Feminism and Economics." *Journal of Economic Perspectives* 9(2): 131–148.

Nelson, Julie A. 1995b. "Economic Theory and Feminist Theory: Comments on Chapters by Polachek, Ott, and Levin." In *Out of the Margin: Feminist Perspectives on Economics*, edited by Edith Kupier, and Jolande Sap, 120–125. London, England: Routledge.

Nelson, Julie A. 1996a, "What Is Feminist Economics All About?" *Challenge* 39(1): 4–8.

Nelson, Julie A. 1996b. "The Masculine Mindset of Economic Analysis." *Chronicle of Higher Education* 42(42): B3.

Nelson, Julie A. 2001. "Feminist Economics: Objective, Activist, and Postmodern?" In *Postmodernism, Economics, and Knowledge*, edited by Stephen Cullenberg, Jack Amariglio, and David F.Ruccio, 286–304. London, England: Routledge.

Nelson, Julie A. 2010. "Sociology, Economics, and Gender: Can Knowledge of the Past Contribute to a Better Future?" *American Journal of Economics and Sociology* 69(4): 1127–1154.

Nelson, Michelle R., and Alexandra M. Vilela. 2012. "Is the Selectivity Hypothesis Still Relevant? A Review of Gendered Persuasion and Processing of Advertising Messages." In *Gender, Culture, and Consumer Behavior*, edited by Cele C. Otnes, and Linda Tuncay Zayer, 111–138. New York, NY: Routledge.

Niederle, Muriel, and Lise Vesterlund. 2010. "Explaining the Gender Gap in Math Test Scores: The Role of Competition." *Journal of Economic Perspectives* 24(2): 129–144.

Niederle, Muriel, and Lise Vesterlund. 2011. "Gender and Competition." *Annual Review Economics* 3: 601–630.

Olsen, Robert A., and Constance M. Cox. 2001. "The Influence of Gender on the Perception and Response to Investment Risk: The Case of Professional Investors." *Journal of Psychology and Financial Markets* 2(1): 29–36.

Otnes, Cele C., and Linda Tuncay Zayer, eds. 2012. *Gender, Culture, and Consumer Behavior.* New York, NY: Routledge.

Ourahmoune, Nacima. 2012. "Masculinity, Intimacy, and Consumption." In *Gender, Culture, and Consumer Behavior*, edited by Cele C. Otnes, and Linda Tuncay Zayer, 311–335. New York, NY: Routledge.

Richardson, Sue. 1996. "Why Women Make Lousy Economists." *Academy of Social Sciences in Australia Newsletter* 15(4): 19–20.

Rose, Hilary. 1986. "Beyond Masculine Realities: A Feminist Epistemology for the Sciences." In *Feminist Approaches to Science*, edited by Ruth Bleier, 57–76. New York, NY: Pergamon Press.

Rosener, Judy B. 1990. "Ways Women Lead." *Harvard Business Review* (Nov./ Dec.): 3–10.

Rosener, Judy B. 1995. *America's Competitive Secret: Utilizing Women as a Management Strategy.* Oxford, England: Oxford University Press.

Rosener, Judy B. 1997. *America's Competitive Secret: Woman Managers.* Oxford, England: Oxford University Press.

Roszkowski, Michael J., and John Grable. 2005. "Gender Stereo-Types in Advisor's Clinical Judgments of Financial Risk Tolerance: Objects in the Mirror Are Closer than They Appear." *Journal of Behavioral Finance* 6(4): 181–191.

Sheman, Naomi. 1983. "Individualism and the Objects of Psychology." In *Discovering Reality: Feminist Perspectives on Epistemology, Metaphysics, Methodology and Philosophy of Science*, edited by Sandra Harding, and Merrill B. Hintikka, 225–244. Dordrecht, the Netherlands: Reidel Publishing Company.

Unger, Rhoda K. 1989. "Sex, Gender, and Epistemology." In *Gender and Thought: Psychological Perspectives*, edited by Mary Crawford, and Margaret Gentry, 17–35. New York, NY: Springer-Verlag.

Weinreich-Haste, Helen. 1986. "Brother Sun, Sister Moon: Does Rationality Overcome a Dualistic World View?" In *Perspectives on Gender and Science*, edited by Jan Harding, 113–131. London, England: Falmer Press.

Williams, Rhonda M. 1993. "Race, Deconstruction, and the Emergent Agenda of Feminist Economic Theory." In *Beyond Economic Man: Feminist Theory and Economics*, edited by Marianne Ferber, and Julie Nelson, 144–153. Chicago, IL: University of Chicago Press.

Zayer, Linda Tuncay, and Cele C. Otnes. 2012. "Climbing the Ladder or Chasing a Dream? Men's Responses to Idealized Portrayals of Masculinity in Advertising." In *Gender, Culture, and Consumer Behavior*, edited by Cele C. Otnes, and Linda Tuncay Zayer, 87–110. New York, NY: Routledge.

Chapter 12

Conclusion

Social theory can usefully be conceived in terms of four key paradigms: functionalist, interpretive, radical humanist, and radical structuralist. The four paradigms are founded upon different assumptions about the nature of social science and the nature of society. Each generates theories, concepts, and analytical tools which are different from those of other paradigms.

All theories are based on a philosophy of science and a theory of society. Many theorists appear to be unaware of, or ignore, the assumptions underlying these philosophies. They emphasize only some aspects of the phenomenon and ignore others. Unless they bring out the basic philosophical assumptions of the theories, their analysis can be misleading; since by emphasizing differences between theories, they imply diversity in approach. While there appear to be different kinds of theory, they are founded on a certain philosophy, worldview, or paradigm. This becomes evident when these theories are related to the wider background of social theory.

The functionalist paradigm has provided the framework for current mainstream in academic research, and accounts for the largest proportion of theory and research in academic fields.

In order to understand a new paradigm, theorists should be fully aware of assumptions upon which their own paradigm is based. Moreover, to understand a new paradigm one has to explore it from within, since the concepts in one paradigm cannot easily be interpreted in terms of those of another. No attempt should be made to criticize or evaluate a paradigm from the outside. This is self-defeating since it is based on a separate paradigm. All four paradigms can be easily criticized and ruined in this way.

These four paradigms are of paramount importance to any scientist, because the process of learning about a favored paradigm is also the process of learning what that paradigm is not. The knowledge of paradigms makes scientists aware of the boundaries within which they approach their subject. Each of the four paradigms implies a different way of social theorizing.

Scientists often approach their subject from a frame of reference based upon assumptions that are taken-for-granted. Since these assumptions are continually affirmed and reinforced, they remain not only unquestioned but also beyond conscious awareness. In this way, most researchers tend to favor the functionalist paradigm.

The partial nature of this view only becomes apparent when the researcher exposes basic assumptions to the challenge of alternative ways of seeing, and starts to appreciate these alternatives in their own terms. To do this, one has to explore other paradigms from within, since the concepts in one paradigm cannot easily be interpreted in terms of those of another.

The diversity of research possibilities referred to in this book is vast. While each paradigm advocates a research strategy that is logically coherent, in terms of underlying assumptions, these vary from paradigm to paradigm. The phenomenon to be researched can be conceptualized and studied in many different ways, each generating distinctive kinds of insight and understanding. There are many different ways of studying the same social phenomenon, and given that the insights generated by any one approach are at best partial and incomplete, the social researcher can gain much by reflecting on the nature and merits of different approaches. It is clear that social scientists, like other generators of knowledge, deal with the realization of possible types of knowledge, which are connected with the particular paradigm adopted.

The mainstream academic research is based upon the functionalist paradigm; and, for the most part, theorists are not always entirely aware of the traditions to which they belong. This book recommends a serious conscious thinking about the social philosophy upon which social research is based and of the alternative avenues for development.

Academic research can gain much by exploiting the new perspectives coming from the other paradigms. An understanding of different paradigms leads to a better understanding of the multifaceted nature of social phenomenon. Although a researcher may decide to conduct research from the point of view of a certain paradigm, an understanding of the nature of other paradigms leads to a better understanding of what one is doing.

Paradigm diversity is based on the idea that more than one theoretical construction can be placed upon a given collection of data. In other words, any single theory, research method, or particular empirical study is incapable of explaining the nature of reality in all of its complexities.

It is possible to establish exact solutions to problems, if one defines the boundary and domain of reality. Functionalist research, through its research approach, defines an area in which objectivity and truth can be found. Any change in the research approach, or any change in the area of applicability, would tend to result in the breakdown of such objectivity and truth.

The knowledge generated through functionalist research relates to certain aspects of the phenomenon under consideration. Recognition of the existence of the phenomenon beyond that dictated by the research approach, results in the recognition of the limitations of the knowledge generated within the confines of that approach.

It is almost impossible to find foundational solution to the problem of creating specific kind of knowledge. Researchers are encouraged to explore what is possible by identifying untapped possibilities. By comparing a favored research approach in relation to others, the nature, strengths, and limitations of the favored approach become evident. By understanding what others do, researchers are able to understand what they are not doing. This leads to the development and refinement of the favored research approach. The concern is not about deciding which research approach is best, or with substituting one for another. The concern is about the merits of diversity, which seeks to enrich research rather than constrain it, through a search for an optimum way of doing diverse research.

There is no unique evaluative perspective for assessing knowledge generated by different research approaches. Therefore, it becomes necessary to get beyond the idea that knowledge is foundational and can be evaluated in an absolute way.

Different research approaches provide different interpretations of a phenomenon, and understand the phenomenon in a particular way. Some may be supporting a traditional view, others saying something new. In this way, knowledge is treated as being tentative rather than absolute.

All research approaches have something to contribute. The interaction among them may lead to synthesis, compromise, consensus, transformation, polarization, or simply clarification and improved understanding of differences. Such interaction, which is based on differences of viewpoints, is not concerned with reaching consensus or an end point that establishes a foundational truth. On the contrary, it is concerned with learning from the process itself, and to encourage the interaction to continue so long as disagreement lasts. Likewise, it is not concerned with producing uniformity, but promoting improved diversity.

Paradigm diversity is based on the idea that research is a creative process and that there are many ways of doing research. This approach leads to the development of knowledge in many different, and sometimes contradictory, directions such that new ways of knowing will emerge. There can be no objective criteria for choosing between alternative perspectives. The number of ways of generating new knowledge is bounded only by the ingenuity of researchers in inventing new approaches.

The functionalist paradigm regards research as a technical activity and depersonalizes the research process. It removes responsibility from the researcher and reduces him or her to an agent engaged in what the institutionalized research demands.

Paradigm diversity reorients the role of the researchers and places responsibility for the conduct and consequences of research directly with them. Researchers examine the nature of their activity to choose an appropriate approach and develop a capacity to observe and question what they are doing, and take responsibility for making intelligent choices which are open to realize the many potential types of knowledge.

To implement paradigm diversity, some fundamental changes need to be directed to the way research is presently managed in academic fields. In other words, paradigm diversity implies and requires changes. The most fundamental change is to understand the multifaceted nature of social phenomena.

An understanding of paradigms provides a valuable means for exploring the nature of the phenomenon being investigated. Furthermore, an understanding of other paradigms provides an invaluable basis for recognizing what one is doing.

It is interesting to note that this recommendation is consistent with the four paradigms:

1. It increases efficiency in research: This is because, diversity in the research approach prevents or delays reaching the point of diminishing marginal return. Therefore, the recommendation is consistent with the functionalist paradigm, which emphasizes purposive rationality and the benefit of diversification.
2. It advocates diversity in research approach: This is consistent with the interpretive paradigm, which emphasizes shared multiple realities.
3. It leads to the realization of researchers' full potentials: This is consistent with the radical humanist paradigm, which emphasizes human beings' emancipation from the structures which limit their potential for development.
4. It enhances class awareness: This is consistent with the radical structuralist paradigm, which emphasizes class struggle.

Knowledge is ultimately a product of the researcher's paradigmatic approach to the multifaceted social phenomenon. Viewed from this angle, the pursuit of knowledge is seen as much an ethical, moral, ideological, and political activity, as a technical one. Mainstream academic research can gain much from the contributions of the other paradigms.

Index

About the Author

Kavous Ardalan is a professor of finance at the School of Management at Marist College, Poughkeepsie, New York, USA. He holds PhD degrees in both economics and finance. His research interests are in the theoretical, practical, educational, social, and philosophical aspects of economics and finance. He is the author of the following seven books: (1) *On the Role of Paradigms in Finance*, (2) *Understanding Globalization: A Multi-Dimensional Approach*, (3) *Paradigms in Political Economy*, (4) *Case Method and Pluralist Economics: Philosophy, Methodology, and Practice*, (5) *Global Political Economy: A Multi-Paradigmatic Approach*, (6) *Equity Home Bias in International Finance: A Place-Attachment Perspective*, and (7) *Understanding Revolution: A Multi-Paradigmatic Approach*. He has also written more than eighty journal articles. Some of his research papers have received awards at international conferences, have been regarded very highly by publishers, have been referenced in the "Handbook of Finance" as well as in many journal articles and books, and have been used as course reading materials at top universities in three different continents.

www.ingramcontent.com/pod-product-compliance
Lightning Source LLC
Chambersburg PA
CBHW022303280326
41932CB00010B/961